Behaviour and Rationality in Corporate Governance

Corporate scandals due to bad accounting happen far too frequently for a system of corporate governance to be deemed effective. This book examines why the safeguards designed to prevent bad accounting so often fail. By studying why the auditors and members of a board of directors regularly fail to deliver the truth about a company's financial state of affairs, this provocative book explores a serious problem in the system of reporting financial information.

Exploring the reasons behind corporate misbehaviour, this book also answers the question of whether recent reforms are sufficient to prevent further scandals from occurring in the future. The author examines the independence of reputable intermediaries in the monitoring model of corporate governance. A special focus is on auditors and board directors, but the findings can be extended to other gatekeepers, including bankers and corporate lawyers. The author demonstrates that conventional policies to reform corporate governance such as increased legislation, stronger penalties, and more codes of practice are necessary but typically underestimate the pressures which intermediaries face from inevitable conflicts of interest and bias in judgement and decision-making.

This book is unique in that it draws together various strands of the literature on corporate governance, accounting, law, cognitive research, psychology, behavioural economics, and conventional economics to shed light on questions regarding the feasibility of independence and impartiality of boards of directors and external auditors as monitors and gatekeepers in corporate governance. The book is essential reading for professional accountants and auditors, directors, regulators, law makers, corporate lawyers, and investment bankers. It will appeal to all those interested in behavioural economics and corporate governance.

Oliver Marnet is a Lecturer in Economics at the School of Management and Business, at Aberystwyth University.

Routledge Studies in Corporate Governance

1 **Corporate Governance Around the World**
Edited by Ahmed Naciri

2 **Behaviour and Rationality in Corporate Governance**
Oliver Marnet

Behaviour and Rationality in Corporate Governance

Oliver Marnet

Routledge
Taylor & Francis Group
LONDON AND NEW YORK

First published 2008 by Routledge
2 Park Square, Milton Park, Abingdon, Oxon OX14 4RN

Simultaneously published in the USA and Canada
by Routledge
270 Madison Ave, New York, NY 10016

*Routledge is an imprint of the Taylor & Francis Group,
an informa business*

Typeset in Times New Roman by Graphicraft Limited, Hong Kong
Printed and bound in Great Britain by Biddles Ltd, Kings Lynn

British Library Cataloguing in Publication Data
A catalogue record for this book is available from the British Library

Library of Congress Cataloging in Publication Data
Marnet, Oliver.
Behaviour and rationality in corporate governance / Oliver Marnet.
p. cm.
1. Corporate governance. I. Title.
HD2741.M247 2008
658.4′2019—dc22
2007037739

ISBN10: 0-415-43752-0 (hbk)
ISBN10: 0-203-92956-X (ebk)

ISBN13: 978-0-415-43752-3 (hbk)
ISBN13: 978-0-203-92956-8 (ebk)

This book is dedicated to my family.

Contents

Boxes, figures and tables

Boxes

Figures

Tables

Preface

This book is concerned with issues of corporate governance following the Enron and other scandals. In particular, it focuses on policy reforms and the independence of reputational intermediaries in the monitoring model of corporate governance. The book questions the traditional economic approach to such issues which is based on the rational actor using available information to make judgements which then guide their decisions. The agency view of corporate governance requires effective monitoring to align the interests of the agent with those of the principal. It is suggested that conventional proposals to reform corporate governance through legislation, codes of best practice, and the like are necessary, but underestimate the pressures which reputational intermediaries face from inevitable conflicts of interest and bias in judgement and decision-making. There are various reasons – many linked with the (economic) psychology literature – why agents, including auditors and members of the board, make decisions or come to opinions which tend to be biased as information is selectively used to support an original decision or confirm a prior view. The original contribution of this book is in drawing together the various strands of the literature on corporate governance, accounting, law, cognitive research, psychology, behavioural economics, and conventional economics to shed light on questions regarding the independence of boards of directors and external auditors as monitors in corporate governance. This work demonstrates how a behavioural perspective can add value to the rational actor model of conventional economics to better understand the causes of failures in corporate governance.

Acknowledgements

I owe a debt of gratitude to Professor John Hudson for his insights, support and encouragement throughout the drafting of this work. Crucial support from Professor John Sessions is gratefully acknowledged. Comments and suggestions by Adrian Winnett and Professor Andy Mullineux are much appreciated. Any remaining shortcomings and mistakes are my own.

Abbreviations

ABA	American Bar Association
ACFE	Association of Certified Fraud Examiners
AFC	Asian Financial Crisis
AICPA	American Institute of Certified Public Accountants
AMEX	American Stock Exchange
APRA	Australia's Prudential Regulation Authority
ASIC	Australian Securities and Investments Commission
BaFin	Federal Authority for the Supervision of Financial Services (Germany)
BCCI	Bank of Credit and Commerce International
BOT	Bank of Thailand
CEO	Chief Executive Officer
CFEs	Certified Fraud Examiners
CFO	Chief Financial Officer
CLERP	Corporate Law Economic Reform Program
CNMV	Comisión Nacional del Mercado de Valores
CONSOB	Commissione Nazionale per le Società e la Borsa
COSO	Committee of Sponsoring Organizations of the Treadway Commission
CPA	Certified Public Accountant
DFAT	Department of Foreign Affairs and Trade
DTI	Department of Trade and Industry
EBITA	Earnings before Interest, Taxes, and Amortization
EBITDA	Earnings before Interest, Taxes, Depreciation, and Amortization
EMH	Efficient Market Hypothesis
EU	Expected Utility
FASB	Financial Accounting Standards Board (US)
FIDF	Financial Institutions Development Fund (TH)
FRC	Financial Reporting Council (UK)
FSA	Financial Services Agency (Japan)
FTSE 100	London Stock Exchange Share Index of the 100 most highly capitalized companies

GAAP	Generally Accepted Accounting Principles
GAAS	Generally Accepted Auditing Standards
GAO	US Government Accounting Office
GCCC	German Corporate Governance Code
IPO	Initial Equity Offering
IRS	US Internal Revenue Service
NASDAQ	National Association of Securities Dealers Automated Quotations
NESDB	National Economic and Social Development Board
OFHEO	Office of Federal Housing Enterprise Oversight (US)
PCAOB	Public Company Accounting Oversight Board (US)
POB	Public Oversight Board (US)
QLCC	Qualified Legal Compliance Committee
SEC	Securities and Exchange Commission (US)
SEU	Subjective Expected Utility
SFAC	Statement of Financial Accounting Concepts
SOE	Seasoned Equity Offering
SPV	Special Purpose Vehicle

1 Introduction

The human capacity for rationalization of own and observed behaviour can be a formidable barrier to rational judgement and decision-making. This book critically investigates the quality of monitoring of the activities of executive management in large corporations. It seeks to provide greater realism in understanding agent behaviour within a corporate governance setting. The argument is developed that an over-reliance on rational choice models of decision-making may prevent a more thorough discussion of unexpected corporate collapse, and corporate governance in general. Policies based on the assumptions of rational models of choice-making may underestimate the intrusion of bias in the decision-making of agents in corporate governance.

This book examines the roles and functions of auditors and directors as reputational intermediaries in corporate governance. These professionals provide verification and certification services to investors. Rational concerns would suggest that a reputational intermediary is motivated to preserve his or her credibility and can thus be a means to reduce the agency costs of corporate governance (Kraakman, 1986). Anecdotal evidence would suggest, however, that such agents frequently neglect their reputation. A behavioural approach to decision-making under uncertainty empirically supports the view that agents may at times deviate from the outcomes predicted by rational models of judgement and choice. This is of importance to the monitoring model of corporate governance as it critically depends on agents' adherence to the rational actor ideal. This book challenges the assumption of, and reliance on, the independence and impartiality of monitors in corporate governance. Further questioned is the near universal application of the rational actor paradigm by governance policy-makers, researchers, and practitioners.

A main argument of the present text is that conventional proposals to reform corporate governance based on the rational model of decision-making may be insufficient in preventing corporate debacles. It is suggested that pressures from conflicts of interest and bias on reputational intermediaries are typically underestimated, and that an understanding of monitor behaviour in corporate governance would be improved by placing it on psychologically more realistic foundations. As gatekeepers (Coffee, 2001), auditors and directors are subject to systematic biases and social pressures which can compromise their professional judgement.[1] This may lead to situations where the outcomes of choice behaviour differ from the predictions of the rational actor model of judgement and decision-making that is conventionally relied upon by economists. It will be shown that gatekeeper failure may, as a result, frequently be less sinister than is commonly assumed. A further conclusion is that legislation which primarily aims at deterrence of consciously deviant behaviour may be less effective than hoped for.

A major motivation for this book is to integrate results from behavioural economics and cognitive psychology with existing economic theory on corporate governance to shed light on the causes of the recurring failure of monitors and gatekeepers. The originality of this approach lies in drawing together diverse strands of the literature to analyse the issue of corporate governance in a way that has not been done before. This work uses insights from agency theory, corporate governance, accounting, law and legal practice, behavioural economics, cognitive research, and standard economic theory to provide an explanation for the failure of gatekeepers. It also suggests extensions to the rational model of choice- and decision-making to obtain a more realistic model of human judgement and choice which will allow for a better understanding of agents in corporate governance. This has relevance also for policy- and law-making with regard to the governance of corporations (Baron *et al.*, 2006). A behavioural perspective can add value to the rational actor model and allow a better understanding of the causes of governance failures.

The corporate governance debate identifies the central problem of the separation of ownership and control in the modern corporation. This debate generally centres on the alignment of the motives of executive managers with those of the owners, the composition and independence of members of the board of directors, and compliance to accounting standards and auditing practices. The agency view of corporate governance requires effective monitors and gatekeepers to align the interests of the agent with those of the principal. This book focuses its investigation on the behaviour of the board of directors and the external auditors as important gatekeeping agents. The collective failure of such gatekeepers is seen as one common denominator in recent corporate debacles (e.g. Enron, WorldCom, Parmalat). The monitoring model of corporate governance is implicitly based on the rational choice model of economics, and the standard debate identifies important aspects for the minimization of the agency problem. Notwithstanding the substantial contribution made by the corporate governance discussion, this may insufficiently account for the significance and persistence of bias in the decision-making and choice behaviour of monitors and gatekeepers. It is suggested that conventional proposals to reform corporate governance (such as codes of best practice, additional layers of oversight, and greater penalties for breaches of relevant laws), while of importance, tend to underestimate the pressures from conflicts of interest and bias faced by reputational intermediaries in their interaction with colleagues and clients.

Rationality has been considered the cornerstone for making decisions and judgements for over 50 years. The economist's conventional model on how individuals form judgements, update their beliefs, and make decisions has been broadly adopted by legal scholars, accountants, and policy-makers. In contrast, behavioural studies suggest that individuals (and groups) regularly and predictably fall short of this normative standard. This has resulted in definitions of decision-making and choice which are based not only on the logical and analytical reasoning of the economist, but also on cognitive limitations, heuristics, and bias. There is a growing awareness in the governance literature of the importance of a better understanding of human decision-making behaviour than may be provided by the neo-classical rational choice model alone. Choice behaviour is not solely based on logical reasoning and a pure application of probability theory, but is also influenced by schemata, framing, and cognitive and judgemental heuristics which can systematically bias judgement (Jolls *et al.*, 1998; Prentice, 2000; Rabin, 2002). If these insights can be shown to be useful in describing how executive managers and their monitors behave, this would seriously question the value of many existing rules and regulations on corporate governance, as these strongly rely on the assumptions of the rational actor model. At the very least, these insights would suggest the need for significant modifications to the monitoring model of corporate governance.

During the second half of the 1990s, exceptionally bright people ran exceptionally successful companies, or so it appeared, and helped create exorbitant expectations among investors. For a short period this induced an atmosphere that, for a broad array of observers, seemed to indicate the suspension of economic laws on risk and return, and the absence of business cycles. This was also reflected in financial reporting practices. Cash flows and real profits were often replaced in perceived importance by quests for market share and imaginary earnings. Ever more innovative, and illusive, earnings measurements including, for example, Earnings before Interest, Taxes, Depreciation, and Amortization (EBITDA) were expected to guarantee corporate success regardless of underlying economic and financial prospects. However, economic reality had not been suspended and increasingly aggressive financial reporting could maintain the mirage of ever increasing earnings, irrespective of real underlying profits, only for so long. A wake-up call came when Enron unexpectedly went bankrupt in December 2001, soon to be followed by WorldCom in 2002.[2] Together with these two companies many other erstwhile corporate success stories in the United States, including HealthSouth, Adelphia, Tyco, Quest, and Global Crossing disintegrated, revealing not mere mistakes or unfortunate business turns, but rot and more rot. This rot, as Susan Koniak (2003a) notes, had a name: accounting scandal. What made this worse was that the problems subsequently identified (including earnings management) were not a prerogative of a small number of rogue companies, or recently created unknowns, but had a firm grip on established blue-chip companies (e.g. Xerox, Shell, Lucent). This strongly indicates the possibility of systemic problems in corporate governance.[3] The deluge of corporate scandals tarnished the reputation of the corporate governance system, in particular that of the monitoring component designed to prevent the managerial fraud and gross mismanagement identified in many cases (Clarke *et al.*, 2003; Coffee, 2003a, b).

The fall of Enron was the most shocking corporate scandal of recent years and one of the biggest corporate collapses in US history. Even more worrying was that this was quickly followed by aftershocks of similar magnitude in the form of WorldCom, Parmalat, and the collapse of Germany's Neuer Markt.[4] These scandals, predictably, led to a great deal of soul searching by policy-makers, commentators, accountants, and academics on both sides of the Atlantic and elsewhere. One result of this was the Sarbanes-Oxley Act of 2002 in the United States and various legislative and regulatory efforts in Europe and elsewhere aimed at preventing a repeat of such debacles. A small, and by no means exhaustive, selection of such efforts outside the US include the United Kingdom's Combined Code of 2003 (FRC, 2003) and the Company Law Reform Bill White Paper of March 2005 (DTI, 2005a); Spain's Aldama Report (CNMV, 2003a) and 2003 Law 26/2003 aimed at improving transparency and corporate governance (CNMV, 2003b); Italy's 2004/5 Reform of Company Law (CONSOB, 2005); Germany's 2002 Transparency and Disclosure Law (Germany, 2002), and the German Corporate Governance Code (Germany, 2007); France's 2003 LOI n° 2003–706 du 1er Août 2003 de Sécurité Financière (France, 2003); various efforts by the European Commission at improving the quality of auditing within the European Union (e.g. EU Directive 2006/43/EC, on statutory audit); and Australia's Corporate Law Economic Reform Program (Audit Reform and Corporate Disclosure) Law 2004 (known as 'CLERP 9'; see ASIC, 2004) and several rounds of governance reforms since 2002 by Australia's Prudential Regulation Authority (APRA).[5]

Enron will remain in the minds of researchers for the magnitude and complexity of the frauds committed, the speed of the subsequent implosion of the firm, and its relevance to the corporate governance discussion.[6] Enron is also remembered for its key role in the demise of its external auditor, Arthur Anderson, a former Big-5 accounting firm. Although the extent and scale of the *ex post* investigation of the collapse of Enron has been unprecedented, the most accessible studies are still those emanating from the internal enquiry set up by Enron shortly after the commencement of the Securities and Exchange Commission (SEC) investigation (the Powers report: Powers *et al.*, 2002) and the enquiries of the bankruptcy examiners (Batson, 2002, 2003a, b, c; Goldin, 2003).[7] The Powers report focuses primarily on the scale of Enron's off-balance sheet activities, transactions between Enron and its unconsolidated Special Purpose Vehicles (SPVs), the use of transactions with these SPVs to seek to protect Enron's reported profitability in the two years immediately prior to its collapse, and the opportunity for improper personal benefit afforded to Enron's senior executives from such transactions.

The bankruptcy examiners' reports give a wider perspective on the extent and manner of the manipulation of Enron's financial reporting in terms of income, cash flows, and the balance sheet.

Enron's corporate governance structure appeared to be a model of good practice. Enron's Audit and Compliance Committee, chaired by Robert Jaedicke, Emeritus Professor of Accounting and former Dean of the Graduate School of Business at Stanford, and including Wendy Gramm, a former chair of the US Commodity Futures Trading Commission, and Lord Wakeham, both a qualified accountant and a previous UK energy minister, was a distinguished one. The external audit was carried out by Arthur Andersen, one of the then Big-5 auditors. There was an active risk and compliance function internal to the firm. The only potential reservation would be that the internal audit function was outsourced to Andersen, the external auditors, a practice which is now prohibited in the United States.[8]

It is arguable whether anything could have prevented the collapse of Enron subsequent to the initial revelations of financial irregularities. Nonetheless, a more effective corporate governance structure might have been able to check management excesses in terms of remuneration and would have both reduced the scale of the loss, and significantly affected where the losses fell by ensuring more appropriate financial reporting practices and the prevention of schemes whereby net cash outflows were incurred for the purpose of financial reporting manipulation. That is, more effective corporate governance may have prevented problems before they became fatally damaging to the firm. With respect to the audit committee, the *ex post* enquiry gave rise to concerns as to its independence (in particular the acceptance by John Wakeham of consulting fees to represent Enron in Europe), close political and social relationships (Wendy Gramm),[9] the amount of time that members were able to devote to their duties, and the level of scepticism and enquiry that they employed in the conduct of their duties. The minutes of the relevant audit committee meetings show a very wide range of business being covered in a relatively short space of time – and with the basic pattern being that of presentations made by executive management. In that executive management controlled the information flows to the committee and the committee did not seek to engage in or commission any independent activity of enquiry or investigation, the committee was largely powerless to contest the assertions of management. Representatives of the external auditors were present at audit committee meetings, but their role was supportive of management. Although the committee members did periodically meet the auditors without any members of executive management being present,[10] at these meetings the external auditors did not raise any of their significant concerns as to the aggressive nature of the accounting practices employed by Enron.[11]

A large number of well-known European companies revealed a comparable pathology to that exposed in the United States (e.g. Parmalat, Ahold, Deutsche Telekom, Royal Dutch Shell, Standard Life, Vivendi), and repeated breaches in corporate governance by a series of listed firms were instrumental in the demise of an entire stock market in Germany (the Neuer Markt). A common pattern is identifiable where increasingly aggressive steps in financial reporting were followed by revelations of accounting practices far removed from presenting a true and fair view of a company's state of financial affairs. Bankruptcies or massive write-downs of capital revealed that reported earnings had frequently been manipulated to provide maximum returns to executive officers by hiding obligations and overestimating assets and earnings of the firm. In misguided quests for performance, mistakenly phrased in terms of 'shareholder value' and, ironically, 'corporate governance', executive compensation was frequently linked to meeting the very figures executives themselves had so imaginatively created.[12] What added to the confusion of observers, and eventual loss of a great deal of confidence in the corporate governance system as a whole, was the customary issuance of unqualified (i.e. approving) audit reports just prior to the announcement of major financial irregularities by the firms' lead auditors.

The Asian Financial Crisis of 1997/98 and the corporate debacles in the United States and Europe in the early years of the new millennium demonstrated a massive divergence in the interests between corporate executive management and those of other stakeholders of the firm. The case of Enron, the Asian Financial Crisis of 1997/98, the debacle of Germany's Neuer Markt stock exchange, and the Parmalat scandal are discussed in greater detail in Chapter 7 for the unique insights these provide to the discussion. The discussion of these cases will allow a reflection on the analytical material of the preceding chapters, and forms a basis for the policy discussion in Chapter 8.

While the near total absence of any real system of corporate governance in Asia at the time of the financial crisis (1997/98) is widely recognized, Europe, the United States, and Australia were frequently assumed to have established mature and highly effective systems to monitor managerial conduct (Shleifer and Vishny, 1997a; Clarke *et al.*, 2003). Sadly this was, and remains, simply not the case.[13] Nor is this a new problem, as the potential for a divergence in the interests of principal and agent has long been well documented in the literature (Smith, 1776; Berle and Means, 1932; Jensen and Meckling, 1976). Waves of corporate fraud have occurred with some degree of regularity throughout history and across very different regulatory regimes. There is little doubt that the more criminally adept members of the corporate elite thrived in the mid- to late 1990s, when a vibrant economy and booming stock market provided ample room for 'irrational exuberance' and 'infectious greed', to paraphrase former Federal Reserve Chairman Alan Greenspan.[14] Promises of financial rewards from artificially inflating stock prices appear to have tempted more than just a few executives to go one step beyond mere greed and to solidly transgress into the territory of fraud by deliberately issuing misleading financial reports.

The more recent cases of corporate misconduct in the United States and elsewhere are merely the latest (if spectacular) examples of accounting frauds that periodically enter public attention, rather than representing a new breed of scandals. Only a decade or so before the Enron cohort of frauds, for example, the United States was engulfed in the Savings and Loan debacle, and the junk bond saga. These had followed defence contractor bribery cases of the 1970s. The latter, in turn, were preceded by the self-dealing of the 1920s that led to the introduction of the 1930s securities laws and the establishment of the Securities and Exchange Commission (SEC). The United Kingdom suffered a string of corporate debacles in the late 1980s and early 1990s, including the collapse of Barings Bank, BCCI, the Maxwell group of companies, and Polly Peck. More recently, UK authorities were investigating the pensions disaster at insurer Equitable Life. Clarke *et al.* (2003) detail corporate collapses over four decades in Australia from the 1960s to the recent past, and emphasize the familiar patterns of the observed cases and subsequent (largely ineffective) legislative responses. Thailand, at the centre of the 1997/98 Asian financial crisis, a decade earlier had bailed out much of its banking and finance sector, only to repeat the exercise on a much larger scale in the late 1990s when the health of its entire economy was affected by widespread banking irregularities and overextensions of loans.

This recurrence of scandals gives rise to the question of whether more fundamental issues are being overlooked. Corporate scandals generally lead to changes in legislation.[15] Often, what are seen as specific and/or unique causes of a scandal are met with specific changes to particular rules, laws, and codes of best practice. Quite predictably, technical fixes are sought for what are presumed to be purely technical issues. Typical responses to corporate fraud, thus, focus on stronger penalties and additional layers of oversight, and more regulation. However, these have been tried in the past with little success (Clarke *et al.*, 2003; Coffee, 2003a). It would appear that the safeguards, rules, and sanctions put in place after a wave of scandals often prove inadequate to prevent the next cohort of frauds, which differ only in technical detail from previous cases. The particular financial instruments or vehicles used in those new cases may have changed, as specific earlier loopholes have been closed by legislation following the previous bout of scandals, but the general patterns remain.[16] Even strong enforcement of strict laws, while no doubt deterring some wrongdoing, does not seem to ensure a satisfactory convergence of the interests of principal and agent.[17] The Sarbanes-Oxley Act 2002, for example, in large parts elaborates standards of existing law which either had not been fully enforced, or were deemed not sufficiently visible (Cunningham, 2003). In comments relating to Parmalat, Ferrarini and Giudici (2005) make a similar argument with regard to the enforcement of corporate governance rules in Italy, emphasizing that law on the books can be very different from its application and enforcement. With particular, but not exclusive, reference to corporate scandals in Australia, Clarke *et al.* (2003) argue that many standards-setting exercises in response to corporate scandals ultimately fail to address what the authors see as the core problems of corporate governance failures.[18]

Common to many of the observed scandals is the near complete failure of the traditional monitors and gatekeepers of corporate governance. The frequent recurrence of corporate governance failures may indicate that the monitoring system of corporate governance, even where it is considered to be relatively advanced, is less reliable than had previously been assumed. Of paramount interest to the present investigation are questions of how and why monitors and gatekeepers so regularly acquiesce to the actions of senior management, or plainly fail to notice the (admittedly with hindsight) obvious. This book sheds light on behavioural and psychological reasons behind this failure of monitors to perform their duties. An argument is made that the fraudulent intentions of monitors and gatekeepers may, at least initially, be of less importance than previously thought as a cause for such failures. Enron demonstrates particularly well that the incentive structure motivating actors in a monitor-based and largely self-regulatory governance system generates less powerful checks against abuse than many observers had assumed. Partly because more about the Enron fraud is in the public domain, this book makes frequent use of this case and the particular US legal and regulatory setting in demonstrating the arguments put forth. However, the focus of the investigation is on human judgement in corporate governance, which obviously is not limited to Enron and the United States. It is suggested that the insights presented here are more widely applicable, and to an extent independent of any particular regulatory regime.

Of major concern are the behavioural foundations for the apparent failure of standard corporate governance mechanisms. A key issue is whether the observed corporate governance failures of, say, the Enron cohort are indicative of common underlying patterns of human behaviour, or constitute aberrant or atypical behaviour. This asks whether the Enron cohort was different in degree only, but not in substance, from other corporate governance failures, in earlier periods or outside the United States. If Enron is not an outlier, but instead indicative of typical behaviour in corporate governance, this would have important repercussions for the interpretation of human choice behaviour in a corporate setting. The traditional monitoring model of corporate governance suffers from inherent weaknesses due to a reliance on a model of human decision-making inappropriate in general, and specifically to the problems at hand. It is suggested that a key issue lies in misleading assumptions with regard to human decision-making, rather than a primarily insufficient implementation of existing governance mechanisms.

Further, this investigation argues that fraudulent behaviour or a lack of ethics are not necessarily the main problems in corporate scandals, though both can and probably do contribute to these. Although a lack of ethics might accompany corporate governance failures, it is difficult to make the point that ethics are in shorter supply than in earlier periods.[19] Instead, systematic cognitive/affective biases and psychological traits of the human mind influence agents' perception, judgement, and behaviour in ways largely ignored by models of choice behaviour which assume utility maximization. Patterns of acquiescence to, and rationalization of, the actions of management, as well as self-rationalization of own actions by monitors, can be explained by recourse to behavioural choice theories.

It is likely that intentional fraud by many participants played a part, and in some cases a major one, in recent accounting scandals, and there remains a need for effective compliance systems and penalties where laws are broken. Rules and regulations narrow the degrees of freedom within which fraudulent behaviour can occur, and penalties can act as a strong deterrent.[20] There is also no doubt that the rational model of decision-making sheds some light on the effects of such incentives on shaping behaviour. Nonetheless, it is suggested that many of the more pernicious and serious problems with corporate financial misreporting may not primarily be due to a lack of rules and regulations, or their insufficient enforcement. This book emphasizes the role of common cognitive and behavioural influences on decision-making in corporate governance which move agents away from the outcomes predicted by traditional rational choice theories. This provides a complementary explanation for failures of corporate governance. It is hoped that this will enrich the standard model of choice-making used by traditional economics.

The emphasis in much of the existing literature on corporate governance is on quantifiable relationships between some measure of corporate performance and traditional remedies to agency problems (such as independent directors, external audits, etc.). Factors in monitoring senior management's performance include the composition and independence of outside board members, transparency, outside reporting, accounting standards, and shareholder composition. The importance of these factors is emphasized in existing empirical research on corporate governance, which typically concentrates on quantifiable relationships between accounting measures of corporate performance and conventional remedies for agency problems (see, for example, Jones, 1991; Peasnell *et al.*, 2000a, b, 2002; Klein, 2002; DaDalt *et al.*, 2003). Suggested remedies include the use of independent directors on a company board and various board committees, and the independence of external auditors. This large body of research identifies important aspects of the problem of minimizing the conflicts between principal and agent. While this body of research identifies some important aspects of the agency problem, the present research raises questions regarding the effectiveness of this conventional approach in monitoring and controlling managerial performance.

This book looks at the human vulnerability to drift away from accepted behavioural norms in certain circumstances (Maccoby, 2000), the tendency of monitors to acquiesce to corporate misdeeds (Coffee, 2001; Langevoort, 2001a), the effect of unconscious bias during the corporate auditing process (Bazerman *et al.*, 2002a, b), and socio-psychological effects of group decision-making on judgement and decision quality (Janis, 1989). These, and more, factors may hide an impending corporate disaster from the eyes of the actors nearest to the events, as well as from the eyes of interested parties until after the facts become public knowledge. It is important to emphasize that unethical business practices (and by extension, fraud) may not always, certainly not initially, stem from a trade-off between ethics and profits, as might be assumed in the rational choice framework of economics. Instead, common judgement and decision-making processes can be a major contributing factor to what ultimately may become fraudulent, imprudent and destructive behaviour of senior management, and the acquiescence (or blindness) to such activities by their monitors and gatekeepers.

One proviso is required at this point. While decisions in corporate governance are frequently made at the individual level, this research is not a reflection of the actions of any particular individual. The 'cult of the individual' is correctly seen as a source of distraction when trying to disentangle corporate disasters (Clarke *et al.*, 2003). In contrast, the focus here is on systematic causes of corporate governance failures, with an emphasis on the choice behaviour of agents.

Any analysis that bases policy recommendations and laws on a set of incentives has to make assumptions on how individuals respond to these incentives. Scholars in the law and economics tradition have long since adopted the assumptions of the economist's rational choice theory (Burrows and Veljanovski, 1981). Much of the prior research on corporate governance, policy recommendations, and standard economic and legal analysis means for minimizing the agency problem are premised on the assumption of strongly rational agents with long-term time horizons and stable and consistent preferences (Fama, 1980; Easterbrook and Fischel, 1991; Shleifer and Vishny, 1997a; Prentice, 2000). Issues of human cognition, perception, and actual choice behaviour under uncertainty receive somewhat less attention in the standard debate of the agency problem.

Members of the board of directors and external auditors are, for example, thought to care about their reputation and their prospects in the job market, which is theorized to discipline their actions. Yet, individuals (and groups) frequently fall short of the normative standards suggested by rational choice theories by, for example, sacrificing their considerable reputation for relatively minor rewards. This book investigates the underlying cognitive and behavioural factors which can lead agents to deviate from the predictions made by rational choice models of decision-making. Crucial questions of this investigation include the following: What makes monitors and gatekeepers deviate from what is expected of them, and from the obligations they have contracted to? How do they justify this to themselves? Are the identified behaviour patterns exceptional, or are these the result of common motivational, cognitive, and affective factors which are an integral part of human choice behaviour? Finally, with respect to the behaviour of agents in corporate governance, is it possible to control for these effects, or at least keep these to a minimum? These questions are discussed with particular reference to the behaviour of two important groups of monitors in corporate governance, the external auditor and members of the board of directors. The inclusion of behavioural aspects in the corporate governance debate can significantly contribute to a more effective understanding of the agency problems caused by the separation of decision and risk-bearing. Basing the analysis of corporate governance on psychologically more realistic assumptions may also lead to better policies to deal with the issues arising from the separation of ownership and control.

The potential shortcomings of rational choice theory on decision-making in explaining actor behaviour have not gone unnoticed in the literature or among practitioners. The law and economics movement in particular appears to be in a paradigm switch from the neo-classical, rather mechanical conception of decision-making, towards one that incorporates psychologically more realistic notions of human nature. Leading scholars and practitioners have become increasingly concerned about diminishing returns from the application of the principles of standard microeconomics to human choice behaviour (Korobkin and Ulen, 2000). Behavioural economics offers one potential extension to the standard economic interpretation of decision-making. This newly emerging branch of economics strives to integrate insights from psychological research into economic science by basing human judgement and decision-making on rigorously testable assumptions. In economics, as in all sciences, it is critically important to determine whether a particular theory is consistent with what happens in the real world. Over the years, many researchers have criticized some of the tenets of mainstream economics as being psychologically unrealistic and in conflict with behavioural evidence (Simon, 1959; Rabin, 2002). Unrealistic assumptions may of course not necessarily be a problem when designing a model to explain core issues in economic research (Friedman, 1957). It is the accuracy of predictions that matters. Where, however, model predictions persistently conflict with observations, it might be unwise to insist that reality conforms to the model.

In this book attention is centred on monitors and gatekeepers, selecting auditors and directors of the board to keep the discussion focused. The role of lawyers and investment bankers as two agents with important gatekeeper functions will, however, be briefly discussed. A key question is whether independence and impartiality of monitors are reasonable assumptions of corporate governance. Arguments are introduced such that departures from arm's length outcomes should, if anything, be expected as the rule, rather than the exception. A wave of large corporate scandals in the early part of the twenty-first century revealed significant, and arguably systemic, weaknesses in the control mechanisms designed to supervise senior management. It is questionable whether reforms based on standard assumptions of behaviour of monitors in corporate governance are sufficient to prevent corporate scandals from occurring in the future. Or are these reforms little more than cosmetic sticking plaster to give the appearance of having righted the corporate ship while leaving it still fundamentally adrift? A somewhat pessimistic conclusion would suggest that they are insufficient. It may be inherent in human nature to gamble imprudently, to cheat, and to lie. Potentially more damaging to the monitoring and gatekeeping function than fraudulent motivations may be the tendency of the human cognitive apparatus to rationalize own behaviour and beliefs, even when in conflict with existing norms or reality. This does, nevertheless, provide some room for optimism as such deviations from the 'rational norm' tend to be systematic in nature, and might be anticipated and reflected in policies and rules. It is strongly suggested that a failure to appreciate behavioural influences on choice and decision-making impedes an effective approach to minimizing the agency problem. The subsequent discussion hopes to provide a more realistic interpretation of monitor failure, and suggests improvements to existing corporate governance regulations.

Chapter 2 introduces the principal–agent problem that arises from the separation of decision and risk-bearing, or more traditionally, the separation of ownership and control. The roles of the board of directors and the external auditors in the monitoring model of corporate governance are introduced. Chapter 3 discusses in some depth the concept of earnings management, with a particular focus on its measurement and economic significance. Chapter 4 describes features of the rational model of decision-making and shows how conventional means to minimize the principal–agent problem are premised on critical assumptions underlying this standard model of economics. This is contrasted with an introduction to insights from behavioural economics and cognitive research. Chapter 5 identifies, discusses, and illustrates a wide range of biases, heuristics, and social pressures that affect the judgement and decision-making of individuals and groups. Chapter 6 assesses potential partial solutions to the agency problem, and discusses questions with regard to the feasibility of independence of the board of directors and external auditors. This is contrasted with findings from cognitive, social and behavioural research that demonstrates how corporate governance mechanisms may be undermined by common human traits. Chapter 7 highlights some recent failures in corporate governance, including Enron, Parmalat, Germany's Neuer Markt, and the Asian Financial Crisis of 1997/98. These descriptive case studies refer back to and support the preceding analytical material. This section also forms a bridge to the subsequent discussion on governance policy. Chapter 8 discusses implications for policy, relevant not only to the two groups of monitors at the centre of the present discussion, but applicable also to other monitors and gatekeepers in corporate governance. This includes corporate lawyers and legal counsel, who have largely escaped allocation of blame, despite their key role in corporate governance and in the scandals under discussion. Another important agent in corporate governance discussed here is investment banks, frequently counterpart to the very business deals at the heart of corporate scandals. Chapter 9 concludes and summarizes the presented findings and discusses open questions.

2 Overview of corporate governance

Definitions of corporate governance

Under investigation is the monitoring model of corporate governance with an emphasis on large corporations where decision-makers do not bear a major share of the wealth effects of their decisions. The principal–agent model is interpreted through the contractual view of the firm (Coase, 1937; Jensen and Meckling, 1976; Fama and Jensen, 1983a, b). A key issue in the agency view of corporate governance is how to align the interests of the agent with those of the principal. Other important issues include the timely minimization of any divergences, and how to balance the need for and the cost of monitoring with the benefits that arise from the separation of control and ownership. An effective system for decision control implies, by definition, that the control of decisions is to some extent separate from the management of decisions (Fama and Jensen, 1983b). That is, meaningful ratification and monitoring of decisions need to be separate from their initiation and implementation. The role of gatekeepers, their effectiveness, and their motivation in monitoring managerial behaviour is central to the discussion.

The principal–agent problem describes a situation where one or many individuals (principals) rely on one or more individuals (agents) to act on their behalf. This includes the stewardship over corporate assets when shareholders hire senior executives to manage companies. In the case of the large corporation, shareholders and other providers of risk capital typically form a widely dispersed group, which necessitates the use of professional management to run the firm. A key issue of the principal–agent arrangement is the potential divergence of interests between the two parties. The actions of the agents are frequently not directly observable, which gives rise to the problem of incomplete and asymmetric information between the two sides. Information asymmetry refers to the situation where one party (or economic 'agents', which includes individuals as well as firms) has more or better information than the other party. Usually, the agent has more information about the state of affairs, including their own performance, than the principal. This introduces, among others, the potential for self-dealing, negligence, and deliberate fraud by the agent.

As agent behaviour is not fully observable, it is not usually sufficient to rely on contracts to control the activities of agents. The use of various forms of monitoring and performance incentive schemes is typically recommended to further minimize potential divergences of interests. The principal–agent problem is found in most employer/employee relationships, and firms typically also have internal principal–agent issues. The internal agency problem refers to the need to monitor the actions of agents acting on behalf of the firm (e.g. employees) to ensure conformance to company objectives. In corporate governance, the conflicts of interest of greatest concern are those between executive management (the insiders) and all parties who have a stake in the firm (the outsiders). These outsiders include shareholders and other providers of capital, but also employees, customers, suppliers, and other stakeholders. Insiders typically have access to privileged information which may be of relevance to outsiders. As corporate governance is concerned about the efficiency with which a company is run on its capital resources, the flow of important financial information between insiders and outsiders and the reliability of financial reporting are important components of the monitoring system.

Agency problems between stockholders and top executives arise as the result of the separation of ownership and control of assets, or, alternatively, where there is a separation of the decision and risk-bearing functions (Fama, 1980; Fama and Jensen, 1983a). The separation of ownership and control is a defining feature of the modern large corporation (Berle and Means, 1932). The minimization of agency problems in the decision process is of particular importance where the decision-makers are not the major residual claimants (Fama and Jensen, 1983b), and therefore do not bear a major share of the wealth effects of their decisions. Fama (1980) emphasizes the difference between a firm's 'owners' and its 'security holders' or 'risk-bearers'. For the most part, these terms are used somewhat interchangeably in this book without significant loss in the main thrust of the argument.

The need for corporate governance

The separation between ownership and management opens the possibility of insider abuse. The use of rules, incentives (e.g. implicit or explicit contracts), and monitoring is designed to align the interests of agents with the desires of principals and thus minimize the potential for insider abuse and mismanagement. Without effective control, decision-makers in the firm might be tempted to take actions that deviate from the interests of residual claimants. The divergence of interests may manifest itself, among other variations, in extravagant or risky investments, insufficient effort, entrenchment, and self-dealing. The requirement to prepare and periodically publish financial reports is one means to provide investors with information on the financial state of the firm. In an ideal world, management would be focused on the performance of the firm (running it as effectively and efficiently as possible), and performance reporting would then be a straightforward matter of following existing accounting standards to produce a picture of a firm's economic and financial reality. However, the considerable discretion provided by accounting standards can result in the devotion of considerable managerial energy to drafting a financial report which suits management interests, rather than providing an accurate reflection of economic reality and the financial performance of the firm.

Contemporary examples of corporate looting and mismanagement by top executives, negligent boards, and accountants' alleged complicity make for good headlines in the popular press and provide a colourful glimpse of human folly. The problem of controlling the manager of a firm is, however, hardly new. Research from Smith (1776) to Berle and Means (1932), and more recently, Jensen and Meckling (1976), Fama (1980), and Shleifer and Vishny (1997a) suggests top management may decide expropriation of the owner/shareholder to be an optimal choice decision. Managers hired by the owners of the firm may systematically make choices that are not in the owners' best interests, as Adam Smith observed over 200 years ago,

> The directors of such companies [joint stock companies] however, being the managers rather of other people's money than of their own, it cannot well be expected that they should watch over it with the same anxious vigilance with which the partners in a private copartnery [corporation or joint stock company] frequently watch over their own.
>
> (Smith, 1776)

Smith's reference to the principal–agent problem highlights the necessity of aligning the interests of these two parties. In a more contemporary setting, Berle and Means (1932) referred to the alignment of the interests between management and the holders of the firm's capital (and possibly other stakeholders).

There is little that effectively explains why a manager should not 'run off with the money' (Shleifer and Vishny, 1997a). Nor why investors expect to get a decent return on their investment, and why investors in common stock part so easily with their money, given the fact that once parted from this capital, they have, with the possible exception of large shareholders, virtually no further say in the running of the company. This is especially puzzling since shareholders are last in line for payment when a company enters bankruptcy proceedings under most corporate bankruptcy law systems.[1] That this is not a mere academic concern is indicated by estimates of the upper bounds of agency costs. Estimates for Russian firms reach as high as 99 per cent of the firm's potential value (Boycko *et al.*, 1995; Black, 2001a). Such estimates, and the central role of corporate governance failures in the Asian financial crisis of 1997/1998, give an indication of the potential damage to the real economy when corporate governance mechanisms are mostly absent.

The rash of highly visible corporate bankruptcies in the United States and in Europe in the early 2000s has shown that fraud and mismanagement in the corporation remains a significant issue in countries where corporate governance systems are considered to be advanced. A firm's value depends not only on its future economic prospects, or how efficiently capital is being used, but also on the effectiveness of control mechanisms, which help ensure that investors' funds are not expropriated or wasted in value decreasing projects. La Porta *et al.* (2002) found that valuation of corporate assets was positively correlated with the quality of shareholder protection for firms across a sample of 27 developed countries. Similar results were reported for US firms by Gompers *et al.* (2003). Klapper and Love (2003) reported a high positive correlation between corporate governance measures and market valuations for firms from 14 emerging stock markets. Black *et al.* (2003) found a positive correlation between corporate governance quality and the valuation of Korean firms. Finally, Drobetz *et al.* (2004) found a strong positive relationship between the quality of corporate governance and firm valuation for German public firms.

These issues would also appear to be of relevance to another important, but somewhat neglected issue – namely the question as to whom the corporation should ultimately be accountable to. The compatibility of shareholder wealth maximization and long-term sustainability of the firm, and indeed that of an entire economy, deserves a thorough discussion.[2] Lazonick and O'Sullivan (2000) and O'Sullivan (2000) identify the significant shortcomings of the shareholder wealth maximization version of corporate governance, and question whether this in fact improves the long-term performance of corporate enterprises.[3] The rate of return on corporate stock may be a poor measure of a firm's performance, especially over longer periods, and also tends to neglect discussion on other stakeholders.[4] Alternative interpretations explore the link between corporate governance and innovation, and ask how the process of innovation leads to increases in the performance of dynamic economies (O'Sullivan, 2000). Emphasized in these investigations is the need for organizational control over the allocation of resources in the economy, and the relationship between resource allocation and corporate governance. O'Sullivan's work (2000) is a challenging examination of the links between the general business environment and the operations, decisions, and organization of firms.

The work of Lazonick and O'Sullivan provides a valuable extension to the contemporary debate on corporate governance which, in their view, largely ignores the implications for the governance of corporations for the development, organization, and strategic allocation of resources of an economy. Highlighted are some of the limitations of the shareholder and stakeholder arguments with respect to the role of the firm in innovation. Further demonstrated are potential shortcomings of the agency view of corporate governance due to looking primarily at a small subset of the issue that arises from the separation of ownership and control of the firm. The question of to whom the corporation should ultimately be accountable to is an important one. However, it would seem that effective monitoring is required irrespective of the different interpretations of the economic goals of a firm. If this interpretation is correct, then it should be useful to have an adequate understanding of motivation and choice behaviour within a corporate setting.

Implementing corporate governance

The identification of means to ensure that principals are not expropriated and also earn a decent return on their investment has been widely discussed in the literature (for an overview, see Shleifer and Vishny, 1997a). Empirical research on corporate governance frequently investigates quantifiable relationships between various measures of corporate performance and specific remedies to agency problems. Of critical importance is the independence of directors of the board or board committee, and the independence of external auditors (Jones, 1991; Peasnell *et al.*, 2000a, b; DaDalt *et al.*, 2003). A variety of instruments, including monitoring, performance bonuses, equity shares, promotions and dismissal of senior management, are designed to help align the agent's incentives with those of the principal. While incentive motivation and monitoring have important roles to play in corporate governance, implementation of these control mechanisms remains difficult. Unfortunately, it would also appear that many of the lessons from research and past experiences of corporate scandals are frequently ignored in real world applications (Langevoort, 1998a, b; 2001a, b; 2002a, b). Worse yet, and of particular relevance to the present research, is the possibility that even when the relevant control mechanisms have been put in place and are implemented as suggested, things can still go seriously wrong (Clarke *et al.*, 2003).

Applied solutions to minimize the agency problem are typically aimed at an effective design of incentive contracts and monitoring systems, realizing that the manager retains a considerable degree of freedom within these constraints (Grossman and Hart, 1986). Important elements of contracts and monitoring systems include the establishment of a board of directors and various board committees, the use of independent directors on the board and committees, the mandating of external auditing, public reporting of audited financial reports, adherence to established accounting rules and principles, supervision of areas of corporate activity by government and non-government agencies, and legal liability provisions. Nonetheless, effective monitoring remains subject to implementation difficulties (Langevoort, 2001a). Issues which frequently complicate effective monitoring include the measurement of performance, and the verification of compliance to contractual agreements. How can gatekeepers ensure that these measures are not manipulated by the agents whose performance is to be measured and monitored? Further, how reliable are the various monitors in judging the performance variables, and in subsequently intervening when remedial action is deemed necessary? Finally, how effective is legal liability as a deterrent, both for managers and for their gatekeepers?

It would be ideal if the two sides to the agency problem could devise a contract that comprehensively regulates what the manager can do with invested funds, how any surpluses will be divided, and what happens if any of the covenants are violated. Since it is not possible to contract for every contingency, complete contracting is not feasible or in fact desirable (Williamson, 1988, 1996). The next best way to minimize agency problems might be through high levels of monitoring. Yet, this is often impractical as direct and indirect costs rise very rapidly with the level of monitoring. Excessive monitoring can also lead to counter-productive responses in the firm (e.g. evasion, and damage to motivation). A critical issue, and one which will be further discussed in subsequent chapters, is that monitors, including external auditing firms, face internal agency problems of their own, which complicate and compromise their monitoring role. Thus, despite contracts and monitoring, the manager has a considerable degree of freedom within these constraints and, for practical reasons, retains the residual control rights.

Means of managerial control

Compensation

It is a cornerstone of modern compensation practices to tie the financial well-being of executive managers to the fortunes of the firm. When designed to reward good managerial performance, this can motivate the manager to take care of the firm's financial well-being (Jensen and Murphy, 1990a, b). If the incentive component of the contract is substantial and appropriately structured, compensation contracts can be useful in minimizing the potential divergences between the interests of the manager and capital providers. Share ownership, stock options, and cash bonuses are examples of incentives that have been utilized to that purpose. To make such contracts effective, the incentive contract will need to specify firm performance measures which are closely correlated to managerial decision-making. Firm performance variables are frequently based on accounting items such as turnover, earnings, return on equity, return on investment, return on assets, and combinations thereof.

Incentive contracts are common in practice and widely discussed in the literature. However, while 'agency theory predicts that compensation will depend on relative performance evaluation, [it] gives little guidance to the form of this contract' (Gibbons and Murphy, 1990: 43). Berle and Means (1932) argued that management ownership in the modern corporation is far too small to make the manager interested in maximizing returns for the investor. Jensen and Murphy (1990a, b) subsequently looked at sensitivity of pay of US executives to performance, and proposed that executives' compensation typically provided an insufficient link to the prospects of the firm. This was seen as evidence of inefficient compensation arrangements and subsequently interpreted as support for an increase in 'at risk' compensation through the use of stock and option grants. The sensitivity of reward to performance is a key motivational aspect in aligning the interests of the manager with those of the capital providers.

While the variation of executive income could be significant (for an alignment of interests), even under the relatively weak link indicated by Jensen and Murphy (1990b), the implied swings in current income might already be unacceptable to risk-averse or even risk-neutral executives. Portfolio diversification considerations alone would advocate against holding one asset only. Thus, an executive manager could be excused for diversifying asset holdings, as represented by corporate compensation. At some point, however, such diversification would appear to defeat the incentive value of risky compensation. This concern is highlighted where firms compensate senior executives for losses in the risk-bearing component of compensation, say by backdating options. This particular practice not only minimizes the risk of losing such compensation, but may also amount to securities fraud, as evidenced by the ongoing investigations of this practice by the US Securities and Exchange Commission (SEC) against US companies.[5]

An additional problem in using accounting variables as a proxy for managerial performance is that the firm's senior executives have considerable discretion and control over these and related accounting measures. Hence, to a degree, the choice of benchmarks against which a manager's performance is evaluated, and their realization (i.e. whether the manager has met them), are endogenous and subject to managerial control (Dechow and Skinner, 2000).[6] One consequence is that the incentive contract, which is meant to control the manager, can provide the motivation and the tools for managerial manipulation of financial reporting. In the extreme, a manager may take steps that allow personal benefit at the cost of other stakeholders of the firm, and even risk the firm's survival.

Yermack (1997) analyses the timing of CEO stock option awards as a method of investigating corporate managers' influence over the terms of their own compensation, and reports that managers receive stock options shortly before good news and delay such option grants until after bad news announcements. These results on the timing of option grants suggest that options may sometimes be misused as a covert mechanism of self-dealing rather than an incentive device (see also Bebchuk and Fried, 2003). This is complicated by the fact that compensation contracts are usually negotiated by a board of directors, the members of which are in turn dependent on, and typically appointed by, the executive whose compensation they determine and whose performance they are meant to monitor. In the optimal contracting view of the world, managers' incentives are closely aligned with those of the shareholders.

> The . . . pay of . . . C.E.O.'s reflects intense competition among companies for the best managerial talent. Stock options and other typical forms of executive compensation are designed to provide incentives for performance. These incentives align the personal interests of managers with those of shareholders.
>
> (Krugman, 2002a)

Krugman refers to the difficulties of effective monitoring with regard to the monitoring of executive performance by the board of directors. Specifically, he asks what happens to corporate governance if senior management captures the board and, thus, voids much of the latter's monitoring functions. An evaluation of the ways in which incentive contracts have been designed suggests that these may, in part, be due to motivations other than a minimization of the agency problem (Krugman, 2002a, b). Much of the notion of stock options disciplining managers, for example, is still based on the assumptions of the efficient market hypothesis (EMH).[7] However, given numerous examples of rewards for managerial underperformance and outright mismanagement, why should the solution to bad management be a bigger pay cheque?

Shortcomings in the motivational value of incentive contracts would appear to be particularly pronounced in cases where the incentive effect (through executive income) from share ownership by executives (through shares or share options) is insufficiently small or incorrectly implemented (Jensen and Murphy, 1990b). An incentive effect would also be weakened by allowing the short-term sale of such instruments, or by hedging, which diminishes the risk of holding such instruments. In this case there is no performance incentive effect and shares/options effectively are an endowment. The ability to exercise shares or exercise option rights (or similar compensation components) before any meaningful performance assessment can take place would seem to largely negate the link between pay and performance.

The optimal contracting model also assumes an adversarial or at least functionally independent role of the directors of the board in setting executive compensation. It is questionable how realistic an interpretation this is. The rent extraction framework can perhaps better explain some of the puzzles that confound the optimal compensation model, which include the uniform use of in-the-money options, widespread managers' freedom to unwind their incentive packages, and the apparently common practice of options reprising, backdating, and reloading. The lack of effective restrictions on unwinding or hedging incentive packages further allows managers to avoid risk that dilutes *ex ante* incentives. This interpretation of the relationship between top executives and the board would lead to the conclusion that many executive compensation schemes might in fact pervert the role of this instrument as a check to the agency problem.

Compensation arrangements are likely to be subject to both market forces (as suggested by the optimal contracting view), which push towards a minimization of the agency costs, and managerial power, which pushes the outcome towards one where the managers can extract rent. Executive pay practices in the 1980s and 1990s may have largely abandoned the link between performance and pay.[8] Indeed, lucrative compensation packages appear frequently to have been rewarded with scant regard to the financial state of the company. This may have undermined the efficiency of incentive contracts as a tool to align managerial interests with those of the providers of capital. Further support for such an interpretation comes from an analysis of executive compensation as a proportion of firm earnings. Between 1993 and 2003, for example, executive pay as a proportion of firm earnings doubled from 5 per cent to 10 per cent of firm earnings for US firms (Bebchuk and Grinstein, 2005). Equity-based compensation grew considerably in this period, without having been accompanied by a reduction in non-equity compensation. Since the increase in the share of a firm's earnings going to executive compensation could not be attributed to changes in size and performance of firms, this raises important issues with regard to the quality of the pay-setting process (Bebchuk and Grinstein, 2005).

The ideal of a board bargaining with the executives at arm's length, and assumptions of executives being constrained by market forces and norms may be far removed from reality. This is reflected in observations that managerial restraint in salaries and perquisites, as it may have existed for the first two decades after the Second World War, no longer seem to apply (Krugman, 2002a). A permutation of Krugman's 'outrage constraint' is found in Jensen and Murphy (1990a) under the term 'political constraint'. In either case, this refers to a limit to executive compensation (the rents derived from being able to set their own contracts) stemming from a perceived reluctance of directors to approve, and the executive to seek, compensation packages that might be viewed as outrageous by outside observers. Even a cursory survey of compensation packages and analyses of income divergence between CEO compensation and average worker pay in the United States would indicate that this constraint has lost much of the moderating influence it might at one time have had (Krugman, 2002a, b).

That 'the near complete absence of relative pay seems to be a puzzle' (Hall and Liebman, 1998: 682, n. 34), referring to the tendency for CEO compensation not to vary much with fluctuations in a firm's fortunes, and generally not to suffer on the downside as a company or the market does badly, is a puzzle mainly for the optimal contract view.[9] The same empirical facts are less of a surprise to the rent extraction interpretation of the managerial power view. As noted earlier, protecting executive compensation from any downside risk, whilst at the same time virtually guaranteeing gains to the upside, would seem to remove the incentive motivation aspects ascribed to pay-for-performance compensation. The expectation that firms will adjust compensation upwardly *ex post* for adverse stock price movements undermines *ex ante* incentives. Where executives get paid their full contractual remuneration on failure, this would indicate a perversion of the pay-for-performance principle.

Worse yet, guaranteed compensation may become a motivator for behaviour which destroys shareholder wealth.[10] If an executive is aware *ex ante* of getting paid a generous severance package, irrespective of performance, as long as no gross negligence or fraud can be determined, the notion of pay for performance and incentive motivation is not only substantially depreciated. Where a compensation package is virtually guaranteed, this can lead to managerial behaviour that effectively widens the divergence of interests between agent and principal. Corporate decisions (and the reporting of their financial impact) then might be based on personal considerations, rather than on benefit to the firm, a situation where private cost–benefit concerns replace corporate cost–benefit considerations. Similarly, insignificant financial (and negligible reputational) cost to the executive from excessive perquisite consumption, or empire-building, may induce excessive risk-taking.

Thus, while theoretical consideration of the agency problem has identified a number of relatively clear and straightforward instruments for implementing a measure of monitoring and control on the principal, theory and practice can diverge significantly. In many instances of corporate debacles, managers' interests were allowed to be in serious misalignment with the interests of the owners of the firm and other stakeholders. Massive golden handshake and golden parachute arrangements that are payable no matter how badly a manager has performed, or indeed whether the company is still a going concern, can be expected to pervert managerial incentives. The spread of such practices and their ultimate effects are a subject for empirical analysis. It is valid to ask whether existing incentive structures may at times have tilted the individual cost–benefit consideration in the direction where appropriately cushioned dismissal was preferable to enhancing corporate performance and continued employment (Johnson *et al.*, 2006).

Reputation

The literature on the separation of security ownership and control (Fama, 1980; Milgrom and Roberts, 1992; Shleifer and Vishny, 1997a) refers to the outside managerial labour market as one additional source of pressure on the performance of the manager. Concerns with regard to reputation, return on human capital, and the competition for managerial talent on the market are thought to provide the manager with an incentive not to deviate significantly from expectations on the marginal product to be achieved by his/her employment by the firm.

Reputation is likely to play some role in the decision-making process. In theory, rational managerial labour markets, efficient capital markets, and rational investors could devise *ex ante* contracts that affect a necessary *ex post* settling up, in order to reflect any divergence from expected and actual managerial performance. The problem remains that 'a game which is fair on an ex ante basis does not induce the same behaviour as a game in which there is also ex post settling up' (Fama, 1980: 296). Another problem with reputation is that it inevitably runs into a backward recursion problem when the future benefits to the manager from being honest are dwarfed by the potential return from being dishonest (Bulow and Rogoff, 1989).[11]

Where full *ex post* settling up is not done or is not feasible, potential losses from separation of ownership and control arise. In addition, this control mechanism loses effectiveness where the weight of a wage revision is insufficient to resolve potential problems with managerial incentives. That is, situations may arise where the anticipated future compensation changes are insufficient to prevent self-dealing, outright theft, or decisions which lack any concern for expected returns.[12] This includes end-game situations (where, for example, the manager is at the end of his/her career), scenarios where the reputational loss accrues mainly to the firm and not to the manager, and where the returns to the individual manager from activities deviating from those of the owners massively outweigh any possible losses in future labour market returns.[13] The discussion will return later to questions regarding reputation as a deterrent to fraudulent behaviour.

Sanctions

Senior managers frequently escape relatively unscathed and with their personal wealth largely intact after a company is tarnished by scandal. Of the hundreds of individuals who benefited generously though their work for, or association with Enron, only a handful have been indicted and sentenced (although heavily in some cases), and it remains open whether any of the other top officers will be forced to surrender much of the financial gains they made during their association with the company.[14] If the past is a reliable guide, it is unlikely that many of Enron's top-200 officers, who received a total of some $1.4bn in salary, shares, and bonuses in the 12 months prior to the firm's collapse, will be forced to give up these financial gains (US Senate, 2003b).[15] This may send out the unfortunate message that white-collar crime, on average, pays handsomely. In any case, the personal wealth of these managers is unlikely to even remotely compensate investors and less fortunate Enron employees for the losses incurred when the firm went bankrupt.

The value of sanctions as a deterrence to undesirable behaviour (including economic crime) has been questioned in general.[16] The conventional economic argument suggests that sanctions act as a deterrent to legal transgressions.[17] A rational actor is expected to conduct an analysis of the expected costs and benefits, where the personal benefit of violating a rule or regulation or participating in excessive risk-taking is balanced against the risk of getting discovered, and the likely magnitude of expected penalties. The value of sanctions as a deterrent, is, however, not obvious, neither theoretically nor empirically. There are three typically suggested ways to deter an objectionable activity: (1) increased policing, (2) increased fines, and (3) increased social stigma attached to the activity. These conclusions are standard, though not universally shared.[18] Conventional economic theory suggests similar measures to deter other forms of objectionable or illegal actions. However, punishment-based deterrence does not seem to work very well, neither as a means to deter repeat offences, nor as a means to prevent first-offenders from committing a wrongdoing.[19] The standard prescriptions face a problem when individuals either, a) apply motivated reasoning to rationalize the probability of detection and/or the likelihood or severity of sanctions to a minimum, or b) fall into cognitive traps which unconsciously prevent an accurate perception of the risks from, or impropriety of, a particular activity (Rabin, 2002).

An additional factor may diminish the deterrence impact of sanctions. If much of the reputational and financial loss from discovered irregularities perpetrated by an individual agent is assumed to fall on the firm, then the choice of an ambitious rational actor might well be to engage in a rogue act (Langevoort, 1998b, 2001a). Indeed, under some circumstances, a rational cost–benefit profit maximization calculation may overwhelmingly point the actor towards a violation of rules and regulations. This is further enhanced if the payoff is either immensely large, or the actor is in an end-game situation. A yet more interesting outcome is presented by actors who go ahead with a violation of rules despite relatively small rewards in relation to significant risks of severe penalties (Viscusi, 1996). Such behaviour may violate the axioms of rational choice behaviour and utility maximization, but may nevertheless be a potent force on current choice behaviour, even if it subsequently leads to regret of own actions (Korobkin and Ulen, 2000). Further deviations from the expected outcomes of models of rational choice and decision-making will be investigated shortly.

Institutional investors

Large investors, including pension funds, mutual funds, venture firms, insurance companies, banks, and more recently, hedge funds, may engage with firms in their portfolio to positively influence outcomes of the managerial process. Within the standard principal–agent framework, the threat of exit by investors and executive incentive contracts are means to align the interests of owners and managers. Unlike the conventional 'arm's-length' approach, activist investors tend to use their ownership stakes to engage with companies that underperform, rather than selling their investments (Parkinson, 1995). Institutional investors may increasingly encourage better performance of companies in their portfolio by engagement with senior management (Hartzell and Starks, 2003; Doidge *et al.*, 2005; Stulz, 2005; Ferreira and Matos, 2006).[20]

An increase in investor activism in the form of engagement suggests that the traditional 'arm's-length' approach favoured by the conventional finance model may be somewhat oversimplified. Under the assumption that company financial performance can be enhanced by improvements in its management practice, institutional ownership can make a contribution to overcoming problems of asymmetric information and incomplete contracts (Myners, 2001). The UK's Companies Act 2006 advocates engagement (following the 'enlightened shareholder value' approach of the 2002 draft bill), emphasizing enhanced shareholder engagement and a long-term investment culture (UK, 2006; also see DTI, 2007). Such an engagement is seen as an additional means of matching investor expectations and actual company practice. There is less of an emphasis on direct intervention with regard to day-to-day managerial decisions.

Investor activism (a term which can generally be applied to investors engaging with the management of companies in their portfolio) may have an especially important role to play in stopping problems before they get out of hand. Institutional shareholder activism has, until recently, not been as strongly supported in the US, apart from some prominent exceptions (e.g. Calpers, the California Public Employees' Retirement System), and has lacked the weight of the generally more coordinated UK engagements. In order to perform their governance function, investors may engage with target firms by exercising their voting rights at general meetings, in formal and informal discussions with management to present views and transfer information, by attaching conditions to the provision of further funds, and through direct takeover of target firms (Black, 1998; Gillan and Starks, 2000, 2002; FRC, 2003).

While there is mixed empirical evidence on the systematic impact of investor activism on firm performance, a glance at the performance of dedicated activist funds suggests that as an investment strategy activism can have a significant impact. A good example may be the original Hermes Focus Fund, which, between 1998 and 2004, outperformed the FTSE all-share index by some 4.5 per cent on an annualized basis (Hermes, 2004). In the US, a fund run by Relational Investors LLC has also outperformed its benchmarks since being launched in 1996 (Hermes, 2004). Institutional investors may have a significant information advantage because they not only refer to the public information released from companies (such as accounting information in annual reports) but also have access to private information through direct and indirect communication with firm management (Holland, 1997, 1998a, b). This allows institutional investors to diagnose potential problems companies face in terms of operating strategy, management quality, effectiveness of board, and financial performance. The form of engagement varies with the goal of engagement, and can range from cooperative dialogue to hostile negotiations (Useem, 1996; Pellet, 1998; Byrne, 1999). The UK Combined Code emphasizes the use of their votes by institutional investors and, where practicable, suggests they enter into dialogue (FRC, 2003, 2006). To go public with concerns is generally considered to be a last step in an escalated effort for institutional investors, as this may signal unwillingness by target management to respond to more cooperative attempts at negotiation (Gillan and Starks, 2000; Prevost and Rao, 2000). Proxy voting (Davey, 1991), media campaigns (Rehfeld, 1998) and shareholder proposals (Del Guercio and Hawkins, 1999) are more public forms of such engagement.[21] An explicit activism strategy is advocated by Myners (2001) and addresses issues such as when to intervene, what approach to use, and how effectiveness may be measured.

The monitoring role of institutional investors in the UK has, historically, generally been more significant and stronger than in the US. Share-ownership in the UK is more concentrated in the hands of institutional investors than in the US, although institutional shareholdings as a percentage of outstanding shares are rapidly increasing in the US. Institutional shareholders hold some 80 per cent of shares in the UK (DTI, 2005b), compared to just over 60 per cent in the US (Conference Board, 2007). Of significance is that institutional investors hold stronger proxy voting rights in the UK. The UK Combined Code provides shareholders with considerable powers to appoint directors to company boards and various board committees, replace CEOs and chairmen, and influence their remuneration, powers which are increasingly exercised through institutional shareholders.

There are some historical reasons for the relatively strong presence of institutional investors in the UK compared to the US. High personal income tax rates during the post-war period suppressed individual retail shareholding in the UK, while tax exemptions for pensions led to a rapid increase in the assets managed by institutional investors and mutual funds. Large institutional shareholders in the UK also supported stronger corporate governance controls and norms. In the United States, federal and state regulation in the first half of the twentieth century limited the equity that banks and insurance companies could hold. This partially explains a higher degree of retail investor participation in US equities markets and a traditionally more reluctant response by institutional investors. The relative weakness of institutional investors and the comparatively large size of the retail investor market have been cited as one reason for greater federal corporate disclosure requirements and more aggressive securities law enforcement in the US.[22]

Institutional investors in the US are increasingly active in engaging with portfolio company management, and the SEC is under pressure to allow institutional investors to be more influential in the use of proxy votes to elect members to the board and the remuneration and audit committees, bringing the US more in line with governance guidelines especially in London but also elsewhere in Europe.[23] Hedge fund managers may be particularly motivated to become active investors. Traditional institutional investors in the US have become more outspoken in recent years, partially due to having, since 2004, to disclose proxy votes. It is too early to say whether shareholder activism in the US will continue to insist on asserting the rights of shareholders to exercise control over managers. However, if the observed pressure for an advisory shareholder vote on executive pay is evidence of an underlying current of greater involvement by investors, this would reinforce the view that the board is accountable to shareholders (see *The Economist*, 2 June 2007).

Specific corporate governance mechanisms

The board of directors

The board of directors is the body of individuals designated to discipline the top management of the firm (Brudney, 1982; Fama and Jensen, 1983a, b;

Hermalin and Weisbach, 1998, 2003). It is a control mechanism of 'professional referees' (Fama and Jensen, 1983a), which, if need be, has the power to replace incumbent management with more effective individuals (Hermalin and Weisbach, 2003). Boards of directors are typically ascribed three main functions (see, for example, Daily *et al.*, 1996; Hermalin and Weisbach, 2003): First there is the role of monitoring, which is part of the traditional agency cost solution.[24] The board formally selects, compensates, and decides on retention of the chief executive officer (Hermalin and Weisbach, 1998), monitors for conflicts of interest, and supervises the process of financial reporting, including external auditing and disclosure. Second, directors have a reputational function (Dechow *et al.*, 1995; Dechow and Skinner, 2000). Assistance in the formulation of corporate strategy can be seen as a third major function for the board (Langevoort, 1998b). Ideally, directors' interests would be appropriately aligned with the interests of shareholders, as the ultimate clients of the board.

The governance debate emphasizes the distinctive contribution that independent directors can make in minimizing the agency problem (Fama, 1980; Fama and Jensen, 1983a, b). Brudney accords to the independent director the role of 'an admonisher of proper behaviour' (1982: 632), where independence implies an adversarial role. Hermalin and Weisbach (2003), in contrast, refer to the board of directors as an endogenously determined institution, and suggest that the reputation of a director as being amenable to a CEO's views is of value to the director. Independent directors, usually defined as non-executive officers with no other ties to the firm apart from their role as directors, can positively influence corporate strategy, risk-taking, human resource decisions, and overall firm performance (Higgs, 2003). The inclusion of independent directors on the board is seen to enhance the viability of the board as a control mechanism, as outside directors are thought to lower the probability of collusion of management to expropriate security holders (Higgs, 2003). Non-executive directors, in helping to separate decision management and decision control, are a potentially significant governance mechanism especially when external constraints on executive behaviour are weak (Fama and Jensen, 1983a; Mayers *et al.*, 1997; Peasnell *et al.*, 2001).

Beekes *et al.* (2004) report that board composition is an important factor in determining the reported earnings quality of UK firms. Specifically, boards with a higher proportion of outside directors were found to be timelier in reporting bad news, and displayed greater earnings conservatism with regard to the recognition of good news. The demand for monitoring by outside directors is predicted by theory to be high when managerial equity ownership is low, especially under conditions of dispersed stock ownership (Jensen and Meckling, 1976; Fama and Jensen, 1983a, b; Jensen, 1993). With increasing managerial ownership, the increasing incentive-alignment effects of equity ownership are predicted to reduce the demand for such outside monitoring (Weisbach, 1988; Denis and Sarin, 1999). Peasnell *et al.* (2001) suggest an incentive-alignment factor will lead to a negative relationship to managerial ownership, until managerial entrenchment reverses the sign of this correlation, and find that the demand for outside directors declines as a decreasing function of managerial ownership.

The likelihood of managers engaging in income-increasing earnings manipulations in order to avoid having to report losses and earnings reductions is thought to be negatively related to the proportion of outside directors (Peasnell *et al.*, 2000a).[25] DaDalt *et al.* (2003) found that the composition of a board in general, and specifically that of the audit committee, is related to the likelihood that a firm will engage in earnings management. Board and audit committee members with corporate or financial backgrounds were associated with firms that have smaller discretionary current accruals. The frequency of board and audit committee meetings was also associated with reduced levels of discretionary current accruals. The authors concluded that board and audit committee activity and their members' financial sophistication might be important factors in constraining the propensity of managers to engage in earnings management. These findings support earlier conclusions by Dechow and Dichev (2002), who found a positive correlation between accruals quality and earnings persistence, primarily due to a positive correlation between levels of accruals and the magnitude of estimation errors, where large accruals signify low quality of earnings, and less persistent earnings.[26]

Non-executive directors have also been found to reduce collusion (Fama, 1980). Board intervention may be particularly important to avoid income-increasing earnings management. The incidence of fraud in financial statements has been found to be negatively related to the proportion of outside directors (Beasley, 1996). Outsider dominated boards are also more likely to remove a CEO (Weisbach, 1988). There may be a positive effect on capital–asset ratios when a firm appoints outside directors (Rosenstein and Wyatt, 1990). The market tends to view the appointment of an outsider to the CEO position more favourably than an insider appointment – and boards with outside directors have been found to be more likely to appoint an outsider CEO (Borokhovich *et al.*, 1996).[27] Comparing earnings management before and after the UK Cadbury Report of 1992 (Cadbury, 1992),[28] Peasnell *et al.* (2000b) found lower incidence of income-increasing accruals management to avoid reporting of earnings losses or earnings declines when the proportion of non-executive directors was high. This is consistent with the view that appropriately structured boards improve the reliability of financial reports (Klein, 1998, 2002).

Ideally, managers' incentives are closely aligned with those of shareholders through the use of efficient compensation contracts and close monitoring of executive performance by the board (see, for example, Grossman and Hart, 1986, for an outline of the optimal contracting view). Recent research, however, contradicts this ideal view of the board's monitoring function. Hermalin and Weisbach (2003) suggest that the reputation of a director as being amenable to a CEO's views is of value to the director. Where independent board directors receive above average compensation for their role and/or are recipients of other direct or indirect financial benefits or remuneration, serious conflicts of interest can develop which point to potentially compromised monitoring roles. The influence of the CEO in selecting board members can have a negative impact on the board's effectiveness (Hermalin and Weisbach, 2003), and board capture has been identified as a significant problem (Krugman, 2002a, b; Bebchuk and Fried, 2003). The Sarbanes-Oxley Act 2002 provides the board's nominating committee with greater powers over the election of directors. The impact of this provision on the functional independence of directors remains to be seen. The call for a board majority of independent directors, and in particular that all members of the compensation, corporate governance, and audit committees must be independent is a well-meant step. Another positive requirement of the Act gives the audit committee the power to engage independent outside advice on accounting matters. The audit committee is now also responsible for the appointment and oversight of the external auditor. Formal independence does not, however, necessarily translate into functional independence. Hence, formal independence may not actually lead to improvements in corporate governance. The functional independence of the board is an important issue to which the discussion will return.

External auditors

External audits serve to evaluate an organization's accounting procedures and provide an opinion on the true and fair state of the firm's financial health (in the UK). They also verify compliance with specific rules and standards, such as the Generally Accepted Accounting Principles (GAAP) of the United States. Specific issues deal with the firm's danger of failing, what particular risks the board and management should focus on, and compliance to existing accounting standards. Materiality, relevance, and reliability of financial information are some of the main qualities in the audit process. Whether financial statements give a true and fair view remains a judgemental matter of the auditor. Crucial ingredients in the value of an external audit, and in accepting the judgements made therein, are the independence and neutrality of the auditor. Reputational concerns are deemed to provide a strong motive for auditors against signing off on financial reports of questionable quality. The underlying assumption in much of the regulation and public discussion on auditing remains that the auditing process can be impartial and free of bias, or that an auditor can successfully counter any bias present in an assessment of the client's books. Recent failures of the auditing process (Enron, WorldCom, etc.) have disturbed this picture, highlighting concerns that assumptions of impartiality and the absence of bias are perhaps too optimistic. The American Institute of Certified Public Accountants (AICPA)[29] seems to be aware of the potential for bias and partiality when it states in its Code of Professional Conduct:

> In the performance of any professional service, a member shall maintain integrity, shall be free of conflicts of interest, and shall not knowingly misrepresent facts or subordinate his or her judgment to others.
> (AICPA Code of Professional Conduct, Rule 102, 2002a)

It remains as an underlying assumption of this statement that the auditing process can be impartial and free of bias, presumably if the auditor only 'watches out' for this. Yet, how realistic is the assumption of impartiality of auditors as long as an auditor conducts an audit 'in a professional manner'? Repeated failures in the financial reporting process have led to a growing cynicism of the investing and lending public with regard to the accounting profession and may lead to the opinion that the profession is either hopelessly crooked, incompetent, or that the ideal of impartiality and the absence of bias is unrealistic. Existing incentive structures within accounting firms, in combination with changes over the last two decades in the accounting industry from a partnership structure towards one organized along the lines of a limited liability partnership, and a perceived commodification of audits due to the increased provision of non-audit services, may have changed the nature of audits from the provision of quality audit services to one of mere certification (Macey and Sale, 2003). This refers to a change in the traditional auditor–client relationship, where the concern for long-term reputation may have been replaced by an emphasis on selling an audit. Governance within accounting firms may be weakened by internal agency problems, which may have contributed to the incidence of bad audits. Individual auditors (i.e. the engagement partners) may, for example, be less independent in their engagement with clients than the audit firm as a whole.[30] At the same time, there is evidence that peer review and internal monitoring have been weakened in the industry (Macey and Sale, 2003).

Perceived shortcomings in the auditing process have lent support to the view that the ideal of impartiality and the absence of bias are largely unrealistic assumptions. Financial incentives can be a serious potential source of bias. It is perhaps no coincidence that the 1990s saw both a massive increase in the provision of non-auditing services by accounting firms and an increase in the number and magnitude of earnings restatements (POB, 2000). An auditor will find it difficult to remain impartial even in the absence of financial incentives since bias intrudes as the result of the close working relationship with the client (Bazerman *et al.*, 1997). The subjective nature of accounting, per se, indicates a vulnerability of auditors to unconscious bias in their assessments of corporate performance due to the close working relationship with the client (Bazerman *et al.*, 2002a, b). A distortion of the assessment in an audited firm's financial status may be due to such unconsciously biased judgements, and need not necessarily be caused by corruption and fraud on account of the auditor. Overall, unconscious bias may represent a more pernicious problem with corporate auditing than is commonly accepted.

Arthur Andersen, the now defunct, former Big-5 accounting firm, may provide an extreme example of the intrusion of bias in the auditor–client relationship. It is not obvious, however, if this particular firm was in any way exceptional, despite being at the centre of one of the most infamous cases of accounting fraud. The simplest explanation would be for Arthur Andersen to have been an outlier or a rogue firm within an otherwise healthy and functional accounting profession. An example of this view can be seen in the complaint of *In re Enron Securities Litigation*, which emphasizes that Arthur Andersen 'is a repeat offender with a history of failed audits, conflicts of interest and document destruction in some of the most egregious cases of accounting fraud in history'.[31] The complaint recounted the auditor's allegedly improper conduct in earlier accounting scandals, and asserted that Arthur Andersen had had a 'callous, reckless disregard for its duty to investors and the public trust for decades'.[32] The firm seems to have routinely succumbed to demands for certification by Enron management. This may at times have been initiated by the local partner and at other times by headquarters. Testimony at the Andersen criminal trial and during the Enron securities litigation supports this allegation, and the court found evidence that Andersen's internal monitoring failed its own standards.[33] Nevertheless, Macey and Sale (2003) point out that Andersen's clients did not restate at significantly different rates to that of other major firms' clients during the period from 1997 to 2001 (see Box 2.1 for a selective listing of large audit failures listed by lead audit firms).[34]

This would indicate that Andersen was not an outlier, and that the identified problems are hardly specific to a particular firm. The surviving Big-4 accounting firms remain subject to the same forces which caused the internal governance failures at the heart of Arthur Andersen's shortcomings. It should be pointed out that the roles of auditors may differ to some degree between the US and the UK regulatory environments, especially with regard to the purpose and focus of the financial accounts. The focus of financial accounts in the UK is frequently interpreted to be closer to serving the interests of the shareholders than is the case in the US, which is seen to be more focused on ensuring accurate market pricing (Bush, 2005; Mullineux, 2007). This difference is significant and implies a concentration in the US on the accounts being consistent with the value of shares traded, contrasted with the focus of the UK approach on the accounts being an indicator of capital being used efficiently (Bush, 2005). The US audit regime was modelled on the UK's 1929 Companies Act to inform investors acquiring new shares (O'Connor, 2004). The British reporting model generally gives the shareholders the right to know any facts deemed significant in order to form an opinion on a firm's stewardship, as distinct from the US regime which is mostly aimed at providing information useful in the forward valuation when shares are exchanged. UK statutory audits are not directly concerned with share values.

The UK auditor reports to shareholders only, whereas the US auditor is appointed by the board and reports to both directors and shareholders, which

Box 2.1 Selected cases of bad audits and settlements by the four largest accounting firms (post Arthur Anderson)

Ernst & Young LLP

- Cendant ($335m settlement 1999)
- PeopleSoft (six month ban on accepting new clients in April 2004)[i]
- Superior Bank
- Computer Associates
- HealthSouth
- Time Warner/AOL ($100m settlement 2005)
- Equitable Life

Deloitte & Touche, DT Tohmatsu and Grant Thornton, DT Singapore

- Adelphia
- Parmalat
- Barings Bank

PricewaterhouseCoopers (PwC)

- Barings Bank (£65m settlement – Schlesinger, 2003)
- Allied Irish Bank
- Tyco
- Royal Dutch/Shell

KPMG

- XEROX
- Computer Associates
- Gemstar
- US Tax shelter fraud ($456m fine in 2005)[ii]
- Royal Dutch/Shell
- Banco Nacional (Brazil)[iii]

Source: various news reports.

Notes

i A 69-page ruling by the SEC called Ernst & Young 'reckless', 'highly unreasonable', and 'negligent' for forming a business venture with audit client PeopleSoft in the 1990s. Ernst & Young was as a result temporarily banned from taking on new business from SEC-listed companies and also ordered to pay a $1.7m fine. Regulators deemed Ernst & Young to have violated the independence requirements from 1994 through 2000 (Street.com, 05/20/2002; *The San Diego Union-Tribune* 17 April 2004). This was the second time the SEC had brought an auditor independence action against Ernst & Young. The firm settled an earlier (1995) SEC action and agreed to comply with independence guidelines.

ii KPMG, admitted to having marketed illegal tax shelters and paid this fine to avoid further prosecution.

iii KPMG had audited Banco Nacional for 15 years, not noticing fraudulent financial statement manipulations for the last eight years prior to the scandal being unveiled in 1995.

creates a potential conflict of interest (O'Connor, 2004; Romano, 2004). However, the UK requires directors to manage auditors on behalf of the shareholders, reintroducing this potential conflict of interest in practice. Nor would the UK audit appear to provide sufficient requirements to identify self-serving valuations and judgements, which may weaken its basis for meeting the statutory reasons for an audit in the UK and other countries whose civil company law is based on that of Britain, such as Australia, Canada (bar Quebec), South Africa, Hong Kong, India, Ireland, and Malaysia (Bush, 2005; Turnbull, 2005). Further, while it has been suggested that the UK system has advantages over the US audit regime in terms of auditor independence (O'Connor, 2004), governance practice in the UK creates conflicts of interests, as auditors tend to treat the directors and the company management as their client, rather than the shareholders (Turnbull, 2005).

UK accounting standards and codes supplementing Company Law, apply to all companies, not only to listed companies as in the US. The UK approach defines key accounting principles through the use of the Combined Code (FRC, 2003, 2006) with an emphasis on substance rather than form, and its focus on a true and fair view of a company's state of financial affairs goes beyond the relatively simple checks for compliance of the audit regime in the US. These and other differences between the US and the UK (and elsewhere) are of importance with regard to policy issues and are at the focus of intense discussions on the role of audit, including the discussion on rules vs. principles (see, for example, Clarke *et al.*, 2003). Chapter 8, on policy implications of the present research, will further reflect on these issues. For a detailed discussion on key differences in purpose and function of US vs. UK (and other regimes) financial reporting and auditing, see Bush (2005).

Summary

The value of properly designed and enforced incentive contracts in minimizing the agency problem should not be underestimated and there is little doubt that most advanced market economies have dealt with the separation of ownership and control with a degree of competence. Yet, the traditional monitors, including directors, auditors, investors, and regulators, appear to have failed comprehensively in the corporate disasters of recent history. Well-known governance failures from Robert Maxwell's group of companies and the Bank of Credit and Commerce International (BCCI), to Enron, WorldCom and Parmalat, share a number of similarities. These include a recent clean bill of health from auditors, little or no active intervention from directors, little active involvement of institutional investors, and attention from supervisory agencies mainly after the fact.

A major contributing cause of the lapses in ethics under investigation may be the perverse nature of many improperly designed contracts between managers and the boards. The self-dealing opportunities in many high-powered incentive contracts may have set up massive moral hazard traps into which managers frequently stepped without much trepidation. At least in some cases, the design of executive contracts appears to have given managers an acute interest in being dismissed. This would clearly be an indication of improper contract design. An additional contributing factor can be seen in inadequate or misguided accounting rules (Clarke *et al.*, 2003), and insufficient oversight (Coffee, 2002, 2003a). A major contributing cause may be the application of an inappropriate model of human decision-making, an argument to which the discussion will return. Before analysing agent behaviour in corporate governance, the discussion now turns to a review of earnings management, the primary tool of corporate fraud.

3 Earnings management

Reported earnings can provide important information about the economic performance of a firm and may serve as a guide to a firm's value. The usefulness of this information is balanced by the wide scope of managerial judgement inherent in existing accounting rules which govern financial reporting. This provides managers with the opportunity to present earnings which coincide with their personal interests rather than with those of the firm's various stakeholders, and allows the reporting of corporate performance in ways which may obscure the firm's true economic situation. The fact that users of financial information deem a particular financial reporting measure of importance gives managers one reason to manipulate this variable (Watts, 2003a, b). Basing managerial compensation on firm performance, measured by accounting variables under the direct control of the very same managers, provides further motivation for manipulation.

It has been suggested that, 'Companies manage earnings when they ask: "How can we best report desired results?" rather than "How can we best report economic reality (the actual results)?"' (Makar *et al.*, 2000: 2). There does not, however, seem to exist a uniform definition of earnings management in the academic literature. Nor is there any agreement in the literature on whether earnings management is widespread, or has a large effect on aggregate earnings. Proponents of the efficient market view might argue that earnings management, if it had significant negative effects, would tend to be driven out of the market. Under this interpretation, any earnings management that occurs either causes no serious damage (or even has positive effects), or there really is no earnings management, as such.

It is indeed slightly embarrassing for the earnings management literature that despite a large amount of work on this subject, academic research has generally failed to provide significant evidence of systematic attempts to manage earnings. Questions regarding the magnitude and frequency of earnings management and its impact on the allocation of resources in the economy have likewise not been settled with great confidence in this literature. The business press, practitioners, and regulators, on the other hand, tend to infer that problems affecting the quality of earnings are much more pervasive and serious than the academic literature would seem to indicate. These disparate views are all the more startling after the massive accounting failures of recent years in the US and Europe where earnings management, and financial statement fraud as its extreme form, played a focal role. Despite differences in definition and assessment, the emphasis of popular definitions of earnings management is on the deliberate attempt to mislead the users of financial information, with less weight given to the more benign interpretation of this practice as potentially providing superior (insider) information.

The debate over the significance of earnings management prompts at least two important questions of interest to the present research. First, is earnings management a problem of sufficient importance to justify such a wide discussion?[1] Second, are the methods applied to the detection of earnings management of sufficient sensitivity to reliably detect manipulations of financial reports? The first question investigates the consequences of earnings management: are these significant in magnitude, prevalent, and widespread? In other words, is earnings management a purely academic problem, or does it cause a significant misallocation of resources in the economy? Despite the corporate scandals of the recent past (and many more before that) resulting in the loss of many hundreds of billions of US dollars, it is not obvious that the corporate system overall is deficient.

There is little argument that senior management hold significant residual powers and have an incentive to diverge from the interests of the principal. It is an entirely different matter to ask whether there actually is a significant amount of earnings manipulations and corporate fraud, and whether this is harmful in the aggregate. Concerns about corporate governance would amount to very little if the consequences of managerial mismanagement were insignificant in relation to the size of capital markets, or if this practice did not actually have serious negative economic consequences, because it were, say, fully incorporated in the decisions of market participants.[2] The second issue concerns the detection and measurement of earnings management. Current research methodologies may not be powerful enough to reliably identify and measure earnings management. Since the definition of earnings management is less than straightforward, it is perhaps not surprising that its measurement is controversial. Specific measurement issues include potential model mis-specifications and typical shortcomings of the time-series and cross-sectional approaches being used. Potentially more serious issues are presented by the generally weak detection powers and poor performance in forecasting earnings management of existing models (Dechow and Skinner, 2000; Dechow *et al.*, 2003).

Definitions of earnings management

The issue of earnings management is as important as it is controversial. Irregularities in the financial statements are frequently at the centre of corporate scandals. Yet earnings management can occur without violating Generally Accepted Accounting Principles (GAAP) or breaching relevant corporate laws, and hence does not necessarily involve fraud in the legal sense.[3] The controversy does not end here, as the detection and measurement of earnings management is also a matter of considerable discussion (Dechow *et al.*, 2003). There does not seem to exist a uniform definition of earnings management in the academic literature. Nor is there any agreement in the literature on whether earnings management is widespread or has a large effect on aggregate reported earnings.

The emphasis of goal-oriented definitions of earnings management is on the deliberate effort to mislead the users of financial information. Earnings management has, thus, been described as 'a purposeful intervention in the external financial reporting process with the intent of obtaining some private gain' (Schipper, 1989: 92). Another popular definition suggests that,

> Earnings management occurs when managers use judgement in financial reporting and in structuring transactions to alter financial reports to either mislead some stakeholders about the underlying economic performance of the company, or to influence contractual outcomes that depend on reported accounting numbers.
>
> (Healy and Wahlen, 1999: 6)

Earnings management can encompass a broad range of actions that affect reported earnings (see, for example, Schilit, 2002; Mulford and Comiskey, 2002; Hribar *et al.*, 2006). Examples of earnings management methods range from real decisions such as changes in productivity efforts or current expenditures, to pure accounting activities including the selection of accounting methods, and changing residual valuations of capital. Accounting-based management of financial reports can be within GAAP, but may include practices that violate GAAP. It is important to emphasize that within-GAAP accounting choices can be considered earnings management, if the users of financial information may be significantly misinformed by such practices (Levitt, 1998, 2000). The flexibility provided to management by existing accounting practices can lead to situations where identical decisions of identical firms may be interpreted as earnings management in one situation and the appropriate application of accounting discretion in the other. Clearly demonstrated by this is the existence of a continuum in the definition of earnings management. It is not surprising that questions over the definition of this form of financial engineering contribute to the difficulties in systematically identifying and measuring earnings management in empirical research.

Accounting judgement, where interpreted as earnings management, can theoretically be used to convey privileged (insider) information to users of financial reports. It is, thus, conceivable that earnings management could, at times, play a positive role in financial reporting. The flexibility provided by existing accounting practices can therefore, where used appropriately, result in the presentation of substance over form to better reflect the underlying trends in the financial performance of a firm (Griffiths, 1986). Managers might, for example, manage earnings to convey privileged information to the market (Healy and Palepu, 1993, 1995; Francis and Schipper, 1999), or to reduce political costs (Watts and Zimmerman, 1990). Unidentified earnings management has also been found to enjoy lower capital costs (Dechow *et al.*, 1995), with the potential to benefit selected shareholders, at least in the short run. Managers and existing shareholders may benefit from manipulation of (new) investors' perceptions of the firm's value (Kellogg and Kellogg, 1991). Earnings management may even be the result of an application of a rational expectations framework, reflecting a rational response by managers to the market's anticipated mistrust in reported figures and the expected subsequent discounting of the value of the firm's stock (Shivakumar, 2000). If the market expects earnings management to occur in any case, then managers, due to the difficulty of credibly signalling the absence of earnings management, may rationally inflate earnings prior to offering announcements. Finally, conservative accounting, typically proposed as a prudent practice in auditing, may constitute a form of earnings management (Watts, 2003a, b).[4]

These and other potentially benign forms of earnings management come with the risk, however, that the practice eventually mutates into a more malicious form and that creative accounting is used to misrepresent the true state of a company experiencing financial and economic difficulties. Once earnings have been deliberately managed in a particular direction, increasingly large steps have to be taken to prevent their reversion in subsequent periods. This cannot continue in perpetuity, but experience of past financial frauds shows that markets can be deluded for many years, even decades, before the scandal becomes public.[5] Parmalat's senior management appear to have successfully fooled markets for more than a decade.

The intention to mislead users of financial information and to obscure the true economic value of the firm remains a core element of the notion of earnings management. This inference echoes former Chairman of the SEC Arthur Levitt, who portrayed earnings management as a 'numbers game', which, 'has evolved over the years into what can best be characterized as a game among market participants. A game that runs counter to the very principles behind our market's strength and success' (Levitt, 1998). The negative potential of earnings management to risk the firm's financial health is also reflected in the introduction to the Blue Ribbon Committee Report on Improving the Effectiveness of Corporate Audit Committees (1999),

> the fact that financial reporting is not an exact science (e.g. Generally Accepted Accounting Principles (GAAP) leave wide areas of discretion), allows managers to make choices in preparing financial reports. While such reports may not violate GAAP, under certain circumstances they may obscure the true condition of the company. Earnings management crosses the line when it is abused to obscure the reality of the company's situation. The question of where the line is crossed, i.e., when the

> financial ceases to be fairly presented and becomes instead fogged, is not definable with an exact precision in all instances for all companies.
>
> (Millstein, 1999: 1059)

This book firmly places its assessment of earnings management in the realm of a distinctly undesirable activity. Hence, while earnings management may, in theory, be a perfectly acceptable practice, it is difficult to prevent this exercise of managerial discretion from crossing the line into the realm of the illegal. When this happens, earnings management may perhaps best be described as earnings manipulation, with far less palatable connotations. Earnings management is the tool of corporate fraud, but it is a tool which still needs gatekeeper acquiescence, unless of course it is used to deliberately confuse the gatekeeper, where we enter slightly grey territory.

Earnings management is only one term to describe manipulations of financial accounts. Creative accounting is somewhat broader in meaning and the term was used in the literature before earnings management. Creative accounting may indicate a deliberate policy by senior management to deceive shareholders and other users of financial information regarding the true state of affairs (Argenti, 1976). Clarke *et al.* (2003) emphasize the distinction between intentional and unintentional outcomes of particular accounting practices, in order to differentiate between deceitful, or what these authors call 'feral', accounting and accidental outcomes of the application of accepted accounting practices and principles. However defined (see Argenti, 1976; and Briloff, 1972, 1976, 1982 for earlier definitions), creative accounting can also refer to a practice which stays entirely within the realm of legal and accepted accounting standards. The crucial characteristic of the more negative form of this practice is the intent to deceive the users of financial information and to defeat the spirit of accounting standards (Jameson, 1988; Walker, 1989; Clarke *et al.*, 2003).

Incentives for engaging in earnings management

Linking firm performance with compensation is a standard approach to motivate managerial effort (Fama, 1980). Stock-based compensation has become an increasingly important component of remuneration packages of senior management (Hall and Liebman, 1998). Managers naturally care about short-term stock prices due to the effects this may have on their compensation levels (Healy, 1985; Holthausen *et al.*, 1995; Dechow and Skinner, 2000). While this does not necessarily mean that executives will manage earnings with the objective of increasing their compensation, or that this will always harm other stakeholders, the motivation can be tempting, and the potential for damage to the firm is given.

Gains to the manager from engaging in earnings management can take the form of increased compensation (Healy, 1985; Holthausen *et al.*, 1995) or the reduced likelihood of dismissal when managerial performance is low

(Weisbach, 1988). Richardson *et al.* (2003) found that capital market pressures motivate firms accused of earnings management to adopt aggressive accounting policies (extending Dechow *et al.*, 1996, who had investigated firms subject to SEC enforcement actions). The authors found that firms forced to restate their financial accounts attempt to attract external financing at lower costs, have higher market multiples, raise cash from equity markets around the time of the manipulation, and display a smoother income path (i.e. they report long quarterly strings of consecutive positive earnings surprises and earnings growth). Restating firms have abnormally high accruals in the years of the alleged manipulation. Insider trading restrictions and equity issue guidelines provide additional motivation (Richardson *et al.*, 2004b).

Further incentives to manage earnings are provided by political factors (Watts and Zimmerman, 1986, 1990), management buyouts (DeAngelo and DeAngelo, 1985), the reduction of regulatory costs (Jones, 1991), and corporate control and proxy contests (Dann and DeAngelo, 1988). Earnings management has been identified due to window-dressing of financial statements prior to public offerings of securities (Rangan, 1998; Teoh *et al.*, 1998a, b),[6] lowering the cost of external financing (Dechow *et al.*, 1996), and the avoidance of debt covenants violation (DeFond and Jiambalvo, 1994; Dichev and Skinner, 2002). Meeting simple capital market benchmarks or thresholds, such as reporting positive earnings, demonstrating sequential earnings increases, and meeting analysts' earnings forecasts has been found to be of significance (Burgstahler and Dichev, 1997; Degeorge *et al.*, 1999; Dechow and Skinner, 2000; Burgstahler and Eames, 2006; Myers *et al.*, 2006).

A smooth reported income stream appears to be rewarded by capital markets (DeAngelo *et al.*, 1994; Dechow *et al.*, 1996). Skinner and Sloan (2002) demonstrate how managers benefit from consistently achieving simple earnings benchmarks (i.e. where firms are perceived as having smooth earnings). Managers have an incentive to avoid earnings restatements, as firms forced to restate their earnings face a severe decline in their market value (Myers *et al.*, 2006). Firms have been found to opportunistically manage earnings upward before stock issues (DuCharme *et al.*, 2004). DuCharme *et al.* (2004) also found that there is a positive relation between abnormally high accruals and the vulnerability to litigation for alleged misrepresentation, while settlement amounts in these lawsuits were found to be significantly positively related to the abnormal accruals.

Practices such as earnings smoothing (providing the illusion of more predicable earnings), managing earnings upward around the time of new stock issues (Rangan, 1998; Teoh *et al.*, 1998a), and managing analysts' expectations (Brown, 1998; Degeorge *et al.*, 1999; Burgstahler and Eames, 2006) become plausible options once factoring in the disproportional decline in stock valuations faced by stocks that slightly miss earnings expectations. Senior executives face incentives to manage earnings in order to avoid negative earnings surprises and the resultant precipitous drop in market valuations. There are indications that the earnings disappointment per se, rather than the magnitude of the shortfall, is the driving factor of this decline (Skinner and Sloan, 2002). This may support a hypothesis that investors are initially over-optimistic about the future earnings' prospects of growth stocks, only to dramatically revise their view when these expectations are not fully met. It is this over-optimism which raises the possibility that investors, even sophisticated ones, can be fooled (at least for a while), providing one additional rationale for earnings manipulations (Collins *et al.*, 2003). Finally, Watts provides a more general explanation for the manipulation of financial reports by managers,

> If investors take the benchmark measures seriously, managers will attempt to manipulate them . . . If investors use estimates of those benchmark earnings in any way to evaluate and reward managers, those managers will try to manipulate the measures to their own advantage and to the disadvantage of other parties.
>
> (Watts, 2003: 215)

Environments of rapid growth in executive compensation, the elevated status of the CEO in the last few decades, and the threat of dismissal for failing to meet ever higher reaching investor expectations form a particularly fertile environment for earnings management. High rewards for the apparently successful executive and the threat of losing access to this wealth provide a strong motive for not disappointing market expectations.

Other reasons for divergences from truthful reporting

Motivation alone does not necessarily result in the breach of rules. Likewise, fraudulent intent is not a requirement for earnings management to occur. As already noted, a breach of accounting rules/standards is not a requirement for corporate scandals either. Clarke *et al.* (2003) comprehensively demonstrate that the proper use of existing accounting rules may result in misleading financial reports. This may occur irrespective of whether or not any fraudulent intent is present. Fraudulent intent and motivation can be, and likely are in cases of corporate fraud, contributing factors to this. However, neither fraud, intent nor inadequate accounting rules are necessary requirements, at least not initially, for producing unreliable financial reports. The fear of a loss of self-esteem and social recognition (status quo), for example, can have a pervasive and distorting influence on cognition and judgement of agents in corporate governance and may result in biased reporting. Risk-seeking behaviour, say in the form of revenue estimates which are unlikely to be met, is more commonplace when a person perceives the possibility of a loss (Kahneman and Tversky, 1979).

Loss aversion typically induces individuals to seek higher risks in order to preserve what they already have (or feel entitled to).[7] Decisions made under severely adverse conditions, when all options are undesirable, often lead to high-risk taking in preference to a sure loss (Kahneman and Tversky, 1979). An expectation of negative feedback may additionally lead to an escalation of commitment, where sunk costs impact on decision-making (Staw and Ross, 1987). The mere perception of a possible loss of position, esteem, and financial compensation can provide a strong motivation, a) to inflate figures, and b) to do almost everything possible to maintain control, even if only by another year or even quarter. What psychologists call self-serving inference or self-justification is a powerful bias of the individual towards accepting and justifying initially small transgressions and eventually allowing for an increasingly large divergence from what is considered right and proper.[8]

The reputational risk of concealment of the true state of a firm's financial situation, both to the firm and its top executives, is not negligible. Given the risks to wealth, reputation, and even personal freedom, the question arises why a manager would lie about the true state of affairs of the corporation. Arlen and Carney (1992) hypothesize that this problem will not arise as long as the interests of the senior management are indeed fully aligned with the long-term interests of the firm.[9] However, the situation can be quite different when management feels that it is in a 'last period' situation, where the benefits from short-term self-dealing massively outweigh any long-term benefits from managerial reputation. This would also appear to be a relevant factor with regard to the quality of monitoring by the firm's gatekeepers. Where, for example, the members of a board of directors are approaching the end of their career, acquiescence to a known fraud by senior management might be a tempting proposition, rather than risk losing the compensation that comes with the position when reporting this. Potential reputational loss may also be lower in value as age increases.

That the ethical lapses revealed by managers of the Enron cohort of corporate scandals could yield so much damage, despite the existing array of means to minimize the agency problem, questions the effectiveness of the standard agency approach. Within the agency perspective of corporate governance, executive pay is one of the main incentive variables to align the self-interest of the manager with the interests of the suppliers of capital. The theory predicts that long-term incentives provide the manager with an inherent interest in maximizing the value of the firm. In contrast to conventional theory, it would appear that the self-dealing opportunities in most high-powered incentive contracts themselves may set up a massive moral hazard trap into which managers can easily fall. It can be argued that the design of some executive contracts may give the manager an acute interest in being dismissed. Why, indeed, should a manager resist immense opportunities for immediate or near-immediate personal enrichment, especially when the risk of detection and the associated penalties are relatively minor, or perceived to be so?[10]

It would be futile to try to create a new human being, ethically infallible, free of faults, and with perfect knowledge.[11] Nonetheless, if one is being paid hundreds of times more than the average salaried worker of the firm, then stakeholders are justified in expecting superior performance from senior management. Successful leadership also depends on ethics and the capitalist system may not work without moral cooperation (Smith, 1776). A valid point raised by the recent corporate governance failures is perhaps that insufficient emphasis has been put on ethics training of executives. In order to decide between 'right' and 'wrong', one needs to first have an anchor, a reference to which one can turn before any mental assessment regarding a trade-off between ethics and profit can take place. This point is an important one, but will remain the topic for another work. Nevertheless, the reader is reminded that a change in corporate culture, with an emphasis on ethical training, may be a further requirement in attempts to prevent corporate scandals.

Accruals accounting in financial reporting and research

Accruals accounting is an attempt to correct the perceived deficiency of cash accounting, recognizing that the ultimate financial effects of a transaction/ event are not necessarily the same as the corresponding cash consequences. In its conceptual framework, the US Financial Accounting Standards Board (FASB) provides the following rationale for using accruals accounting,

> Information about enterprise earnings and its components measured by accruals accounting generally provides a better indication of enterprise performance than information about current cash receipts and payments. Accruals accounting attempts to record the financial effects on an enterprise of transactions and other events and circumstances that have cash consequences for an enterprise in the periods in which those transactions, events, and circumstances occur rather than only in the periods in which cash is received or paid by the enterprise. It recognizes that the buying, producing, selling, and other operations of an enterprise during a period, as well as other events that affect enterprise performance, often do not coincide with the cash receipts and payments of the period.
>
> (FASB, 1978, para. 44)

This accounting method involves the accrual and deferral of past, current, and anticipated future cash receipts and disbursements (respectively). Income and expense items are recognized and entered in financial accounts as these are earned or incurred, which can differ from when they have actually been paid or received. The rationale for accruals accounting, thus, is the attempt to match costs with related revenues, to better reflect underlying economic performance (Statement of Financial Accounting Concepts No. 1, para. 44, FASB, 1978b).

The use of accruals accounting is not equivalent to earnings management. The abuse of the flexibility given by accruals accounting with the aim to deceive users of financial data, however, is. One advantage of accruals-based accounting over cash-based accounting should be the minimization of noise in the cash flow of a firm (Dechow, 1994).[12] Empirical research on the informational content of accruals indicates that accruals-based earnings can offer information about future cash flows which is superior and incremental to that provided by purely cash-based accounting measures (Dechow, 1994; Dechow *et al.*, 1998a). Superior information, in this instance, refers to the correlation between earnings and future firm performance or future stock returns. It has been shown that earnings can have a stronger correlation with future stock returns than cash flows (Dechow, 1994).[13] Unfortunately, the use of accruals introduces judgement and assumptions with regard to future cash flows, both of which can be subject to error, bias, and direct manipulation. As a result, accruals are prone to both deliberate and unintentional error, which introduces noise to this measure of financial performance.

Accruals tend to be less persistent than cash flows, due to the greater subjectivity of accruals, and cash flows can have greater predictive powers regarding firm performance for larger samples than aggregate earnings (Sloan, 1996). The magnitude of this divergence, in turn, reduces the informational benefit of accruals (Palepu *et al.*, 2000). High levels of accruals may indicate low quality (i.e. non-persistent) earnings (Dechow and Dichev, 2002). Less reliable categories of accruals have been found to lead to lower earnings persistence (Richardson *et al.*, 2004b), and a disaggregation of accruals into various components may provide for better predictive powers of future earnings (Barth *et al.*, 2001). Collins and Hribar (2000) note the tendency for the level of standardized accruals to be negatively related to abnormal returns over the subsequent year (see also Sloan, 1996). The less verifiable the information incorporated in various accruals categories, the less useful (in terms of reliability) these are for users of financial information. Hence, while accruals accounting can provide more relevant information to investors, it also introduces a potentially greater scope for error and bias, deliberate in the case of earnings management, yielding less reliable financial information (see SFAC, 2002, paragraph 42).[14]

As accruals are typically based on estimations and assumptions, these estimations, where found faulty, need to be corrected in subsequent financial reports. Such reversals will affect accruals and earnings in future periods. Reversals are a defining feature of accruals-based accounting, and negative serial autocorrelations in accruals are typical (Hochberg *et al.*, 2003).[15] If, for example, certain costs were underestimated for the projected period (i.e. earnings were overestimated), this will have to be accounted for once that period has passed (impacting negatively on reported earnings). Likewise, an overestimation of likely costs in a prior period will boost earnings in a subsequent reporting period. Such estimation errors (or deliberate manipulations) merely tend to shift reported earnings from one period to another, and accruals typically reverse over time. This would imply that earnings manipulations cannot be maintained indefinitely, as the reversal of accruals tends to undo the effects this has had on earnings (Healy and Wahlen, 1999). While it is generally correct that many important types of accruals sum to zero over time and, hence, are predictable and less persistent (Sloan, 1996), this may also provide managers with incentives to create additional transactions to prevent this reversal, or to structure transactions so that reversal does not occur at all.

One critical implication lies in the possibility that market participants may fail to consistently appreciate that the accruals component of earnings is typically less persistent than cash flows (Sloan, 1996). Markets appear to overreact to earnings that contain a large accruals component (both positive and negative). Subsequent downward reversals in valuation when (lower) earnings are reported in the following year, after the market realizes that the earnings of the previous period are not sustainable, are seen as evidence for market participants systematically failing properly to estimate the future earnings implications of the accruals and cash flow components of quarterly earnings (Sloan, 1996; Collins and Hribar, 2000).[16]

Differentiating between the various types of accruals can be of importance in the detection and measurement of earnings management, since different types of accruals carry varying amounts of information with regard to future earnings (Barth *et al.*, 2001). High levels of accruals may indicate poor quality of earnings, that is, earnings that are less persistent and will likely reverse (Sloan, 1996). Firms with high levels of accruals have been found to be more likely to experience earnings declines in the future, as these accruals reverse (Dechow *et al.*, 1996; Sloan, 1996; Dechow and Skinner, 2000; Bradshaw *et al.*, 2001). Detection is complicated by the fact that certain forms of earnings management are indistinguishable from legitimate accruals accounting choices. A reliable separation of intentional manipulations from the valid use of managerial accounting discretion remains problematic.[17] Financial reporting inevitably rests on judgements with regard to the value of the timing and magnitude of the underlying transactions, and it is not obvious that a distinction between intentional manipulations and errors in judgement can be made in a consistent and reliable manner. Empirical research on the field is further hampered by possible model mis-specifications, differences in samples, and differences in sample size or sampling period (Hribar and Collins, 2002). Even where earnings management has escalated into fraud, this may not always be detected. It is likely that detected fraud cases represent only a fraction of the total incidence of fraud, and an even smaller fraction of the total amount of earnings manipulations.[18]

Detecting and measuring earnings management

Empirical testing for abnormal accruals typically hypothesizes that earnings management takes predictable forms in response to various incentives and motivations (Watts and Zimmerman, 1986; Schipper, 1989).[19] Accruals prediction models generally use the assumption that forecast errors represent earnings management (Jones, 1991; Dechow, 1994; Peasnell *et al.*, 2000a, b; DaDalt *et al.*, 2003).[20] Earnings management is inferred if actual earnings differ from expected earnings in the direction favoured by the identified incentive (Jones, 1991; Dechow *et al.*, 1995). A number of proxies and control variables are used to distinguish between the typical accruals needs of the firm and abnormal accruals, and to adjust for business cycle patterns. This approach defines accruals as the difference between earnings and cash flows from operations, decomposing total accruals into expected (or non-discretionary) accruals and abnormal (or discretionary) accruals.[21] The residual (variously phrased 'unexplained', 'unexpected', or 'abnormal') component of total accruals is then interpreted as evidence of earnings management.[22]

Time-series as well as cross-sectional models are applied, with both types of models displaying typical specific weaknesses. Time-series models frequently suffer from survivorship bias and selection bias. Cross-sectional models, in contrast, primarily identify firms with negative accruals relative to the industry benchmark, potentially missing some negative abnormal accruals if earnings management is correlated across sample firms. Event-specific earnings management studies typically test the mean abnormal accruals across event firms to determine whether the mean is significantly different from zero, which would be interpreted as being consistent with earnings management. This literature includes studies on the relative value relevance of cash flows versus accruals (Rayburn, 1986; Wilson, 1987; Dechow, 1994; Holthausen and Watts, 2001), the pricing of discretionary versus nondiscretionary accruals (Guay *et al.*, 1996; Subramanyam, 1996), tests of earnings management and income smoothing (Healy, 1985; Jones, 1991; DeAngelo *et al.*, 1994; Dechow *et al.*, 1995; Rees *et al.*, 1996; DeFond and Subramanyam, 1998; Erickson and Wang, 1999), and the market's mispricing of accruals (Sloan, 1996; Bradshaw *et al.*, 2001; Xie, 2001; Hribar and Collins, 2002; Richardson *et al.*, 2004a, b).

An alternative approach assesses attributes in the distribution of earnings in large samples as evidence consistent with earnings management (Degeorge *et al.*, 1999; Dechow and Skinner, 2000; Myers *et al.*, 2006).[23] This tries to avoid the problems associated with the direct measurement of accruals, and concentrates instead on differences in earnings distribution patterns. Examples of this work include Burgstahler and Dichev (1997), who found a high incidence of earnings management to avoid small annual losses and earnings decreases. Bartov *et al.* (2002) note an increase in the percentage of firms that met or beat analysts' estimates for the period 1983–1997. Burgstahler and Eames (2006) and Degeorge *et al.* (1999) found an unusually high percentage of zero and small positive earnings surprises. Small reported losses and small declines in reported losses have been found to be unusually rare (Hayn, 1995; Burgstahler and Dichev, 1997). Degeorge *et al.* (1999) found evidence for earnings management being used to meet or beat a simple hierarchy of performance thresholds: first to avoid having to report losses, then to report increases in quarterly earnings, and finally to meet analysts' earnings forecasts. Executives may engage in earnings management in order to maintain a smooth growth history, and to avoid the severe declines in market valuations when such a series is broken (Myers *et al.*, 2006).[24]

The accuracy of popular accruals prediction models in detecting earnings management has been widely questioned in the literature.[25] Accrual models still play a central role in empirical research on earnings management, but suffer from weaknesses in identifying earnings management practices, and tend to perform particularly poorly in terms of forecasting the accuracy of financial reporting (Thomas and Zhang, 2000). Popular models suffer from mis-specifications and low power (Dechow *et al.*, 1995; Kothari *et al.*, 2005; Ball and Shivakumar, 2006). It is generally recognized that existing techniques for measuring earnings management tend to misclassify some nondiscretionary accruals as discretionary (Bernard and Skinner, 1996; Dechow *et al.*, 1998b; Healy and Wahlen, 1999). As a result, accruals prediction models tend to estimate discretionary accruals with considerable imprecision (Dechow *et al.*, 1995; Guay *et al.*, 1996; Dechow and Skinner, 2000; Thomas and Zhang, 2000).[26]

The misclassification of nondiscretionary accruals as discretionary, and imprecision in estimating discretionary accruals, can lead to the false detection of earnings management (Dechow *et al.*, 1998a, b). Guay *et al.* (1996) re-examined the models earlier investigated by Dechow *et al.* (1995) and found that all models under investigation (e.g. Healy, 1985; DeAngelo, 1986; Jones, 1991) estimated discretionary accruals imprecisely. The misclassification of nondiscretionary accruals as discretionary can lead to a false detection of earnings management (Dechow *et al.*, 1999), and allows replication of significant results found in earlier earnings management studies (e.g. Healy, 1985; DeFond and Park, 1997) in the absence of earnings management. This suggests that evidence apparently consistent with earnings management may partially be attributable to research design (Jeter and Shivakumar, 1999; Dechow *et al.*, 2003; Durtschi and Easton, 2005; Hribar and Nichols, 2006).

The model used by Jones (1991), for example, tries to partially avoid this misclassification by taking into account the effects of sales on nondiscretionary accruals, under the assumption that nondiscretionary accruals depend on the change in sales. Nevertheless, this model is thought to misclassify some nondiscretionary accruals as discretionary accruals due to unusual or extreme financial performance and business events (Dechow *et al.*, 1995; Bernard and Skinner, 1996; Dechow *et al.*, 1998a, b). As a result of this measurement error, abnormal accruals estimates in the Jones model capture both unusual nondiscretionary accruals and discretionary (including managed) accruals. Controlling for major unusual accruals events (e.g. mergers and acquisitions) may lead to a more refined measure of abnormal accruals, which may more clearly identify earnings management, but potentially serious estimation errors remain (Bernard and Skinner, 1996; Collins and Hribar, 2000; Xie, 2001; Hribar and Collins, 2002).

Thomas and Zhang (2000) further question the power of accruals prediction models by concentrating their focus on the general capability of different accruals models to forecast accruals, without particular reference to earnings management. Popular models used in the literature can be particularly weak in out-of-sample predictions. A balance sheet approach to measuring accruals, with particular relevance to tests for earnings management, may introduce pervasive and significant measurement error to accruals estimates (Hribar and Collins, 2002), especially when the presumed articulation between the balance sheet and the income statement breaks down.[27] It has been suggested that it may be necessary to control for major unusual accruals events which are typically not linearly related to changes in revenues, in order to better proxy for managerial discretion (Hribar and Collins, 2002).

The use of less reliable types of accruals may result in less persistent earnings, which has prompted calls for a categorization of different accruals with a rating of each category according to the reliability (persistence) of the underlying accruals (Richardson *et al.*, 2004b). With particular reference to the Healy (1985) model, Richardson *et al.* (2004b) suggest that accruals-based research should incorporate such less reliable accruals components to increase the reliability of accruals-based testing for earnings management. This assessment strengthens Sloan's conclusion (1996) that the accruals component of earnings is less persistent than the cash flow component of earnings.[28] The implications for the verifiability (and hence reliability) of information in accounting numbers (Watts, 2003a, b) highlight the costs introduced by the use of less reliable accruals (Richardson *et al.*, 2004a, b).[29] Watts (2003a, b) emphasizes issues of reliability of financial statements in a proposal for a stronger use of conservatism in accounting (for an elaboration, see Francis and Krishnan, 1999). The asymmetrical verification requirements for gains and losses, typical of conservatism, require a higher degree of verification for gains, which according to Watts (2003a, b) limits the ability of managers to introduce bias and noise into value estimates.

There are additional conceptual reasons for questioning the rationale behind some of the frequently applied accruals predictions models. The earnings management literature typically relies on the notion of shifting accruals between time periods, despite the tendency for accruals to sum to zero over time. One may ask why managers would engage in such short-term earnings manipulations, since they can be expected to reverse and thus quickly undo most manipulations (Dharan, 2003).[30] Managers might hence be motivated to use accruals which compromise the tendency to reverse by, for example, shifting accruals from current to non-current assets ('category-shifting'; Dharan, 2003), or between the firm and outside entities ('entity-shifting'; Dharan, 2003). Entity-shifting categories include divestments, mergers, acquisitions, and discontinued operations, giving rise to income from non-operating items and special items.[31] This view seems to be supported by evidence showing that income from non-operating and special items seem to have increased over the last three decades relative to operating income (Givoly and Hayn, 2003).

As an example, one-time charges, including restatements, can result in shifting accruals from one category to another. This may be evidence of earnings management, as large positive accruals due to earlier earnings projections can in this way be reversed through restatements without affecting normal income statement items (Richardson *et al.*, 2003; Dharan, 2003). While the shifting of accruals from one period to another presents management with the problem of reversal, the Enron cohort of corporate accounting scandals provided examples of highly innovative financing and investing strategies in attempts to completely shift accruals off the balance sheet. Frustrating the predictable tendency of accruals to reverse, this indicates the need for investigators to clearly distinguish between traditional accounting techniques which shift operating accruals between time periods, and more complicated financial transactions which shift accruals across accounting categories and entities (Dharan, 2003). Accruals that do not rely on merely shifting between periods may not sum to zero as quickly over given time intervals. This suggests that traditional techniques of financial statement analysis which focus on accruals' reversal may be inadequate in monitoring the performance of firms and testing for earnings management.

The difficulty in detecting earnings management and the general failure of predicting it may also be an indication of the potential inappropriateness of the predominant use of positive economic methodology in accounting (Williams, 2004). Despite the relative ease of producing scholarly papers based on empirical analysis of corporate data, this has not resulted in successes when directed at the prediction of earnings management and financial fraud. The preceding sentence presumes a link between earnings management and fraud, which needs some clarification. Earnings management can encompass a broad range of actions that affect reported earnings, not all of which constitute fraud. As noted earlier, accounting-based management of financial reports can be within Generally Accepted Accounting Principles (GAAP), but can also include practices that clearly violate GAAP. Notwithstanding the considerable disagreement in the literature on the damage caused by earnings management, fraudulent statements typically are the most costly form of occupational fraud (ACFE, 2002, 2004, 2006).[32] Cases of massive corporate fraud tend to centre on financial statement manipulations (Coffee, 2003b). It is the potential for earnings management to obscure the true financial state of the firm which justifies the concern with this 'numbers game' (Levitt, 1998).

The detection and measurement of earnings management remains controversial. Questions on the magnitude and frequency of earnings management and its impact on the allocation of resources in the economy have not been settled with great confidence.[33] Research has generally failed to provide significant evidence of systematic attempts to manage earnings, despite the assumed significance of this problem and the large number of empirical studies on the subject (Dechow *et al.*, 1995; Healy and Wahlen, 1999; Dechow *et al.*, 2003; Larcker *et al.*, 2005). Getting around this problem may require some rethinking with regard to the causes of and motives for earnings management. If earnings management is widespread, significant, and key to corporate financial fraud, then the difficulty in detection and measurement is hardly encouraging. Typical structural indicators of corporate governance used in academic research to explain the link between managerial behaviour and firm performance may have very limited explanatory power (Larker *et al.*, 2005).

Much of the existing research in this area relies (at least implicitly) on the assumption of the rationality of individuals and markets (Dechow and Skinner, 2000). Assuming rationality of economic agents, managers should not, for example, risk their reputation and future income for relatively small gains from earnings manipulations. Reputational intermediaries (including external auditors and board directors) would, likewise, be constrained by rationality. A cost–benefit calculation based on rational expectations may suggest that the costs measured, say, in terms of loss of prestige, outweigh the benefits of fraudulent practice. For example, ignoring considerations of 'honesty' and 'professional integrity', an individual auditor, gatekeeper, or director can be expected to engage in fraudulent practice if:

$$\sum_{t=0}^{T} p_t U(GAINS_t)\delta_t => \sum_{t=0}^{T}(1 - p_t)U(DETECTION_t)\delta_t + U(ADVERSE\ REPORT)$$

Where, the utility of the gains $U(GAINS_t)$ is dependent upon the nature of the gains, the extent of the profits and possibly the extent to which the act is in divergence with commonly perceived ethical modes of behaviour coupled with the individual's degree of honesty. P is the probability of not being caught, which will vary over time. $U(DETECTION_t) < 0$, i.e. the detection of behaving in an unethical fashion, carries adverse consequences. δ_t is a discount factor by which the individual places increasingly less weight on events in the future. U(ADVERSE REPORT) is the utility of filing an adverse report on the firm or otherwise refusing to endorse the firm. It may be negative or positive. It will be negative if other firms are unwilling to employ a gatekeeper who has a reputation for being non-compliant. On the other hand, a reputation for honesty and integrity may become a valuable asset, when this would take on a positive value. U(ADVERSE REPORT) is path dependent. If the individual has previously given the firm a clean bill of health, then suddenly failing to do so may raise questions about previous decisions.[34]

Following the rational actor model and the assumption of efficient markets, users of financial information, in turn, would not be fooled by managed earnings figures and would price securities accordingly, negating the incentive to manipulate financial reports. Arbitrage would take care of any remaining deviations from an optimal solution. Such assumptions may have led empirical research to concentrate on variables where 'fooling' investors, due to high information costs for example, is more likely to succeed, but where earnings management is difficult to detect and measure (Dechow and

Skinner, 2000). This also tends to neglect incentive variables which, if the assumption of rationality is relaxed, may be important in the incidence of earnings management. Dechow and Skinner (2000) suggest that current research methodologies are not efficient at identifying earnings management because this research may have focused on managerial incentives that are not overly useful in identifying earnings management behaviour. A more useful approach for research might be to concentrate on managers' incentives to manage earnings, and on the incentives and motivations of their monitors/gatekeepers to acquiesce. We will return to these arguments when the discussion turns to the influences on agent judgement and decision-making.

The incidence and cost of earnings management

As was the case with regard to the detection of earnings management, the determination of its costs yields considerable conceptual and empirical difficulties. Critical difficulties are partially due to problems of distinguishing where legitimate managerial discretion in estimating a firm's financial reporting variables turns into a deliberate attempt to misrepresent the firm's fortunes. Earnings management may also be undertaken partially to convey insider information and thus has the potential, at least in theory, to benefit the users of financial information. In addition, users of financial information may 'see through' any attempts at misrepresenting the true state of a firm's financial affairs and adjust their decisions accordingly, thus pre-empting potential harm.

A cost calculus goes beyond the immediately affected parties, such as employees, shareholders, and other providers of financial capital, and has to include economic misallocation of capital (Bar-Gill and Bebchuk, 2003). Earnings management adds to uncertainty, and causes additional monitoring costs. The affected firm can suffer from discoveries of manipulations of financial statements, which would likely increase the cost of capital, and yield a loss of client confidence. Other costs include those incurred by users of financial information as they seek to supplement the information on the firm, to compensate for unreliable information given by the firm's own data, and also to compensate for the increased degree of uncertainty which will almost certainly follow from the discovery of firms having engaged in deceptive earnings management. There are the additional costs incurred by the authorities and regulators as they seek to police the system. Despite arguments that emphasize the efficiency of markets, users of information may be consistently fooled over long periods of time by accounting manipulations. Widespread earnings manipulations can have a negative impact on the overall valuation of capital markets.

One possible approach to tally the costs of earnings management investigates the cost of occupational fraud, which can be defined as 'The use of one's occupation for personal enrichment through the deliberate misuse or misapplication of the employing organization's resources or assets'

(ACFE, 2004: 1). Earnings management could be interpreted as a subset of occupational fraud. Fraudulent statements, measured in the Association of Certified Fraud Examiners (ACFE) studies, in turn, form a smaller subset of the total incidence of earnings management. The number of cases detected and eventually reported is a smaller set yet. Hence, indications of the occupational fraud damage caused by fraudulent statements are likely to underestimate the true incidence and cost of earnings management. Nonetheless, estimates of occupational fraud may provide a rough indication of the potential cost of the manipulation of financial reports. Estimates of the incidence and cost of occupational fraud vary widely, in part because no comprehensive studies have been conducted to systematically measure the damage. For the United States, the US Government Accounting Office, for example, estimated that fraud and abuse in the workplace consumed about 10 per cent of the $1 trillion expenditure on the nation's health care in 1995 (ACFE, 1996). One difficulty in any attempt to quantify the cost of fraud is that not all cases are discovered or reported, or they are discovered only after they have gone on for some years which complicates quantification. In addition, not all reported fraud cases are fully disclosed or properly recorded. Hence, any existing tally of the cost of occupational fraud is likely to be a conservative estimate.

The ACFE categorizes cases of fraud and abuse by method, type, duration, and cost of fraud, as summarized in a series of *Fraud Reports* (ACFE 1996, 2002, 2004, 2006). These surveys also investigate characteristics of the perpetrators, list what resulted in the eventual detection of the cases, and theorize about the reasons why frauds went undiscovered for the various lengths of time. During 2003/2004, median losses of some 6 per cent of annual firm revenue to fraud and abuse were reported in the typical organization, which included private and public firms, government offices and non-profit organizations (ACFE, 2004). Similar results were obtained for the 1996 and 2002 reports, and again for the 2006 report. Given the size of the US economy, this yields an estimated loss for organizations in the US in excess of $660bn in 2004 (ACFE, 2004). International comparisons yield loss estimates of similar magnitude. Businesses in the UK, for example, have been estimated to have lost £40bn in 2003, some 8 per cent of firm revenue, as a result of economic crime.[35] Generally, surveys of this type find that the majority of occupational fraud cases involve asset misappropriations, but that fraudulent statements were by far the most costly type of fraud (ACFE, 2004).

The 2002 ACFE report, for example, notes total damage from 663 reported cases of $7bn. One single case of fraudulent statements from that sample alone had accounted for $5.4bn in losses.[36] An alternative metric also demonstrates the heavy cost of fraudulent statements: while over 85 per cent of all cases in the 2002 report were asset misappropriations with a median loss of $80,000, the 5 per cent of cases attributed to fraudulent statements suffered median losses in excess of $4m. Cases involving fraudulent statements were also notable for having the longest median duration of all fraud cases. Very similar proportions had been found in the 1996 survey. The 2004 and 2006 ACFE surveys, again, confirm asset misappropriations as the most common type of fraud (constituting over 90 per cent of the cases reviewed), but with the lowest median loss of the three types of fraud. The latest two surveys confirm the 1996 and 2002 results that financial statement frauds have by far the highest median loss, and as the recent financial statement scandals re-emphasize, have the potential to cause the most significant economic damage.

Capital markets impose substantial costs on firms that have been discovered to be earnings manipulators. Firms identified by the SEC as violators of financial reporting requirements face an increase in their future costs of capital (Dechow *et al.*, 1996; Palmrose *et al.*, 2001). Dechow *et al.* (1996) found an average drop in stock price of 9 per cent at the initial announcement of the need for earnings revisions in their sample of firms subject to SEC enforcement actions. Similar market reactions (minus 13 per cent of share value) were found by Feroz *et al.* (1991). The firms' financial credibility also suffered, as is evident in an increase in the bid-ask spread, increase in short-term interest, and substantial increases in the cost of capital for firms identified as having managed earnings.[37] Public discoveries of earnings management may be interpreted as a signal that the firm's economic prospects are poorer than previously assumed, and market reactions are especially strong for firms that have reported a long string of earnings growth (Myers *et al.*, 2006). Richardson *et al.* (2003) found a large negative market reaction (averaging minus 11 per cent over a three-day window) at the announcement of earnings restatements in their sample of 452 earnings restatement firm-years for the period 1998–2000, complementing and extending findings by Dechow *et al.* (1996) who reported on a sample of 66 firms. The US Government Accounting Office (GAO) found immediate window abnormal returns of minus 9.5 per cent and minus 18 per cent over an intermediate window, from 60 trading days before to 60 trading days after an announcement (GAO, 2002). Immediate market capitalization losses of the restating companies of the sample reached a combined total of approximately \$100bn. Intermediate losses totalled around \$200bn. Firms that restate experience a substantial increase in the cost of capital (Johnson *et al.*, 2006), and are more likely to be subject to class action lawsuits (Jones and Weingram, 1997; DuCharme *et al.*, 2004). Turner *et al.* (2002) confirm that firms may experience a large market reaction to their earnings restatements, with three companies examined in their study (MicroStrategy, Cendant, and Sunbeam) shedding more than \$23bn in combined market value in the seven-day period around the announcement of the restatement. For firms making a corrective downward disclosure, Griffin (2003) estimates an average loss of nearly 27 per cent in the value of a firm's stock in the three days around disclosure, and a combined loss of over \$500bn (over the same three days) for the firms in the study (731 firms selected for facing class action suits). Violations incur significant additional indirect costs to the firm. In a study of SEC accounting enforcement actions, Feroz *et al.* (1991) found that the median effect of reversing the improper accounting procedures was to lower the reporting firm's income by 50 per cent. In 36 per cent of the cases the income effect of the error was greater than the entire income reported in the previous four quarters.

Nevertheless, empirical research has not consistently demonstrated that earnings management is pervasive or that it has had a significant effect on average on reported earnings. While practitioners (and regulators) frequently see earnings management as a pervasive and problematic phenomenon, academics often fail to recognize the same severity or assume that markets will quickly mitigate any deviations (Dechow and Skinner, 2000). Current research methodologies applied by academics tend to use statistical definitions of earnings management that a) may not be very good at identifying misstatements, and b) may miss out much more subtle forms of earnings management.

Hence, two competing views about earnings management exist at opposite ends of the spectrum of research and opinion on this topic (DuCharme *et al.*, 2004). On the one hand, managers are seen to opportunistically manipulate earnings higher in order to increase the proceeds from issuing stock and successfully fool investors about it. They fully accept that subsequent earnings would tend to disappoint.[38] Such an opportunism hypothesis is contrasted with a notion of market efficiency where managers use earnings management only to signal a fair value of the firm's earnings. Under this latter scenario, investors are not fooled by the discretionary accounting choices of the firm, and value the firm's stocks properly. Proponents of the efficient contracting perspective tend to view accounting scandals mainly as minor aberrations, or even as a healthy correction of an efficient market, in relation to the overall size of capitalization and number of firms on the market (see Benston, 2003b).[39]

A benign view of earnings management holds that the accounting scandals in the US and in Europe overstate the problem, and are not indicative of fundamental flaws or shortcomings in the corporate governance setting. The difficulties in detecting and measuring earnings management lend some support to the argument that earnings management is not as prevalent as commonly assumed (Benston, 2003b). This might be corroborated by research which finds that, on average, managers do not seem to abuse the accounting discretion they hold as a result of existing accounting rules and principles at the expense of shareholders (Bowen *et al.*, 2006).[40] Similarly, Benston (1985, 2003a) and Benston and Hartgraves (2002) suggest that the recent accounting scandals in the US may largely reflect inadequate or misaligned accounting and auditing rules, which provided managers with too much freedom to assess the value of certain assets and liabilities. Somewhat inadequate auditing tools (e.g. insufficient use of statistical sampling), rather than examples of gatekeeper acquiescence, are seen to add to the difficulty of providing good audits. This line of thought would appear to suggest that much of the recent financial misreporting was due to mis-specified GAAP rules and Generally Accepted Auditing Standards (GAAS), and that closing such windows will greatly reduce the problem (see also Black *et al.*, 2003).[41] Nonetheless, accounting scandals which involved financial statements that were clearly in violation of basic GAAP requirements and which should have been detected by the lead auditor (as arguably was the case in the Arthur Anderson/Enron debacle) may disturb this somewhat optimistic interpretation (Benston, 2003c).[42]

An interesting, though not entirely convincing, argument is introduced by Deakin and Konzelmann (2003) who suggest that the interpretation of Enron as a failure of monitoring is a mistake. In their view, Enron demonstrates the limits of monitoring due to the complexities of modern business operations. This leads to the argument that Enron was engaging in business activities too complex for the board of directors to fully understand. The resultant inadequacy of the risk management system at Enron, as these authors see it, was the main cause of the company's downfall, rather than the manipulations of earnings per se. While this interpretation accepts that Enron's board had ultimate responsibility for the company's accounting policies, and in overseeing a human resource strategy which mitigated against open and effective communication, the main charge against the directors is that they allegedly failed to make an appropriate assessment of the risks inherent in Enron's business dealings. Deakin and Konzelmann's interpretation (2003) would seem to run counter to the view that places the manipulation of financial reports and gatekeeper acquiescence at the heart of Enron's downfall (Coffee, 2003a). Indeed, Deakin and Konzelmann (2003) raise the rational actor argument that directors have too much reputational capital to lose (and too little to gain) from allowing any conflict of interest to neglect their duties as gatekeepers. This, however, raises the question of why Enron's directors turned a blind eye to the 'intelligent gambling' of the firm's accounting practices, or why they would accept financial reports which they did not understand.[43] If the members of the board did not understand the accounting issues at hand, and could not fathom the associated risks, why did they not consult the experts, that is, the external auditors?

What Deakin and Konzelmann (2003) do not explain either, is why Enron's board did not insist on the implementation of an enterprise risk management system to better assess and monitor these risks. The importance of an adequate internal control framework to prevent financial fraud had been emphasized over a decade earlier by the influential Treadway Commission Report (1987). The specific need for an enterprise risk management system was subsequently identified in the COSO report (COSO, 1992) which picked up on the Treadway Commission's findings. Deakin and Konzelmann's interpretation (2003) also does not explain why the directors waived the company's code of conduct on several occasions to allow self-dealing by the CFO, a decision which obviously violated conflict of interest provisions.

Does earnings management fool investors?

Perceptions of the incidence of earnings management differ between academics and practitioners in part because these two groups emphasize different variables. Practitioners in the field of corporate governance tend to concentrate on actual fraud cases, which might bias them towards overemphasizing the incidence of earnings management (Dechow and Skinner, 2000). Academics, in contrast, tend to assume that earnings management is not actively practised by most firms, or that earnings management which does occur should not necessarily be of great concern to investors (especially if the earnings management is observable). One possible explanation for these different assessments can be seen in the emphasis academics place on the mitigation effect of rationality on agent behaviour. Assumptions of market efficiency and the rationality of economic actors might mitigate the incidence and the effects of earnings management. This can lead to the argument that earnings management does not cause any great damage as long as it is fully disclosed.

A rational actor would properly interpret and weigh new information in, say, a Bayesian fashion to update views on expected financial returns and would strictly follow the axioms of subjective expected utility. The reliance on the rational model of choice behaviour may not generally be advisable, and it is suggested that real-life deviations from the predictions of this model are pervasive and serious to the degree where alternative models of inference and decision-making should be brought into consideration. Behavioural economists would argue that earnings management could still fool people even if it is clearly visible in earnings reports. Some research demonstrates that investors (even sophisticated ones) rely on a relatively small set of heuristics and simple earnings benchmarks in assessing the value of a firm:

> market participants respond to whether earnings meet fairly simple benchmarks; managers appear to practice earnings management to meet these simple benchmarks; and market participants can be 'fooled' by relatively simple earnings management practices.
>
> (Dechow and Skinner, 2000: 247)

Degeorge *et al.* (1999) attribute evidence of earnings management to the distribution of earnings in terms of just meeting or exceeding certain thresholds, premised on the assumption that efforts to meet and exceed certain thresholds yield particular patterns in reported earnings. As expected by a hypothesis of threshold driven earnings management, these researchers find too few earnings reports directly below a threshold, and too many at or directly above it. Managers, in turn, are seen to strive to meet these benchmarks, using earnings management if necessary, suggesting that market participants can be fooled by relatively simple (and obvious) earnings management techniques. 'Fooled' here refers to an improper Bayesian weighing of new information. Evidence for this may be seen in the fact that earnings management that is revealed to market participants typically leads to harsh drops in share prices of the affected firm (Sloan, 1996; Johnson *et al.*, 2006). This indicates that investors may be systematically fooled by common earnings management practices even where these are openly recorded, explicitly indicated, and well known. This would run counter to the assumption that investors make efficient use of easily and cheaply available information in forming their assessments.

Dechow and Skinner (2000) explain extreme market reactions to small deviations from earnings forecasts as possible evidence of a correction of earlier over-optimism by investors, and question assumptions of investor rationality. It would appear that investors can be consistently fooled (surprised) by earnings numbers, despite the knowledge that these numbers are possibly subject to earnings management which ultimately leads to reversal. Burgstahler and Dichev (1997) resort to prospect theory (Kahneman and Tversky, 1979; Tversky and Kahneman, 1992) to help explain why investors rely on heuristics in assessing a firm's prospects. It is hard to understand why investors could consistently be fooled if they are rational in the economist's sense (Dechow and Skinner, 2000). Sloan (1996) had earlier concluded that investors misjudge the quality and persistence of accruals-based earnings and are fooled by relatively simple (as well as transparent) earnings management practices. Results by Barth *et al.* (2001) would seem to confirm that investors (and securities analysts; see Richardson *et al.*, 1999) typically do not incorporate all available information into value assessments. Rather, investors tend to follow a simple heuristic in assessing the persistence of accrual and cash flow components of earnings, and largely ignore the general tendency for accruals to reverse.

Initial information, regardless of its likely validity, may act as an anchor for people's perception, from which they later insufficiently adjust (Tversky and Kahneman, 1974). Even though market participants, including professionals, may be able to 'see through' earnings management (which may even be explicitly highlighted in financial reports), they are likely to still be influenced by initial figures. An example of a frequently used reporting variable which may mislead investors is EBITDA (Earnings before Interest, Taxes, Depreciation, and Amortization). This allows for the presentation of a firm's financial status which ignores one-time write-offs, asset impairments, and other costs deemed to be non-recurring.[44] Stock-based compensation expenses (e.g. options) were historically also ignored in EBITDA calculations. EBITDA is not generally accepted under US GAAP, and the SEC requires that companies registering securities with it (and when filing its periodic reports) reconcile EBITDA to net income, in order to avoid misleading investors. Despite the fact that financial reports had to clearly indicate that EBITDA is not an acceptable or reliable indicator of the firm's financial performance and true economic condition, investors frequently focused on this variable. During the dot-com and telecom boom of the late 1990s, companies typically used this technique (and also pro forma earnings, a related measure which excludes 'unusual and nonrecurring' expenses) to recast losses as profits, or at a minimum to show smaller losses than GAAP compliant accounting would have allowed.[45]

High levels of (positive) accruals, resulting in high projected earnings, can also act as an anchor for an initial assessment of a firm's future prospects. Anchors are typically insufficiently adjusted, despite the fact that firms with high accruals are more likely to experience future earnings problems (Tversky and Kahneman, 1974). Confirmation bias (Wason, 1960), the tendency to notice, seek, and overvalue information which confirms one's beliefs, and to ignore, dismiss, or undervalue the relevance of contradictory information, may also contribute to the discounting of new information which conflicts with financial figures seen earlier.[46] Reliance on professional intermediaries may not alleviate investor bias in the assessment of firm value. Financial analysts seem to be subject to anchoring and insufficient adjustment, and resulting over-optimism, and may thus not reliably signal future earnings problems of firms with high accruals, despite the fact that high levels of accruals are indicative of future earnings declines (Dechow and Skinner, 2000; Bradshaw *et al.*, 2001; De Bondt and Thaler, 2002). This would seem to corroborate views that investors have difficulties in anticipating future earnings problems of firms (Sloan, 1996). Further evidence consistent with the assertion that investors are 'fooled' by overly optimistic earnings reports and analysts' assessments is provided by empirical studies on earnings management, which demonstrate that seasoned equity offerings (SOEs) underperform the market in the subsequent years (Rangan, 1998; Teoh *et al.*, 1998a).

Summary

The view that recent examples of gross financial statement manipulations may only be aberrations in an otherwise healthy corporate landscape cannot be easily dismissed. Of some 12,000 companies listed on the New York Stock Exchange, for example, only a minority are found guilty of serious earnings management or fraud in any one year. Earnings restatements, likewise, form a relatively small (if growing) fraction of all financial reports, and compared to the total market value of all listed firms, the capitalization of firms which experienced massive governance failures constitutes a minor fraction. It may, nevertheless, be somewhat premature to conclude that earnings management (and, in its extreme form, financial fraud) is of a negligible magnitude and of limited impact, and that this practice will be quickly weeded out by efficient markets.

Such a simple arithmetic ignores, or at least would appear to significantly underestimate, a number of important costs. These include the substantial losses to individual investors who are not perfectly diversified and the losses for employees who have the misfortune to work for the affected companies (especially if they had company stock in their retirement fund and were restricted in selling the stock, as in the case of Enron). Increased uncertainty about the trustworthiness of financial reports adds to market uncertainty, and increased monitoring and financing costs. One more cost is that of complying with new regulations put in place after a wave of corporate scandals. The average annual cost of compliance with the Sarbanes-Oxley Act 2002, for example, has been estimated to be around $5m for a sample of companies (Korn/Ferry International, 2004, 2005). In a related survey of 217 companies with average revenues of $5bn conducted by Financial Executives International, total costs for the first year of compliance with section 404 of the Act alone averaged $4.36m. Company size affected compliance costs, and companies over $25bn in revenue on average spent $14.7m on section 404 compliance (FEI, 2005).[47] In sum, costs of earnings management include, but are not exclusive to, market capitalization losses of the affected firms, market uncertainty resulting in generally lower valuations, higher funding charges and higher monitoring costs for all firms, rent abstraction, various monetary losses due to fraud, higher litigation, and regulatory costs (both by the affected firm and the public), and economic misallocations.

Investigations by New York Attorney General Spitzer in 2003/2004 into inappropriate behaviour of the US mutual funds industry and the US insurance industry in late 2004 re-emphasize the view that this kind of problem is not going to go away, and that it is not a negligible or one-time problem.[48] The public was again reminded of this more recently when, in May 2006, US mortgage giant Fannie Mae was fined $400m for accounting irregularities which overstated earnings and capital by some $11bn.[49] According to the Office of Federal Housing Enterprise Oversight (OFHEO, 2006), Fannie Mae engaged in accounting manipulations of firm performance variables which were tied to executives' bonuses from 1998 to 2004. Fannie Mae's board was accused of failure in its oversight responsibilities and lack of independence from the company's former chairman and chief executive. Fannie Mae violated accounting and corporate governance standards, engaged in income-smoothing, and had poor risk management (OFHEO, 2006). The OFHEO had already in 2003 levied a $125m fine against Freddie Mac, Fannie Mae's smaller rival in the home mortgage securitization market, for understating earnings by $5bn between 2000 and 2002 (OFHEO, 2003).

This leaves open the question of the ultimate damage from earnings management, as a precise quantification would appear to be elusive. Many cases of earnings manipulation come to light only after a firm announces earnings restatements, or reveals serious financial difficulties. Many more incidences of earnings management are likely never noticed or never reported, which points to the possibility that the aggregate cost of manipulated accounting figures is greater than the cost of an occasional earnings restatement, or firm bankruptcy. A rich area for future research is implied by this. For now, the discussion will concentrate on the core issues of this research, namely, how to further minimize corporate disasters due to insider fraud by reference to more realistic models of agent behaviour.

4 Rationality or rational behaviour?

No reality please, we are economists
(Blaug, 1998: 13)

The rational actor

The standard economic model of individual choice assumes that individuals have stable and consistent, well-defined and time-invariant preferences. Individuals are expected to rationally maximize those preferences. It is further assumed that the individual applies these preferences to final outcomes (but not to changes), maximizes expected utility, applies exponential discounting to future outcomes, and in general is capable of rational choice behaviour in accordance with a number of normative decision-making rules (axioms). These rules include the perfect definition of a problem and knowledge of all alternatives, the identification of all relevant criteria and their accurate weighting, an accurate assessment of all alternatives, and finally, the accurate computation and choice of the alternative with the highest expected value (Friedman, 1957; Rabin, 2002).

One of the foundations of the rational model of choice-making is rooted in von Neumann and Morgenstern's seminal treatise on choice under uncertainty (1944).[1] In an attempt to axiomatize agents' maximization behaviour over different ventures with random prospects, their work on decision-making (in addition to launching the field of game theory) proposes mathematically that decision-makers maximize expected utility if they consistently follow a particular set of decision rules. The explicit set of assumptions, and axioms, underlying this model have become central to the economist's interpretation of human decision-making and choice behaviour. Ellickson characterizes the influence of von Neumann and Morgenstern's theoretical work on the basic economic model of individual decision-making:

> The economists' model, in its purest form, is based on elegantly simple propositions about both cognitive capacities and motivations. The model assumes that a person can perfectly process available information about alternative courses of action, and can rank possible outcomes in order

> of expected utility. The model also assumes that an actor will choose the course of action that will maximize . . . personal expected utility.
>
> (Ellickson, 1989: 23)[2]

The rationality assumption implies that agents form unbiased forecasts about their prospects. Subsequently these forecasts might be updated in a Bayesian fashion.[3] Generally, when rational agents form judgements on probabilistic outcomes, this assumes that they will take into account all information available at the time, and incorporate new (posterior) information in an unbiased way to improve their judgements.[4]

With 'subjective expected utility', or SEU, Savage (1954) extended expected utility theory to allow for subjective probabilities of outcomes. Probabilities in expected utility theory had initially been treated as objective probabilities in the classical sense (based on relative frequencies). Savage (1954) generalized this to include individuals' subjective probabilities of certain outcomes, reflecting the degree of belief of an individual in an uncertain outcome or proposition. A basic assumption of SEU theory is that choices are made to maximize the expected value of a given utility function from a fixed set of alternatives, with (subjectively) known probability distributions of outcomes for each alternative.

As is the case with expected utility maximization, a rational decision-maker is assumed to have a well-defined utility function to which cardinal ordering can be applied. In addition, it is assumed that the decision-maker is aware of a well-defined set of alternatives to choose from. The decision-maker is also thought to be capable of assigning a consistent joint probability distribution to all future sets of events. Finally, the decision-maker would choose the alternative that will maximize the expected value, in terms of his utility function, from the set or events consequent on the strategy. A probability distribution of future scenarios that can be used to weight the utilities of those scenarios is associated with each strategy (see Box 4.1 for a summary of the assumptions of SEU theory).

Box 4.1 Axioms of SEU theory

Key assumptions of SEU:

- Completeness and transitivity over all lotteries
- Cardinalization. Existence of a certainty equivalent allows creation of an arbitrary cardinal index of utility. Index is unique up to a linear transformation (monotonic transformation in usual case)
- SEU is increasing in pay-offs
- SEU is increasing in probabilities
- Choice between lotteries is independent of context

The principal components of the SEU model include a cardinal utility function, a probability distribution for the future associated with each strategy, and a policy of maximizing expected utility. Subjective expected utility theory is a normative theory of decision-making. It suggests how people should make decisions under uncertainty, and has become a central descriptive element of neo-classical theory of rational economic behaviour.[5]

The assumption that the rational individual is a self-interested utility maximizer, who follows the prescribed axioms, has powerful implications. A major appeal of rational choice theory is that it lends itself to formal modelling, allows rigorous econometric analysis, and enables forecasting. The theory is universally applicable, parsimonious and unifies economics (see Box 4.2). That it lends itself to mathematical modelling makes rational choice theory particularly appealing to economists as an analytical tool of behaviour, and it has become the paramount tool to analyse choice behaviour.

Although there does not seem to be a single widely accepted definition of rational choice theory, the various conceptions have been categorized as points along a continuum which differ in the strength of their predictions. Korobkin and Ulen (2000) borrow a thin/thick dichotomy from Green and Shapiro (1994), with a rational choice theory spectrum reaching from a (thin-end) definitional version, via expected utility and self-interest, to the (thicker-end) wealth maximization version. The thicker versions make increasingly more specific predictions over the means and ends of individual decision-making and the preferences at its base. Thick versions of rational choice theory assume maximization of certain ends, and are plagued by pronounced implausibilities. Thin versions make fewer claims as to behavioural predictions, but suffer from a certain inadequacy in specification. McFadden (1999) formulates the three core components (stable and consistent preferences, utility maximization, use of appropriate tools to update information) of the standard model as perception rationality, preference rationality, and

Box 4.2 The appeal of rational choice theory

Rational choice theory

- Lends itself to formal modelling and econometric analysis
- Is simple and powerful
- Allows rigorous analysis
- Meets the parsimony ideal
- Allows for the creation of precise models
- Allows for predictions to be made from basic assumptions of maximizing behaviour
- Is universally applicable
- Unifies economics

process rationality. The methodological and conceptual convenience of the rational approach has made this an important tool for economic analysis and policy where it has been successfully applied to salient aspects of agent behaviour. In general, assumptions of a model might not need to be overly valid or realistic as long as the model has reasonably predictive powers (Friedman, 1957). It is nevertheless important to recall that an economist's model is an abstract simplification of the real world and that

> Economics has succeeded in creating an imaginary social world described by a system of mathematical equations which allegedly explain the well-ordered behaviour of humans pursuing exclusively their own, narrowly understood, self-interests to the optimal benefit of all.
>
> (Williams, 2004: 996)

The key question is to ask what degree of realism is lost and whether this is significant to the usefulness of the model. A real and pervasive danger in the use of modelling is to take a simplified theoretical construct and assume that this represents reality. Calabresi and Melamed noted that

> Framework or model building has two short-comings: The first is that models can be mistaken for the total view of phenomena, like legal relationships which are too complex to be painted in any one picture. The second is that models generate boxes into which one then feels compelled to force situations which do not truly fit.
>
> (Calabresi and Melamed, 1972: 1128)

The near exclusive use of mathematical formalization in economics is also not without criticism, as mathematical elegance can, at times, take the primary role in research efforts at the cost of a proper description of underlying reality. In the extreme, this can result in the construction of models to yield the stylized results observed by a researcher, regardless of relevance to real economic problems or contribution to knowledge. John Hey, managing editor of the *Economic Journal*, commented on the flaws of this development,

> it is still disheartening that so many economists seem to be playing the 'journal game', i.e. producing variations on a theme that are uninteresting and which do not enlighten . . . it often appears that the model has been constructed for no other reason than to produce a result which is a stylised fact of the author . . . Simply producing a model that comes up with a desired result is a test of the cleverness of the author, not a test of the relevance of the theory.
>
> (Hey, 1997: 3)

Mark Blaug has long criticized this perceived preoccupation of the field with formal technique to the exclusion of relevance as an 'intellectual game played for its own sake and not for its practical consequences' (Blaug, 1998: 14), a phenomenon he calls 'the disease of formalism' in modern economics'.[6] Blaug is highly critical of the near exclusive emphasis in contemporary economics on mathematical logic as a proxy for rigorous proof of a model at hand. This may at times hinder a realistic description of the behaviour of agents. With a reference to the use of economic principals in legal research, Korobkin and Ulen (2000) similarly comment that mathematical elegance may often become the primary goal, at the expense of the usefulness of the analysis. That economic research may, at times, emphasize the elegance of mathematical modelling over realism and relevance is of course a general complaint, and would not on its own demonstrate evidence for or against the value of rational choice theory. The mathematical correctness of any model (especially, perhaps, when it proves the stylized facts of the model), should, however, never be confused with relevance, or proximity to reality.

Alternative interpretations of rational behaviour

Rational choice requires actors to infer facts about the world by applying principles of deductive logic that make use of all known, relevant information, and the complete ordering of their preferences. The theoretical and empirical adequacy of this concept of human choice-making has since its inception invited considerable scepticism (see Zafirovski, 2001, 2003; see also Archer and Tritter, 2000, 2001, for a recent critique of rational choice theory). Early critics of the rational model argued that it did not provide a very accurate description of the actual decision-making process of individuals, since actual thought processes, cognitive limitations, emotional/visceral factors, and perception and judgement biases are largely ignored, or assumed away (Simon, 1955, 1957).

The models introduced by von Neuman and Morgenstern (1944), and then Savage (1954), provide a conceptual and mathematical framework used to analyse decisions under uncertainty. Consistency of decision-making across a wide range of diverse situations and states of mind is a central assumption of these models. Such models are primarily theories of behavioural consistency, rather than empirically valid descriptions of actual decision-making (Nau, 2007). Proposed as a normative theory of behaviour, utility maximizing suggests how people *should* behave if they want to maximize utility, it is not intended to be a psychologically accurate description of real choice behaviour. Hence this states how people would and should behave if they adhered to certain requirements for rational decision-making, rather than describing how people actually behave.

Long-standing critiques of the descriptive and normative validity of the assumptions underlying SEU do not completely invalidate this model, but suggest that decision-making is also subject to situational differences, attributes of the decision, characteristics pertaining to the decision-maker, and other influences. The limitations of the representative agent model in a

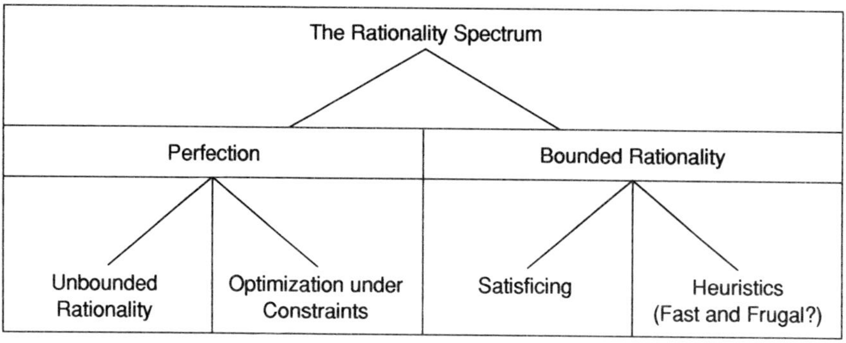

Figure 4.1 Different visions of rationality
Source: adapted from Gigerenzer and Todd (1999).

world of heterogenous actors also needs to be emphasized (O'Donoghue and Rabin, 2005). These concerns suggest that the rational actor model may not be universally applicable to all choice decisions, either with respect to the decision-making of one individual, or across different individuals. Instead, a large number of influences can lead to significant and persistent deviations from the predictions of rational choice models. This can be applied to decisions in corporate governance and has important policy implications. A wider range of interpretations of rationality, which recognizes that rationality may come in many forms, is shown in Figure 4.1.

With the concept of bounded rationality, Simon (1955) provides a strong alternative to the strictly rational model, referring to an understanding of the limits to the human mind where agents are 'intendedly rational, but only limitedly so' (Simon, 1961: 24). The underlying suggestion in this concept is that decision-making can be better understood by investigating the actual decision-making processes, and that descriptive theories of choice and standard rational utility maximization models can complement each other to provide a more complete picture of choice under uncertainty. Simon (1955, 1961) suggests that many of the assumptions that must hold for the SEU theory to work are unlikely to be realistic. Simon's concept of human rationality allows for the fact that human cognitive abilities are not infinite. People often make decisions in the absence of perfect information or a clear understanding of the information they do have, and when probabilities about outcomes are uncertain. As such, bounded rationality contrasts sharply with the (hyper-)rationality commonly assumed in standard microeconomic models (Simon, 1978).

It is important to note that bounded rationality does not mean irrationality in the dictionary sense. However, the rationality reflected in standard economic theory is thought to be hardly attainable, and may not be very useful in describing how human beings actually behave. While it is not always necessary for a theoretical model to accurately describe actual behaviour, it should allow for reasonably accurate predictions. If a model ignores persistently observed violations of its axioms and predictions, it may, at the very least, require appropriate modifications, and perhaps would need to be replaced by a framework which better fits observations. The reality of the human decision-making process makes it near impossible to use the conceptually brilliant SEU model in real-world situations.[7] At best, the SEU model may provide a crude approximation of human decision-making, or a polar ideal, and it should be asked what procedures human beings actually use in decision-making and what relation those actual procedures bear to the SEU theory.

Gigerenzer and Todd (1999) introduce the notion of 'fast and frugal heuristics', by which they refer to set of domain-specific decision-making rules which take into account limitations of time, knowledge, and computational capacity (see also Gigerenzer and Goldstein, 1996). This interpretation of heuristics differs somewhat from that represented by the heuristics and biases tradition (Kahneman *et al.*, 1982) which investigates departures from classical norms of inductive reasoning. Taking into account Simon's concept of bounded rationality (1956), the fast and frugal view places an emphasis on finding simple decision rules based on a set of principles, an 'adaptive toolbox of specialized cognitive heuristics' (Gigerenzer and Todd, 1999), that can be called upon to efficiently make decisions or inference (Chase *et al.*, 1998).

Despite its convenience in use and success in the colonization of economists' minds, the standard economic model of choice behaviour ignores at its own hazard overwhelming behavioural evidence against its universal applicability (McFadden, 1999). Arlen adds this comment to the discussion of the general applicability of the rational choice model,

> The experimental literature presents a compelling case that people are not necessarily rational utility maximizers but instead may exhibit certain predictable, systematic biases. This evidence, at a minimum, suggests that law and economics scholars cannot necessarily assume that results derived from a rational choice model apply to the real world.
>
> (Arlen, 1998: 1765)

Nonetheless, many economists have for some time displayed a reluctance to incorporate descriptive economics and the insights from behavioural and cognitive sciences in their work.[8] Understanding the actual behaviour of economic agents has sometimes been of less interest to mainstream economics if it threatened to disturb the clinical exactness of established econometric models of behaviour. Major support for this reluctance came from Friedman (1957) who argued that in positive economics the realism of assumptions was secondary to the importance of having falsifiable predictions. Abstraction, of course, is central to economic inquiry, and the concept of rationality, as used by economists, is somewhat removed from the dictionary definition of rational behaviour. In a very real sense, 'rationality means little more to an economist than a disposition to choose, consciously or unconsciously, an apt means to whatever ends the chooser happens to have' (Posner, 2003: 17). This makes the model practically unassailable, as almost any behaviour can thus be interpreted as the outcome of rational choice. A problem arises, however, if the assumptions pertaining to the rational agent are accepted without necessitating contact with empirical data and reality.

Traditional economic theory is primarily concerned with a definition of rationality which emphasizes a static outcome defined in terms of utility maximization and framed in mathematical precision. There has, until recently, been less interest in developing a richer model of behaviour which takes into account what happens to choice-making when individuals do not meet the strict criteria of the rational model, or do not apply these in a strict and consistent manner. A number of potentially important questions should be asked in investigations on actual decision-making. How are decisions influenced when individuals have, for example, less than perfect knowledge about alternatives and future outcomes, and have to cope with limited cognitive abilities? What happens when they have limited time in which to make decisions? What if individuals do not even have stable preferences, have priorities other than the maximization of expected utility, are subject to emotions, and also subject to conflicts between their present and future selves? Common to efforts at enhancing the understanding of human decision-making is the realization that the individual may not always, perhaps not even primarily, act in accordance with the axioms of the economist's rational choice model (Rabin, 2002). Instead of always seeking to maximize utility, individuals may, for example, judge prospects for gains and losses from mental reference points that may shift over time and may also depend on the situation.[9]

Economists also tend to object to a concern about individual decision-making. Predictions on choice in orthodox economics are largely based on the mean, rather than the variance, of sampled observed behaviour. Hence, under this definition, variance in individual behaviour may be of less interest to the economist, as irrational behaviour by any single individual is assumed to be counter-balanced by the behaviour of other individuals. Markets indeed have remarkable recovery properties, most of the time, under many circumstances (Smith, 1991). However valid this assumption might be, this reliance on what essentially is mean-reversion would appear to be misleading where the focus of interest is on the crucial importance of individual decision-making. This would also appear to ignore the potential importance of heterogeneity among agents, with reference to observed time-inconsistency and with regard to the design of incentives.[10]

Decisions within the corporation, including decisions with regard to monitoring and control functions, are often taken at the level of the individual, or small group. A few managers, lawyers, bankers, auditors, and board directors each, then, make decisions at the individual or small group level, their judgement subject to biases, heuristics, affect, visceral factors, and social pressures. To expect, in such a disjointed decision-making environment, an overall judgement and choice process of careful (and flawless) deliberation as envisaged by rational choice theories might be optimistic. Simon was critical of economists' apparent lack of concern about the paucity of empirical support for the rational model:

> As an example of what passes for empirical 'evidence' in this literature, I cite pp. 22-23 of Friedman's *Essays in Positive Economics* (1953), which will amaze anyone brought up in the empirical tradition of psychology and sociology, although it has apparently excited little adverse comment among economists.
>
> (Simon, 1959: 254)

Institutional economics has a long tradition of fundamental criticisms of some of the core assumptions of mainstream economics, in particular the strict assumptions about rationality and utility maximization. The unease of this school with the neo-classical assumption of perfectly optimizing behaviour of agents predates the discussion of human cognition and decision-making under uncertainty. From its beginnings in the nineteenth century, the institutionalist school has had an emphasis on seeing humans as cultural beings with all the limitations of physical and social creatures (Knight, 2000). Rational thought is seen to be limited in terms of both physical capacity and also the fact that thought processes are developed within specific social and cultural contexts. To a degree, individuals are taught what to do, how to do it, and how to think about a problem.

The process of acculturation conditions individual choice. This places constraints on behaviour and may constitute a determinant of cognitive abilities (Knight, 2000). Institutional economics regards the notion of individuals as utility-maximizing agents as erroneous, or at least misleading. Mayhew discusses arguments for the view that humans are not exclusively focused on utility maximization, and suggests that the assumed regularities of behaviour described in neo-classical economics are specific to time and place, and exist as a result of social conditioning, culture, and institution 'rather than because of some innate and constant human characteristics' (1987: 588).

More recently, the empirical adequacy of the rational model of decision-making has been questioned by research on behavioural decision-making (Rabin, 2002). Behavioural economics and cognitive research suggest that context, situation, and emotional state influence and condition behaviour and thought processes. Behavioural decision theory emphasizes the importance, among others, of heuristics, perception, and human cognition on judgement, which introduce the potential for systematic deviations from the predictions of the neo-classical rational model. Empirical evidence (including falsifiable hypotheses) assembled since the 1970s by behavioural economists and cognitive psychologists leaves little doubt that human decision-making under risk and uncertainty can depart widely and systematically from the prescriptions of SEU theory (see, for example, Tversky and Kahnemann, 1974). Human beings appear to have neither the facts, nor the reasoning power, nor the consistent structure of preferences to apply SEU principles to the extent necessary to satisfy utility maximization as postulated by the rational choice model. As a result, individual decision-making may not consistently approximate rational choice-making, either as a guide to strategy, or in outcome.

The latest challenge comes from neuroeconomics (see Camerer *et al.*, 2004b, 2005 for surveys of the field). Neuroeconomics reveals that different areas of the brain may be activated by different characteristics and attributes of decisions, including immediate vs. delayed rewards, gains, and losses, and certainty vs. uncertainty (Westen *et al.*, 2006). Cognitive processes and affective processes are very distinct in this framework. This further challenges the notion of the brain as a simple calculating engine. A further complication arises from a suggestion that cognitive decision-making (including rational choice) seems to critically depend on affective processes (Damasio, 1994). One additional (if currently tentative) outcome from research in this area is that probability may not necessarily be separated from utility (Glimcher *et al.*, 2005).

To sum, substantial evidence from over 40 years of behavioural research demonstrates numerous systematic departures from rationality in judgement under uncertainty. These show how individuals (and groups) fall short of the strict rationality standard of the rational choice model, and how predictions based on rational choice theory can be wrong in important aspects.[11] These insights are well expressed by Tversky and Kahneman, who ask,

> How do people assess the probability of an uncertain event or the value of an uncertain quantity? . . . people rely on a limited number of heuristic principles, which reduce the complex tasks of assessing probabilities and predicting values to simpler judgmental operations. In general, these heuristics are quite useful, but sometimes they lead to severe and systematic errors. Behavioural research on judgment under uncertainty teaches us that people are not nearly as rational as economists assume.
> (Tversky and Kahneman, 1974: 1124)

Uncomfortable with discrepancies between behaviour as predicted by rational choice theories and observed behaviour, scholars and legal practitioners increasingly suggest an interpretation of rationality that accepts the complexity of human decision-making, even if it makes the analysis of human behaviour somewhat more of a challenge.[12] Ultimately, the rational choice model implies that decision-makers maximize their subjective expected utility if they act in a manner consistent with the prescribed axioms. There is nothing wrong, per se, with the theoretical propositions of this model. What should be objectionable, however, is the assumption, widely taken for granted in neo-classical economics, that this model is descriptively valid and practically synonymous with rational behaviour in the dictionary sense. Implicit is the assumption that people will actually behave in ways that will maximize the mathematical construct of expected utility. As beautiful a concept as this might be, this conventional assumption of economics seems to be at odds with a large body of evidence from cognitive and behavioural research. While it might be highly desirable to have a model of behaviour that is both simple and correct, the conventional model of the economist is not in this position as its predictions are frequently wrong.

It would appear that judgement, decision-making, and behaviour are simply not exclusively based on logical reasoning. Instead they are also subject to numerous heuristics and biases (Tversky and Kahneman, 1974; Kahneman and Tversky, 1979; Nisbett and Ross, 1980; Fischhoff, 2002), affect (Slovic *et al.*, 2002, 2004), visceral factors (Schelling, 1984; Loewenstein, 1996; Loewenstein and Lerner, 2003), and pressures towards conformity with the group or authority (Asch, 1951; Milgram, 1963; Janis, 1972, 1982). Divergence from utility maximization over time adds a temporal dimension to this literature (Strotz, 1955; Schelling, 1978; Thaler, 1981; Laibson, 1997).

Such influences tend to steer human judgement, inference, and behaviour away from the outcomes predicted by expected utility theory, and can lead to systematic violations of the fundamental normative assumptions central to the economist's concept of rationality. As the subsequent discussion will show, it would be misleading to label these various influences on judgement and choice-making as 'errors'. Their continued existence in human evolution may instead indicate that they are of significant value in allowing the quick processing of a complicated environment and in successfully economizing on time as a scarce resource.

A large and growing body of evidence demonstrates that individuals make use of quick decision tools when faced with common choice problems, rather than exclusively relying on the strict optimization approach suggested (and usually presumed without question) by rational choice theory.[13] This allows for the possibility of persistent divergences from the results expected by the theory of utility maximization, and questions some of the key assumptions of law and economic theory with regard to choice behaviour. This, in turn, may require law and economics scholars 'to acknowledge that in some circumstances actual policy decisions should not be based on the assumption that people are rational' (Arlen, 1998: 1768). The result is that rational choice theory may provide an inadequate understanding of many aspects of decision-making.

At the very least, the theory's view of human choice behaviour would appear to be incomplete, as it fails to take into consideration that various cognitive, perceptual, motivational, situational, and experiental factors may systematically distort human judgement and inference. The underestimation of context dependency of an action and all forms of thought and problem-solving might be a particular weakness of the rational model of decision-making. This fails to incorporate situational, individual, and cultural influences, which have a strong effect on decision-making (Archer and Tritter, 2000). The assumption of fixed, well-ordered preferences and perfect information assimilation may also be empirically incorrect (Rabin, 2002). This combination of concerns raises serious doubts about the universal applicability of the rational model of decision-making to human choice and judgement.

Specific challenges to the rational model

A detailed categorization of challenges to the rational model is provided by Rabin (2002), who ranks these challenges by how serious a problem they represent to the standard economic model of judgement and decision-making. A relatively modest challenge is represented by extensions required to the form of the utility function to make it more realistic. For example, a person's preferences may often be determined by changes in outcomes relative to reference levels, not merely by absolute levels of outcomes (Kahneman and Tversky, 1979). Relative to a reference point (e.g. the status quo), the experienced disutility from losses tends to be significantly larger than the utility from equivalent-sized gains. This has repercussions for predictions with regard to loss aversion and attitudes to risk. Individuals who are in a loss frame tend to be risk-seeking, which is contrasted by risk aversion when the individual is in a gain frame (Kahneman and Tversky, 1984, 1986).

More of a challenge to the rational model is presented by the observation that people make systematic errors in their attempts to maximize utility. Individuals are frequently influenced by biases in judgement under uncertainty (Kahneman and Tversky, 1974), fail to consistently take account of base rates when estimating probabilities (Tversky and Kahneman, 1982), or make incorrect use of base rates[14] (Birnbaum, 2001), tend to infer more than evidence warrants (Rabin, 2002), and typically interpret evidence as confirming prior beliefs or hypotheses (Bruner, 1957; Wason, 1960, 1968; McHoskey, 1995). While the rational model might be able to accommodate some of these qualifications to its axioms (into an arduous utility function), it is questionable whether the resulting framework still deserves the 'rationality' label.

Bayesian updating and the use of base rates

In calculating the probability of an event, it would appear crucial to correctly apply base rates, which reflect the proportion of events out of the total population that meet a particular condition (e.g. the true proportion of a population having some condition or attribute). Suppose an individual tests positive for Disease X during a physical exam, and that the accuracy of the test is 95 per cent. It may appear that the probability of having Disease X (once tested positive) is therefore 0.95. However, due to the possibility of misses and false positives, more information about the accuracy of the test is needed. If an individual has the disease and the test failed to detect it that would be a miss. A false positive refers to the situation where an individual does not have Disease X but the test indicated that the individual did. The miss and false positive rates do not need to be the same. The test accurately indicates the disease in 99 per cent of individuals with the disease, and accurately indicates no disease in 91 per cent of people who do not have it. This means, that the test has a miss rate of 0.01 and a false positive rate of 0.09. This may lead to a revision of judgement and a conclusion that the chance of having the disease is 0.09 rather than 0.05. This would be true if half the people in the same situation (people who show up for a regular physical exam) had Disease X. The analysis becomes complicated if more or less than half the people in that situation have Disease X. The proportion of individuals in a given population who have the disease is the base rate. Now, assume that Disease X is a rare disease, and only 2 per cent of the population have it. How does that affect the probability of having the disease? Or, more generally, what is the probability that someone who tests positive actually has the disease? With the assumption that one million people were tested, out of this only 2 per cent, or 20,000 people, on average would have the disease. Of these 20,000 with the disease, the test would accurately detect in 99 per cent of cases. This means that 19,800 cases would be accurately identified. Of the one million people 98 per cent (980,000) do not have the disease. Since the false positive rate is 0.09, 9 per cent of these 980,000 people will test positive for the disease. That is, a total of 88,200 people are incorrectly diagnosed as having the disease. To summarize, 19,800 people who tested positive (out of one million) would actually have the disease and 88,200 people who also tested positive would not have the disease. This means that of all those who tested positive, only 19,800/(19,800 + 88,200), or about 0.18 per cent would actually have the disease. Hence, the probability that an individual who tested positive has the disease is not 0.95, or 0.91, but only 0.18. These results are summarized in Table 4.1. Of the one million people tested, the test was correct for 891,800 of those without the disease and for 19,800 with the disease, indicating that the test was correct 91 per cent of the time. However, looking only at the people testing positive, only 19,800 (18.33 per cent) of the 108,000 testing positive actually have the disease.

Table 4.1 Diagnosing disease X

	True condition		
No disease – 980,000		*Disease – 20,000*	
	Test results		
Positive – 88,200	Negative – 891,800	Positive – 19,800	Negative – 200

Source: adapted from David Lane for The Connexions Project. Licensed for use under the Creative Commons Attribution License.

The same result can be obtained using Bayes' theorem. Bayes' theorem considers both the prior probability of an event and the diagnostic value of a test to determine the posterior probability of the event. For the current example, the event is that an individual has Disease X (event D). Since only 2 per cent of all people have Disease X, the prior probability of event D is 0.02. Formally, P(D) = 0.02 (where P stands for probability). If -D represents the probability that Event D is false (i.e. not having the disease), then P(-D) = 1 – P(D) = 0.98. To establish the diagnostic value of the test, requires the definition of another event: that an individual tests positive for Disease X (event T). The diagnostic value of the test depends on the probability an individual will test positive given that the individual actually has the disease, written as P(T | D), and the probability the individual tests positive given that the individual does not have the disease, written as P(T | -D). A representation of Bayes' theorem shows the calculation of P(D | T), the probability that the individual has the disease given that the individual tests positive for it:

Bayes' Theorem:

$$P(D \mid T) = \frac{(P(T \mid D) \times P(D))}{(P(T \mid D) \times P(D)) + (P(T \mid -D) \times (P(-D))} \qquad (1)$$

Probabilities for the various terms are:

- P(T | D) = 0.99
- P(T | -D) = 0.09
- P(D) = 0.02
- P(-D) = 0.98

Therefore,

$$P(D \mid T) = \frac{(0.99 \times 0.02)}{(0.99 \times 0.02) + (0.09 \times 0.98)} = 0.1833 \qquad (2)$$

as computed previously.[15] Individuals seem to frequently fail to correctly incorporate base rates when information is presented in terms of probabilities rather than frequencies (Tversky and Kahneman, 1982).[16]

Own knowledge of preferences

A quite serious problem for the rational model is the observation that people may not always be good at evaluating their own preferences. Individuals do not always accurately predict their own future preferences, nor accurately assess experienced well-being from past choices. The human mind appears to be influenced by framing effects (whether something is presented as a gain or a loss) and presentation effects (the order of questions, for example, may affect the answer). This can, for example, lead to preference reversals (Lichtenstein and Slovic, 1971, 1973), which describes situations where individuals prefer one option to another when the choice is elicited one way, but reverse their choice when it is elicited another way (Tversky and Thaler, 1990). This may indicate that individuals may not have stable, well-defined preferences that can be rationally maximized, even if maximization were a reliable assumption. Individuals frequently make choices in order to rationalize earlier decisions, rather than on the basis of underlying preferences. Self-serving biases, motivated cognition and reasoning influence our beliefs and judgement (Miller and Ross, 1975; Nisbett and Ross, 1980). Prior beliefs influence perception (Lord *et al.*, 1979; Nisbett and Ross, 1980, 1991), and individuals are typically subject to temporal inconsistencies (Strotz, 1955; Schelling 1984; Laibson, 1997).

Satisfaction with own objective circumstances is significantly affected by how these own circumstances compare with those of others (Festinger, 1957). Further, satisfaction with an outcome depends on how this compares with original expectations (Atkinson, 1964). Finally, people appear to be affected by how their objective outcomes compare to imagined outcomes (Kahneman and Tversky, 1982). This means that a person's objective achievements may often matter less than their subjective interpretation. Coming second in a race, for example, may not be interpreted as a triumph over many, but as a loss to one (Gilovich *et al.*, 2002b; Langer *et al.*, 2006). Hence, the same outcome can yield very different utilities, even for the same individual. Utility would appear to be conditioned by the situation and subjective interpretation. The objectively same outcome can either excite or disappoint, depending on how it is interpreted by the individual.

Economic research typically requires models that concentrate on a small number of salient variables in order to gain insights into their economic implications. It is a mistake, however, to ignore robust and tractable research findings that expose important shortcomings of the rational actor model. Individuals tend to be, for example, more sensitive to changes with regard to specific reference levels than to absolute levels, that is, changes in wealth may be more salient than absolute wealth (i.e. levels), which contradicts the rational model's assumption that only final outcomes matter (Kahneman and Tversky, 1979). One implication of this is that same-sized losses weigh heavier than gains, leading to the concept of loss aversion (Kahneman and Tversky, 1979). In a wide variety of domains, people may be more averse to losses than they are attracted to same-sized gains, which can lead to risk-seeking in the negative region and risk aversion in the positive region (Kahneman and Tversky, 1979). The greater displeasure from a monetary loss compared to the pleasure of an equal-sized gain is also implied by the standard concave utility function. Loss aversion is different to conventional risk aversion, however, due to the characteristic of the Kahneman-Tversky value function to abruptly change slope at a reference level, which indicates that people are significantly risk averse even for negligible amounts of money (Kahneman and Tversky, 1979, 1982).[17] Earlier observations found that the expected utility framework (the standard concave utility function) cannot simultaneously explain both small-scale and large-scale risk aversion attitudes (Mehra and Prescott, 1985; Epstein and Zin, 1990; Rabin, 2000a). Instead, the Kahneman-Tversky value function might better explain some observed risk attitudes than the conventional expected utility framework (Rabin, 2000a, b, 2002).

Loss aversion is related to the endowment effect (Kahneman *et al.*, 1991; Thaler and Benartzi, 1995; Thaler, 2000), which describes how possession of a good immediately increases its value over the value prior to possession. Closely related is the status quo bias (Knetsch and Sinden, 1984; Samuelson and Zeckhauser, 1988), which holds in multiple-good choice problems. Loss aversion here implies that an individual's willingness to trade one object for another depends on which object is initially held. Individuals tend to strongly prefer the status quo to changes. This holds even for some situations where losses in some dimension are coupled with larger gains in another dimension (Korobkin, 2003). Results from experiments with random allocation of goods (Knetch, 1992) and observations in real life negotiation settings (Babcock, *et al.*, 1996; Babcock and Lowenstein, 1997; Korobkin and Guthrie, 2004), with transaction costs being held minimal, suggest that the observed behaviour may reflect preferences that are induced by the initial allocation. That individuals place a higher value on entitlements in their possession, and tend to prefer a state of affairs identified with the status quo over an alternative (Korobkin, 2003), has implications for property rights and allocative efficiency (Korobkin and Guthrie, 2004). Much of the law-and-economics theory on property law, for example, is based on an assumption of the Coase Theorem (Coase, 1959, 1960) that the allocation of property rights is irrelevant (given certain conditions, including the absence of transaction costs) in order to reach a Pareto efficient outcome.[18] However, the endowment effect and the related status quo effect suggest that individuals are likely to arrive at estimates of value that depend on the initial allocation of these property rights, consistently setting a higher value upon the perception of ownership (Arlen *et al.*, 2001). This effect results in individuals placing a higher value on their endowment than on something they seek. Hence, ownership can lead to perceived property rights which are more sticky, and resistant to change, than rational choice would indicate (Korobkin and Ulen, 2000).

Individuals typically display diminishing sensitivity to changes in utility, which reflects that the (marginal) change in perceived well-being is of greater magnitude for changes close to the reference point than for changes further away from it. One implication of the diminishing slope of the utility function over wealth with increasing distance from a reference point is that individuals tend to be risk averse over gains and risk-loving over losses. According to Kahneman and Tversky's Prospect Theory (Kahneman and Tversky, 1979), an individual's first priority is not to lose, with gains being secondary to the 'no loss' rule. Whether the loss is actual or potential, or merely imaginary, is irrelevant for this to hold. Decisions are systematically affected by the way

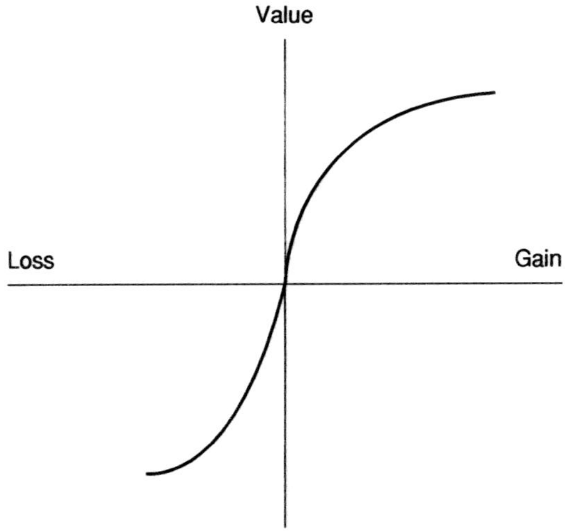

Figure 4.2 Kahneman and Tversky's value function
Source: adapted from Kahneman and Tversky (1979).

in which a situation is presented. Framing a decision in terms of a possible loss motivates a person more than framing the same decision in terms of a possible gain. Kahneman and Tversky (1982) plotted the psychological relationship that exists between value, gains and losses (see Figure 4.2).

With their value function, Kahneman and Tversky (1979) suggested that individuals based values on gains and losses relative to a reference point, displayed diminishing sensitivity to gains and losses, and were subject to loss aversion. While the shift in choice behaviour around a reference point can be shown to be inconsistent with expected utility theory (von Neuman and Morgenstern, 1944), it is consistent with the common observation that decision-makers frequently avoid risk with regard to gains and seek risk with regard to losses.[19] According to prospect theory, two elements determine risk attitude: 'value' ('utility' in the expected utility framework) and a 'reference point'. Of significance is the framing of outcomes by the decision-maker. Here, this refers to the conceptualization of an outcome as either a loss or a gain relative to a reference point, with subsequent effects on risk attitudes. A robust example of framing effects was illustrated by Tversky and Kahneman's 'Asian Disease' problem (1981), where respondents were asked to choose between two problems with logically equivalent outcomes. Tversky and Kahneman (1981) found that the majority choice was risk averse if the problem was framed in terms of 'saving lives'. Changing the description of outcome states (the frame) from patients saved (a gain) to patients lost (a loss) was sufficient to shift behaviour from risk aversion to risk-seeking. This indicates that the presentation of information can influence how it is processed and perceived. Thus, the framing of a problem can shape risk preferences and choices, which contradicts what expected utility theory would predict.

Heuristics and biases

The seminal work of David Kahneman and Amos Tversky transformed the study of human judgement when they introduced the 'heuristics and biases' approach to a wider audience with their work on Prospect Theory (Tversky and Kahneman, 1974; Kahneman and Tversky, 1979). This provided a strong challenge to the economist's concept of rationality, and their work demonstrated that when faced with decision-making under uncertainty people often rely on a limited number of heuristic principles and judgemental operations rather than on complex processing based on optimization axioms. These findings challenge the adequacy of the rational choice model, which assumes that the individual will strictly follow the rules of probability when assessing probabilities.

Heuristics-based reasoning would appear to violate some of the axioms of the rational choice model, and indicates that the way individuals form judgements and make decisions may be categorically different from that presumed in the economist's standard model of choice behaviour. It can be demonstrated that individuals, in many instances, do not follow the predictions of normative or prescriptive models (e.g. Bayes' rules). The work of Tversky and Kahneman demonstrated that individuals persistently employ heuristics such as availability, representativeness, and anchoring and adjustment to make judgments, and that the use of these mental tools can lead to systematic deviations from the rational choice model. The use of such heuristics provides a quick and fairly efficient way to reasonably assess the surrounding environment, and frequently results in accurate judgement. At the same time, it allows the intrusion of systematic bias and error in judgement (Tversky and Kahneman, 1974).

Assessments are frequently made on the basis of how similar a given instance is to an earlier experience ('Representativeness', Tversky and Kahneman, 1974), and on the ease of recollection of earlier experiences of a similar type ('Availability', Tversky and Kahneman, 1974). At other times, judgement is unduly influenced by first impressions. This can lead to situations where decision-makers focus on an initial value (an 'anchor'), adjust their responses after receiving additional information in the right direction, but typically do so insufficiently ('Anchoring and Adjustment', Slovic and Lichtenstein, 1971; Tversky and Kahneman, 1974). Historical precedent, the formulation of a problem, and random information can, thus, result in an initial value or belief. Even uninformative initial values can form an anchor that individuals insufficiently adjust for when subsequent information allowing updating becomes available (Slovic and Lichtenstein, 1971; Tversky and Kahneman, 1974). This implies that individuals are not always accurate or systematic Bayesian updaters.

It is important at this point to emphasize that heuristics are sensible estimation procedures and by no means irrational (in the dictionary sense), even when they can lead to patterns of systematically biased judgements. Heuristics draw on highly sophisticated underlying mental processes, and are normal and common intuitive responses to cognitive questions which have been adopted as mechanisms in successfully dealing with an uncertain world. Heuristics have been interpreted as an ecologically rational adaptation to a particular environment (Gigerenzer and Todd, 1999). Rather than relying on strategies which advocate the use of all available information and extensive computation of all probabilities and utilities, heuristics economize on inputs and decisions to render fast, and generally accurate, judgements (McKenzie, 1994).

Theories of optimization, in contrast, rely on more formal decision rules which are more resource intensive in terms of information, computational power, and time. Standard models of optimization assume that all decision-making tasks and choice behaviour can be compressed into a common denominator, namely quantitative probabilities and utilities. Mathematically convenient, this allows for a straightforward manipulation of data using standard statistical methods. However, such computational intensive and time-consuming optimization strategies, where more information is always preferred, do not necessarily perform better in real-life settings than a heuristics-based process.

Most economists assume that individuals update a prior belief with new information in a Bayesian fashion. The fact that individuals may dismiss or incorrectly assess prior probabilities is sometimes ignored, as is the reliability of new information. If individuals rely on a perceived relationship between prior and new information, this may violate Bayesian principles. A prior may be interpreted as an estimate with a confidence level around this estimate. Once new information is received, this is used to revise the prior, yielding a posterior probability of an event. Most decision updating may then be seen as updating an existing estimate of probability (the prior probability, view, or belief) with new information. Under Bayes' rule, a prior is updated according to this simplified formula,

$$\text{prob}(A \mid \text{new info}) = \frac{\text{prob}(\text{new info} \mid A)^{*}\text{prob}(A)}{\text{prob}(\text{new info})}$$

Where,

- prob(A) is the prior probability before new data is provided
- prob(new info | A) is the likelihood of the new data (given the prior), and
- prob(A | new info) is the updated (posterior) probability after the new data has been incorporated.

In words: posterior = k(prior × likelihood), giving the normalized posterior distribution (where k is a normalization parameter).[20]

Under Bayes' rule, a prior expectation is updated by an estimate of the likelihood of the new information with respect to a prospect. Standard economic theory on choice behaviour presumes that when individuals get new information, they would correctly update their prior beliefs (i.e. probabilities) of an event. Key assumptions for this to hold include knowledge and accurate assessment of the prior probability, a correct judgement of the relationship between prior and new information, and estimates of the reliability of the new information. The reliability of the new information relative to the reliability of the prior information is of central importance.[21] A problem arises where the likelihood of the new information is incorrectly assessed relative to its correct value. For example, a person may be deemed more likely to be a member of a particular group if that individual displays attributes typical of a member of that group. The application of the representative heuristic typically leads to an overweighing of the likelihood of, say, a professor being forgetful, due to an underutilization of base rates which reflect how many professors there actually are in the general population. That is, given that individuals make use of the representative heuristic, they may overweight salient new data relative to base rates in judging posterior probabilities. It is not necessarily the case that base rates are completely ignored, but individuals may give more weight to representativeness than to base rates when assessing probabilities. Even uninformative information may lead to a relative neglect of base rates (Tversky and Kahneman, 1974).

Closely related to the neglect of base rates is 'the law of small numbers' (Tversky and Kahneman, 1973), where individuals expect close to the same probability distributions for small samples as they do for large samples. Thus, individuals may incorrectly estimate how closely a small group will resemble the population or underlying probability distribution which generates the group. Observations by flight-training instructors of performance deterioration subsequent to praising pilots for smooth landings was frequently contrasted by performance improvements subsequent to criticizing pilots for poor landings. This resulted in assumptions of a correlation between performance and particular means of motivation, leading to the view that negative reinforcement (penalties) is a stronger motivator than praise. What these flight instructors ignored was regression to the mean, the fact that random effects alone will tend to lead to a deterioration after good landings and improvements after a poor one (Tversky and Kahneman, 1974). Faulty statistical reasoning, in this case, led to an incorrect theory of incentive motivation (for a general discussion, see Rosenthal and Jacobson, 1968; also Snyder *et al.*, 1977).

One partial explanation for base rate neglect argues that the human mind, rather than neglecting base rates (or overweighting new information), may simply not be very good at calculating probabilities as required by Bayes' rule (Chase *et al.*, 1998; Gigerenzer and Todd, 1999). Accepting that people frequently provide non-Bayesian responses, it is argued that individuals could become better at using Bayesian inference if information were presented in terms of natural frequencies (frequencies which have not been normalized with respect to base rates) rather than probabilities. Box 4.3 provides a comparison of a problem first solved using Bayesian probability inference and then using natural frequencies, with results of a number of studies which tested for performance between the two forms of presentation. This demonstrates how base rate neglect may, in some circumstances, be mitigated by varying the way information is presented.[22]

The conjunction fallacy is another demonstration of an incorrect assessment of such a likelihood. It occurs when specific conditions are considered to be more likely than general ones. As the amount of detail in the description of an event increases, its probability steadily decreases. Its representativeness and, hence, its apparent likelihood may, however, increase, affecting judgement. An often cited example of this fallacy originated with Tversky and Kahneman (1983):

> Linda is 31 years old, single, outspoken, and very bright. She majored in philosophy. As a student, she was deeply concerned with issues of discrimination and social justice, and also participated in anti-nuclear demonstrations.
> Which is more likely?
>
> 1 Linda is a bank teller.
> 2 Linda is a bank teller and is active in the feminist movement.

Of the subjects asked, 85 per cent chose option 2. However, the probability of two events occurring in conjunction is at most equal to the probability of either one occurring on its own. Tversky and Kahneman (1983) argue that most people get this problem wrong because they use the representativeness heuristic in their judgement, where option 2 seems more representative of Linda based on the earlier description of her, although it is mathematically less likely.

Another example of the effects of unrelated information on judgements of likelihood can be seen in the availability heuristic. The availability heuristic is a strategy to estimate probability based on the ease of recollection of similar events. Recollection, in turn, is heavily influenced by the vividness and emotional impact of an event (Tversky and Kahneman, 1973). Availability affects estimates of the frequency of events, where easily retrieved events are judged to be more frequent than events which are more difficult to retrieve from memory. This simple strategy for the estimation of frequencies can lead to errors in judgements of probability.[23] For example, an individual may have an opinion on how likely they are to be a victim of a tsunami (the prior). After a devastating flood destroys thousands of homes and lives, an event followed by vivid pictures on television and reports of similar catastrophes, how safe now, in the revised opinion, is a trip to a similar part of the world perceived to be? In an investigation of judgements of mortality rates, Lichtenstein *et al.* (1978) demonstrated that

Box 4.3 Probabilities vs. frequencies

Assume the probability of breast cancer in a female of a particular age participating in routine screening to be 1 per cent. If a female has breast cancer, the probability is 80 per cent that she will have a positive mammography. The probability of a false positive (no cancer, but a positive mammography) is 9.6 per cent. If a female in this age group had a positive mammography, what is the probability that she actually has cancer? Applying Bayes' rule gives a posterior probability, p(cancer | positive), of 7.8 per cent. Eddy (1982) found that 95 per cent of physicians given this problem estimated the probability to be between 70 per cent and 80 per cent (left panel).

p(H) = 0.01 (prob. cancer)
p(D | H) = 0.80 (prob. pos. mam., given cancer)
p(D | -H) = 0.096 (false positives)

$$p(H \mid D) = \frac{p(H) \times p(D \mid H)}{p(H) \times p(D \mid H) + p(-H) \times p(D \mid -H)}$$

Hence,

$$p(H \mid D) = \frac{(0.01 \times 0.80)}{(0.01 \times 0.80) + (0.99 \times 0.096)} = 7.8\%$$

	1000		
10		990	
8	2	**95**	895

Hence,

$$p(H \mid D) = \frac{8}{8 + 95} = 7.8\%$$

When expressed in natural frequencies, the mammography problem can be expressed as follows (right panel): Ten out of every 1,000 women of this age participating in screening have breast cancer. Eight out of these ten women with breast cancer will get a positive mammography. Of the 990 women without the disease, 95 will get a positive mammography. Given a new representative sample of women of this age who have a positive mammography in routine screening, how many can be expected to actually have the disease? When Gigerenzer and Hoffrage (1995) presented this format to subjects who had never been exposed to Bayesian inference, 46 per cent correctly solved this problem, whereas only 16 per cent of students who received the problem in terms of probabilities solved the problem correctly. Of physicians with an average of 14 years professional experience, 46 per cent made the correct response when presented with frequencies, compared with only 10 per cent correct answers for the group given probabilities (Hoffrage and Gigerenzer, 1998).[i]

Source: adapted from Eddy (1982) and Chase *et al.* (1998).

Note

i See Kotchekova and Messier (2001) for an investigation of auditors' probabilistic judgements based on this approach. Specifically, Kotchekova and Messier ask whether auditors are more likely to make such judgements in accordance with Bayes' rule and less likely to neglect base rates when making assessments in a frequency format. Their preliminary results broadly confirm the results of Hoffrage and Gigerenzer (1998).

people frequently get the probability of such events wrong, and found that individuals can both underestimate or overestimate, respectively, the likelihood of particular diseases. Availability was the key explanatory concept in this study, which illustrated the potential disassociation of event frequency and ease of memory recall, leading to distortions in frequency judgements.

While the classical view of choice behaviour equates rationality with adherence to the laws of probability, behavioural research emphasizes the investigation of the choice-making process. This broader view of rationality takes into account how individuals actually form judgements, and investigates the effects of environment, situation, and state of the decision-maker, and what choice processes individuals adopt in order to arrive at a decision. In view of the behavioural challenges to the classical rational model, economists may be well advised to broaden their horizons beyond traditional assumptions on inference and choice behaviour. McFadden (1999), for example, suggests expanding the assumptions associated with 'Chicago man' (the rational maximizer associated with the free market theories developed at the University of Chicago), by incorporating the constraints and additions associated with 'K-T man' (the actor associated with heuristics and biases introduced by Kahneman and Tversky).

This argument does not propose that individuals are incapable of the application of formal utility maximization strategies, but it emphasizes that cognitive (also affective, social, etc.) effects operate on perception and on the processing of information (McFadden, 1999).[24] The argument that simpler, more informal, judgement strategies may at times be less accurate than more normative strategies can hardly be used to dispute their actual application by real people. Another point to consider is that the accuracy of particular heuristics-based judgement strategies may well depend on the environmental conditions under which the strategy is used, and that different strategies will be applied in different environments to increase judgement and decision-making efficiency (Simon, 1956; McKenzie, 1994; Gigerenzer and Todd, 1999).

Biases in judgement

An individual's opinions are unconsciously influenced by own self-interest. Correcting for this bias is an imperfect process (Kunda, 1990; Bazerman *et al.*, 2000). The human mind also tends to underuse base rates, frequently infers too much from too little evidence, and typically misreads evidence as confirming previously held beliefs and hypotheses (Nisbett and Ross, 1980). People have a persistent tendency to go beyond the information given, to perceive matters as they expect to see them, in accordance with prior theories and beliefs (Bruner, 1957). Once people have an idea about something, they 'evade facts, become inconsistent, or systematically defend themselves against the threat of new information relevant to the issue' (Watson, 1982). Francis Bacon commented on this tendency towards belief perseverance nearly four centuries ago,

> The human understanding when it has once adopted an opinion (either as being the received opinion or as being agreeable to itself) draws all things else to support and agree with it. And though there be a greater number and weight of instances to be found on the other side, yet these it either neglects and despises, or else by some distinction sets aside and rejects; in order that by this great and pernicious predetermination the authority of its former conclusions may remain inviolate.
>
> (Bacon, [1620] 1960: 50)

People often rationalize prior beliefs and chosen decisions, rather than apply rational analysis to evidence and arguments presented (Katz, 1960).[25] Typically, perceptions are also biased by hopes, emotional states, and self-interest. This may lead to inevitable disparities between, for example, perceived and actual risk probabilities.

Research on dissonance reduction (Festinger, 1957) demonstrates how people rationalize their actions and views to reduce discrepancies in their belief system, hence, 'Decisions . . . are often reached by focusing on reasons that justify the selection of one option over another' (Shafir *et al.*, 1993: 34). This highlights the potential of situational and contextual factors to erect barriers to rational judgement. Even when individuals earnestly try to attend to the facts and arguments and strive to be open to another opinion, they may become more polarized in their beliefs (McHoskey, 1995). This happens when arguments and evidence congruent with own interests and beliefs are accepted at face value (or interpreted as such), while critically scrutinizing, undermining, and minimizing evidence that threatens those interests and beliefs. Further complications arise from a tendency to readily recognize bias in others, but not in oneself, and to typically underestimate the influence of bias on own interpretations (McHoskey, 1995). Some fifty years earlier, Ichheiser noted that

> We tend to resolve our perplexity arising out of the experience that other people see the world differently than we see it ourselves by declaring that these others, in consequence of some basic intellectual or moral defect, are unable to see things 'as they really are' and to react to them 'in a normal way.' We thus imply, of course, that things are in fact as we see them, and that our ways are the normal ways.
>
> (Ichheiser, 1949: 39)

That is, people typically fail to recognize the operation of biases in their own judgements and decisions. While it is generally recognized that others see the world differently, individuals are often unable to accept that their own view of the world is as subject to bias as that of others. The belief that one sees the world objectively frequently leads to the conviction that if others cannot see things 'the way they are', these others must be subject to bias or wilful misinterpretation, be irrational, or influenced by ideology or self-interest. People persist in feeling that their view of a situation enjoys particular authenticity, which others will or should share if they are 'attentive', 'rational', 'fair', 'objective,' and 'open minded'. Hence, delusions of own enlightenment tend to be balanced by the firm belief that others suffer from distorted objectivity. This typically leads to overestimates of the importance of dispositional factors (i.e. factors related to personality) and underestimates of situational factors when judging actions of others.[26]

This can be applied to individual decision-making in corporate governance. Agents may frequently convince themselves of the correctness of their actions. The notion of self-serving inference (Kunda, 1987, 1990) is a fundamental construct in social cognition which plays into this. When there is enough ambiguity to permit this, people have no difficulty in seeing what they want to see. And what they want to see is typically something that is in their self-interest, not a threat to either their self-esteem or career prospects. Such a threat is stressful, and, in group decision-making, upsets cohesion. It is normal, and to a certain degree healthy, therefore, to resist it. This can be one reason why anti-social behaviour in business settings may frequently be less the product of base moral corruption than of the ability of normal people in stressful environments to distort and rationalize their judgement and actions.

It is difficult to avoid bias. Individuals are subject to unconscious bias even when this is clearly demonstrated to the individual, where steps are taken to ensure that the concept of bias was clearly understood, and where individuals are explicitly instructed to avoid bias (Babcock *et al.*, 1993, 1995). At the very least, people tend to significantly underestimate their vulnerability to bias. Bias typically enters unconsciously at the perception stage, where people form an opinion or judgement on a matter, and reflects the individual's self-interest. The same facts are filtered, weighted, and interpreted differently when presented to different individuals, to support their respective prior held views or to match their current association. Individuals may interpret the same information differently in different situations (Kunda, 1987). Hence, when presented with identical facts, people can interpret these very differently. Interpretation would appear to depend on the individual's position, prior beliefs, context, and when they are being asked, and may be influenced by the order of the presentation (Jones and Nisbett, 1971; Nisbett and Ross, 1980).[27]

Belief perseverance and confirmatory bias refer to the tendency of people, once having formed a strong hypothesis, to frequently pay less attention to relevant new information which contradicts their hypothesis (Kuhn, 1970). This can lead individuals to maintain a hypothesis formed on weak (and even false) evidence, even if later evidence should lead them to its rejection. Information may be misinterpreted to support initial hypotheses, regardless of the validity of the hypothesis, even when this additional evidence is contrary to a prior held belief.[28] The biased assimilation processes underlying this may include a propensity to remember the strengths of confirming evidence and the weaknesses of disconfirming evidence. Further, confirming evidence tends to be interpreted as relevant and reliable but disconfirming evidence as irrelevant and unreliable. Confirming evidence thus is frequently accepted at face value, while disconfirming evidence is critically scrutinized. Even completely inconsistent and random data has been shown to possibly lead to the maintenance or reinforcement of prior beliefs, especially where such information is ambiguous (Lord *et al.*, 1979). Identical information may, thus, move judgements further apart if individuals differ in their initial beliefs on a topic.

The literature on escalation of commitment shows that decision-makers can become over-committed to prior decisions, and in the process increase allocations of resources to failing projects (Staw, 1976). Individuals who confront negative consequences (based on earlier views or actions) tend to cognitively distort these to a more positive looking outcome. They also regularly go to great lengths, including taking higher risk positions, hiding losses, cheating and lying, to avoid the recognition of a loss (Krawiec, 2000; Bratton, 2002). Biased assimilation of information can lead to attitude polarization, where a prior belief is reinforced by selective interpretation of information (McHoskey, 1995).[29] This reflects both the selective attention and differential weighting of information of cognitive processes (e.g. hypothesis confirmation; see Snyder, 1984), and also motivational accounts such as cognitive dissonance theory (Festinger, 1957). Opposing prior beliefs can be reinforced by a subjective interpretation of the same information. A related mode of information processing inducing confirmatory bias is the selective scrutiny of evidence, leading to an inappropriate interpretation of consequent evidence as further evidence for initial hypotheses ('hypothesis-based filtering'; see Rabin, 2002).

Lord *et al.* (1979) illustrate polarization in a study where two groups of individuals, after reviewing the same information, were strengthened in their support of a prior position with regard to the death sentence (i.e. for or against). Hastorf and Cantril (1954) analysed the selective perception of two groups watching the same (American) football game. Respective supporters of each team (incorrectly) interpreted the other team to be playing more unfairly, evidence for Hastorf and Cantril of an active construction of differing realities, and for a selective interpretation or perception of evidence that is of significance to an egocentric view of a particular topic. The inability to accurately identify correlations is one of the most robust shortcomings in human reasoning and people easily imagine correlations between events when no such correlation exists (Smedslund, 1963; Chapman and Chapman, 1967, 1969, 1971; Nisbett and Ross, 1980).

In forming estimates of uncertain numerical quantities, judgement can frequently be influenced by random numbers that form an anchor to subsequent adjustments (Slovic and Lichtenstein, 1971). Later adjustments to initial assessments, while frequently in the right direction, are typically insufficient. Tversky and Kahneman (1974) provide the following demonstration of the anchoring effect and insufficient adjustment. Subjects were asked to estimate various quantities, stated in percentages (for example, the percentage of African countries who are a member of the United Nations). For each quantity, a number between 0 and 100 was determined by spinning a wheel of fortune in the subjects' presence. The subjects were instructed to indicate first whether that number was higher or lower than the value of the quantity, and then to estimate the value of the quantity by moving upward or downward from the given number. Different groups were given different numbers for each quantity, and these arbitrary numbers had a marked effect on estimates. The median estimates of the percentage of African countries in the United Nations were 25 and 45 for groups that received 10 and 65, respectively, as starting points. Payoffs for accuracy did not reduce the anchoring effect. Tversky and Kahneman (1974) point out that anchoring can occur as a natural part of the assessment process itself. Opening offers in negotiations, for example, can form anchors which influence the outcome of subsequent negotiations (Oesch and Galinsky, 2003).

Another strong demonstration of anchoring is found in Bruner and Potter (1964), who exposed subjects to blurred pictures that were gradually brought into sharper focus. With the pace of the focusing and final degree of focus identical, different subjects began viewing the pictures at different stages of sharpness. Of those subjects who began their viewing at an early stage (where the picture was severely blurred), less than a quarter eventually identified the pictures correctly, whereas over half of those who began viewing at a later stage (where the picture was significantly less blurred) were able to correctly identify the pictures. This allows a conclusion that 'Interference may be accounted for partly by the difficulty of rejecting incorrect hypotheses based on substandard cues' (Bruner and Potter, 1964: 424).

When weak evidence is used to form initial hypotheses, individuals might have difficulties in correctly interpreting subsequent, better information that contradicts those initial hypotheses. This seems to contradict a central theme of rational economics, namely that more information is better, in as much as it should allow a Bayesian updater to improve assessments. As the aforementioned experiments demonstrate, however, more information may, instead, bias subsequent perception and inference. This may occur even if the information presented would allow the individual to come to a better assessment using Bayesian type adjustment of a prior. That is, valuable new information may be ignored once a judgement is made or an opinion is formed. Information or attributes irrelevant for the determination of product quality or the discrimination of brand choice, for example, can influence consumer decisions (Brown and Carpenter, 2000).

The influence of irrelevant information has also been shown when consumers were explicitly made aware of the irrelevance of the information (Shafir *et al.*, 1993; Brown and Carpenter, 2000). Even the process of learning (e.g. knowledge of appropriate statistical methods, or having potential biases expressly pointed out) may at times exacerbate errors in judgement and decision-making, as there may be a positive relationship between expertise and overconfidence (Wilson and Schooler, 1991; Griffin and Tversky, 1992; Braun and Yaniv, 1992).

Is maximizing utility the correct model?

In sharp contrast to the assumption of the rational model of fixed and immutable preferences, behavioural research suggests that preferences may be temporary, subject to change, and context dependent. Models of utility maximization may, however, still be able to (awkwardly) incorporate this in the analysis. A more serious problem is that failures of perception rationality and process rationality may leave preferences, even if they were stable and known to the individual, less relevant as a basis for observed choice behaviour than is assumed by conventional theory (McFadden, 1999).

It has been proposed that rational choice may involve two guesses, a guess about uncertain future consequences and a guess about uncertain future preferences (March, 1978). A broad class of findings from behavioural research demonstrates violations of preference models (including rational choice), due to a strong dependence of choice and preferences upon information processing considerations and situational context (Archer and Tritter, 2000; Rabin, 2002; Parisi and Smith, 2005). This questions the concept of immutable and known preferences. Contrary to predominant neo-classical theory on human behaviour, this suggests that preferences may not be absolute, stable, consistent, precise or unaffected by the choices they control. At least, there may be important circumstances and situations in which preferences do not adhere to rational choice precepts. Even when individuals correctly perceive the consequences of their decisions, people may systematically misperceive the well-being they derive from such outcomes. There may exist an

> explicit distinction between two notions of utility. The experienced utility of an outcome is the measure of the hedonic experience of that outcome . . . The decision utility of an outcome, as in modern usage, is the weight assigned to that outcome in a decision.
>
> (Kahneman, 1994: 21)

This suggests that people may not always, at least not consistently, be aware of their own utility function.

The way choices are elicited can influence the choices people ultimately make, as different ways of uncovering preferences may lead to changes in preference ordering (Rabin, 1998). Preferences may be influenced and even constructed by the very process of choice and judgement, and subject to context, situation, and procedure in which choices take place (Tversky and Thaler, 1990). Framing effects, for example, have been shown to be robust when stakes are large, when the framing of the appropriate choices is understandable, and when the decision context refers to everyday decisions (Cameron, 1995;

Fehr and Tougareva, 1996). A greater challenge to the economist's model of choice-making may result from the observation that, rather than merely confusing people in establishing stable preferences, framing may influence the determination of preferences (Rabin, 2002). Preference reversal and context effects raise strong doubts about the definition and stability of preferences. Results by Simonson and Tversky (1992) cast additional doubt on the assumption that consumer preferences among alternatives are independent of their choice menu. The addition of a new option to a set of choices may alter the choice between the existing options (for examples, see Simonson and Tversky, 1992: 281 and 287). The principle that an unattractive (third) option can enhance the attractiveness of the other (two) options is well known among salespeople.

A standard assumption of economic models on intertemporal choice is that an individual's preferences do not change over time. However, it has been suggested that preferences may be time-variant (Phelps and Pollak, 1968; O'Donoghue and Rabin, 2001, 2005). The widespread phenomenon of procrastination indicates that people typically prefer immediate rewards and delayed costs, to immediate effort and delayed rewards (Akerlof, 1991). The traditional modelling in economics of such observations by exponentially discounting streams of utility over time implies a time-consistency of intertemporal preferences (Green *et al.*, 1994). This assumption of time-consistency is less than satisfactory and frequently quite wrong (O'Donoghue and Rabin, 2003).

When considering trade-offs between two future time periods, individuals frequently give stronger relative weight to the earlier period as it gets closer. The preference for immediate gratification in large part reflects psychological findings that a person discounts near-term incremental delays more severely than distant-future incremental delays of the same magnitude. Hence, an individual's preferences today over future delays may be different from the same individual's future preferences over those same delays, which make preferences time-inconsistent (O'Donoghue and Rabin, 2005). This is also inconsistent with the discounted utility mode (see Thaler and Loewenstein, 1989, for an overview). Such temporary preferences for poorer, earlier alternatives when they are immediately available may indicate self-defeating behaviour (Ainslie and Haslam, 1992; on problems of self-control, see Rachlin, 2000; and Bickel and Johnson, 2003). The preference for immediate gratification has been approximated by hyperbolic rather than exponential discounting of future payoff streams (Chung and Herrnstein, 1967; Ainslie, 1975, 2001; Mazur, 1987; Loewenstein and Prelac, 1992; Loewenstein, 1996).

Time-inconsistency is a more general phenomenon and the use of the specific hyperbolic functional form is only one model used to describe this.[30] Time-inconsistency has been modelled and analysed without assumptions about structural form (see, for example, Strotz, 1955; Phelps and Pollak, 1968; Loewenstein, 1996). Phelps and Pollak (1968) capture the preference for immediate gratification with a non-hyperbolic, two-parameter model that slightly modifies exponential discounting but also captures the observed dynamic inconsistency. The behaviour predicted by models of time-variant preferences often differs dramatically from the behaviour predicted by the exponential model. While time-consistent individuals may be assumed to primarily respond to long-term incentives, more time-inconsistent individuals tend to be more influenced by short-run incentives, possibly at the cost of long-term benefits (O'Donoghue and Rabin, 2003).

The preceding discussion would appear to have implications for the fine details of projects, regulations, and legal structures. Not all people will react to the ostensibly same incentive in the same predictable way, as might be assumed by a strictly prescriptive decision theory. Nor can it be assumed that individuals are completely aware of these self-control problems (O'Donoghue and Rabin, 2001). Taken together, these results would imply that behaviour is likely to vary across situations that economists generally consider identical, and add to the discussion on the heterogeneity of agents.

A critique of the behavioural view

Some aspects of the behavioural view of decision-making have been heavily criticized. Mitchell (2002), for example, asserts that proponents of behavioural decision theory assume that actors always behave inconsistently with rational choice theory. Professor Mitchell seems to have a particular dislike for the heuristics and biases approach. He criticizes what he interprets to be the claim of this approach, that individuals are deemed to always be uniformly subject to heuristics, regardless of personal disposition, emotional state, cognitive ability, and situation. It would, however, be difficult to actually find such claims being made in the behavioural decision theory literature. Quite to the contrary, most studies in this area emphasize that while individuals exhibit systematic and predictable cognitive biases, the various influences on the decision-making process can vary in their effect, and in some instances counterbalance each other.[31]

Mitchell (2002) contrasts uniformly perfect rationality found in the law and economics tradition, with a presumed assumption of uniformly imperfect rationality in behavioural decision theories.[32] He notes further that not all deviations in outcomes from those predicted by rational choice theory can or should be ascribed to biases and heuristics in their entirety (but then, nobody in this latter tradition has made this claim), nor are any observed deviations always present to the same degree. This seems to be acknowledged by Mitchell when he notes that situational and individual variations have a strong influence on the outcomes of the choice and decision process:

> differences in education, training, cognitive capacity, thinking dispositions, sex, and cultural background across individuals appear to be reliably associated with different levels of cognitive performance. Furthermore,

> emotional differences, developmental differences, and different forms of mental processing appear to be associated with different levels of cognitive performance within individuals. Therefore, depending on the characteristics of the individual and the system of thought activated in a particular decision-making situation, the behaviour of different groups of individuals and the behaviour of the same individual over time may vary considerably, from perfect rationality to seeming irrationality.
>
> (Mitchell, 2002: 31)

This, however, is hardly disputed by behavioural decision theorists. The view that decision-making is subject to many different, and at times conflicting, effects is integral to the behavioural approach and one of the crucial points for the critique of the rational choice model. This refers to differences between individuals, as well as to differences within individuals (both for decisions within one time-period and across time), and to situational and contextual differences, which emphasize that the individual can behave according to the rational choice axioms, but is also subject to a number of heuristic, affective, and situational effects. Rational choice and behavioural decision-making may form polar modes in a spectrum of human choice behaviour. De-biasing, training in statistical methods, incentives and accountability, may lead to somewhat better performance in such tasks (where this means less biased), though the evidence on this is not clear (Camerer and Hogarth, 1999; Seidenfeld, 2001).[33] Mitchell makes a considerable contribution to the debate by noting the importance of individual and situational differences, which can lead to wide variations in individual performance of judgement and choice tasks.

Rationality and mental health

Systematic deviations from outcomes predicted by rational choice theory are significant, robust, and evident in important dimensions. These deviations are themselves subject to further, at times contradicting, influences. It is not immediately obvious that such violations of the rational model are necessarily inferior to neo-classical maximization, or are subject to adverse selection in an evolutionary process. Heifetz and Spiegel (2001), for example, find that individuals who have moderate perception biases and update their beliefs in a non-Bayesian fashion may not only survive in the long run but prosper and take over an entire population. This shows that individuals who hold (moderately) biased perceptions about their prospects and fail to update in a Bayesian fashion can gain a strategic advantage over rational rivals who revise their beliefs using Bayesian updating.[34] This would seem to counter claims that Darwinian-type selection would necessarily root out behaviour patterns deemed inconsistent with the classical concept of rationality (Sandroni, 2000).[35]

There is substantial evidence, for example, that people consistently exhibit overconfidence in their abilities or susceptibility to future events (Kruger and Dunning, 1999).[36] While individuals may be expected to learn (eventually) from their mistakes, overconfidence has proven to be a persistent feature of the human psyche. The maintenance of self-esteem appears to be a motivational factor in this bias. Own successes are typically attributed to skill, diligence, superior intelligence, and other personal attributes. Own failures, by contrast, tend to be attributed to adverse circumstances outside the individual's control (the fundamental attribution bias). A string of good luck can easily lead to self-reinforcement of such attributional biases, increasing self-confidence and diminishing the informational value allocated to adverse events or contradictory information.[37]

The likelihood of catastrophic failures in such settings increases, however, when the individual progressively underestimates risk and neglects warning signals. Self-serving inference and wishful thinking are only two of the factors that can move the individual to accept increasing levels of risk. Over time, the successful agent may gradually exceed established targets, and an ever-higher level of performance becomes necessary to maintain acquired levels of status and self-image. In a highly competitive setting the fear of falling behind peers, or the mere perception that others are moving ahead, can trigger a cascade of risk-seeking. Learning in a setting of success is made more difficult if this success is attributed to own skill, irrespective of the underlying causes of success. At the same time, prudence and care become less desirable qualities (risk-taking is considered a positive quality especially in a business setting). Goal-setting can motivate unethical behaviour (Douma *et al.*, 2004), and overconfidence and self-serving rationalization can contribute to such behaviour (Schweitzer *et al.*, 2002).

Contact with reality is often seen as essential to mental health. Rational choice models assume that the well-adjusted individual would gather data in an unbiased manner, properly weigh the evidence, and update prior beliefs in an appropriate Bayesian fashion. Rather disturbingly, however, overly positive self-evaluations and unrealistic over-optimism may be fundamental to mental health, and prevalent in normal human cognition (Taylor and Brown, 1988; Heifetz and Spiegel, 2000). An accurate perception of reality, rather than being evidence of mental health, might indicate an individual who is less than well adjusted (Taylor and Brown, 1988). Hence, a degree of optimistic self-delusion might be indicative of mental health, and a factor in successfully coping with difficult situations.

Over-optimism (and a related underestimation of risk) may carry evolutionary benefits. Research on organizational behaviour indicates that the most successful person, on average, tends not to be the realist, but rather the optimist, irrespective of the potentially disastrous effect of unrealistic optimism on the organization (Kahneman and Lovallo, 1997, 2003). Managers who display an optimistic outlook are more highly rewarded than those with a more realistic outlook. Part of this may be due to a positive motivational effect of over-optimism. Weick tells of a Hungarian army detachment lost in the Alps during a snowstorm, which found its way out by consulting a map of the Pyrenees:

> When you are confused . . . any old strategic plan will do. Strategic plans . . . animate . . . people. Once people begin to act, they generate tangible outcomes (that) help them discover what is occurring . . . and what should be done next.
>
> (Weick, 1995: 345)

The ability to focus and the formation of a strategy may at times be more important than precise information and a detailed utility calculation. This indicates that confidence, morale, and motivation can rank higher in certain situations than absolute realism in the appraisal of situations. Positive illusions have been found to foster creativity, motivation, and performance (Taylor and Brown, 1988). Moderate levels of optimism and self-delusion may positively contribute to the ability to cope with challenges and difficult situations. This suggests that realism may come at a motivational cost (Seligman, 1991). The cited research also indicates that overly positive self-evaluation, illusions of control, and unrealistic optimism might be characteristics of a healthy human mind and crucial to productive thought.[38]

Individuals low in self-esteem, or who are moderately depressed, appear to be less vulnerable to illusions of control (Abramson and Alloy, 1981; Watson and Clark, 1984; Greenberg and Alloy, 1989), and are less likely to be over-optimistic (Ruehlman *et al.*, 1985).[39] The individual who experiences mild forms of subjective mental distress may be more likely to process self-relevant information in a relatively unbiased and balanced fashion (Taylor and Brown, 1988). Realism can be pathological and self-defeating if it undermines motivation and effort (Kahneman and Lovello, 1997, 2003). Positive illusions appear to provide functional benefits (Taylor and Brown, 1988), as people with positive illusions may be healthier (Taylor *et al.*, 2000), and illusions may bring benefits against stress (Cohen and Edwards, 1989). Hence, instead of being selected out in a Darwinian fashion, undue optimism, illusions of control, and overly positive self-evaluations (all, presumably, to some moderate degree) may yield benefits to the individual, and promote mental health and the ability to perform successfully. Such results are, however, inconsistent with the traditional notion that realistic perceptions of the self are characteristics of mental health.

This raises troubling questions regarding risk management in a corporate setting, where a high level of optimism by agents is typically considered advantageous, regardless of the danger of this leading to an undue negligence of risk and a devaluation of negative feedback. Over-optimism in the corporation can lead to disaster. In a discussion on failure avoidance management, Landau and Chisholm (1995) comment on the high costs of mistakes in organizations. These authors strongly denounce what they call the 'arrogance of optimism', which denies the very possibility of failure. This may be at the centre of management disasters, and may also be an element of poor group decision-making (Janis, 1972).[40]

This points to a genuine dilemma for organizational decision-making. While an optimistic bias appears to be an essential mark of a healthy mind, and (mildly) optimistic judgements of risks (i.e. underestimates) and of opportunities (i.e. overestimates) would appear to be typical of human behaviour, in the extreme, however, downplaying the risk element in decisions and ignoring danger signs leaves an individual and organization open to catastrophic failures. The present research will shortly return to discuss issues relating to the pathological neglect of risk and danger signals by individuals on their own and within organizations.

Summary

The economist's rational choice framework provides one model of optimal performance under uncertainty. It has many strengths, including a relative ease of modelling and the ability to make forecasts. The rational actor model can be a useful way of looking at the expected behaviour of individuals and groups and can provide valuable insights into decision-making. Nevertheless, economic agents ultimately have to make judgements based on their cognitive apparatus and emotive state, and within a social context. This makes decision-making far messier and more complicated than a simplified model of optimal choice behaviour may capture. Studies on human judgement and decision-making effectively demonstrate how individuals (and groups) can systematically depart from the expected utility framework of the economist. Hirsch *et al.* noted,

> By precluding attention to non-rational elements of human behaviour, economists leave themselves no mechanism for learning about the crude and messy empirical world that so defies their models. Economists pay a heavy price for the very simplicity and elegance of their models: empirical ignorance, misunderstanding, and, relatedly, unrealistic and bizarre policy recommendations.
>
> (Hirsch *et al.*, 1987: 320)

In human judgement and choice-making, myopia often trumps foresight, the immediate typically dominates the important, and people tend to have a preference for gratification sooner rather than later. These characteristics of human behaviour, taken together with bounded cognitive capacity and the use of heuristics, regularly interfere with the rational decision-making ideal of the traditional economic model. If 'complex economic organization is explained in large measure as a response to the problems that are posed by the basic attributes of human actors' (Williamson, 1999: 35), then understanding these basic attributes may enable observers to provide better predictions of human behaviour in a corporate setting.[41]

Individuals may not consistently update their beliefs in a Bayesian fashion, nor, over time, learn to do so. At the very least, insights from behavioural decision theory suggest that Bayesian updating is only one tool of many that individuals use in forming and refining their judgement and decision-making. At the same time, it would be misleading to call heuristics a mistake. Instead, these findings add weight to an evolutionary explanation for certain cognitive and perception tools which nonetheless can at times lead to bias. Despite the predominance of the rational model in economic thinking, empirical evidence from experiments and observations suggests that human inference and decision-making bears little resemblance to the normative model of traditional economics. Rather, information processing is subject to incomplete data-gathering, mental shortcuts, situational conditions, inconsistencies over time, biases, prior expectations, and self-serving interpretations (Nisbett and Ross, 1980).

The human mind is subject to self-enhancing biases in a wide range of matters. These can manifest themselves in the form of motivated cognition and self-serving reasoning, belief perseverance (the tendency to cling to one's belief's in the face of contrary evidence), and confirmation bias (the tendency to seek information that confirms one's own view and to overlook or discount evidence that disconfirms these prior beliefs). Individuals tend to be over-optimistic regarding their susceptibility to illness (Weinstein, 1980, 1984; Kunda, 1987), feel less vulnerable to risk than others (Perloff and Fetzer, 1986), and tend to feel more responsible for successes than for failures (Miller, 1976). Individuals often feel superior to others (Klein and Kunda, 1993) and deem themselves better at controlling risk (Klein and Kunda, 1994), better drivers (Svenson, 1981), and more ethical than others (Messick *et al.*, 1985; Liebrand *et al.*, 1986; Tyson, 1990; Morgan, 1993).

Beliefs are intertwined with the preferences individuals have concerning those beliefs. The literature on cognitive dissonance examines how people avoid information that they find unappealing, and demonstrates that people often prefer to avoid or distort information that challenges comfortable beliefs (Festinger, 1957; Sherman and Gorkin, 1980). The human mind has the ability to subconsciously screen out unattractive signals, which contrasts sharply with the standard economic presumption that people care about information only for its instrumental value, and hence always prefer more of it to less. Anchoring and adjustment behaviour shows that more information may actually result in less accurate decisions and that irrelevant choices may bias decision-making (Tversky and Kahneman, 1974; Simonson and Tversky, 1992).

Rational choice theories on decision-making and behavioural decision theories would seem to be located on opposite poles of a wide spectrum of possible choice behaviour. This does not necessarily make these views mutually exclusive. Individuals might at times be largely rational. Nevertheless, evidence from behavioural economics, psychology, decision theory, cognitive psychology, and related fields demonstrates that the standard economic model overstates the rationality of the economic actor, pointing to the possibility that 'at the individual level EU [expected utility] maximization is more the exception than the rule' (Schoemaker, 1982: 552).

The insights on human decision-making presented in this section will next be applied to reputational intermediaries in the corporate governance setting. The next chapter will show how these effects tend to steer the judgement and decision-making of these agents away from the outcomes predicted by the rational choice model. Cognitive, affective, situational, and social effects will be discussed. Gatekeeper susceptibility to bias will be further developed in Chapter 6. The insights from this discussion have significant repercussions for the impact of governance policies and rules discussed in Chapter 8.

5 Behaviour and rationality in corporate governance

Homo Economics meet Homo Sapiens[1]

This chapter asks why some of the standard means of monitoring the activities of senior decision-makers in large corporations seem prone to periodic failure. Key factors in monitoring managerial performance include the composition and independence of the board of directors, issues of transparency, outside reporting, accounting standards, and auditing quality. It is suggested that an over-reliance of legal and economic theory on the standard rational model as applied to reputational intermediaries may lead to overconfidence with regard to the feasibility of independence of the two groups of gatekeepers under investigation. As a result, rules based on the presumed rationality and independence of these agents may be less reliable than is frequently assumed.

The two means of corporate supervision of primary interest to this research are the board of directors and the external auditor. The role of corporate lawyers and legal counsel, somewhat neglected agents in the corporate governance discussion, is not, at this time, investigated in depth. Lawyers and legal counsel are involved in every aspect of running a corporation, and are instrumental in the setting up of contracts and the provision of opinions with regard to the compliance of contracts with the law. Lawyers should be responsible when they have provided an opinion on the legality of a contract which subsequently is found wanting. This is highly significant to the governance discussion, or at least it should be.

Sale (2005) comments on the role of banks in corporate scandals. As is the case with legal counsel, the role of banks in corporate debacles has not been widely acknowledged. A number of large investment banks have settled (without, as is customary, admitting guilt) with US authorities to avoid further litigation with respect to their association with Enron and WorldCom (SEC, 2003d).[2] Nevertheless, the banking industry did not receive the scathing, and in the case of Arthur Andersen vindictive, criticism bestowed on the auditing profession. Nonetheless, investment banks had a central role in the recent corporate scandals (Batson, 2003b, c; Sale, 2005). The role and responsibilities of legal counsel and bankers in enabling corporate misdemeanour will be commented on in Chapter 8 which discusses the policy implications of this research.[3]

Behaviour in corporate governance

It is important to emphasize the distinction between problems with individual actors' behaviour and problems in the way in which actors interact. The present chapter primarily discusses critical issues with regard to individual perception, judgement, and choice-making. While group decision-making is introduced, a more detailed discussion on group dynamics is the focus of Chapter 6, which investigates the interaction of actors with colleagues, peers, and clients. Questioned in both chapters is the assumption of the rational model that individuals and groups consistently respond appropriately to incentives and information. Individuals vary in the degree to which they are susceptible to various biases, self-control problems, and temporal inconsistencies. Heterogeneity in choice behaviour between agents, of course, complicates the design of incentive systems. This is compounded by evidence which indicates that individuals themselves may not act consistently when they face choices under uncertainty, but may instead vary in their responses depending on situation, context, and mood, and with regard to intertemporal decisions. The potential for heterogeneity and inconsistency between and within agents indicates a need for flexibility in incentive design, and strongly suggests the need for attention to details which the conventional model would assume to be essentially irrelevant (O'Donoghue and Rabin, (2005).

The following sections discuss behavioural and cognitive causes leading to persistent divergences from the rational model of judgement and decision-making within a corporate setting. The main argument is that these persistent features of human behaviour can critically undermine some of the assumptions and outcomes of corporate governance models based on rational choice theory. Agents within a corporate setting may not strictly adhere to the axioms of the rational theory on decision-making. Thus, predictions with regard to agent behaviour made on the basis of the rational actor model may be misleading in important ways. As a result, rules and regulations formed on the basis of flawed assumptions *re* choice behaviour may be less reliable in preventing corporate fraud than generally predicted. The behavioural approach is viewed as adding value to the rational actor approach, but is, for the most part, not intended to represent a wholesale replacement.

Heuristics and the nature of bias

Heuristics are mental shortcuts, or rules of thumb, that have their origin in human evolution, an origin they share with the human capacity for rational and analytic thinking (Slovic *et al.*, 2002). Heuristics are useful means for quickly coping with complex situations. In general, heuristics provide good outcomes, but sometimes lead to serious errors, or bias (Bazerman, 1986). There are two broad classes of bias of particular interest to the present investigation. One is the kind of bias arising naturally from bounded rationality, constraints on cognitive-processing ability, affect, and context. An individual's perception and judgement tends to be unconsciously influenced by a set of heuristics and is subject to limits to cognitive processing. One reason why such simple heuristics may lead to bias is that they are based on rules appropriate to the past. The second class of bias is the motivated one, with the notion of self-serving rationalization as a fundamental construct. People tend to 'see what they want to see', and threats to self-image are typically resisted (Yariv, 2002). In a group setting, threats to group self-image upset cohesion, something that is actively discouraged.

Correcting for bias is an imperfect process (Kunda, 1990; Bazerman *et al.*, 2000). Individuals continue to be subject to unconscious bias even when its operation is clearly demonstrated to the individual, where the concept of bias is clearly understood, and where individuals are explicitly instructed to avoid bias (Babcock *et al.*, 1993, 1995). Bias typically enters at the perception stage (when people form an opinion or judgement on a matter) and often reflects the individual's prior beliefs. Motivation may affect reasoning through a choice of a biased set of cognitive processes whereby an individual may chose those cognitive processes that lead to the desired conclusions (Kunda, 1990). Under this interpretation, rational thought and reasoning may often be an instrument to justify an earlier decision. The use of processes inappropriate for the task at hand, while highly useful in conserving one's prior beliefs, can exaggerate bias. Affective reactions also guide subsequent information processing and judgement (Zajonc, 1980).

Tversky and Kahneman (1974) describe three major heuristics that form the basis for numerous biases resulting from a reliance on these specific mental shortcuts. The *availability* heuristic refers to the tendency to assess frequencies and probabilities of events on the basis of ease of their recollection. This method is fallible because availability of information not only is subject to irrelevant factors, but also has been found to typically disregard base frequencies. The *representative* heuristic reflects judgements based on stereotypes or preconceived categories. Decisions and assessments are made on the basis of how representative a given instance is to an earlier experience. *Anchoring and adjustment* refers to the phenomenon that an initial value, or starting point, typically influences assessment value, irrespective of the likelihood or relevance of this initial value. Historical precedent, the formulation and presentation of a problem, or random information can form an initial value (anchor). No matter how extreme the initial value may appear, even where it is fully recognized as irrelevant, individuals tend to insufficiently adjust for this subsequently (Slovic and Lichtenstein, 1971; Tversky and Kahneman, 1974). The discussion will demonstrate shortly how gatekeepers are subject to these, and more, heuristics, and the negative effect these can have on the quality of monitoring in corporate governance.

Belief perseverance

Belief perseverance, or cognitive conservatism (Nissani, 1990), is a bias towards the status quo. Once a belief (opinion, theory) is formed, it tends to be insufficiently revised by evidence that runs counter to the initial impression, as 'beliefs tend to sustain themselves even despite the total discrediting of the evidence that produced the beliefs initially' (Nisbett and Ross, 1980: 192). Humans have the ability, and the strong tendency, to selectively filter out and overweigh information that supports a view, and at the same time discount evidence that contradicts an initial opinion. If belief perseverance has something to say about how human beings evaluate new evidence, then they may not merely be Bayesian updaters, and may instead go beyond objectively updating a prior with new information. As people ignore and discount evidence at variance with a prior belief, and overweigh supportive data. (Lord *et al.*, 1979), the weight given to new data would seem to depend on whether it supports or contradicts an implicit theory. The same information is differently evaluated depending on prior opinion towards an issue. Information supportive of a position is uncritically accepted, whereas contrary information is typically discredited. Hence, individuals may read more, or less, into the same information, depending on a preconceived view.

Systematic bias in the processing of information reflects both the selective attention and differential weighting of information of cognitive processes (e.g. hypothesis confirmation; see Snyder, 1984), and also motivational accounts such as cognitive dissonance theory (Festinger, 1957). Biased assimilation of information can lead to attitude polarization (McHoskey, 1995). Thus, prior beliefs and expectations can filter and shape perception in such a way as to support and preserve earlier held views (Nisbett and Ross, 1980), which can lead to self-serving attributions and motivated reasoning. Individuals typically are unaware that they are highly selective in their perception and frequently deny that they are interpreting information in a self-serving fashion (Diekmann, 1997; Diekmann *et al.*, 1997). In other words, 'when faced with choice between changing one's mind and proving there is no need to do so, almost everyone gets busy on the proof' (ascribed to John Kenneth Galbraith). This would appear to run directly counter to the assumptions of Bayesian updating, discussed earlier. Belief confirmation theory implies that the individual will typically process new information subjectively. With regard to corporate governance disasters, what may appear as clear warning signs to the outside observer, especially in hindsight, can quite easily be discounted as noise or nonrepresentative (and even supportive) of an interpretation by management and its gatekeepers.

Once executives have committed to a course of action, their subsequent survey of information is strongly biased to support their choice. This would also appear to apply to the behaviour of gatekeepers. The literature on escalation behaviour shows that bolstering evidence is actively sought, while disconfirming information is subconsciously resisted (Staw, 1976, Staw and

Ross, 1987). Further shown in this literature is that negative consequences may actually cause decision-makers to increase their commitment and risk further negative consequences. This changes the objective function of the individual. Individuals who confront negative consequences may, instead of changing their behaviour, cognitively distort the negative consequences to a more positive looking outcome. Potentially aggravating this bias is the typical reaction of individuals who perceive themselves in a loss situation ('loss frame') to increase their willingness to take risks, and become relatively more risk-seeking (Tversky and Kahneman, 1974). Loss aversion, explained in the following section, is a closely related phenomenon which can introduce further bias to the interpretation of information.

Loss aversion

With prospect theory, Kahneman and Tversky (1979) demonstrate that individuals may not strictly adhere to one of the central tenets in economic theory, namely that sunk costs should be ignored when forming decisions on future resource allocation. Standard economic theory posits that decisions on the allocation of resources should only take expected (future) returns into consideration. Past investments should be disregarded as these are irrelevant to future returns. In contrast, prospect theory (Kahneman and Tversky, 1979) demonstrates that for individuals, sunk cost might not be sunk at all. According to this theory, humans have a strong aversion to losses, and the propensity for risk-taking depends on an individual's position relative to a potential loss. Gains and losses are not considered in the same way, nor given the same weight. Under prospect theory, an individual's first priority is not to lose. Gains are secondary to the 'no loss' rule. Framing an outcome in terms of possible loss motivates a person differently than framing the same outcome in terms of possible gain. Negative (loss) framing makes the person more risk-seeking (Tversky and Kahneman, 1981).

Loss aversion can help explain a wide range of phenomena that seem at odds with standard economic theory on individual choice. For example, individuals will go to great lengths, including taking higher risk positions, lying, and hiding losses, to avoid the recognition of a loss (Langevoort, 1996, 1998b, 2002b; Krawiec, 2000; Bratton 2002). Initial small losses can set an individual off on a path of increasingly risky attempts to hide subsequent losses. Sunk costs, interpreted as losses, can thus form a negative reference point or loss frame (Tversky and Kahneman, 1981), from which new decisions are made. Even imaginary or potential losses may induce extreme risk-seeking. This would be considered by many economists as an error, as only the future costs and benefits of a decision are considered relevant to the standard economic theory. Decision-makers, however, do not seem to strictly follow this advice. Instead, a loss is often seen as unacceptable, especially by those responsible for the earlier decision that led to an initial loss (Staw, 1976). Once a situation begins to deteriorate, an individual is likely to undertake further steps, and take further risk, to avoid the detection of losses (or sub-par performance) by peers or supervisors (Staw, 1976). Cognitive dissonance considerations (Festinger, 1957) can lead to an escalation of commitment (Weick, 1964; Staw, 1981; Brockner, 1992) where steps are undertaken to try to turn a failing situation around, allocating resources beyond what a purely rational analysis (and subsequent hindsight) would recommend.[4]

Risk-seeking behaviour is more commonplace when a person perceives the possibility of loss or makes comparisons of relative position (Kahneman and Lovallo, 1997, 2003). Loss framing may be especially prominent in settings of social comparisons. Not to fall behind others is a potent motivator and can easily lead to fears of loss of status or financial security. Prospect theory predicts that people take up more risk to keep up with others rather than to move ahead of them. In a loss frame, a small actual loss can put the actor under considerable strain to try and 'make up' for the loss. Cognitive behaviour studies (see Rabin, 2002) show that under such circumstances, individuals become increasingly risk-seeking. A tournament environment (Rosen, 1981) may be the ultimate loss frame setting, where the missing of a set goal by even a small margin can have a significantly negative impact on a career. Meeting or exceeding the goal, in contrast, is extremely well rewarded, and the gulf between winners and losers, while possibly small in terms of performance, can be large in terms of rewards (Rosen, 1981). The tournament setting acts as an incentive to high-risk takers or those comfortable with high-risk taking, and may increase unethical behaviour (Douma *et al.*, 2004).[5]

Escalation of commitment

Decision-makers frequently become overcommitted to prior decisions, increasing the allocation of resources to failing projects (e.g. Staw, 1976; Fox and Staw, 1979; Staw and Ross, 1987). Individuals who confront negative consequences (of earlier views or actions) frequently distort these to a more positively looking outcome, and may go to great lengths, including taking higher risk positions and hiding losses, to avoid the recognition of a loss (Krawiec, 2000; Bratton, 2002). This is further aggravated by belief perseverance, the bias towards the status quo, which can reinforce self-serving attributions and motivated reasoning in order to avoid or reduce cognitive dissonance (Festinger, 1957).[6] Commitment to a prior belief or decision is one of the fundamental concepts of both individual and organizational psychology (Nisbett and Ross, 1980). Once committed to an idea or course of action, there is a strong motivation to resist evidence contradicting an initial position. Self-confidence and external image are both threatened by introducing a troubling awareness of the possibility of having made a mistake. This may also necessitate a public reversal of one's position, which not only questions one's competence, but calls into question one's reputation for consistency, a highly valued asset in our economic culture. Cognitive dissonance theory predicts that once a commitment is made, attitudes and beliefs will shift to preserve consistency.

Krawiec (2000) explains the potentially disastrous consequences to the firm of the action of a rogue trader partially in reference to an escalation of commitment problem. In her view, the combination of serial decision-making and substantial sunk costs can lead to a situation where the rogue trader is trying to cover up increasingly large losses, while his or her supervisor/manager is under psychological pressure to interpret the rogue's behaviour in positive terms. Perception and judgement biases, impression management, and loss aversion are at the root of escalatory behaviour. Of primary importance to the present discussion is that an individual's decisions are systematically affected by the way in which a situation is presented, or framed (and subsequently interpreted). While agents may indeed be irrational by 'throwing good money after bad', this phenomenon is sufficiently prevalent that it cannot simply be dismissed as an aberration to expected behaviour.[7] Where a decision-maker is responsible for an earlier investment or judgement, this may lead to escalation of commitment (Staw, 1976), the tendency to invest resources beyond what a neutral observer would consider reasonable.

Escalation of commitment has been investigated as 'entrapment' (Fox and Staw, 1979; Brockner and Rubin, 1985), 'too much invested to quit' (Teger, 1980), and 'throwing good money after bad' (Garland, 1990). Individuals are especially prone to escalation if they are responsible for the initial decision to go ahead with a project. The management literature (see, for example, Nisbett and Ross, 1980) strongly suggests that once executives have committed to a course of action, their subsequent survey of information is strongly biased to bolster their initial decision, especially when their choice is public and they can be held accountable for their decisions. Managers (and decision-makers in general) frequently come to believe in the efficacy of projects for which they are responsible, despite evidence that advocates abandonment. This typically leads to behaviour where bolstering evidence is actively sought, while disconfirming information is subconsciously resisted.

Such behaviour patterns would also seem to apply to auditors and members of a board of directors with regard to earlier decisions. Once a judgement has been made and a decision is taken, or suggested, a reversal of opinion would potentially signal an earlier error, and possibly a lack of steadfastness. People often commit the greatest amount of resources for a previously chosen course of action when they are personally responsible for negative consequence (Staw, 1976). Rationalizing previous behaviour or decisions is a process of self-justification. A Bayesian updater might be expected to reverse decisions once negative feedback is used to update a prior. This is contrasted with observations that negative consequences may actually cause decision-makers to increase the commitment of resources and undergo the risk of further negative consequences (Staw, 1981).

According to rational decision-making models, escalation of commitment to a failing cause stems from the decision-maker's failure to recognize that the time, money, and effort already expended are sunk costs that cannot be recovered. This results in the neo-classical assumption that the current decision should be made by evaluating only the future costs and benefits of the contemplated action. This may not always hold if wealth maximization is only one of many variables of importance to the individual. Status would appear to be very highly rated among decision-makers within trading institutions (Krawiec, 2000), and it can be assumed that this is also of importance in the general corporate setting. If recognizing a loss results in reduced status (say, by obtaining a reputation for inconsistency), then accepting higher risk in an attempt to eliminate the loss may be a reasonable attempt to maximize utility, but not necessarily wealth. By committing additional resources, it may be possible to 'turn a situation around' and to show the ultimate rationality of an original decision. Staw (1981) finds that even where the effort ultimately leads to failure, an apparent norm for consistency rewards persistent behaviour higher than the indecisiveness perceived from a 'change of horses in mid-stream'. The desire to appear rational and consistent may be one motive for selectively filtering information to maintain commitment to a course of action (Festinger, 1957; Tversky and Kahneman, 1974; Nisbett and Ross, 1980).

Justification for previous decisions and a perceived norm for consistency may thus combine to give a powerful incentive for adhering to a committed path. Even measures specifically introduced to control overcommitment may increase the likelihood that decision-makers fail to acknowledge project deterioration (Bromiley *et al.*, 2002). External demands for success constitute one variable which can foster escalation of commitment. External performance assessment of decision-making and consequent effects on the decision-maker's prospects can lead to surreptitious behaviour by the individual hoping to avoid negative repercussions from having made a bad decision.

Practical implications immediately follow from the analysis presented in the preceding paragraphs. The dangers from cognitive dissonance reduction efforts (Festinger, 1957), and escalation of commitment (Staw, 1976), suggest that changing auditors and directors on a regular basis would reduce problems in two ways. First, the new auditor/director is unencumbered by the weight of decisions made by the previous auditor/director. Second, knowing that one will only be in office (as the engagement partner or on a board) for three years, at which time someone else will come in to check the books and past decisions, means that any gambles taken must pay of within that time frame. This suggests the need for regular rotation of people in charge of decisions, including auditors, board directors, and other monitors and gatekeepers.

Group decision-making

With 'groupthink' Janis (1972, 1982) described how bright people in highly cohesive groups can end up making bad decisions. Groupthink tends to occur when groups are highly cohesive and under pressure to come to a decision. Various social and cognitive pressures intervene to result in bad decision-making. Shared illusions, including a sense of invulnerability, presumptions of unanimity, suppression of personal doubt (self-censorship), and taboos against antagonizing existing and new members of the group conspire to lead to selective bias towards accepting the status quo, and a suppression of alternative interpretations. Additional pathologies of this phenomenon include the failure to seek alternatives, not seeking expert advice, a high degree of selectiveness in information gathering, and a lack of critical evaluation of presented ideas. This can lead to a state of affairs described by Janis (1972: 9) as 'a mode of thinking that people engage in when they are deeply involved in a cohesive in-group, when the members' strivings for unanimity override their motivation to realistically appraise alternative causes of action'.

Groupthink, one of the most extreme forms of mutual agreement, gradually merges the opinion of each member of a group with what they deem to be the group's consensus (Stasser *et al.*, 1989). Groups may not exert a moderating effect on their members. Contrary to earlier held assumptions, group discussions can intensify attitudes, beliefs, judgements, and values (Pruitt, 1971a, b; Myers, 1982). Discussions may lead to polarization, rather than moderation in views (Myers and Bishop, 1970; McHoskey, 1995; Baron, 2005). Belief positions after group discussions have been found to be more extreme (Myers, 1982), typically reinforcing earlier held group beliefs (Lord *et al.*, 1979; Diekman, 1997). Persuasion (Stasson *et al.*, 1988), social-comparison (Myers, 1978), decision schemes (Davis *et al.*, 1989), and normative influence are thought to combine to generate group polarization (Isenberg, 1986). In the extreme, this can render group decision-making highly inefficient and counterproductive.

Factors that magnify the potential problems of groupthink include a high degree of cohesion, which increases the pressures for conformity towards a single goal and increases the reluctance to speak out against decisions. Cohesion can foster an atmosphere of cordiality and friendly relations with other group members, where questioning the performance or conduct of another member is seen as being impolite and inappropriate. Groups increase their susceptibility to faulty decision-making through isolation from the outside world and by working only with members of their group. This reinforces group cohesion, but also prevents rigorous testing of alternatives. A group leader is frequently biased towards the decision he or she would like to see as the outcome of the deliberations. As such, the leader typically sets the agenda, limits the discussion to preconceived options, and may actively discourage dissent by urging agreement. Various insecurities felt by individual members may be minimized by placing responsibility on a collective decision. In sum, group and situational factors can combine to result in faulty decision-making, where potential initial misgivings by individuals give way to unanimous, but potentially flawed, decisions (Cox and Munsinger, 1985).

While a degree of conformity is necessary for group bonding, pressures to conform may become aggressively overwhelming in groupthink situations where even the least dissent is frowned upon. This can lead to self-appointed 'mind-guards' (Janis, 1972) who shield the group from information which could potentially disrupt the consensus view. Individual members of the group also tend to engage in a type of self-censorship, preventing them from disturbing the atmosphere of unanimity. A combination of group pressures, self-censorship, and highly selective information gathering may lead to the minimization and suppression of private misgivings (Janis, 1989).

Boards of directors can be seen as the ultimate corporate in-group and can be highly prone to the groupthink phenomenon. The nature and composition of a board (e.g. similar social background of the members and an emphasis on consensus decisions), typically result in a high degree of conformity, and the incidence of a minority opinion against a seemingly unanimous majority is negligible (Asch, 1956). Unqualified support for the chief executive is often seen as an unspoken norm of boards (Zarowin, 2005), despite the danger of passive directors failing to provide the oversight necessary to avoid mismanagement and corporate disasters. With a tendency for over-optimism in the assessment of own capabilities, and frequent illusions of invulnerability and superior morality, boards may suffer from biased perceptions towards the quality of own decision-making. Warning signs with regard to the quality of decision-making may be dismissed or rationalized to a minimum.

Sub-optimal monitoring

Given the potential liability and reputational threats to the firm from an accusation of lax monitoring of its employees where such individuals are found to have engaged in fraud or gross negligence, a firm would rationally be expected to implement an effective system of internal controls. Against this stand arguments that a firm has to balance legal sanctions and reputational loss with the costs of compliance initiatives (Langevoort, 2001a). The costs of compliance initiatives include the direct costs of monitoring and supervision. A greater cost can be the effects of increased monitoring on the firm's internal incentive and motivation structures. Courts and standard setters may generally underestimate the direct and indirect costs of such compliance within the firm (Langevoort, 2001a). Compensation contracts are frequently based on meeting measurable targets. One side effect of this is, however, that the stronger performance based incentives are, the less likelihood there might be for an adequate regard for strict legal compliance (Langevoort, 1996, 1998a, b, 2001a, b).

The question remains why, given the potential for disastrous costs due to employee fraud, a firm would implement a less than effective system of internal controls. Two answers are suggested here. One is that it is efficient to do so. If society under-enforces the law in such a way that firms do not fully internalize the risk of noncompliance, then it would be rational to have a system that tolerates some level of 'profitable' violations. In addition, the act of monitoring itself is likely to uncover some violations that otherwise might remain hidden, thus increasing the firm's exposure. The second answer is related to internal agency costs, where managers face an asymmetry in their incentives. Managers may not want to implement efficient systems because they can benefit substantially from the potential profitability associated with undetected violations but, on the whole, may suffer little in terms of personal exposure when value destroying violations by subordinates are detected.

Successful monitoring very much depends on supervisor motivation. Conflicting pressures at work can undermine this effort, motivated inference being one of these. It is psychologically unpleasant to discover a breach in compliance and have to confront a colleague, especially if one personally hired that staff member. Discovery of a wrongdoing would question the judgement of the manager who hired the wrongdoer, which can lead to efforts to rationalize the wrongdoer's actions. The unpleasantness of discovering a breach and having to confront a colleague about it can explain some level of sub-optimal monitoring and, by extension, negligent and/or fraudulent behaviour (Prentice, 2000; Coffee, 2002, 2003a). Krawiec (2000) comes to a similar conclusion with regard to the incentives a rogue trader faces in evading a firm's controls, and the line manager's incentives to allow this to happen. The connections between esteem, wealth, and risk-taking may be even more pronounced in a 'superstar' setting, which defines an environment where a disproportionate share of benefits go to the top performer in his/her class (Rosen, 1981).

Rational economic considerations alone (both by the firm and the employee) may lead to sub-optimal monitoring. Biases (by the agent and the monitor) can subsequently contribute to further weaken judgement, and interfere with a proper recalibration of risks and rewards of a policy of undermonitoring. This indicates a challenge to achieving the desired level of compliance. Direct supervision can break down where the supervisor is motivated by contractual and market forces to aim at an appropriate level of monitoring. Where good compliance is considered to start with hiring, the difficulties relate to imperfect information. Hiring is a heuristic process, fraught with mostly unconscious shortcuts that rely heavily on a small number of salient hints (Kahneman and Tversky, 1979). The reader may be familiar with the dictum that 'first impressions count', which refers to the tendency to place too much weight on initial impressions in making predictions on future performance of others. Perhaps even more important are psychological forces that subsequently interfere with an objective assessment of a candidate's job performance. Observed behaviour that runs counter to an initial judgement or held belief can result in cognitive dissonance, which an individual typically wishes to minimize. This can lead to self-justifying interpretations, rationalizing the behaviour observed in others (or oneself).

McNair (1991) looks at the inherent internal control problems faced by audit firms, and suggests that firms often rely on time budgets to monitor the quality of an audit.[8] This, however, exposes the firm and the individual auditor to the dilemma of trying to meet time budgets on the one hand, and quality concerns which would merit greater time investment in audits on the other. McNair concludes that firms appear to place a major reliance on the ethical character of the auditor, despite findings that ethical development may not be highly rewarded by firms (Ponemon, 1990), and that auditors are not ranked particularly high in ethical development scores.[9] The collapse of Barings Bank and Enron, the trading losses at Allied Irish Bank, Orange County and Daiwa, and the forced closure of Arthur Andersen show, however, that there is a high, and potentially terminal, risk to firms from sub-optimal monitoring and supervision, especially with regard to the monitoring function of the external audit.

Affect and visceral factors

Despite its empirical weaknesses, economists have broadly adopted expected utility theory and Bayesian updating as normative and descriptive models of decision-making under uncertainty. Under this interpretation, individuals consistently apply a probability calculus and formal logic in assessments and subsequent updates. Yet, even when people are aware of their choices, have stable preferences, are consistent when asked about their preferences, and would appear to meet all the requirements of the perfectly rational utility maximizer, they will not always choose what is rationally optimal for them.

Individuals frequently find themselves in situations where they are torn between what they believe they should do and what they finally end up doing (Loewenstein, 1996). Observed discrepancies between actual behaviour and perceived self-interest have been somewhat neglected by decision theories (Miller *et al.*, 1960). This is a serious shortcoming, as such discrepancies can be significant and persistent (Nisbett and Ross, 1980). Individuals can be fully aware of this conflict but still continue to act against their self-interest (Loewenstein, 1996). To bridge this gap between self-interest and behaviour, Slovic *et al.* (2002, 2004) propose that people use an affect heuristic to make judgements, where affect may act as a cue for decisions, just as vividness and similarity can serve as cues for probability judgements (i.e. the availability and representativeness heuristics). In explaining various anomalies concerning impulsivity and self-control problems, an affect heuristic may help explain the gap between perceived self-interest and actual behaviour (Slovic *et al.*, 1982, 2002).[10]

People may observe themselves behaving contrary to perceived self-interest (Loewenstein, 1996), a behaviour they and others subsequently may come to call irrational. Control over actual behaviour is frequently subject to a struggle between myopic decisions that provide an immediate benefit, and decisions more focused on maximizing future considerations of utility (Schelling, 1984). These deviations between self-interest and behaviour may stem from an internal conflict between a visceral response and a more reasoned cognitive response (Loewenstein, 1996). In hindsight, and with temporal distance to the conflict, people often regret their actual (emotive) response to a particular situation. Despite the best intentions, people frequently misjudge visceral and emotional effects and underestimate their impact on human behaviour. Affect may influence decision-making when the outcomes to be evaluated are visceral in nature.

Visceral factors include states such as hunger, thirst, sexual desire, emotions, moods, fear, pain, and various addictions. Although these states produce strong feelings in the present moment, these feelings are difficult to accurately recall or anticipate (Loewenstein, 1999).[11] Visceral impulses demand immediate gratification, while reasoned cognitive considerations allow for the postponement of gratification. Accounting for visceral reactions may allow an understanding of apparent irrationalities when analysing divergences between self-interest and actual behaviour. Decision theories that neglect the impact of visceral factors on behaviour do not recognise that these effects may severely limit an individual's ability to make rational decisions.

Loewenstein (1996) identifies three forms of attention-narrowing from visceral factors. The first is to focus attention and motivation on activities and forms of consumption that are associated with the visceral factor. This may happen to the degree of eliminating all forms of behaviour that do not lead to the satisfaction of the visceral factor (e.g. extreme anti-social and self-destructive behaviour due to a severe addiction). A certain tunnel vision induces the marginal rate of substitution between goods associated with the visceral factor and all other goods to become negligibly small. A second form of attention-narrowing is the collapse of one's time-perspective towards the immediate present, where the satisfaction of an immediate need takes strong precedence over longer-term goals (where the urgent may trump the important). A third form of attention-narrowing involves increased focus on the self, which causes a narrowing of focus towards the inward and a strong tendency towards becoming selfish. Box 5.1 lists seven propositions which describe the relationship between deliberation and action due to visceral factors, as suggested by Loewenstein (1996), summarizing the disproportionate effect that visceral factors can have on behaviour.

Physical and temporal proximity with an object of desire (such as a promotion, a bonus, targets, etc.) may lead to impulsive behaviour quite contrary to longer-term rational considerations. Individuals tend to respond more emotionally and less rationally when they are at the moment of decision in a conflict than they do when they are either anticipating a conflict or thinking back on a conflict (Bazerman *et al.*, 2002c).[12] A future conflict is frequently anticipated to be dealt with in a reasoned and rational manner. However, it is more likely that the actual conflict situation will be dominated by mutual emotional responses, undermining intentions of a reasonable and rational response, especially in the absence of predetermined credible and workable 'circuit breakers' that defuse a situation. When people discount the influence of emotional factors, they are likely to fail to plan for dealing with their emotions in conflict situations (Schkade and Kahneman, 1998; Bazerman, 2002c).

Box 5.1 Seven propositions on the impact of visceral factors (VF) on behaviour

1 Differences between actual value of an action or good and desired value increase with the intensity of the VF.
2 Future VF are perceived to have limited influence on future value. This is consistent with hyperbolic discounting. However, hyperbolic discounting does not explain why some forms of consumption more commonly associated with impulsivity, such as physical proximity and sensory contact are important cues.
3 Immediate VF are more powerful than a delayed VF. This shows the effect of vividness on valuations.
4 VF, even if temporary, can influence decisions for the future.
5 People underestimate the impact on their own future behaviour of VF.
6 People forget the degree of influence of VF on past behaviour. Past behaviour under the influence of VF subsequently seems perplexing.
7 The first six propositions extend to interpersonal comparisons.

Source: based on Loewenstein (1996).

Schwartz (2000: 433–7) examined the interplay of affect and decision processes from a number of different perspectives: (1) the role of affect at the time of decision-making, (2) post-decision affect, (3) the impact of anticipated affective states on decisions, and (4) the impact of memories of past affective states on decisions. Negative moods were found to frequently induce normative information processing and decision-making methods, in contrast to optimistic states, which were typically associated with heuristics-based information processing.[13] Post-decision effect can be incorporated in the decision-making process as emotive states (such as regret or disappointment about past decisions) and thus affect current and future decisions.

The call for the recognition of the affect heuristic in human judgement is strengthened by the indication that positive and negative emotions towards an issue may serve as cues for judgement (Slovic *et al.*, 2004). Subliminal effects, for example, have been found to potentially lead to a more positive judgement of a person or situation than would be warranted by a rational assessment (Winkielman *et al.*, 1997). Induced or acquired preferences tend to persevere (Sherman *et al.*, 1998), may explain preference reversals (Tversky *et al.*, 1990), and have been used to explain insensitivity to probability and risk (Frederick *et al.*, 2002). This indicates that a thorough evaluation of all relevant options may at times be precluded by affect (Shafir *et al.*, 1993).

Temporally inconsistent behaviour

Problems of incompatible personal goals are especially apparent with regard to decisions with a temporal dimension. The impact of visceral factors on future behaviour is typically underestimated (Loewenstein, 1996; Bazerman *et al.*, 2002a, b). Once the future has become the present, these factors again impact disproportionably on decision-making:

> Unlike currently experienced visceral factors, which have a disproportionate impact on behaviour, delayed visceral factors tend to be ignored or severely underweighted in decision-making. Today's pain, hunger, anger, etc. are palpable, but the same sensations anticipated in the future receive little weight.
>
> (Loewenstein, 1999: 240)

In a sense, most actual decisions are made in the immediate presence, and the future remains firmly in the distance, where individuals perceive themselves as being rational. Best intentions might, however, be voided when the future collapses to the present, and a discounted utility maximizer who does not discount at a constant rate may systematically deviate from prior consumption plans (Strotz, 1955). Temporally 'myopic' or impulsive behaviour can result from this time-inconsistency when the deviation from constant discounting involves a higher discounting rate for the nearer term.

That the capacity for rational decisions is challenged when there is a temporal dimension would seem to be inconsistent with the standard discounted utility model widely used by economists, and may be an example of self-defeating behaviour.[14] For example, Viscusi (1992: 11) asks: 'at the time when individuals initiate their smoking activity, do they understand the consequences of their actions and make rational decisions?' Given people's preferences, this essentially asks whether individuals are incorporating available information about risks and benefits of an activity in a manner that is congruent with rational decision-making. Quite regularly, the future-self does not appreciate own decisions made in the past. This emphasizes a distinction between decision utility and experience utility, which refers to the observation that the quality and intensity of the experience that actually occurs at a future date often differs substantially from the utility predicted or expected at the time of the decision (Kahneman and Snell, 1992; Loewenstein and Schkade, 1999). Schelling illustrates the internal inconsistencies that people experience in their preferences in terms of multiple selves battling for control over behaviour:

> Everybody behaves like two people, one who wants clear lungs and long life and the other who adores tobacco, or one who wants a lean body and the other who wants dessert . . . the 'straight' one often in command . . . but the wayward one needing only to get occasional control to spoil the other's best laid plans.
>
> (Schelling, 1984: 290)

This would imply one 'self' being focused on the present and favouring immediate benefit, whereas the other 'self' is more focused on maximizing future or long-term benefit. An alternative interpretation describes intrapersonal conflict in terms of two different utility functions existing within an individual (Bazerman *et al.*, 2002c). The 'want self' focuses on the present and prefers immediate gratification. The 'should self', in contrast, is more future oriented and emphasizes future benefits. Unfortunately, it seems that just as the individual approaches that future, the 'want self' is again a strong favourite for control over choice. Of course, the individual is not composed of several different selfs, yet the outcome is that individuals often do not behave in ways that are strongly (or even remotely) rational, but may engage in activities that are damaging to their prospects, and that they might well be aware of it.

Temporal distance to an event typically solicits a more reasoned (self-interested/rational) response. The more impulsive visceral (want self), however, places very strong emotional pressure on the individual as the event becomes immediate (Schelling, 1984; Lowenstein, 1996; Bazerman *et al.*, 1998; Bazerman *et al.*, 2002c). The human mind may perceive reality in two fundamentally different ways or modes, the intuitive and the analytical or rational (Slovic *et al.*, 2002). Accordingly, in response to an event, a person makes use of emotions associated with related events, which in turn motivates perception, interpretation, and action. Epstein suggests that

> people apprehend reality in two fundamentally different ways, one variously labelled intuitive, automatic, natural, non-verbal, narrative, and experiential, and the other analytical, deliberative, verbal, and rational.
>
> (Epstein, 1994: 710)

The experiental system would appear to have an affective basis, and is deemed to allow faster reactions to situations that require an immediate decision. Relying on images, associations, experience, emotions, visceral factors, and affect, an 'experiental system' (Epstein, 1994) can provide a rapid, intuitive, mostly subconscious and automatic way to perceive and assess risk (see Table 5.1, which compares this intuitive system with a rational/analytical system).

In a similar vein, Kunda suggests two modes of thought that explain individual variations over time in the propensity to engage in rational behaviour:

> Researchers in several areas of social cognition have developed dual-process models of cognition. Although these models differ in their details, they share the broad assumption that people alternate between different modes of thinking. Sometimes we engage in careful, detailed, and elaborate processing, devoting all of our attention to the problem at hand and aiming for the best possible solution. On other occasions we engage in more cursory, superficial processing, devoting little time and attention to the problem, aiming only for a quick and easy, albeit less than perfect, solution.
>
> (Kunda, 1999: 107)

Table 5.1 Two modes of thinking – comparison of the experiential and rational systems

	Experiential System		*Rational System*
1	Holistic	1	Analytic
2	Affective: pleasure–pain oriented	2	Logical: reason oriented (what is sensible)
3	Associative connections	3	Logical connections
4	Behaviour mediated by 'vibes' from past experiences	4	Behaviour mediated by conscious appraisal of events
5	Encodes reality in concrete images, metaphors, and narratives	5	Encodes reality in abstract symbols, words, and numbers
6	More rapid processing: oriented towards immediate action	6	Slower processing: oriented towards delayed action
7	Self-evidently valid: 'experiencing is believing'	7	Requires justification via logic and evidence

Source: adapted from Epstein (1994).

Zajonc (1980) earlier noted that affect guides information processing and judgement, forming an anchor to subsequent information processing and judgement. Affect (mood and emotions) may affect judgement and decision-making regardless of changes in situation.[15] Cognitive processing may change with affective state, and even moderate fluctuations in feelings have been found to affect cognitive processing (Ashby *et al.*, 1999).[16] Rather than being seen to interfere with reason, as a strict rationality view might infer, affective images embedded through lifelong learning in the brain ('markers') have been found to increase the accuracy and efficiency of the decision-making process (Damasio, 1994). Such markers are intuitively utilized to quickly provide incentives or disincentives in interpreting a situation. Rational decision-making may depend on an integration of emotion and reason, and affect may be a crucial element of rational judgements (Damasio, 1994).[17]

An alternative interpretation of deviations from the predictions of the standard economic model with respect to intertemporal choices is provided by the mental accounts model (Tversky and Kahneman, 1981; Kahneman and Tversky, 1984; Thaler, 1980, 1985, 1999). The mental accounts model describes how people record, analyse, and perceive the results of financial transactions and events. Put simply, mental accounts help people keep track of money and expenditures. This can be shown to differ significantly in outcomes compared to those predicted by conventional economic theory. The mental accounts model can enhance our understanding of choice-making. Mental accounting has been described as 'the set of cognitive operations used by individuals and households to organize, evaluate, and keep track of financial activities' (Thaler, 1999: 183). Broadly defined, this may refer to the process of perception, interpretation, categorizing, and evaluation of financial events. The three components of mental accounting of most relevance to an analysis of decision-making include the following. How outcomes are perceived, experienced and judged, and how decisions are made and subsequently evaluated. This particular accounting system provides the inputs to *ex ante* and *ex post* cost–benefit analyses. A second component involves the assignment of activities, events, and expenditures to specific accounts. Both the sources and end-uses of funds are perceived in terms of mental accounts (in addition to real accounts). The third component refers to the frequency with which accounts are evaluated. Accounts can be evaluated more or less often and can be defined narrowly or broadly. These components of mental accounting violate the economic principle of fungibility, and thus are of importance to the economic analysis of choice behaviour.[18]

An example from consumer theory may serve to demonstrate how mental accounts models can be utilized to explain actual behaviour which involves choices over time.[19] Economists tend to analyse the consumption-saving decision under assumptions of rational behaviour and would expect that consumers smooth their consumption over time. A standard model is the life-cycle theory of consumption.[20] In its simplest form, the life-cycle theory of consumption suggests that individuals' consumption depends on the present value of their wealth. Individuals are assumed to compute the present value of all wealth, including current and future income, and net assets, and consume a constant amount of money that could be afforded from an annuity purchased with that level of wealth. One implication is that individuals should engage in consumption smoothing. A further result (in the absence of transaction and other costs) is that the marginal propensity to consume all types of wealth is supposed to be equal, which extends into future income streams.

A crucial assumption of the life-cycle theory is fungibility, the notion that various income streams (i.e. different assets) can be concentrated into one common denominator, which allows the collapsing of all components of wealth into a single figure. This approach to consumer behaviour naturally appeals to economists as it incorporates traditional notions of economic rationality, is theoretically tractable, and allows for the generation of readily testable predictions. As elegant, simple, and logical as this theory would seem to appear, empirically it fares less well (Mankiw, 1981; Thaler, 1990; Thaler and Benartzi, 2004). Two types of anomalies are frequently cited in the savings literature. First, consumption appears to be more sensitive to current income than predicted by this theory (the old and the young, for example, tend to consume too little). Second, different forms of income and wealth do not appear to be as close substitutes as the theory would suggest.

The behavioural life-cycle model (Shefrin and Thaler, 1988) emphasizes self-control, mental accounting, and framing. This model suggests that individuals maintain mental accounts that lead them to treat various components of their wealth differently (nonfungible).[21] One implication is that an individual's consumption decision will be affected by asset composition as well as total wealth. This model of self-control rests on an observed preference for present consumption, the setting up of mental accounts for different assets with varying marginal propensities to consume, and a form of framing whereby individuals' consumption not only depends on levels of wealth but also on the type of account from which funds can be accessed. This suggests that there are psychological as well as financial transaction costs associated with spending from different types of accounts. Shefrin and Thaler (1988) suggest that individuals divide wealth into three mental accounts – current income, current assets, and future income. Individuals seem to be less reluctant to spend from current income and have a lower marginal propensity to consume from future income. The theory also predicts that certain types of income are allocated to certain types of consumption. It can be shown that, as a result, the marginal propensity to consume differs between various mental accounts and that consumption closely tracks current income. This sensitivity of consumption to current income is, however, incompatible with lifetime concepts of permanent income.

Risk perceptions

An area of particular interest is the compound effect of judgement errors on risk perception. Individuals are widely susceptible to framing effects, and display overconfidence in their own ability to avoid risks. As a means to minimize the mental anguish of engaging in an action perceived to be in conflict with legal, ethical, or professional guidelines, cognitive dissonance might cause individuals to discount risk in an inappropriate manner. Individuals might ignore or downplay their own information about the level of risk in order to minimize the resulting dissonance.

Perceived risk and perceived benefit have been found to be negatively correlated, which suggests the use of an affect heuristic in judgements on risk and benefit (Slovic *et al.*, 1982, 1999, 2004; Alhakami and Slovic, 1994). Alhakami and Slovic (1994) found an inverse relationship between perceived risk and perceived benefit of an activity which was linked to the strength of positive or negative affect associated with that activity. This implies that people may base their judgements of an activity not only on what they think about it but also on what they feel about it. Emotions were found to negatively affect the perception of risk. If the benefits of an activity were considered high (if one 'liked' the activity), then the risk from it was considered low. A dislike led to a low-benefit/high-risk perception.

Time pressure exacerbates this effect (Finucane *et al.*, 2000), and the affect heuristic has been shown to also affect experts' risk assessment (Slovic *et al.*, 1999).[22] Even if people are accurate in the perception of a particular risk in general, their actual behaviour towards that risk still does not have to correspond to this. It is important to bear in mind that economic analysis traditionally relies on generalized rather than personal perceptions of risk. Individuals may have a separate schedule of actual behaviour towards risk in contrast to the risk perception. Individuals may regard others as more susceptible to exogenous influences than they themselves are. Thus, even where people accurately estimate generalized risks, they might still underestimate their own personal susceptibility to the same risk.

The intrusion of behaviour

Rationality in corporate governance

The view that individuals are rational actors has dominated and shaped the economic analysis of choice for much of the last 50 years. The assumption of rationality of economic agents, in turn, underlies much of the view that independent and neutral monitors should be strongly motivated by reputational and legal concerns. Such considerations should encourage these agents to withstand various pressures to comply with the self-motivated views of senior management in the interpretation of financial data (Shleifer and Vishny, 1997a). Law and economics scholars, practitioners and judges may at times assume a descriptive validity of the rational model of decision-making where none is warranted. This can subsequently filter into policy and rule-making.

It is not surprising that academic accounting, too, has long since adopted neo-classical economics as one of its cornerstones. While the adoption of neo-classical paradigms may have provided academic accounting with a notion of scientific rigour, it remains open whether it has provided the field with an appropriate tool set for the job at hand. Williams (2004) identifies the colonization of accounting by 'positive economic science' as one possible contributing cause to the frequent involvement of auditors in corporate fraud. He notes that the application of neo-classical economics to accounting may have introduced an appearance of scientific rigour, but that this has not made accounting better at preventing financial misrepresentation and fraud. It may, however, have changed the interpretation of the accounting function, from one with a strong emphasis on moral and legal values, to one that primarily relies on technical mechanisms (Williams, 2004).

The role of accounting in corporate governance may not be served well by an uncritical adoption of scientific methods if the assumptions on which these are based miss critical elements of human choice behaviour. An over-reliance on technical means to verify compliance of financial statements, for example, may come at the cost of diminished efforts to seek out earnings manipulations and outright fraud. Too much trust may generally be placed in mathematical models to estimate compliance with technical guidelines such as GAAP. Such reliance may have taken accounting and auditing away from a moral and legal role, exposing it to the danger of irrelevance in the detection and prevention of fraud (Williams, 2004).[23] Revisions of accounting standards, procedural rules, and sanctions in response to past audit failures have not greatly improved the quality of accounting, at least not in the prevention of sudden and unexpected corporate failures (Clarke *et al.*, 2003).

The accounting profession as a whole was unable to detect or prevent the more recent cases of corporate misdeeds, and a reliance on rational theories of decision-making may partially have contributed to this poor performance.[24]

Many traditional means designed to enhance corporate governance assume that the main problem is one of conscious corruption. Much of the existing and proposed legislation also primarily aims at preventing or minimizing fraudulent intentions and penalizing legal transgressions. Economic analyses of the principal-agent problem still strongly rely on the rational model of decision-making. Less attention is focused on the issue of subconscious bias in the judgement and decision-making process of agents. The continued reliance on the ideal of the rational utility maximizer is somewhat odd, given the many robust examples of human behaviour which conflict with the axioms and predictions of rational choice theory. Concerns regarding the empirical validity of rational choice models of decision-making have led to questions as to whether the rationality assumption unduly limits the analysis of the agency problem in corporate governance (Langevoort, 1998b, 2001a, b; Coffee, 2001).

Failures in corporate governance appear to occur far more frequently than the presumably high standards of corporate governance in countries with a well-developed system of property rights, law, and regulatory agencies might suggest (Turnbull, 2000; Clarke *et al.*, 2003). The affected companies typically have clean audit reports, certified by leading accounting firms just prior to the announcements of the financial irregularities or the discovery of fraud. This has created an academic literature on an 'audit expectation gap', which tries to partially absolve the accounting profession from responsibility in cases of corporate fraud (Walker, 1991a, b; Guthrie, 1992; Guthrie and Turnbull, 1995). According to this interpretation, the auditor's role as a gatekeeper is of secondary importance, as the senior management of a corporation can easily and systematically 'fool' the auditor due to the former holding superior information. Hence, the auditor should not, in this view, be blamed for breaches in corporate governance, at least not in cases where the auditor did not knowingly collude (Young, 2001).

An example of this argument is given by Morrison (2004) who points out that Arthur Andersen, a former Big-5 auditing firm, was not actually responsible for the auditing of the Chewco, LJM1 and LJM2 special purpose vehicles (SPVs) at Enron, instrumental in the firm's accounting irregularities. Instead, it was auditing firm KPMG which (lead-) audited LJM1 and LJM2 (Chewco, according to Morrison, had not been properly audited at all). Morrison forcefully claims that Arthur Andersen itself was defrauded by Enron executives, and that Andersen was merely a scapegoat in the Enron case, held responsible and abruptly terminated by US authorities. While there is considerable merit in this argument, Morrison also emphasizes that an auditor should, in general, not be blamed for an auditee's fraud. Thus, she claims that 'the most rigorous audit cannot uncover collusion to defraud' (Morrison, 2004: 372), and elsewhere, 'Even a perfect audit will be unable to detect the widespread collusion among officers, employees, banks *et al.*, exemplified by the Enron frauds' (Morrison, 2005: 66). This would seem to support the 'auditors can easily be fooled' view expressed by expectations gap theorists. This would also appear to be an attempt to completely absolve auditors from blame in any audit failure in general, as long as the auditor cannot be shown to have been actively involved in the fraud (which would be very difficult to do). Andersen, under this interpretation, was the victim of a fraudulent client, which questions the prosecution's case against the accounting firm.

Turner (2005) critically responds to Morrison's article and holds Andersen accountable for failing to deliver a quality audit for Enron.[25] Turner cites Andersen's role as lead auditor in several major corporate frauds including Baptist Foundation of Arizona, Sunbeam, Waste Management, Qwest, Global Crossing, HIH, and WorldCom, the last example representing the largest bankruptcy in US history. In most of these audit failures Anderson at least partially admitted responsibility by agreeing to substantial financial settlements (without admitting or denying guilt with regard to the legal charges made).[26] It is a valid question to ask of what use, if any, the accounting profession would see itself, if it were indeed so easy to hide fraud and collusion from highly trained audit professionals during an audit. A further question might be what, if anything, would justify auditing fees paid by firms (and ultimately their shareholders) if audits are deemed mostly superfluous tools in corporate governance, of less than marginal value to users of financial information.

In an interesting twist to the Arthur Andersen/Enron saga, the US Supreme Court in May 2005 overturned the 2002 obstruction of justice verdict against Andersen which had destroyed the firm.[27] This adds credence to Morrison's argument (2004) that Andersen was made a scapegoat for the accounting profession. This may well have been the case, and it can be shown that Andersen was hardly an outlier in terms of bad audits in the accounting profession, but this does not absolve Andersen from blame in this, or in other cases. It is mildly ironic that the infamous shredding of working papers ultimately hindered an investigation of what was known by Andersen auditors about the true state of financial affairs at Enron, and how relevant items were interpreted during the audit. It would seem that the destruction of working papers robbed Andersen of any chance of a defence, which questions the professionalism of the in-house lawyer who allowed (and possibly encouraged) this. For now it would appear that the abrupt termination of Andersen prevents a reliable analysis of the causes of the internal governance failures of this accounting firm. These, arguably, were at the core of Andersen's troubles, and may contribute to audit failures in general.

In defence of the firm, and to the disgrace of the surviving large auditing firms, Arthur Andersen appears to have been responsible for a slightly less than proportionate share of earnings restatements compared to the (then) Big-5 accounting firms in the five years prior to its demise. Between 1997 and

2001, Andersen audited 21 per cent of Big-5 audit clients, while it was responsible for only 15 per cent of the restatements experienced by the Big-5 accounting firms (Coffee, 2002). Disclosed settlements also appear to be spread evenly across the big accounting firms. This is not a new phenomenon:

> The accounting profession is dominated by the [then] Big Six accounting firms, all of which have been sued for substantial sums in connection with securities fraud claims, making differentiation by reputation difficult. The difference between Coopers and Lybrand, which disclosed $145 million in settlements in 1992, and KPMG Peat Marwick, which disclosed $4.5 million in the same year, is discernable but also debatable, particularly in view of the fact that, in the following year (1993) Coopers and Lybrand disclosed $25.90 million in settlements whereas KPMG Peat Marwick disclosed $55.32 million . . . [F]or a large accounting firm a securities suit is simply one more suit to be settled or litigated.
>
> (Painter and Duggan, 1996: 239)[28]

While it is difficult to see how Andersen could be completely absolved of blame, given the long string of audit failures the firm had been involved in (Turner, 2005), it does not appear that this auditor was particularly worse than the other firms in producing bad audits. The single-minded destruction of the firm by the prosecutor's actions is another matter. This may well have prevented a deeper understanding of the factors within Andersen which led to the internal governance failures at the heart of the many poor audits. It would also seem to hinder an analysis of the internal monitoring weaknesses the remaining Big-4 accounting firms are subject to.

Responses to accounting scandals

A time-honoured response to major corporate failures is the establishment of committees of inquiry, the recommendation of new codes of best practice, and the introduction of additional rules and legislation. These steps typically react post-hoc to problems, and new waves of unexpected corporate debacles tend to shake public confidence in the existing system of corporate governance relatively soon thereafter. This, yet again, leads to questions about the adequacy of existing rules, which, in turn, result in the formulation and implementation of new rules and regulations. One detects a circularity in the actions and reactions where incidences of corporate fraud are followed by formal inquiries and subsequent regulatory responses. The recurrence of waves of fraud should prompt the question whether some crucial elements in human behaviour are perhaps being missed in the standard approach to the agency problem.

Crucially, this begs the question whether the assumption of monitors as rational actors can safely be relied upon. Research in the fields of cognitive psychology (Neisser, 1967, 1976), decision theory (Gigerenzer and Todd, 1999), managerial power (Bebchuk and Fried, 2003), and auditor independence (Bazerman *et al.*, 2002a, b) suggests that some of the traditional means of minimizing the agency problem might be flawed in their description of how individuals behave in real life. Policies and rules based on such flawed models of human decision-making may, as a result, suffer from shortcomings.

Legal scholars have increasingly become critical of the behavioural assumptions proposed in the rational actor model, turning instead to the findings of psychologists and behavioural economists to increase the accuracy of legal analysis of behaviour within corporations (e.g. Jolls *et al.*, 1998; Hanson and Kysar, 1999). Langevoort, for example, discusses reasons why securities brokers may exploit the trust clients place in them (1996) and investigates why corporations commit securities fraud (1998b). More recently, he has analysed sub-optimal monitoring 2002a, and examined the tendency of boards of directors to acquiesce to management decisions (2001b). Coffee (2001, 2002) elaborates the acquiescence rationale with regard to reputational intermediaries – with an emphasis on auditors and board directors – and defines conditions under which the watchdog role is likely to fail. In particular it is asked under what conditions a gatekeeper might deem it rational to reduce, rather than preserve, reputational capital (Prentice, 2000; Coffee, 2002). Research on corporate governance has also turned to the findings of psychology and behavioural economics for answers (Jolls *et al.*, 1998; Hanson and Kysar, 1999; Prentice, 2000). Bazerman *et al.* (2002a, b) discuss the unlikely probability of auditor independence and demonstrate the vulnerability to unconscious bias during the corporate auditing process. Bebchuk *et al.* (2002a, b) and Bebchuk and Fried (2003) dispute the independence of directors in view of pressures from managerial power and strongly question the broad applicability of what the authors call 'the optimal contacting approach', where managers are provided with efficient incentives to maximize firm value.

The accounting literature has joined the call for a critical review of the broad applicability of rational choice theory to auditing and accounting (Briloff, 2004; Williams, 2004). A thorough analysis by Prentice (2000) investigates whether it is always irrational for an auditor or an auditing firm to audit recklessly or fraudulently. Prentice's discussion introduces cognitive and behavioural explanations why auditors might rationalize their actions and delude themselves with regard to the risk of sanctions from making misstatements. Krawiec (2000) develops this line of thought in an analysis of rogue traders in financial scandals, where the trader typically evaded an employer's risk and loss limits. Supervisors and managers are seen to have made a conscious decision to tolerate some level of such transgressions. In the extreme this can lead to situations where firms are no longer 'rational, risk-averse wealth maximizers who, by definition, naturally behave in a manner that enhances their own self-interest' (Krawiec, 2000: 109). These efforts suggest that the rational model of decision-making may at times fall short in explaining real world choice behaviour in a corporate environment (see also

Posner, 2003; Parisi and Smith, 2005). At the very least, these findings may indicate the need to significantly qualify the monitoring model of corporate governance.

Monitors and rationality

Monitors are typically assumed to be rational actors, disciplined by concerns about their reputation, future incomes, and prospects in the job market. (Fama, 1980; Easterbrook and Fischel, 1991; Shleifer and Vishny, 1997a; Prentice, 2000). Notwithstanding the theoretical merits of the rational model of decision-making, research findings introduced in the preceding text demonstrate that the human mind is subject to a large number of influences, which tend to steer inference, judgement, and choice behaviour away from the predicted outcomes of expected utility theory. These influences can lead to systematic violations of the normative assumptions central to the economist's rational model. As noted, the corporate governance literature and the legal tradition have increasingly joined the discussion of behavioural causes for managerial fraud and monitor acquiescence (see, for example, Arlen and Carney, 1992; Langevoort, 1996, 2002a, b; Hanson and Kysar, 1999; Prentice, 2000; Coffee, 2001, 2002; Posner, 2003).

The legal profession's usual method in the allocation of guilt for a crime in question is to look for motive and opportunity. Yet, there need not be a crime or criminal intent for corporate disasters to occur, although one would assume that there was plenty of criminal and morally challenged behaviour in the Enron cohort of bankruptcies. There may well be a tendency for successful executives to move towards a disengagement from the world around them (Maccoby, 2000), and a tendency for those around the executive to acquiesce to their activities and behaviours. More damaging yet for a reliance on the independence of gatekeepers is the realization that these monitors may frequently fail to notice their acquiescence to fraud (Prentice, 2000; Coffee, 2002, 2003b).[29]

Individuals are selective in their assimilation and interpretation of information (Lord *et al.*, 1979; McHoskey, 1995). Short-cuts used by the human mind to facilitate cognition and judgement often yield self-reinforcing patterns that in themselves may be trivial and harmless. In their sum, however, these can lead individuals and groups to unconsciously, and later perhaps more consciously, manufacture significant gaps between what reality is and what they would like it to be (Staw, 1981; Rabin, 2002).[30] This reflects both the selective attention and differential weighting of information of cognitive processes (e.g. hypothesis confirmation; Snyder, 1984), and also more motivational accounts such as cognitive dissonance theory (Festinger, 1957). Hypothesis-based filtering induces an individual to interpret ambiguous evidence in light of an initial hypothesis (Rabin, 2002). This, in turn, can reinforce belief in the hypothesis, increasing the likelihood that further ambiguous evidence is interpreted to be consistent with the initial hypothesis.

Such biased assimilation of information may lead to attitude polarization, where a prior belief is reinforced irrespective of the supportive value of additional information (McHoskey, 1995). This bias also operates at the group level where it can be reinforced by social pressures (Janis, 1972).

Individuals are typically unaware that they are highly selective in their perception and tend to deny that they are interpreting information in a self-serving fashion (Diekmann, 1997; Diekmann *et al.*, 1997).[31] This can skew their perception, and the resulting interpretation, even in situations when this is pointed out to the individuals. Goals and desires influence reasoning even before external pressures exacerbate issues of impartiality and independence. Critically, people find it very hard to overcome their self-interest and prior beliefs, even when they accept the explicit goal of being impartial. Self-serving bias may be a potent factor against impartiality (Westen *et al.*, 2006). This is especially significant for those areas of human interaction where impartiality would appear to be of particular importance. Bias in the auditor/client relationship can severely compromise the independence of an external audit (Bazerman *et al.*, 2002a, b). The past few years have demonstrated that the economic incentives of auditors in combination with a raft of biases may have skewed their performance. This has happened despite all the rules for conducting audits, auditing and professional standards, high levels of training, and liability threats. A similar argument may be applied to assumptions of independence and impartiality with regard to the work of members of a board of directors.

A weakened regulatory system

The presented arguments should not be interpreted to mean that properly designed and enforced rules and incentive contracts are irrelevant in minimizing the agency problem. Of course, there should be penalties for breaking the rules, and sanctions can provide some deterrence to unacceptable behaviour. The legal environment limits the degrees of freedom of engaging in illegal activities, and an effective incentive contract can assist in aligning the interests of the various parties. However, past experience shows that individuals can rationalize away with relative ease the risks associated with a particular activity.[32] The frequent concentration of scandals would appear to indicate structural deficiencies of the system of corporate governance.

Changes to the system of corporate governance clearly contributed to the latest wave of corporate misconduct. Enron was highly successful in lobbying for a legal and regulatory environment that suited its immediate objectives. Enron's exemption from oversight in trading certain energy-related derivatives, and the ease with which it was able to set up largely unsupervised special purpose vehicles, are potential examples of regulatory failure (Coffee, 2003a). With reference to the United States, a number of legal and regulatory developments weakened the corporate governance system during the 1990s. These included changes to the financial incentives of senior executives and auditors, the rise of equity-based compensation of senior management, and the relaxation of the rules on stock option exercise. The Private Securities Litigation Reform Act (PSLRA) 1995 and the Securities Litigation Uniform Standards Act (SLUSA) 1998 are considered to have weakened the deterrence effects of the law on particular agents (Coffee, 2003a, b).

The literature on the changing regulatory environment is an important one, and provides further insights into failures of corporate governance systems. Coffee (2002: 6) suggests that one starting point for a discussion about corporate governance debacles should be not to ask: 'Why did some managements engage in fraud? But rather . . . why did the gatekeepers let them?' One obvious answer to Coffee's question about why gatekeepers were complicit is that it was profitable to them, or at least appeared to be so. A more comprehensive explanation suggests that changes to the regulatory and economic environment in the preceding decade or so may have had a significant impact on the incidence of corporate fraud. Thus, Coffee (2002) suggests that auditor independence in the United States had become compromised by a confluence of circumstances that include:

1 The diminishing legal risks from fraudulent or negligent audits throughout the 1990s (undermining deterrence and increasing acquiescence).
2 The massive increase in the provision of non-auditing services (exposing the auditor to low-visibility sanctions, creating the possibility of auditing services being offered as a loss leader, placing increasing pressure on auditing to become a profit centre).
3 Increasing concentration in the auditing industry (inducing a 'race to the bottom', where no auditing firm finds a competitive benefit from increasing its integrity).
4 The stock market boom of the late 1990s (leading to an exuberant market where auditing might have been considered a mere nuisance by management, and of little value to the euphoric investor).
5 Principal/agent problems within the auditing firm due to the use of incentive fees and bonuses in conjunction with the increase in consulting services (providing a strong incentive to the individual partner to circumvent internal monitoring).
6 The over-reliance on a simple certification of compliance to GAAP rules rather than the provision of an opinion of a firm's true and fair financial position.

Another major contributing cause of the more recent corporate governance failures was the effective absence of corporate governance mechanisms long recommended in the literature, including functionally independent directors and board committees, auditor rotation, and properly designed incentive contracts.[33]

In an attempt to explain corporate failure, care should be taken not to a focus strongly on the deficiencies of any particular individual in management, the board, or the auditing process. This would obscure the discussion of systemic problems that underlie the frequency of such scandals (Clarke *et al.*, 2003; Langevoort, 2003). To concentrate on a few 'rogues' or 'bad apples' would be a serious mistake. This 'cult of the individual', meaning a concentration on a single person or group of persons in allocating blame for a corporate disaster, leads to a seriously mistaken analysis. Whether a *particular* individual consciously or unconsciously turns fraudulent is truly irrelevant. Blaming individual members of the board or the auditing partner allows for quick identification of scapegoats, but would be somewhat myopic and avoids recognition of the core issues. Such a conclusion, which merely places blame on the individual(s) involved, without looking at the deeper causes behind the frauds, misses the point and condemns itself to experiencing another cycle of scandals just a few years later (see Coffee, 2003b for further discussion). Of course, where blame for committed crimes can be rightfully allocated to individuals, they should face the appropriate penalties. What this book suggests, however, is that fines and penalties do not seem to work sufficiently well to prevent corporate scandals, as individuals have the ability to rationalize the potential future costs of current activities to a minimum.

Behavioural causes for monitor failure

This research is concerned with the ease with which existing systems of corporate governance can be undermined. One of the causes for this is seen in the inadequacy of the rational model of judgement and decision-making in describing the full range of human behaviour in a corporate setting. It is of major importance to understand the limits to independence and impartiality of monitors and gatekeepers, as the monitoring model of corporate governance critically relies on this for its effectiveness. Rules and regulations put in place in response to scandals still largely ignore the effect of bias. This is particularly the case with regulations that merely serve up more of the same. It was noted earlier that the typical reaction to corporate accounting scandals is to increase the number of standards, raise penalties, impose additional layers of supervision, and so on. None of these were sufficient to prevent the corporate frauds at the start of the new millennium. Nevertheless, much of the legislative and regulatory approach continues to be based on assumptions of the rational actor model.

It might be useful to define the principal-agent problem as an issue of human relationships and human behaviour, set within an environment of laws and regulations, contracts, and social constructs. Thus, a proper understanding of human behaviour, judgement and decision-making, by individuals and by groups respectively, would appear to be useful in the design of effective rules and instruments governing the conduct of agents. The American Institute of Certified Public Accountants was aware of the potential for bias when it noted (in reference to a 1988 AICPA statement) that

> In the performance of any professional service, a member shall maintain integrity, shall be free of conflicts of interest, and shall not knowingly misrepresent facts or subordinate his or her judgment to others.
> (AICPA, 2002a, 01 Rule 102 – Integrity and Objectivity)

The underlying assumption at the time was that the auditing process can be impartial and free of bias, as long as the auditor pays close attention to this problem. Yet, auditors still missed what was going on at, say, Enron and Parmalat. There is some evidence that legislators and standard setters are starting to recognize bias as a much more serious and persistent problem. For example, the 2002 Statement on Auditing Standards No. 99 (SAS 99) (AICPA, 2002b) highlights the persistence of bias in auditing.[34]

The US Sarbanes-Oxley Act 2002 also goes some way towards mitigating bias in auditing by mandating lead audit partner rotation, and prohibiting the provision of certain services by accounting firms to firms which they audit. However, the punitive legislation incorporated in this Act is also evidence of a long-established, but possibly ineffective, tradition of primarily raising the cost of crime. Regulations that merely serve up more of the same, such as additional regulations, larger penalties, and stronger oversight, have failed in the past and it is difficult to see why they should work now.

Rational choice in law and accounting

Despite considerable concerns with regard to the general applicability of rational choice theory, this perspective has had a significant impact on the interpretation of agent behaviour in fields outside economics. The desire for scientific rigour has successfully introduced positive economics to academic accounting (Zeff, 1978; Williams, 2004). Economic principles have also been applied to, and used in, law for several decades (Posner, 2003; Krecké, 2003). The economist's view of rationality of the individual has been adopted by legal interpretations of behaviour of auditors and auditing firms with respect to corporate governance issues in United States courts, at least pre-Enron.

A number of court decisions have had a major impact in cementing rationality assumptions with regard to the motives of defendant auditors accused of complicity or gross negligence in their client's accused fraud. In *DiLeo* v. *Ernst & Young* (901 F.2d 624, 7th Cir. 1990), Judge Easterbrook discarded the plaintiffs' aiding and abetting claim against the defendant auditor, in part for lack of sufficient allegations of motive and opportunity. After noting that securities fraud plaintiffs must supply grounds 'to conclude that the defendant has thrown in his lot with the primary violators' (901 F.2d, at 629, quoting an earlier case, *Barker* v. *Henderson, Franklin, Starnes & Holt*, see below), Judge Easterbrook found that,

> The complaint does not allege that [the audit firm] had anything to gain from any fraud by [its client]. An accountant's greatest asset is its

> reputation for honesty, followed closely by its reputation for careful work. Fees for two years' audits could not approach the losses [the auditor] would suffer from a perception that it would muffle a client's fraud . . . [The audit firm's] partners shared none of the gain from any fraud and were exposed to a large fraction of the loss. It would have been irrational for any of them to have joined cause with [the client].
>
> (901 F.2d, at 629)

Judge Posner, a leading proponent of law and economics (see, for example, Posner, 2003), had anticipated the *DiLeo* decision, in *Barker* v. *Henderson, Franklin, Starnes & Holt* (797 F.2d 490, 497, 7th Cir. 1986), by reasoning with respect to auditors that 'it is inconceivable that they joined a venture to feather their nests by defrauding investors. They had nothing to gain and everything to lose' (797 F.2d, at 497). This line of thinking is indicative of a particular mode of legal analysis, which relies on the normative underpinnings of expected utility theory as it evokes the presence of the calculating rational utility maximizer. This maximizer would not succumb to what, with 20-20 hindsight, presumably amounts to irrational behaviour.[35]

This raises the question of whether people (including auditors) are so rational (and law-breaking so irrational) that fraud and recklessness cannot occur. If people (and firms), however, do succumb to temptation, then one would have to consider whether people and firms are not always quite as rational as expected utility theory assumes, or whether it might at times be rational to defraud others, or both (Prentice, 2000). As Williamson (1991: 159) puts it, 'reputation effect mechanisms are no exception to the general proposition that all theories of economic organization must eventually be confronted by the realities'.

Behaviour in legal thought

Findings from behavioural research have undermined some of the assumptions of law and economic theory that humans are rational utility maximizers (in the classical sense). This would suggest that the results derived from Neumann and Morgenstern's expected utility maximizing model (1994) may, at times, conflict with real world behaviour. A growing unease with the apparent inability of rational choice theory to accurately predict human behaviour in important areas (Arlen, 1998) has led to increased efforts to capture psychologically more realistic notions of choice behaviour and introduce these to economic and legal analysis. Legal scholars in particular seem to be dissatisfied with the behavioural assumptions of the rational actor model, and have increasingly turned to the findings of cognitive psychologists and decision theorists for insights.

Several important articles demonstrate the value that behavioural research brings to legal analysis. Some of the most comprehensive include an investigation by Jolls *et al.* (1998) into the potential impact of behavioural research on the law; Langevoort's (1998b) more focused behavioural explanation of why executive officers commit securities fraud; his look at the human nature of boards (2001b); and Hanson and Kysar's (1999) discussion of product liability law.[36] Prentice (2000) makes the point that it is not necessarily irrational for an auditor to behave in ways that run counter to the tenets of rational utility maximization, and questions the basic behavioural assumptions made in economic and legal analysis. Shared in these articles are doubts about the strict and general applicability of the rational maximizer model.

Considerable care should be taken when applying highly specific models to general conditions. Abstraction and theory, as valuable as they are, cannot be confused with reality. Simon reflected on this difference and proposed that in order

> to predict the short-run behaviour of an adaptive mechanism, or it's behaviour in a complex and rapidly changing environment, it is not enough to know its goals. We must know also a great deal about its internal structures and particularly its mechanisms of adaptation.
>
> (Simon 1959: 255)

Much of the analysis of and policy recommendation for improving corporate governance, however, continues to depend on the premise that actors are strongly rational agents, with stable and consistent preferences. This also applies to much of the legislation introduced after the latest round of corporate scandals.

Logic, for example, would predict that a gatekeeper would not sacrifice considerable amounts of reputational capital for a small amount of financial gain from a single client. Yet, gatekeepers have been observed to jeopardize their reputation for financial gains that are far smaller than potential losses. What moves a gatekeeper, or monitor, to acquiesce in managerial fraud and risk sanctions and loss of reputation that far exceed any potential gain from acquiescence? It is intriguing to ask why none of the conventional remedies to the agency problem worked sufficiently well to prevent corporate disasters such as Enron and Parmalat. On paper, Enron's corporate governance was admirable. It had split the roles of the chairman and the chief executive (advocated in the UK and elsewhere as one of the pillars of good corporate governance – and rightly so – but still somewhat resisted in the US), had distinguished individuals on its audit committee, and had a commendable corporate governance code.

Enron's lead external auditor (Arthur Andersen) was, despite a widespread belief to the contrary, no more negligent than any other of the (then) Big-5 auditing firms, nor more often the target of regulatory investigations (Cunningham, 2002). Enron would also have satisfied many of the requirements of the Sarbanes-Oxley Act 2002 on corporate governance and accounting, which introduced new regulations on corporate conduct as a reaction to the actions that brought down this company, and others. Yet,

Enron's directors did not raise any concerns until after the company started to implode under a string of accounting irregularities. They were 'asleep at the wheel' (*The Wall Street Journal*, 5 May 2002, p. A3). Arthur Andersen, Enron's lead auditor, meanwhile, was accused of aiding and abetting in the financial frauds, and ultimately convicted (and destroyed) for obstruction of justice.[37]

While the frauds committed at Enron were to an extent unique (as each crime is somewhat unique), they share sobering pathologies with many corporate governance debacles of the recent and more distant past. One of these similarities was acquiescence by the main groups of monitors and gatekeepers to the actions of senior executives. Recent corporate scandals underline the importance of understanding human psychology and cognition in forming beliefs and making decisions. A selection of biases in perceptions and judgement that can contribute to failures in fiduciary duties is discussed in the following section.

Summary

It is not easy to disentangle the causes and motivations underlying ostensibly unethical or fraudulent behaviour in corporate governance. The attraction of money (i.e. the greed argument) alone is perhaps not sufficient in explaining why ordinary people engage in white-collar crimes or neglect their duties as monitors and gatekeepers. It is doubtful that individuals always perform a rational cost–benefit analysis when engaging in questionable activities, especially perhaps where the financial rewards are significant. In the case of financial fraud or negligence of gatekeeper duties, reputation, entire careers, and personal freedom may be lost by actions that yield relatively small financial rewards. It would appear that individuals are prone to mentally minimize the realization that own behaviour is unethical and potentially damaging to longer-term interests. It may also be that a strong sense of competition and a desire to win in all situations lead individuals to engage in activities they subsequently regret.

The insights presented by research into affect and visceral factors prompt the assumption that one guide to judgements, decisions, and behaviour in corporate governance might be the emotional responses of the moment, rather than reasoned considerations with regard to legal compliance and potential consequences of actions. Individuals do not always recognize the ethical issues of a matter, or they may have a strong sense of entitlement to the prospective financial rewards, however negligible these may be. Auditors and members of a board of directors are no less subject to tendencies for immediate gratification than ordinary individuals, at times ignoring potential negative future consequences from current actions. The gratification from, say, a financial bonus, promotion, a bigger office, re-election to the board, renewal of an auditing contract, the prospects of employment in the client's firm, and meeting a deadline or a quota is certain and experienced in the immediate or near future. Likewise, potentially negative consequences from actions that are awkward for the client, superiors or senior management, such as refusing to look the other way or asking critical questions, disputing an accounting interpretation, or refusing to sign off on a misleading financial report, are felt immediately and are highly predictable. In contrast, potential legal sanctions from acquiescence or participation in fraud, and the potential costs from such actions on others, are uncertain, and in the future. Such costs might be rationalized to a minimum. Since potential sanctions are in the 'distant future', their impact is discounted, and further reduced in perceived severity by self-serving justifications and over-optimism. One further consideration illustrates the qualitative difference between (real) present benefits and (merely potential) future costs: benefits fall on the individual and his or her immediate social and professional environment, while costs can frequently be assumed to fall on faceless strangers.

The (naïve) optimism bias plays directly into this by providing the illusion of control over random or exogenous events (Langer and Roth, 1975; Muren, 2006).[38] Affect can compound such an illusion of control and lead to an inverse relationship between the perceived benefit of an event and the associated perceived risk (Alhakami and Slovic, 1994; Slovic *et al.*, 2004). These cognitive and emotive biases can lead to an overestimation of the influence of the individual over the likelihood of events. The insights from behavioural research summarized on the preceding pages suggest that individuals and groups may systematically fall short of the rational model of human choice behaviour. Since these factors are likely to also influence executive managers and their gatekeepers in forming judgements and decision-making, this could seriously question the usefulness of the monitoring model of corporate governance. This chapter has raised serious questions regarding the efficacy of the conventional approaches in monitoring and controlling managerial performance. The following chapter aims to show that the inclusion of behavioural aspects in the corporate governance debate can significantly contribute towards a more effective understanding of monitor and gatekeeper failure. Specifically, the insights from behavioural economics and social psychology will be applied to the work of auditors and members of a board of directors.

6 Independence of auditors and directors

This chapter investigates some of the conventional partial solutions to the principal–agent problem. Crucial to the minimization of agency problems is the independence of gatekeepers and monitors. The present discussion concentrates on the potential for independence of a) the board of directors, and b) external auditors. Reference is made to the cognitive and psychological factors introduced in the preceding chapters. Problems in ensuring the independence of monitors are highlighted. The independence of non-executive directors is discussed with an emphasis on problems of board capture and issues arising from social bonding and group decision-making. Auditor independence is discussed with particular reference to cognitive pressures which potentially lead to bias in interpretation by individual auditing partners, as well as to pressures within auditing firms to engage in sub-optimal monitoring of partner performance.

This chapter suggests that these reputational intermediaries may not perform as effectively as the traditional economic model predicts. Especially questioned are assumptions of and reliance on notions of independence and impartiality by these monitoring agents. This chapter will take a close look at the feasibility of independence of the board of directors and the external auditor. Reliance on a simplistic and in many aspects misleading model of human behaviour also extends to policy and legal decisions on corporate governance. It is suggested that the solutions conventionally relied upon to minimize the agency problem may be less reliable than is commonly assumed, and that the inclusion of behavioural perspectives can assist in better understanding actual agent behaviour. These perspectives lead into the policy issues discussed in Chapter 8.

Partial solutions to the problem I: the board of directors

The design of effective contracts and monitoring systems is part of the solution to the agency problem. For practical reasons, the manager keeps a considerable degree of freedom within contractual constraints (Grossman and Hart, 1986). It is, thus, of importance to find ways and means to effectively minimize the abuse made possible from holding residual control rights

(Fama, 1980). A board of directors and the specialized board committees, particularly the auditing and compensation committees, form an important element in a system based on contracts and monitoring (Cadbury, 1992). The board has control functions over the public reporting of audited financial reports, the use of external auditing of the firm's financial state of affairs, compliance with established accounting rules and principles, and the adherence to auditing standards.[1]

The need for independence of the board of directors

It is frequently suggested (and mandated by a number of corporate governance laws) that a board be made up of a mix of independent and executive directors with an adequate professional background and integrity (Cadbury, 1992; Sarbanes-Oxley Act 2002; Higgs, 2003). Specialized committees including auditing committees staffed with qualified and (frequently exclusively) independent directors complement board compositional requirements. A positive correlation between the independence of board members and the quality of corporate governance is generally assumed (Peasnell, 2002). Peasnell *et al.* (2001) support earlier conclusions (Fama and Jensen, 1983a, b; Mayers *et al.*, 1997) that outside directors, in helping to separate decision management and decision control, are a potentially significant governance mechanism when external constraints on executive behaviour are weak. Independence of the board, closely associated with 'outside', 'independent', or 'non-executive' directors, that is individuals not otherwise affiliated with the firm, can reduce insider pressure, and thus impact positively on measures of company performance (Fama and Jensen, 1983a, b). The inclusion of independent directors on the board can also enhance the viability of the board as a control mechanism (Fama, 1980; Fama and Jensen, 1983a, b). Finally, independent directors may lower the probability of collusion of management to expropriate security holders, and their role has been interpreted as that of a professional referee (Fama, 1980; Fama and Jensen, 1983a, b) who oversees top management, and, if necessary, replaces it with more effective individuals.

The degree of independence of a board may depend on the bargaining power between the board and the CEO (Hermalin and Weisbach, 2003). A CEO may prefer a weaker board (less independent), while the board might be seen to prefer stronger independence. The lower the managerial equity ownership, the higher the demand for monitoring by outside directors is predicted to be, especially under conditions of dispersed stock ownership (Jensen and Meckling, 1976; Fama and Jensen, 1983a, b; Jensen, 1993). With an increasing share of managerial ownership, incentive-alignment effects of equity ownership are predicted to reduce the demand for such outside monitoring (Weisbach, 1988; Denis and Sarin, 1999). An incentive-alignment factor typically leads to a negative relationship between managerial ownership and the demand for outside directors, until managerial entrenchment may lead to a positive relationship (Peasnell *et al.*, 2001).[2] Empirical research finds statistically strong relationships between various interpretations of board independence and a number of accruals measures (see Jones, 1991; Pearsnell *et al.*, 2000b, 2001, 2002; and Klein 2002). This link has been empirically tested for data on US and UK firms regressing board independence against a number of variables including residual income (Dechow *et al.*, 1999), earnings management (Peasnell *et al.*, 2001; Klein, 2002), SEC accounting enforcement actions (Dechow *et al.*, 1996), the incidence of financial statement fraud (Beasley, 1996), as well as timeliness and conservatism in income recognition (Beekes *et al.*, 2004). Board size has been negatively correlated with firm performance (Yermack, 1996; Eisenberg *et al.*, 1998), supporting the view that larger boards may be less effective than smaller boards (Lipton and Lorsch, 1992; Jensen, 1993).

The 2002 Sarbanes-Oxley Act emphasizes the independence of the board audit committee. While this is in tune with recommendations for the independence of boards and especially audit and compensation committees in other legislations, including, for example, the United Kingdom (Cadbury, 1992; Higgs, 2003; FRC, 2006), Australia (ASX, 2003, 2007) and Germany's Corporate Governance Code (Germany, 2007) it does not appear to be necessary for all directors to be independent in order to achieve markedly lower incidences of earnings management (Peasnell *et al.*, 2002).

Formal and functional board independence

Despite empirical findings which suggest a positive effect of independent directors on governance measures, Hermalin and Weisbach (2003) suspect that the causality might run from the functional form of independence to the observable characteristics of independence (the formal form). This caveat is of importance, as there is a discomforting lack of empirical evidence supporting a clear statistical correlation between measures of board independence as a governance indicator and actual corporate economic performance (Mehran, 1995; Klein, 1998; Bhagat and Black, 1999, 2000, 2002).[3] Functional independence, in the sense of directors being professional referees (Fama, 1980) or board monitors (Fama and Jensen, 1983b), is difficult to measure. Testing for the presence of directors defined as independent in the traditional definition is relatively straightforward, but this should not be equated with independence in an objective and functional sense, since 'outsider domination may simply create a carefully calculated illusion of board independence' (Langevoort, 2001b: 801).

The lack of family relationships and pecuniary ties of directors with respect to senior management are frequently used as proxies for independence in empirical testing and in legal interpretation. The relationship between monitoring quality and board, or committee, composition would appear, however, to be more complex. Of primary concern to the present discussion is the difficulty of effectively bringing to board monitoring the high degree of sceptical objectivity and constructive criticism that the concept of independence implies. This of course complicates a correlation calculation, and indicates the need for a definition and identification of true director independence. In other words, director independence, to be effective in the sense of directors being professional referees (Fama, 1980), monitors (Fama and Jensen, 1983b), and gatekeepers (Coffee, 2001), must be in the mind. Subsequently, this then needs to be translated into independent action. There is a distinct difference between independent position and independent behaviour (see, for example, Clarke *et al.*, 2003). Formal independence, as demanded by many statutes on corporate governance, is simply not the same as functional independence. Functional independence is not easily implemented, and greater outsider (i.e. independent directors) presence on the board (which can empirically be tested for quite easily) cannot be equated with greater independence in an objective sense.

Limits to board independence – capture and social bonding

True functional independence may for the most part be an illusion, and various heuristics, group, and social pressures interfere with the ideal role of the board as a professional referee (Fama, 1980), even where functional independence is an active goal. In the optimal contracting view (Grossman and Hart, 1986), managers' incentives are closely aligned with those of shareholders. This should be reflected in board actions to monitor and control executive compensation. However, the benefits to a director of attempting to curb excessive executive compensation are relatively low, uncertain, and in the future. The potential costs to the individual director, in contrast, are high, definitive, and in the present. Even though stock-based compensation for board members has been increasing, the direct benefit to directors of curbing CEO behaviour seen as damaging to shareholders is limited. Directors are unlikely to hold more than an insignificant level of shares (in terms of shares outstanding), while the cost to themselves of trying to curb such behaviour could be considerable. The limits to board effectiveness with regard to executive compensation points to the limits of board monitoring in general (Bebchuk *et al.*, 2002b). This includes one of the essential monitoring functions of the board, namely controlling for managerial conflicts of interest (Langevoort, 2001a). A board is subject to potential problems of dependence, and, in the extreme, senior management may capture the board and thus void much of the latter's monitoring functions. The typical selection for membership on boards of directors is heavily based on compatibility, fit, consensus, and cooperation (Langevoort, 2001b). Jensen reflects on board culture as an important component of failure of board function when he describes an atmosphere of

> courtesy, politeness and deference at the expense of truth and frankness during board meetings, reflecting a general reluctance of confronting

> a CEO regarding management decisions, which is seen as both a symptom and cause of failure in the control system.
>
> (Jensen, 1993: 863)

An overly strong emphasis on teamwork and conflict-avoidance by boards may be evidence of capture by the CEO. This is contrasted with the independence, scepticism, and loyalty to the shareholders (and other stakeholders) of an idealized monitoring board (Fama and Jensen, 1983a). The problem is that a director generally wishes to be re-elected, and also might wish to be elected to the board of other firms. A reputation as a troublemaker would severely undermine such chances. The typical CEO is closely involved in selecting the board (Shivdasani and Yermack, 1999), and in granting directors' remuneration and perks.[4] The close involvement of the CEO in selecting and rewarding board members can have a seriously negative impact on the board's independence and effectiveness as monitors and gatekeepers (Hermalin and Weisbach, 1998, 2003). This is consistent with the view that control by the CEO over board selection decreases the board's independence (Bebchuk *et al.*, 2002a, b). Executive managerial influence over own compensation packages (i.e. rent extraction) further questions the validity of the optimal contracting approach.

Ideally, boards design and negotiate efficient compensation deals to provide managers with incentives to maximize firm performance. In sharp contrast, Bebchuk *et al.* (2002a, b) and Bebchuk and Fried (2003) argue that numerous compensation features may be used to extract rent and to cover up (or 'camouflage') the saliency of compensation arrangements. The managerial power view (Bebchuk and Fried, 2003) interprets a number of typical compensation practices as evidence of the agency problem, rather than a remedy for it. Brenner *et al.* (1998) investigated the self-dealing nature of options by examining the practice of resetting the terms of previously issued executive stock options, and found that resetting of options has a strongly negative relationship with firm performance even after correcting for industry performance.

Concerns highlighted in research on managerial power and board capture question the broad applicability of the optimal contacting approach, under which managers are provided with efficient incentives to maximize firm value (Bebchuk and Fried, 2003). Managers have substantial power and discretion over setting their own compensation. In the extreme this may result in rent extraction, rather than the outcome of the more traditional model of optimal contracting (Bebchuk *et al.*, 2002a, b). Boards may not adopt optimal compensation arrangements if they are captured by, or at least strongly sympathetic to, senior management. Where capture occurs, this can shape the preference for compensation structures and processes to allow a degree of concealment of compensation practices and their magnitude to demonstrate a degree of constraint (Bebchuk *et al.*, 2002a, b; Krugman, 2002a). Rather than mitigating the principal–agent problem between shareholders and managers, existing compensation practices for top management may thus be part of the agency problem itself (Bebchuk, 1999; Bebchuk *et al.*, 2002a, b; Bebchuk and Fried, 2003).

Board capture provides the CEO with significant powers to engage in activities which may be to the detriment of other stakeholders (Bebchuk *et al.*, 2002a, b). This interpretation of managerial power would seriously undermine the arm's length model of boards and their crucial watchdog function, and is in stark contrast to the optimal-contracting view where directors take an adversarial position against management (Bebchuk *et al.*, 2002a, b). In support of the argument of Bebchuk *et al.* (2002a, b) and Bebchuk and Fried (2003) that existing compensation practices do not minimize the agency problem, Wan (2003) found that firm and industry differences largely explain variations in executive pay, and that greater representation of independent directors on boards does not impact materially on pay for performance ratios. This casts doubt on the presumption that formally independent directors automatically are better monitors. Increasing the percentage of independent directors would thus not necessarily reduce executive pay or enhance corporate performance (Bhagat and Black, 2002).

The very psychology of a board is tilted towards supporting the chief executive. Short of firing the CEO, open dissent is rarely found in board meetings. The role of the board of directors in monitoring agent behaviour may be further devalued where the position of CEO and Chairman are combined. If the CEO/Chairman can select the members of the board, how independent can they be, and how well can they undertake their role as monitors?[5] Board capture is not the only influence bearing against independence. Groups such as boards of directors are highly subject to groupthink (Janis, 1972) and polarization (McHoskey, 1995), with potentially negative effects on the quality of decisions. The pressures on a board of directors towards consensus opinions make it subject to the (negative) consequences of groupthink (Janis, 1972, 1982). An ideal board would act to counter the groupthink tendencies of an in-group (Janis, 1982), while group social effects are a potent influence against critical opinion. The social dynamics that exist in any group move members towards placating other group members, and to come to a consensus view. This acts as a strong counter-weight to the potential for group decision-making to moderate an extreme position, and instead can lead to further polarization (Janis, 1972; Myers, 1982; McHoskey, 1995).

Cognitive research shows that escalation of commitment is a particular problem for the individual or a group responsible for an initial decision (Staw, 1981; Brockner, 1992). To counterbalance the pressure for escalation, an outsider who is not connected to the set of decisions that have described the course of action to date should be consulted for an objective opinion. Hence, the ultimate decision on whether to continue with a project or not is best left to somebody who is not responsible for previous losses and not subject to internal or external justification needs. An outsider, thus, is more likely to better assess the benefits and costs of further commitment of resources. Rotating the decision-maker, or the organization, in charge of resource allocation or policy determination can reduce the likelihood of disastrous commitment. Groupthink tendencies of highly cohesive groups, as represented by the typical board, make recourse to outside opinion less likely. They would also be a barrier to creating a healthy degree of heterogeneity of opinions within the group.

The collapse of Enron shows the shortcomings of meeting the letter, but not the spirit of the various rules and recommendations on board composition. In many respects, Enron had a model system of corporate governance. Its board and audit committee consisted mostly of independent directors (independent at least by the going definition), most had highly relevant business experience, and some had qualified backgrounds in accounting. In particular, Enron's audit committee consisted of six well-qualified outside directors. Enron had a corporate conduct code that would have been the envy of most companies and was, on paper, in compliance with some of the more recent governance stipulations, for example those provided by the Sarbanes-Oxley Act 2002. Unfortunately, the board of directors also granted suspensions of the code of conduct on several occasions, to allow senior management to set up and run some of the SPVs instrumental in bringing down the firm.[6] That the board subsequently claimed that 'they knew nothing about the companies questionable financial reporting',[7] and had no qualms about waving the firm's code of conduct when this suited senior executives, is extraordinary, and indicative of a negligent or actively complicit board.

While available evidence does not allow a definitive verdict on the complicity of Enron's board, it would appear to match findings from cognitive psychology that monitors might simply not recognize problems or risks due to systematic perceptual filters (Aronson, 1968a, b), which is one of the arguments of the present research. Enron's directors either did not know what was going on and should have, or the board knew and failed to stop it. The former would suggest that the board members were incompetent, the latter would implicate the board as an accessory to fraud. Neither of these interpretations is necessarily correct, while both might be, and certainly neither is very flattering. Without a doubt, the directors failed to carry out their responsibilities to Enron's shareholders, employers, customers, and the wider community. It would appear that there was no effective system, and perhaps not even an ethic, of checks and balances in place when important decisions were made.

Members of the board are normally expected to possess a minimum level of competence, knowledge, and power to investigate matters of concern if they are to fulfil their duties appropriately. Specifically there is a perceived need for directors, particularly the independent directors, to possess an adequate knowledge base, whether pre-existing or as a result of search and evidential inquiry, to allow the formation of an independent opinion as to the quality of financial reporting and managerial performance. Further, board members are expected to be sceptical and ask questions if they do not understand a transaction. Insufficient technical knowledge and expertise may not always be at the heart of the issue however. Without a critical approach to managerial monitoring, a board's performance may degenerate into no more than an acceptance of management representation, adding little value as a governance instrument. In the case of Enron, no deep accounting or legal knowledge was required to conclude that crucial transactions lacked an economic, legal, and ethical base, just a healthy dose of common sense and a notion of scepticism before signing away shareholders' money.

Massive conflicts of interest at Enron were compounded by a general lack of due diligence as the board conducted only the most cursory and ineffective reviews of major executive decisions. Allowing the blatant conflict of interest of Enron's chief financial officer in running several of the special purpose vehicles which broke the company is one of the more visible failures to maintain independence.[8] This fiduciary failure was hardly due to a lack of qualifications or the inexperience of the involved directors. Enron's audit committee, for example, included Robert K. Jaedicke, a Stanford University distinguished professor emeritus of accounting[9] (Jaedicke was chairman of Enron's audit committee between 1985 and 2002, a total of 17 years); Mrs Wendy Gramm, George Mason University, who was instrumental in including the 'Enron Point' in the passage in 2000 of the Commodity Futures Modernization Act, granting the complete exclusion for energy trading companies from financial or disclosure requirements respecting portfolios of over-the-counter derivative securities; Dr John Mendelson, President of the Anderson Cancer Centre, University of Texas; and Sir John Wakeham, former UK Secretary of State for energy and a member of the House of Lords. The almost complete absence of board oversight and the near total breakdown of the corporate governance duties of the board of directors of Enron are well documented in the literature (see, for example, Batson, 2002, 2003a, b, c; Benston and Hartgraves, 2002; Powers *et al.*, 2002; Coffee, 2003a; and Prentice, 2003).

The cognitive dissonance (Festinger, 1957) displayed by members of Enron's board is complemented by the board's failure to even partially understand the instruments the company was using to maintain the charade of profits (Powers *et al.*, 2002; Deakin and Konzelmann, 2003). Nonetheless, the failure of the board of directors to notice or to stop the activities which led to the collapse of Enron is, to a large extent, indicative of the biases in judgement and decision-making any individual and any group of individuals is subject to. If one does not understand a particular instrument, or is uncertain about the validity of presented figures, but one is required to sanction their use, why not ask for an explanation?

The failure to investigate may occur at the perception stage of the involved agents, at least initially, and would appear to reflect a two-stage process of bias intrusion on the formation of judgement in general. At stage 1 unconscious bias affects the formation of an opinion rather than deliberate cheating. While at stage 2, more conscious and motivated bias influences subsequent judgement, as the (initial) basic opinion or evaluation becomes a reported or public one. This may be close to cheating, because the gatekeeper is adjusting what they believe in order to meet clients' (say, management's) wishes, as well as own past judgements.[10] Hence, fraudulent intentions are not initially part of this argument, but may enter at a later stage.

It would appear that the issue of low visibility sanctions against director's independence was present at Enron (Gordon, 2002). The failure to re-nominate a director is highly visible and may reflect negatively on the company, whereas the failure to contribute to one of a director's causes or projects is not. The size of a director's financial compensation, in itself a threat to independence (since a director would not like to lose this income), is not the only venue for sanctions. Low visibility sanctions could be the sanction of choice in managerial efforts to discipline a director. To counter such threats, it could be recommended for a director not to undertake consulting, nor to accept donations for a charity or cause in order to lower susceptibility towards such soft sanctions. Low visibility sanctions have repercussions with regard to the definition of 'independence' of directors. There is a general move towards mandating the independence of directors sitting on the auditing board, and on the nominating and compensation committees. It may, however, be difficult to ensure true independence when directors' affiliations with the company make them a target of sanctions that fly below the radar screen of analysts, investors, and other outside observers.

Even individuals who want to increase their reputation during most of their professional career may lose much of this motivational incentive once they reach the end of their career. Any reputational capital will then be of limited use (unless it can be transferred to another venture) and may prompt opportunistic behaviour. The critical issue is the diminished future value of reputation where an individual is near the end of his or her career life.[11] Hence, there might, at least from some age onwards, be a negative correlation between agent age and reputational value of deterrence.

The average age of a board director in the United States for 2005/2006, for example, was about 56 years (Directorship, 2006), matching results of an earlier study which reported a median age of directors of 51–60 years for some 60 per cent of reporting institutions in the banking industry, and a median range of 61–70 years for the remainder (Professional Bank Services, Inc., 2001).[12] Reputation may indeed be of limited value, and hence of limited effect on deterrence, where a director faces the trade off between acquiescence (or at least a less than critical stance) to managerial behaviour, and the potential loss of fee income associated with a board position that may result from overt opposition. This argument can be extended to other gatekeepers.

Partial solutions to the problem II: auditors

An external audit evaluates an organization's accounting procedures and is intended to certify the financial statements as a true and fair representation of the firm's financial status. This includes compliance certification with specific accounting rules such as the Generally Accepted Accounting Principles, and assurance of the auditing process to conform to Generally Accepted Auditing Standards (GAAS). How well an audit performs depends not only on the technical qualifications and experience of the auditor, but also on the feasibility of independence in the relationship with the audit client.

Bias in the auditor–client relationship

A crucial ingredient in establishing the value of an external audit, and in accepting the judgements made therein, is the independence of the auditor. An underlying assumption is that the auditing process can be impartial and free of bias. Presumably, this can be achieved if an auditor of 'good standing', 'watches out' for potential conflicts of interest and bias, and tries 'hard enough' to be neutral. The more recent failures of the auditing process have, however, once again, disturbed this idealized picture and have led to a growing cynicism about the accounting profession. Repeated audit failures highlight concerns that assumptions of auditor impartiality and the absence of bias are perhaps somewhat unrealistic. The magnitude and persistence of bias in this relationship tends to be underestimated in rational actor models, and would seem to represent a much more persistent problem in the auditor–client relationship than is generally appreciated.

Financial incentives can be a serious source of conflict of interest in the auditing process, and may lead to deliberate collusion, or self-serving inferences (Frankel *et al.*, 2002). It is perhaps no coincidence that the second half of the 1990s saw both a massive increase in the provision of non-auditing services by accounting firms and an increase in the number and magnitude of earnings restatements. Consulting fees paid by audit clients during the 1990s rose significantly. According to the US Public Oversight Board's Panel on Audit Effectiveness (2000: 102), 'audit firm's fees from consulting services for their SEC clients increased from 17% . . . of audit fees in 1990 to 67% . . . in 1999'. A *Chicago Tribune* survey noted that the largest 100 corporations in the Chicago area paid consulting fees to their auditors that were on average over three times the audit fees they paid (Kidd-Steward and Countryman, 2002).

Possibly related, the incidence of earnings restatements in the United States has increased significantly in recent years (FEI and Wu, 2002; Wu, 2002; GAO, 2002, 2006). Averaging slightly under 50 cases per year from 1990 to 1997, restatements increased to about 156 in 2000, to 225 in 2001, and to 330 in 2002 (Bratton, 2002; US Senate, 2002c; Huron Consulting Group, 2003). The trend continued through 2005 (GAO, 2006). Figure 6.1 summarizes the nearly fivefold increase in financial restatements in the US from 1997 through September 2005.

Over the same time, the proportion of companies listed on the New York Stock Exchange (NYSE) restating their financial results increased from less than 1 per cent in 1997 to over 7 per cent in 2005, with comparable increases

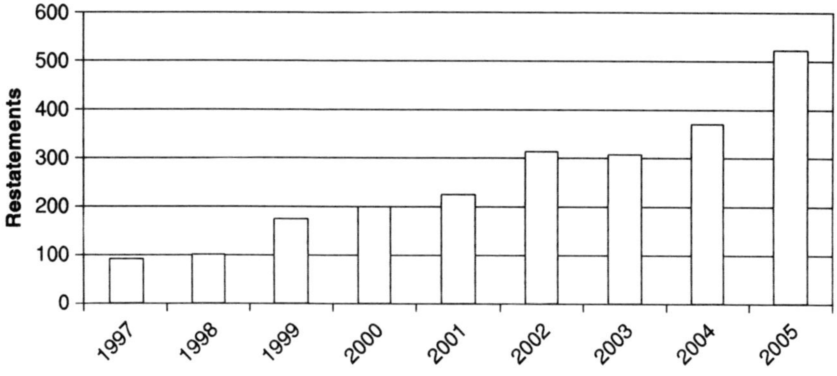

Figure 6.1 Total number of restatement announcements identified, January 1997–September 2005

Source: GAO (2006).

at the other two main Stock Exchanges in the United States, AMEX and NASDAQ (see Figure 6.2).

It would certainly be desirable for auditors to live up to the rationality ideal as outlined in the conventional model of economics. However, limitations on information and processing capacity are especially pronounced in the complex and variable environment in which auditors operate.[13] Since 'judging and deciding are inherent in every phase of the audit process' (Solomon and Shields, 1995: 139),[14] an auditor would appear to be the classical decision-maker under uncertainty. This is especially true in light of 'the general tendency to view the entirety of GAAP . . . as laws or rules to be interpreted and manipulated, rather than applied in a spirit of professional judgment' (Hendrickson and Espahbodi, 1991: 26).

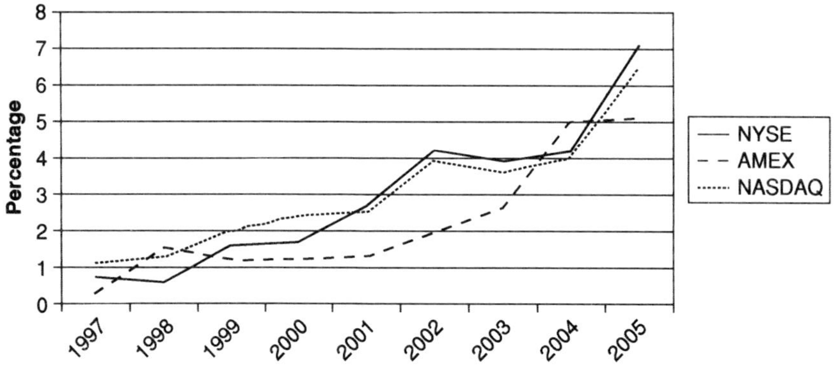

Figure 6.2 Percentage of listed companies restating, 1997–September 2005

Source: GAO (2002, 2006).

Accounting uncertainty has been found to negatively impact auditor objectivity despite the potential damage to auditor reputation (Mayhew *et al.*, 2001). Uncertainty may motivate auditors to agree with clients' interpretations (Hackenbrack and Nelson, 1996), and the tendency towards clients' interpretation has been found particularly pronounced where prior precedence was mixed (Salterio and Koonce, 1997). This places auditors in the unenviable centre of complex interactions between a raft of heuristics and cognitive influences, which question the feasibility of an auditor's work escaping self-serving bias. Independence issues may be aggravated by increased competition in the auditing industry, particularly by the increase in importance of non-auditing services provided by accounting firms.

The intrusion of bias in the client working relationship may be inevitable even in the absence of financial incentives and motivation. This would make auditor impartiality an impossible ideal (Bazerman *et al.*, 1997; O'Connor, 2002), and suggests the need for additional instruments to counter bias, including periodic auditor rotation (at partner and at firm level) and increased auditor peer review. As the result of selective interpretation of ambiguous information that goes into a financial report, and the weight of earlier interpretations, an auditor's judgement is almost certainly biased in favour of their own and clients' interests (Bazerman *et al.*, 1997). Self-serving bias in an auditing setting can be exacerbated by a number of factors. These include the distance and anonymity between the potential victims of misrepresentation and the auditor, as opposed to the closeness and familiarity of the people in the client firm who could be hurt if a negative audit opinion were issued. Also, repercussions from a negative opinion are likely to be immediate and substantial, as opposed to the temporally distant and only potential negative repercussions from having made a misstatement.

Bazerman *et al.* (1997, 2002a, b) identify three structural aspects of accounting which encourage biased judgment.[15] These are of particular relevance in an accounting setting:

- Ambiguity, the more leeway there is in interpreting accounting rules, the more bias.
- Attachment, auditors have strong incentives to remain in the good books of clients, for follow-up business and to gain other income from the client.
- Approval, an auditor is more likely to accept more aggressive accounting from a client than if an assessment were made in a vacuum.

In addition, the authors identify several aspects of human nature that reinforce unconscious biases:

- Familiarity, people are more likely to harm a stranger than an individual they know, and the more familiar the auditor is with the client, the more biased judgement tends to become.

- Discounting, which refers to the time value of money, where people are more responsive to immediate consequences than delayed ones.
- Escalation, correcting a bias may require admitting prior errors. This would force individuals to admit that they had initially made a bad decision. Even if this would represent only a minor error of judgement, the more likely response is to cover up the mistake, or to mentally picture this as a success in the making, to justify additional effort.

While the existence of various self-serving biases can hardly be used as a blanket amnesty for cases of misleading reporting, it does point towards the fallacy of expecting perfect impartiality. These insights can be applied to the individual auditor as well as to the auditing firm. Monitoring itself is fraught with problems. The line-supervisor too suffers from cognitive biases. Monitoring is costly, with regard to direct and indirect costs.

Prentice (2000) questions the assumption that an accountant always adheres to the rational actor ideal, and dismisses the view that the potential or actual loss of reputation is a reliable deterrent to fraudulent or negligent auditing. Auditors tend to satisfice (Simon, 1955), rather than optimize. This might be inconsistent with a Bayesian application of probability, but is entirely rational from a cognitive cost–benefit perspective as it economizes on the cost of analysis (Asare and Wright, 1997; Gigerenzer and Todd, 1999). Auditors use rules of thumb, or heuristics, to guide them, even when objective methods could be more effective (McDaniel and Kinney, 1995; Asare and Wright, 1997). Auditors have been found to utilize a number of specific heuristics, including the representativeness heuristic (Uecker and Kinney, 1977; Kellogg and Kellogg, 1991; Smith and Kida, 1991), anchoring and adjustment (Joyce and Biddle, 1981a, b; Bonner and Pennington, 1991; Bedard and Wright; 1994; Hirst and Koonce, 1996), and availability (Bonner and Pennington, 1991; Haynes and Kachelmeier, 1998). Auditors are subject to cognitive dissonance and escalation of commitment (Weick, 1983). Auditors display a strong tendency to seek and use confirmatory rather than disconfirmatory evidence (Waller and Felix, 1984), and to self-rationalize decisions (Peecher, 1996).

Memory is critically important to avoiding audit errors, and overconfidence in their memories can lead auditors to commit reckless errors by failing to check working papers before reaching conclusions (Ramsay, 1994). General audit experience may not improve memory tasks (Johnson, 1994). Compounding this, there seems to be little correlation between auditors' confidence in their ability to make going-concern judgements, and their accuracy in actual judgements (Kida, 1984). This reflects overconfidence in their own abilities (Kent and Weber, 1998) and possibly also in self-perceptions of ethics (Cohen *et al.*, 1995). Tax professionals (including accountants) have been found to be highly susceptible to biases towards the client preference (Kahle and White, 2004). Auditors' risk-taking tendencies have been found to generally conform to the predictions of prospect theory (Kahneman and Tversky, 1979) with regard to risk preferences, where a decision-maker tends to be risk averse in a gain situation, and risk-seeking in a loss situation (Jegers, 1991; Schisler, 1994; Cohen and Trompeter, 1998). Affective reactions can somewhat reverse this behaviour of risk avoidance (seeking) in gain (loss) contexts, indicating that such contextual variables may have a significant influence on risky behaviour (Moreno *et al.*, 2002).[16]

The way in which an auditor combines a prior with new information has a number of implications for the way auditors perform their jobs. First, bias may arise when auditors place too great a weight on prior beliefs and insufficient weight on current information. This may, from some point onwards, be done deliberately because the auditor, when forming an opinion, takes into consideration the implications for their own career of contradicting an evaluation arrived at in previous years. Second, information gained from prior audits has relevance for the current period only in as far as it is still valid. If the validity of prior information decays over time, then such information should have a built-in decay factor which reflects that information from, say, three years ago has limited relevance for the firm's current position. The (assumed) fact that a firm's accounting was reliable during a previous period should be understood to be only an approximate guide to the quality of current figures. This link between past and present quality of information (in terms of current relevance of prior information) may get less reliable with time, hence the need to discount the value of such prior information. The incorrect application or absence of such a decay factor is a further potential source of evaluation bias. In sum, the subjective weight given to prior and new information, and the relevance of prior information (incorporated in the form of a decay factor) will be of importance in the formation of an audit opinion.

A gatekeeper's initial hypothesis has an important influence on subsequent perception and judgement related to the same issue. Confirmation bias describes a bias towards an initial belief. However, an individual may also overestimate the importance of new information if this is more salient and appears to be more informative than initial data. More weight may also be given to a client's (or a peer's) view. Motivated reasoning is likely to enter this process at some point, and may then influence a gatekeeper's opinion. This presents a problem for a prescriptive interpretation of judgement and choice-making. Sequential evaluation of an event or updating of a view can be described by a two-stage process, where an initial evaluation on the basis of evidence is likely to be unconsciously influenced by own past decisions or a prior belief. At a second stage, the individual not only may again tend to seek confirmatory evidence to support this earlier view, but may also more consciously bias towards conformity with earlier opinion and/or expectations of the people around the individual. In this way, unconscious bias can turn into deliberate fraud, lying, and cheating.

In stage 1 (Year t), gatekeepers make their evaluation on the basis of the evidence, but are influenced, perhaps unconsciously, by their own past decisions and by knowledge of what the client wants.[17] Factors likely to influence this process include reputational concerns, in terms of both a reputation for being honest and a reputational stake in an earlier public opinion; potential sanctions from a bad audit, as well as sanctions from a client (likely to be perceived as being executive management – not the shareholders) when issuing a qualified audit opinion; perceived benefits from being honest as well as from being fraudulent; the perceived relevance of prior and new information, and the quality and relevance of either (see Figure 6.3 for an illustration of this process).

In stage 2 (Year t + 1) gatekeepers make public their evaluation. This may not be the same as their stage 1 evaluation, and may lean even further to what the client wants and takes account again of earlier decisions. This may be so perhaps because any evaluation is subject to uncertainty, as is the case in the audit process. While a best guess of the true position might be X, the true value could, with some likelihood, also be X + 1 (or indeed X – 1). If the client would prefer X + 4, to give them X + 1 'may after all be right'. This is likely to be subject to anchoring.

This framework would imply (at least) two forms of major bias: unconscious bias at stage 1 in the formation of an opinion, but not (primarily at least) deliberate cheating. This may then be followed by more conscious and motivated bias at stage 2, where the basic opinion or evaluation becomes a reported one. This can be close to cheating, because gatekeepers are adjusting what they believe in order to meet clients' wishes and own past judgements. Once the gatekeeper agrees to figures which are knowingly wrong, or agrees to procedures which are knowingly in conflict with, say, GAAP, this may in a subsequent stage then turn into fraud. This highlights that the way new information is processed and used to update a prior may not always be as straightforward as suggested by prescriptive models based on probability rules.

The presented analysis abstracts from considerations of how much information the auditor uses. Such information is not costless to obtain and

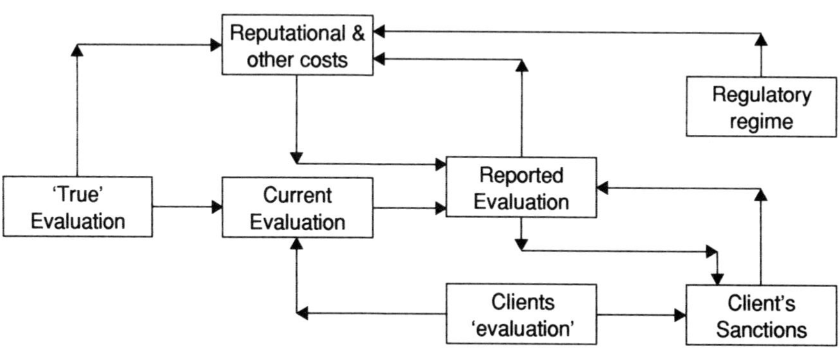

Figure 6.3 Stage 1: formation of opinion in Year t

it is unlikely that the auditor will make use of all the information which is potentially available. Thus, given a favourable prior (acting as an anchor), and positive information signals which are easy to obtain (confirming a prior belief), the auditor may reach an opinion that further work in accessing information is unjustified.[18] The problem with this is that for firms who are both in trouble and have dishonest managers, obvious or low cost information may well have been falsified or biased. Belief confirmation theory would suggest that an auditor is likely to overweigh information which confirms a prior, and conversely underweigh information which is in conflict with a prior. Hence, auditors might be expected to accept easily obtainable information at face value, especially where this seems to confirm a prior view. It should be noted that an auditor is susceptible to biases towards a client's view even where this conflicts with a prior (Kahle and White, 2004). This emphasizes that context and situation can influence the processing of information and ultimate judgement.

Once more this analysis leads us to conclude that the regular changing of an auditor is a good regulatory practice, as a new auditor would be less encumbered by a prior interpretation, and an earlier public opinion. Although even here the new auditor may use the conclusions of the previous auditor in the formation of a prior. Nevertheless, a new auditor would be somewhat less likely to escalate commitment as there is no responsibility for a prior judgement, especially where this was made public, and would have less reputational investment from a previous decision.[19] Mandatory rotation of audit firm would reduce potential conflicts of interest with regard to future business retention. A prohibition for a lead auditor to join the client firm until a minimum time interval has passed may reduce bias further. Such steps will not eliminate bias, but can go some way to minimizing it.

Auditing practice and regulation should take the persistence of bias into consideration in order to increase the reliability of financial reports. This seems particularly relevant as the discussion has shown that self-serving judgements, fraudulent intentions, and deliberate misleading are not necessary for the provision of false, incorrect, or grossly misleading audits, at least not initially. Bias can be strictly separated from motivation, though motivation may (and usually does) subsequently contribute to further biased perception and judgement. Mere proximity to the client is sufficient to introduce bias in the perception, interpretation, and judgement of the professional, and result in audit interpretations favourable to the client (Zajonc, 1968; Bazerman *et al.*, 2002a). Subsequent pressures to self-justify initial acceptance of accounting interpretations tend to lead to yet closer affiliation with the client's view. Hence, while it may only involve small steps from initial bias to self-serving motivation and finally to fraudulent behaviour, bias can affect audits before any motive and intent for fraud enters the equation. This is in stark contrast to the assumption of deliberate intent by individuals of rational choice theories, and policy making and legal practice based on its predictions. It must be recognized that bias affects the perception and cognitive processing stages long before any conscious choice takes place. Traditional economic theory generally assumes that choice is a process of consciously weighing the costs and benefits of an event or decision. While this may be the intention of an individual, and can certainly form one part of the choice-making process, biased perceptions and information processing would appear to influence this process long before (as well as during) such deliberations.

Current legislation may not sufficiently consider impartiality in the audit process. The Sarbanes-Oxley Act 2002, for example, is aimed directly at fraud, but fails to strongly address the problem of bias.[20] It is not obvious how unconscious bias would be deterred by the threat of increased punishment (Bazerman *et al.*, 1997, 2002a, b). This refers to 'a growing consensus that the law must do something more (or different) than simply relying on its conventional strategy of vicarious corporate liability in order to induce good monitoring' (Langevoort, 2001a: 2). The problem for policy makers is how to minimize the unconscious biases the auditor is subject to in everyday dealings with clients, and at the same time enhance the impact of rules on more conscious and motivated bias, and fraudulent intent.[21] Impartiality is difficult to achieve, some would say impossible, as all individuals are biased towards their own interests or prejudices, and affected by proximity to peers and clients. While an auditor may indeed be of very high integrity, and consciously strive towards providing judgements that are 'true and fair', behavioural research points to the difficulty of escaping bias and heuristics that skew perception. There is no reason to assume that stronger penalties alone would deter activities where deterrence has failed in the past, as a gatekeeper can be expected to rationalize (i.e. distort the objective interpretation of) their own actions to comply with accepted norms, and may downplay potential risk from penalties, as outlined throughout this book.

A mandatory requirement to rotate auditors, at the individual partner and at the auditing firm level, a requirement partially implemented under the Sarbanes-Oxley Act, may help to reduce bias. It is doubtful whether this will sufficiently eliminate bias, as rotation is currently only required at the lead audit partner level. Even if repeat audits at firm level and the provision of all non-auditing services were disallowed completely, an auditing firm would hardly risk losing future contracts with this or other clients by having a reputation of being overly adversarial in negotiations with the senior management of audited firms.[22] The individual audit partner still has an incentive to upset neither his superiors, nor what may become a future employer.[23]

This has wider repercussions for the provisioning of audit functions by private sector accounting firms, and the general issue of impartiality of monitors in corporate governance. When scandals occur repeatedly in a profession, this would indicate a serious dysfunction. Cramton (2002) and Koniak (2003a, b) make a related point with regard to legal liability of lawyers in corporate governance (see also Fisch and Rosen, 2003; Sargent, 2003, 2004; Spiegel and Ohl, 2005). This emphasizes the reduction in liability in the United States, due to changes in the legal framework, an argument also noted by

Coffee (2001) with regard to auditing, and conflicting interpretations of legal and ethical obligations between various states, federal law, courts, and the bar. Sale (2005) emphasizes the central role of banks and financiers in many corporate governance failures, highlighting similar agency problems.

Reputation as a deterrent

As the discussion has shown, the auditing accountant, as a gatekeeper in corporate governance, is subject to incentives and biases that may negatively impact on the function of protecting the interest of investors and shareholders. The principal forces thought to provide an incentive to the gatekeeper rest primarily on reputational capital and liability. Traditionally it is assumed that the gatekeeper is motivated to preserve and to enhance the reputation gained from professional certification and a past track record. This is thought to enhance an auditor's success in accessing a future income stream from providing professional services. The motivational effect of reputation is further enhanced by the potential of liability from sub-standard or fraudulent service provision. There is of course considerable validity to the liability argument, and the absence of legal liability may well cause an agent to engage in greater levels of illegal or socially unacceptable behaviour. The absence of legal liability for one's actions may contribute to a rise in fraudulent or criminally negligent behaviour (Cramton, 2002).

Reputational considerations ideally provide managers and control agents with an incentive not to deviate significantly from expectations with regard to performance (Jensen and Meckling, 1976; Fama, 1980; Fama and Jensen, 1983b). Yet, the value of liability as a deterrent can be subject to immense pressures and cognitive biases, which can lead the gatekeeper to engage in practices that run counter to own long-term interest. This is made worse by the divergence of interests between individual accounting partners and the firm itself (this also applies to partners in a law firm and to employees of a bank). Even the destruction of the firm may not be much of a threat to the individual. To make the point, most Andersen partners likely found gainful employment with the remaining big accounting firms without significant loss of income or status, or retired with their pensions intact.

There are profound and deep running forces that may encourage a gatekeeper to behave in ways that do not easily fit in the traditional gatekeeper model. For the gatekeeper model to hold, Coffee (2001) identified three elements which have to be present together:

1 The gatekeeper's work must be observable (if it is not, then how can failure be detected?).
2 The gatekeeper must be a repeat player (otherwise the temptation to take the chance and run with the money might be too overwhelming).
3 The individual client must not be material to the gatekeeper's income (or else the independence of the gatekeeper is, by definition, compromised).

Another element crucial to the functioning of the model can be added:

4 Gatekeepers must be aware of the failure of meeting their duties. Where such agents, due to biased perceptions and judgement, fail to recognize the error of their ways, damage to reputation and threats of penalties fail as a deterrent.

Gatekeepers may, at least initially, not be aware of any deviation from norms or laws, if they are subject to cognitive and perceptual biases which cloud their judgement of risk, and legal and ethical behaviour. Reputation as a motivator for acceptable behaviour would be weakened if the individual is not aware of the threat to reputation from a particular action or severely misjudges the associated risk. This could be due to self-serving interpretations of own actions. Since biases are an inevitable result of working closely with the client, and by their very nature intrude unconsciously (Festinger, 1957; Staw, 1976, 1981; Bazerman *et al.*, 1997, 2000, 2002a, b), sanctions may be greatly diminished in affecting behaviour.

It also matters how reputation is defined and interpreted. An accounting firm (or an individual accountant) might have an interest in maintaining a certain reputation. But a reputation as what? Being honest? Adhering to the law? Being cooperative with the client? Maximizing profits for the client? Finally, who does the auditor ultimately deem him or herself to be accountable to – shareholders, or senior management? An auditing firm that has a reputation for being rigidly law abiding, to the degree of reporting the client to the authorities at the slightest hint of a legal breach, will hardly find much sympathy or business in the market. Likewise, a firm that has a reputation for being honest but does not make any money for the client (or not as much as a firm less afflicted by qualms over honesty) might find it hard to find business.

This is further complicated by the observation that reputational impairment may not be a serious obstacle to future business opportunities (Davis and Simon, 1992). If one excludes the exceptional demise of Arthur Andersen, a controversial case at best as the decision which led to its demise was subsequently overturned, it is not obvious that accounting firms sanctioned for bad audits subsequently suffer significant penalties in terms of loss of income. SEC disciplinary actions, for example, tend to be rather light when involving large accounting firms, and may have no significant lasting impact on fee income.[24] Several empirical studies demonstrate that audit failures cause minimal damage to auditor reputation, and that auditing firms generally do not witness a lasting or significant loss of market share after being sanctioned by regulators. Painter and Duggan (1996), for example, found that major UK accounting firms admonished by the Department of Trade suffered no serious negative impact in fees charged. Wilson and Grimlund (1990: 58) report that while audit firms disciplined by the SEC tend to lose some market share and clients, overall their study provided 'only weak support for the hypothesis that an auditor's ability to attract new clients' suffered from SEC disciplinary sanctions.[25] Firth (1990) found that UK audit firms continued to gain clients after being disciplined, although they temporarily lost some market share in comparison to rivals. Hence, reputational value may be of somewhat limited value as a deterrent to questionable practices in the accounting industry. While Arthur Andersen's case might caution otherwise, the likelihood of one of the Big-4 firms suffering a similar fate seems to be remote. Andersen, it would appear, while hardly an innocent victim, really was extremely unlucky in its association with Enron and WorldCom, the two largest bankruptcies (and frauds) in US corporate history.

Overall, significant obstacles would appear to diminish the value of reputation as a deterrent. Future benefits from being honest (the reputational value argument) can be dwarfed by the potential returns from self-dealing or negligence. This can include endgame situations where, 1) the individual is at the end of his career or assignment, or a firm faces imminent closure; 2) the reputational loss accrues mainly to the firm but not to the employee (an internal principal–agent problem); 3) the returns to the individual from non-contractual activities outweigh any expected future losses (which may be a rational argument for deception); 4) the risk from an action largely falls on others; and 5) the risk from such actions or their expected penalties is miscalculated (an individual may not be aware of the magnitude and likelihood of the risk to reputation, or might rationalize these to a minimum).

In the case of an endgame, game theoretical considerations would predict that a gatekeeper might be inclined to mine or liquidate reputation rather than to preserve it in perpetuity. Time-value of money theory further diminishes the value of reputation. Benefits from acquiescence are of greater value to the individual as these are closer (and more certain) in time than any (uncertain and merely potential) damages from a bad audit. Benefits are immediately tangible (and pertain to oneself), whereas negative repercussions are further away in time and less certain (and may, with some luck, fall on others, perhaps even on strangers). The combination of temporal closeness and personal ownership of benefits, in contrast to the distribution and temporal remoteness of any potential damage, weakens reputation as a motivator. Cognitive dissonance reduction (the tendency to see events in a more positive way) by the individual auditor (and their control agents) further diminishes the deterrent value of reputation.

The motivational value of reputation suffers a particular weakness if the benefits from an action mainly accrue to the individual, but most of the potential damage to reputation (among other costs) accrues to the firm. This creates a moral hazard framework, with an emphasis for the firm on internal monitoring. The dichotomy in interests and perceived threats between the individual auditing partner and the firm, per se, may further diminish much of the threat of legal liability on the individual due to auditing negligence or fraud. Maintaining reputational capital is a particular problem for the large dispersed firm where individual partners deal with a client with a high degree of independence. An individual may distinguish between the private return from an action and reputational damage to the firm, and in absolute terms the firm has more to lose from a ruined reputation than the individual.

Litigation as a deterrent

Deterrence in the form of litigation is the second leg supporting the gatekeeper model (in addition to reputational concerns), and is assumed to work by imposing additional costs on the agent in case of a breach of duties. For deterrence to work, the threat of liability has to be credible and substantial. Where litigation risks are diminished, financially negligible, or lower than the expected return from acquiescence to, or active involvement in, say, earnings management, then this threat is diminished. Agents' misperceptions with regard to the severity and likelihood of penalties further weaken the value of punitive action. For example, the US accounting profession gained substantial protection from litigation through a number of legislative changes implemented during the 1990s. The Private Securities Litigation Reform Act (PSLRA) 1995 raised pleading standards in securities cases, introduced proportionate liability rules (in contrast to the earlier 'joint and several' liability, which could result in much higher penalties), adopted a protective safe harbour for forward-looking statements, and also restricted the use of RICO in securities litigation.[26] Further reductions to the costs and probability of potential litigation (and hence deterrence) resulted from the Supreme Court's *Lampf, Pleva* decision (1991),[27] which shortened the statute of limitations applicable to securities fraud; the Supreme Court's *Central Bank of Denver* decision (1994)[28], which eliminated private aiding and abetting liability in securities fraud cases; and the Securities Litigation Uniform Standards Act 1998 (SLUSA)[29], which abolished state court class actions of securities fraud.[30] Through the diminished likelihood of successful litigation by private and public parties, these changes tended to undermine the second leg of the gatekeeper model with respect to auditor liability.[31] It is evident that this did not, however, protect Andersen once it had been tarnished by the Enron case.

More subtle reasons can lead to bad audits, as the earlier discussion on the intrusion of bias in the auditing process showed. Audit failure may of course be the result of deliberate collusion of auditor with clients, the result of neglect, corruption, or incompetence.[32] A more pernicious problem is the question of whether impartiality and objectivity on the part of the auditor is an illusionary ideal. The problem for policy recommendations then becomes how to minimize the unconscious biases the auditor is subject to in everyday dealings with clients. Impartiality is difficult to achieve, perhaps impossible, as individuals tend to be biased towards their own interests or prejudices. While an auditor may indeed be of very high integrity, and consciously strive towards providing judgements that are 'true and fair', behavioural research points to the difficulty of escaping bias and heuristics that skew perception. Bias in the working relationship may not easily be countered by moral suasion and/or the threat of sanctions. Such threats can be further rationalized to a minimum by misperceptions about their likelihood and severity. It is very difficult to disregard self-interest even when there is strong ethical pressure for and an explicit goal of impartiality. Joseph Berardino, Arthur Andersen's last chief executive, expressed as much in his congressional testimony on the Enron collapse and Andersen's role as the lead auditor:

> many people think accounting is a science, where one number, namely earnings per share, is the number, and it is such a precise number, that it could not be two pennies higher or two pennies lower. And I come from the school that says it really is much of an art.
>
> (Joseph Berardino; US House of Representatives, 2001)

As a public relations statement, this was a catastrophic display of cynicism, even if it was not intended as such. While technically correct, this somewhat disingenuous attempt at defending questionable behaviour (and a history of bad audits) raises a number of important questions: Why, knowing that an engagement partner is subject to errors in interpreting accounting treatments, was the level of internal monitoring and quality control set at such a low level (and, during the Enron audit, repeatedly waived) that catastrophic auditing failure could occur? Further, why was the highly damaging shredding of working papers allowed to happen? The shredding of important internal auditing documents, which could have proven Andersen's innocence against the prosecution's case, was a fatal mistake. If an auditor has nothing to hide, it is of utmost importance to keep all documentation to be able to defend decisions taken against potential liability suits. Since Andersen's top management claimed to have been aware that accounting is more akin to an art than a precise science, together with the general assumption that auditors are under intense pressures to approve financial statements, it would appear that Andersen failed miserably in its internal monitoring duties.[33] Low levels of effective internal monitoring may be endemic within the accounting profession and elsewhere:

> What we have learned is that, perhaps in the exercise of bona fide business judgment, firms choose compliance structures in which the values of motivation and cohesion (not to mention worries about out-of-pocket costs) often trump high-powered monitoring, thus opting for higher compliance risk because it is the most sensible strategy. While I wouldn't necessarily force them to abandon that strategy, I wouldn't pay much attention to pleas of innocence or victimization, either.
>
> (Langevoort, 2001a: 39)

It is now known that internal opposition to certain treatments of Enron book entries by some Andersen auditors and risk control officers was overruled by Andersen management. There is also no excuse for the destruction of evidence which could have saved the firm from an obstruction of justice verdict. It is difficult to imagine feasible reasons for its destruction. Unless, of course, these papers contained evidence of the complicity of Andersen personnel in Enron's fraud, or knowledge thereof. In this case, internal monitoring failed completely by allowing this to happen in the first place, which recalls the possibility of strategic failures in internal monitoring, where the risk to a firm from poor (or risky) audit is deliberately balanced with the potential benefit from this. An alternative interpretation would suggest that the rot went all the way to the top of this auditing firm.

Low visibility sanctions

Gordon (2002) refers to the phenomenon of low visibility sanctions when discussing shortcomings of the gatekeeper function of monitors. This is contrasted with highly visible events, such as the firing of a member of the board, or a lead auditor, material events that must be disclosed (in the US on a 'Schedule 8-K' form). Even if such an event were not subject to disclosure, it would likely result in a considerable amount of public scrutiny and inquiry. The potential harm to the audited firm from such increased public scrutiny can be greater than the potential harm to an auditor's reputation (in fact, such action may even enhance the latter's reputation). Similar damage to the audited firm could arise from the voluntary resignation of the auditor. The senior management of a firm is less likely to press for a visible event. Instead, it is more likely that management would make use of a variety of low visibility sanctions. Low visibility sanctions include the non-renewal of a contract, or not awarding a consulting contract in the first place (neither action has to be publicized in proxy statements by the client firm).

These types of sanctions are particularly applicable when the accountant is receiving forms of compensation from the firm in addition to the audit fee.[34] More subtle pressures can be exerted on the gatekeeper the more involved he or she is in the company. Disciplinary measures that are not subject to disclosure increase the credibility of threats against a gatekeeper who disagrees with management on a particular issue. Auditor impartiality is severely compromised where an accountant submits to the loss of independence by agreeing to a clients' accounting interpretation. This may lead to a race to the bottom (Gordon, 2002) where accounting firms see a competitive advantage in setting the bar of professional credibility and independence ever lower. Arthur Andersen may have fallen into this trap as the firm changed over the years from a group of independent auditors with a high ethical standing to a profit centre unit.[35]

Dismissing the accounting firm, in contrast, is a high visibility sanction (as this has to be disclosed in financial filings). Such an action may well cause more harm to the sanctioning company than to the accountant, and is thus a less credible threat to an accountant who disagrees with management about a material accounting matter. Too vigorous an effort by management to force a particular accounting treatment may trigger an accountant's resignation, an event that also has to be made public. In contrast, low visibility sanctions carry no such publicity penalty. The susceptibility to low visibility sanctions can be magnified, by allowing accounting firms to cross-sell various other consulting services, such as tax advice and internal auditing, to their audit clients. With regard to low visibility sanctions and the increased provision of non-auditing services, Gordon (2002) argues that it is not simply that the accountant now has more at stake in the relationship.[36] Nor that the accountant may now have a particular reason to please, or at least not alienate, the client who might buy additional services. Rather, senior management now has more credible threats against an accountant who disagrees on an important issue.

The moral hazard implications are yet more pronounced in a situation where the individual partner's income is cross-linked with sales of services other than accounting to the same client. During the 1990s, accounting firms in the US increasingly relied on income from non-accounting services (POB, 2000). These non-accounting services have outgrown accounting income for these firms in recent years (SEC, 2000a, b, 2003a). During the later 1990s, the revenue mix of the then Big-5 auditing firms shifted strongly towards consulting services. Figure 6.4 illustrates the growth of consulting services, showing firms' mix of practice as a percentage of gross fees. For SEC audit

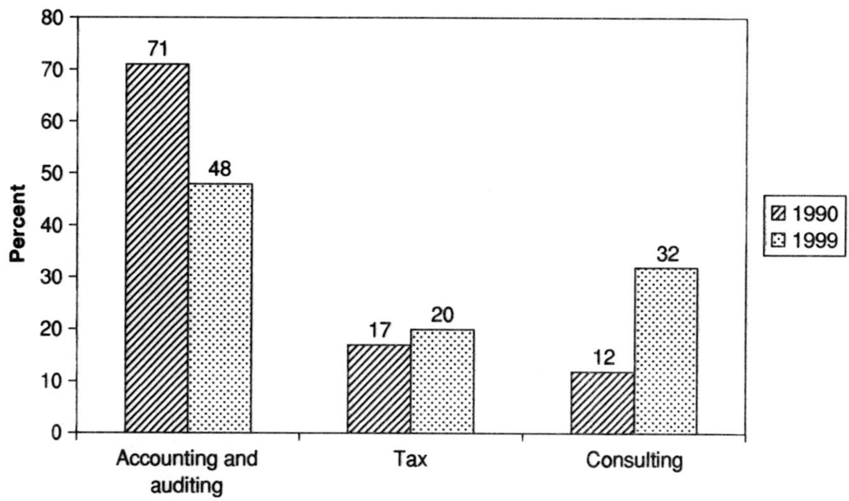

Figure 6.4 Firms' mix of Big-5 practice as a percentage of gross fees, SEC audit clients
Source: Public Oversight Board (2000).

clients, the ratio of accounting and auditing revenues to consulting revenues dropped from approximately 6 to 1 in 1990, to 1.5 to 1 in 1999, and revenues from all non-audit services exceeded revenues from traditional accounting and auditing services towards the end of the decade. Intensified competition in the auditing industry and the combination of auditing services with consulting and tax auditing may have sharpened auditor focus on the potential consequences of losing a client.

Concerns about the simultaneous provision of audit services and consulting are widely discussed in the literature (Coffee, 2002; Clarke *et al.*, 2003; Macey and Sale, 2003). The issue is whether consulting services performed by external auditors impair auditor independence. Problems of measurement and definition would appear to complicate the analysis, which brings to mind the difficulties regarding the detection and measurement of earnings management discussed in Chapter 3 (see Dechow and Skinner, 2000). It is hardly surprising that opinions on the effect of consulting fees on auditor independence are somewhat disparate. One polar view holds that audit failure rates are near zero, demonstrating that the simultaneous provision of consulting and other non-audit services does not compromise the quality of audits (Reynolds and Francis, 2001; DeFond *et al.*, 2002; Francis, 2004; DeFond and Francis, 2005). This view is indicative of a belief in the absolute integrity and independence of the accounting profession (in combination with liability and reputational concerns), which has also been the long-standing opinion of the industry and AICPA, its representative body in the United States.[37] It is likely that the accounting professions of other countries and their respective representative bodies also place faith in this assumption. As was shown earlier, the legal profession too was long of the opinion that reputational concerns would be a sufficiently strong deterrent to providing a poor audit.

An opposing view suggests that the auditing process is essentially broken, that is, no longer producing reliable opinions, and that the provision of non-audit services has contributed to this deterioration in audit quality (Coffee, 2002; Gordon, 2002; Clarke *et al.*, 2003; Macey and Sale, 2003; Cousins *et al.*, 2004; Basioudis *et al.*, 2006). This view, broadly shared by practitioners in the field, would suggest that the massive periodic failures of the auditing process should caution against a naïve belief in the efficiency of market-based incentives. Results of studies which try to establish whether non-audit services compromise independence would appear to be highly sensitive to research design choices.[38] While this is not the place to go into a detailed discussion of the econometric and theoretical issues of particular studies, the reader should bear in mind noted problems with the endogeneity and simultaneity bias of studies which correlate the level of non-audit fees with, say, going concern opinions or abnormal accruals.[39] Further, a concentration on firms under distress might overlook the importance of unexpected corporate failures (Clarke *et al.*, 2003). In many such cases, affected firms announce problems or suddenly restate earnings not long after they have issued unqualified financial reports (i.e. reports approved by the external auditor).

The watchdog role of the auditor may be greatly diminished by the auditor's increasing dependence on income from the consulting side of the firm. The risk to the independence of the auditor is increased as a result of supplying additional services to the client, especially where these additional services carry increasingly greater weight than the audit revenue itself. An individual partner may be forced to choose between the potential loss of a large part of his or her income (by non-acquiescence), or to acquiesce to an accounting treatment not normally accepted. An individual then has to choose between the guaranteed loss of being sanctioned by the firm (loss of job, promotion, case, etc.), or the potential loss through litigation.[40] While even a large client may only be a relatively small contributor to the accounting firm's total income, such a client is likely to be a significant and in some cases sole source of income to the individual partner. This violates one of the essential elements of gatekeeper independence.

In the case of the Andersen/Enron relationship, it was the Houston partner who primarily dealt with this client. The compensation of this individual was significantly tied to his Enron billings, and indirectly with respect to the non-audit services Andersen was supplying to Enron. The continued provision of such services depended, at least to some degree, on a favourable audit. Enron might have been a relatively minor consideration for the totality of Andersen (approximately 1 per cent of overall firm revenue in the last full year of its existence), but it was the largest client for its Houston office, and for the Enron relationship partner, the key source of income.[41] The disparity between a local partner's share in the company's reputation and the financial value to the individual partner's client relationship points towards a classic moral hazard problem which compounds the impact of the low visibility sanctions discussed earlier. The (immediate and real) benefits from acquiescence largely fall to the relationship partner, while any (delayed and merely potential) costs in terms of sullied reputation and legal liability may mainly fall on the group.[42] This has obvious implications for the internal monitoring system of large firms charged with corporate governance monitoring and certification duties.

Internal monitoring may well have been weakened with the spread of the limited liability partnership (LLP) within the accounting industry (Macey and Sale, 2003). In essence, internal monitoring systems that were adequate for a time when a sense of professional integrity and ethics put restraints on an individual's behaviour may no longer be sufficient in a setting of profit-maximizing large firms. This potential conflict is aggravated where partner remuneration is linked to turnover. The consequent threat to the partner's independence and the resulting risks to the auditing firm's reputation (and in the extreme, as Arthur Andersen showed, possibly its very survival) are predictable and would strongly suggest the implementation of an appropriate internal monitoring mechanism.

Prior to the passage of the Sarbanes-Oxley Act, consulting services supplied by auditing firms to their audit clients were not necessarily seen as impairing auditor independence. Under section 201(a) of the Act, however, it became unlawful for an accounting firm that performs an audit for a public company to provide the company with certain types of non-audit services, such as a) bookkeeping or other services related to the maintenance of a company's accounting records or financial statements; b) financial information systems design and implementation; c) appraisal or evaluation services, fairness opinions or evaluations of contributions in-kind; d) actuarial services; e) internal audit out-sourcing services; f) management functions or human resources functions; g) investment banking services such as broker-dealer services and investment advisor services; h) legal services and other expert services unrelated to the audit; and i) other services that the newly created Public Company Accounting Oversight Board determines by regulation to be impermissible.[43] This removes one area of conflict of interest from the auditor–client relationship, although a number of venues for the intrusion of bias in this relationship remain.

Summary

Auditors, by the very nature of their work and the competitive pressures of the accounting industry over the last 20 odd years, are likely to have frequent and close contact with their clients. The offices of the lead partner of an external audit team are often in the client's headquarters. Conflicts of interest, for example from the provision of non-audit services, need not be present for bias to influence an auditor's opinion (though this is likely to further compromise independence). It generally takes only a slight affiliation with a partisan to create sympathetic leanings and bias, even when agents try to be objective and impartial (Thompson, 1995).

The Sarbanes-Oxley Act disallows many of the consulting tasks that accountants had performed for their audit clients, and increases their potential liability from involvement in a poor audit. Further, the Act stipulates a rotation of the lead auditing partner (but not of the auditing firm). This will reduce some of the factors that have weakened the gatekeeper model. The Act also requires some evidence that auditing firms improve their internal monitoring. The risk of economic coercion in the form of low visibility sanctions may be reduced by the prohibition of many non-audit services traditionally provided by accounting firms. This separation of services had previously been vigorously and successfully opposed by the accounting industry. After the collapse of Enron and WorldCom, and the alleged involvement of Andersen in both accounting frauds, the profession lost much of the political support for its opposition to this reform. The provisions of the Act with regard to improvements of auditing firms' internal monitoring are commendable.

Notwithstanding its considerable merits, the Act does not specifically address the issue of bias. Auditor rotation is limited to a change in the lead engagement partner. There is no provision to rotate the firms which conduct audits. To comprehensively restore trust in the role of the system of auditing will require practices and regulations that strongly recognize and counter the existence and effects of bias in the relationship between auditors and auditees. One such requirement is audit firm rotation. However, as there remain only four big accounting companies, and given the fact that an auditing firm wishes to gain future clients, even rotation at firm level may be of limited value. Industry consolidation has led to a concentration of the industry, with potentially negative consequences with regard to the quality and independence of audits. Future intervention may be required to reverse potential impediments to competition from industry concentration.

The Act has increased the independence requirements for a board of directors. The most relevant requirements are aimed at the independence and power of the audit committee. All members of the audit committee must now be independent. The committee is empowered to retain independent counsel, and has been given the sole mandate to select, supervise, and terminate the external auditor (a function pertaining to management prior to the passing of the Act). Qualification requirements have been raised, and at least one committee member must be a financial expert. These requirements formalize and incrementally extend existing recommendations and statutes. Not addressed by the Act are the issues of functional independence, the intrusion of bias, group pressures to conformity, and the potential for suboptimal decision-making due to a synchronization of views. Questions of board diversity are also not addressed. There is very little in the Act which suggests that the board is a body that should actively challenge management on behalf of shareholders and other stakeholders. Given the various pressures on a board to concur with managerial interpretation, it is not obvious how the requirements for minimum qualifications and the power to select and monitor the external auditor alone will lead to significantly better gatekeeping by the board. The Act does not pre-empt or override the protections afforded to directors by (US) state law. Whether higher penalties and liability risks for directors will significantly increase their vigilance is doubtful, given the discussed cognitive biases which work against the recognition of own improper behaviour.

7 Recent corporate governance failures

The revelation of missing funds at Italy's Parmalat in late 2003 was a strong reminder, if one was needed, that massive breakdowns in corporate governance are not limited to the United States or to a particular period in time. Two more recent cases of earnings misrepresentation underline this argument. Japan's financial regulator, the Financial Services Agency (FSA), banned ChuoAoyama PricewaterhouseCoopers (then part of the international auditing firm of PricewaterhouseCoopers) from performing audits of listed companies for two months starting in July 2006 for its faulty audit of regional bank Ashikaga Bank, which had manipulated earnings (with the help of ChuoAoyama auditors) to conceal its insolvency.[1] This is the harshest penalty ever dealt to a large auditor in Japan and highlights persistent problems with auditing irregularities and the policing of securities laws in Japan. In an unfolding of events reminiscent of the problems of Arthur Andersen with regard to its involvement with Enron, the FSA had already in 2005 criticized the internal monitoring system of the auditor for failing to detect that its accounting partners had helped falsify the accounts at Kanebo, a failing cosmetics company.

In late May 2006, Fannie Mae, a US-based mortgage corporation, agreed to pay a $400m fine for failures in corporate governance that had resulted in a $6.3bn net overstatement of profits due to earnings management.[2] James Lockhart, Acting Director of the OFHEO, described the company as having an 'arrogant and unethical corporate culture', and a senior management that 'manipulated accounting; reaped maximum, undeserved bonuses; and prevented the rest of the world from knowing' (Lockhart, 2006; see also OFHEO, 2006). The external audits performed by auditor KPMG failed to note Fannie Mae's significant departures from US GAAP. KPMG had been aware of the non-GAAP provisions of particular Fannie Mae accounting practices and policies, but still issued unqualified opinions on Fannie Mae's financial statements for the years 1998–2003, when respective statements included failures to comply with GAAP (OFHEO, 2006). Lastly, KPMG failed to properly take into account allegations of fraud raised by a former insider (OFHEO, 2006).

These two cases suggest that problems related to managerial oversight are not likely to go away. Systematic failures in the mechanisms designed to monitor and control the actions of executive managers can and do happen even where such systems are considered to be advanced. An entire stock market in Germany (Neuer Markt), for example, was dissolved in late 2002, after a string of corporate frauds had severely undermined investor confidence in that market. Even less protection is provided in countries where managerial oversight is largely characterized by its absence (Black, 2001a, b; Black *et al.*, 2003). It is, for example, generally recognized that one of the root causes of the Asian Financial Crisis of 1997/98 was the virtual absence of an effective system of corporate governance (Krugman, 1998). On reflection, failures in corporate governance occur far more frequently than might be expected given the wide range of institutions, rules, and laws designed to prevent them. This is particularly puzzling for markets with presumably high standards of corporate governance and well-developed systems of property rights, law, and regulatory agencies (Turnbull, 2000; Clarke *et al.*, 2003). What underlines such concerns is the fact that affected companies typically issued healthy (i.e. unqualified) audit reports just prior to announcing the bad news. That markets and investors are typically surprised by corporate scandals does not bode well for an accounting and auditing system designed to prevent corporate fraud (Clarke *et al.*, 2003).[3]

This may also raise questions with regard to the validity of the efficient market hypothesis and the rationality assumptions of actors in financial markets. Unwarranted optimism by senior management, and overly enthusiastic investors, would appear to be more widespread than an assumption of (strongly) rational agent behaviour might predict. Over-optimism on the part of market participants may persist over long periods of time, despite what presumably is the widespread appreciation of the fact that a corporate strategy based on sheer luck and an absence of sound financial foundations is eventually bound to run into trouble. Most actions by executives to avoid reporting undesired financial results ultimately depend on an unsustainable amount of luck, and this precious commodity tends to run out in a time-honoured fashion.[4] Observations of the stock boom of the late 1990s show that projections of ever increasing profits were eagerly anticipated and rewarded by the market (and in terms of managerial compensation packages). Meanwhile, the effects of financial misreporting, a common companion particularly of exuberant markets (Greenspan, 1996), were mostly ignored and discounted until after the boom had started to turn into a bust.

Arguments that the damage caused by corporate scandals is relatively minor and hence does not warrant significant analysis might be supported by assessments of the total capitalization of companies affected by financial scandals in relation to the total capital market which, by some metric, indeed appear to be relatively small (Treadway, 1987). Still, the impact of a relatively small number of highly significant and visible failures (or near failures) of large well-known companies on the overall health and value of capital markets can be more wide-reaching. This damage exceeds the capital value of the companies directly involved. The loss in confidence of the investing public in capital markets in the United States and in Europe as a result of the revelations of corporate financial misdeeds contributed to, and possibly worsened, the broad cyclical downturn in economic activity which accompanied the end of the internet and telecom booms. The corporate governance failures in Asia during the late 1990s quickly threatened the social and economic fabric of a whole region and impacted financial risk assessments elsewhere. The fallout from the Asian Financial Crisis (AFC) was not limited to a single country or region and was felt further afield. Russia, for example, defaulted on its debt obligations in 1998, partially as a result of risk reassessments for emerging market debt subsequent to the events in Asia. The near collapse in 1998 of the US-based hedge fund Long Term Capital Management (after placing wrong bets on emerging markets' debt and losing a total of $4.6bn) prompted the US Federal Reserve Bank to arrange a bailout by private sector lenders, to prevent system-wide damage to the US financial system.[5]

The potential for corporate governance failures to lead to significant disruptions of financial markets warrants an analysis of corporate governance failures.[6] The losses are real, not mere paper losses. Another cost to an economy from corporate mis-government is the potential closure or even bankruptcy of viable honest firms due to, for example, rising capital costs, loss of investors' confidence, and increased regulatory costs. The disruptions and financial losses from a firm's collapse faced directly by thousands of individuals, including investors, shareholders, employees and pensioners, and customers and suppliers alone provide justification for an analysis.

What follows is a brief review of major corporate governance failures in recent memory. These cases reflect the analytical material of the preceding chapters and form a basis for the policy discussion in Chapter 8. First to be discussed is the Asian Financial Crisis, followed by a closer look at the events which led to the collapse of Enron. The review continues with the failure of Germany's technology stock exchange, the Neuer Markt, and concludes with a brief analysis of the fraudulent bankruptcy of Italy's Parmalat. While this is not the place to provide a detailed review of any particular scandal, these case summaries highlight commonalities in behavioural patterns discussed in the preceding analysis. Enron and the events leading to the failure of this company are explored in somewhat greater detail, and reference to this case is made throughout this research, for a number of reasons. First, more about what transpired at this company is in the public record.[7] Second, Enron demonstrates that the underlying causes leading to a firm's demise can be widespread, indicating systemic weaknesses in the corporate governance paradigm. This particular scandal also resulted in massive changes in governance legislation in the United States and elsewhere.

The Asian Financial Crisis of 1997/1998

One of the key causal factors in the Asian Financial Crisis (AFC) of 1997 was the near total absence of effective corporate governance mechanisms in many of the affected countries. The scale of self-dealing provides rich insights into the problems arising from the separation of ownership and control when monitoring, transparency, and the enforcement of existing rules are largely non-existent. Of course, the AFC had multiple root causes (which applied in different degrees across the affected counties) including, among others, a slowdown of exports, overvalued pegged currencies, and the various structural and socio-economic weaknesses of the economies under observation. These aggravated the direct factors of unhedged and mostly short-term foreign borrowing by large parts of the financial sector, underdeveloped and insufficiently regulated financial markets, investments conducted regardless of return on equity considerations, an absence of enforceable bankruptcy laws (e.g. in the case of Thailand), and misguided government policies leading to moral hazard.[8]

Common to most of the affected economies was a lack of transparency, oversight, and monitoring of managerial decision-making in the financial and corporate sector. Collusion, or at least benign neglect, by key oversight authorities and law-makers frequently played into the hands of the private sector actors. Minority shareholder rights protection was, and largely remains, an unknown. Governments around the region were seen to have embraced the (now much criticized) Washington Consensus which emphasized the liberation of trade in goods and services and the opening of financial markets. Unfortunately, most governments had largely neglected to strengthen their financial oversight capacities as they deregulated financial markets. Domestic financial institutions stepped into the vacuum this created, often with scant regard to financial prudence, economic viability of funded projects, considerations of risk, and the well-being of minority shareholders. With the benefit of hindsight, many financial institutions and companies in the region (and, to an extent, the international financial intermediaries which provided much of the capital), ultimately played the age-old game of privatizing gains and socializing losses.[9]

For the present research it is of less importance whether the causation of the various crises went from an exchange crisis to a banking problem, or whether banking problems led to an exchange crisis. While the latter interpretation might better explain the contagion to other countries in the region and further afield after the AFC started in Thailand, weaknesses in corporate governance would appear to be common to either explanation. Krugman (1998) notes that financial intermediaries, whose liabilities were perceived as effectively having a government guarantee, were central causes of the crisis. Directly playing into this was insufficient supervision of financial institutions by the relevant authorities, including the respective central banks. This is probably an oversimplified view of the AFC, but systemic weaknesses of domestic financial systems would appear to be a significant cause of the crisis (Krause, 1998).

Many, if not most, decisions on credit issuance in the crisis countries were based primarily on personal relationships and trust, or government fiat (as in the case of South Korea where political pressure fostered lending to favoured conglomerates, the 'chaebols'). Moral hazard problems stemming from an assumed bailout with public resources, in combination with inadequate bankruptcy laws, added to the tendency of financial intermediaries to lend to projects with low expected returns but high risks.[10] The observation that economies in the region with relatively well-developed banking and control systems – Singapore, Hong Kong, and Taiwan – came through the AFC with limited damage indicates the instrumental role of a financial system with relatively strong internal and external controls, and a corporate sector that places at least some value on corporate governance (Garrido, 2005).

The asset destruction that followed the outbreak of the AFC was enormous. For some 15 years, Thailand, for example, provided an apparently enviable picture of economic development, with the county's GDP expanding at an annual rate of some 10 per cent. The capital city of Bangkok, hub of the national economy, was transformed into a modern looking metropolis with 50-storey high-rises, modern shopping malls, and elevated highways. Asset prices had increased rapidly, reflecting the booming economy and large inflows of capital. Through much of the 1980s and 1990s, this caused increasing property speculation, in part sustained by continued capital inflows. The availability of cheap foreign funds, the assumed stability of the exchange rate, and high growth rates (some of which, in the later years, were fuelled by the inflow of foreign funds) led to massive overinvestments, especially in the property market but also in a number of other non-tradable assets.

All this came to a dead halt on 2 July 1997, when the peg of the Thai baht to the US dollar, in place for over one decade, was abruptly withdrawn, despite massive prior support actions by the Bank of Thailand (the country's central bank). By December of that year the depreciation had resulted in a 50 per cent drop in the value of the baht. During 1998, Thailand's GDP contracted by some 10 per cent compared to an already stagnant 1997 (NESDB, 1999). During its ill-conceived defence of the currency peg with the US dollar, the Thai central bank had spent nearly its entire stock of official reserves (nearly $30bn were committed to forward contracts to purchase the Thai currency), leaving the country with just $2bn in reserves (approximately two-week's import cover). Very quickly it became clear that the country needed a massive financial bailout, which was ultimately orchestrated by the International Monetary Fund to the tune of some $17.2bn.[11]

That some of the foundations for Thailand's meteoric growth were, for much of the 1990s, built on weak foundations (Krugman, 1994, 1998) was not initially obvious, at least not to the average observer of the newly found wealth and conspicuous consumption. For several decades, the country had grown by a massive workforce expansion in its manufacturing and export industry. Millions of farmers' sons and daughters had left the countryside to find employment in the country's rapidly expanding industrial sector.[12] Very little of this significant economic success, however, seems to have been based on improvements in productivity (Krugman, 1994). Compounding this, as the 1990s progressed, was the significant contribution of overinvestment (fuelled by easily available foreign loans at low rates) on the economy's growth rate. As early as 1994/95, standard financial variables, including total debt to GDP ratios, the rapidly rising foreign indebtedness, and the strengthening US dollar to which the Thai currency was pegged (negatively affecting Thai exports), indicated that not all was well with the economy.

A large number of warning flags with regard to the sustainability of this growth record were visible long before the events of spring and summer 1997. These included crony capitalism, a blatant disregard for credit and currency risk or returns on investment considerations, the structural problems of the Thai economy, the country's comparatively low (post-primary) education levels versus its main competitors, a worsening income distribution, outright theft of corporate assets, and financial authorities turning a blind eye to imprudent lending practices. A visiting delegation from the IMF had already sounded warnings on the risks associated with Thailand's pegged exchange rate system in early 1994. In spring 1996, the local financial press ran a series of reports on the precarious state of Thailand's economy.[13] By June 1996, the IMF pointed out that Thailand's widening current account deficits were increasingly exposing the country to currency speculation. These warnings not only went unheeded, but were vociferously disputed by government agencies, most notably the county's central bank.

Export growth had significantly dropped in 1996, and would continue to wane in 1997. Some of the largest financial institutions had run into financial difficulties in 1996 and early 1997. In 1996, the Bangkok Bank of Commerce, one of the supposedly more advanced financial institutions, was closed down after the discovery of massive insider fraud and overstated earnings. Finance One, the largest of the so-called finance houses, and 15 other finance houses were quickly to follow. By December 1997 the government had shut down a further 56 financial institutions. Finance houses were financial institutions allowed to borrow and lend funds, but not allowed to offer a range of other banking products. As a result these institutions frequently borrowed short (including low interest foreign funds) and lent long (primarily in domestic currency), operating under an illusion of low risk, in the firm belief that a) the baht peg to the US dollar was sacrosanct, and b) that the government would bail them out in case of threatened insolvency (as it had a decade earlier during another banking crisis). An additional factor was that none of the money at risk was their own, and that private assets could, to a large extent, not be seized, as the country had no provisions in its bankruptcy laws to allow for this.[14] At the time, the initial closures of finance houses were still largely interpreted as isolated events. The near collapse of the economy after July 1997 came as a surprise to many national and international observers.

Ultimately, the economy's economic deflation led to the permanent closure of two-thirds of the county's finance houses, mergers and takeovers of several commercial banks, a severe credit retrenchment, massive asset deflation, repeated re-capitalizations of the surviving financial institutions, and the socialization of the larger part of the existing private commercial sector debt. In the process of defending the Thai currency from waves of speculation against it prior to July 1997, the Bank of Thailand (BOT) had used up over 95 per cent of the country's foreign reserves. The total cost of keeping the financial system afloat was immense.[15] From early 1997 to mid-1999 the BOT, through the Financial Institutions Development Fund (FIDF), delivered an estimated $40bn (some 22 per cent of GDP) in emergency funds to some of the very same finance institutions that had been instrumental in causing the crisis in the first place. Some of these finance institutions initially (prior to 2 July 1997) used these funds not to repay their debts but to put further pressure on the currency by swapping them into foreign currency and subsequently siphoning these emergency funds off to foreign accounts.[16] Most of these emergency funds were never repaid or recovered upon the closure or forced merger of these finance institutions, and eventually were added to the public debt burden.

Several factors had conspired to lead to the state of national insolvency. Of paramount importance was the combination of fraud and government complicity (many of the owners of the family-run finance houses had close links to the government, were part of it, or included members of parliament).[17] This was aided by supervisory ineptitude (by defending the currency peg to the last, and effectively lending funds to the very same domestic players who had speculated against the currency) and massive overinvestment in assets of dubious value (leading, for example, to a 50 per cent oversupply in office space in 1997–1999).[18] Many domestic observers perceived the acceptance of the emergency IMF bailout package, and the associated conditions, as a humiliating step. Not surprisingly, the IMF was soon blamed for the economic woes the country found itself in, while the crisis itself was mainly blamed on foreign arbitrageurs and hedge funds.

Enron

While not the largest bankruptcy case to date (WorldCom soon proved to be bigger), Enron ranks among the most infamous examples of earnings manipulations and corporate fraud in history. The speed of the firm's implosion was nothing short of amazing. Fifteen years of work to create a market capitalization of nearly $70bn (at its peak) were destroyed in a mere six weeks after the first official announcement of inconsistencies in the firm's financial accounts. The company, based on a supposedly unique skill set, set out to be the embodiment of the proverbial 'wind of creative destruction' (Schumpeter, 1934).[19] In the end, Enron was described as having artfully managed expectations (Langevoort, 2002a). Company executives had for several years woven a web of high growth expectations, while engaging in accounting manipulations to cover up the less brilliant financial reality of the firm.

At one time Enron was a sound business with a solid core.[20] This also extended, to a degree, to the newer business lines the company engaged in. While the meteoric rise of the company's stock valuation must be seen in the context of the stock market's expansion of the mid- to late 1990s, Enron did have a viable, if easily threatened, business plan (with reference to its post-pipeline business), with real profits. Originally a gas distributor with its own network of pipelines, the company had started life in the mid-1980s through a merger between two gas pipeline companies, Houston Natural Gas and InterNorth. With its stock peaking at around $90 in August 2000, it briefly became the seventh largest US company by market capitalization.

On the verge of transforming itself into a virtual company by divestiture of most of its physical assets, Enron was considered to be an example of the New Economy of the 1990s. In an effort to reduce its reliance on a low margin capital intensive business, the company strove to become a trading platform connecting suppliers and wholesale consumers of energy, with the aim of doing so more efficiently (and cheaper) than the market would. To achieve this, the company proposed to internalize the operations of the free market, borrowing vast amounts of capital to guarantee supplies and prices. Enron traded its first unit of electricity in 1994 and in November 1999 launched EnronOnline, the first global commodity trading website based on a proprietary trading platform.[21] Expanding on this first venture into electronic trading, the firm would soon attempt to cover anything that could be traded, including pulp and paper, metals, broadband services, and online movies. Enron also started dealing in and selling risk management products, including over-the-counter derivative contracts to cover its customers' exposure to price risks.

Essentially, the company was in the process of transforming itself into a trading company dealing in financial derivatives. Access to capital was crucial to carry out this line of business, which, in turn, meant that an outstanding financial rating was of paramount importance for its continued survival. This rating depended on various ratios calculated from the figures in the published financial statements. The value of Enron stock was crucial to maintaining the firm's financial viability and the pressure to maintain high stock valuations was likely a key factor in the earnings management which senior executives engaged in. To consistently match (and exceed) expectations became crucial to maintaining the ability to engage in business. In the process, Enron not only pushed the envelope of innovation with regard to its actual business transactions, but also started to aggressively push the envelope of traditional accounting methods. Ultimately, however, the firm's senior management went beyond cutting edge accounting and transgressed into financial fraud.

A major threat to Enron's business model was the relative ease with which competitors could create competing markets, resulting in diminishing profits and a perpetual search for new markets in which to operate. A trend towards lower operating margins, combined with ever larger debt positions and a worsening quality of assets, resulted in a push for revenue growth at all cost. Falling margins in its trading business in combination with a number of unsuccessful deals, and increasing amounts of debt to cover daily transactions and past acquisitions, eventually threatened to affect Enron's financial rating. This led to the creation of financial constructs for reasons that had less to do with economic reasoning and more to do with creating illusions of profitability. Enron increasingly relied on overstating earnings and the value of assets to maintain its financial standing.[22]

Enron frequently booked hypothetical future revenues as real present earnings. That many of these hypothetical future revenues from anticipated business deals might be unlikely to ever come about did not bother Enron's executives or, apparently, its auditors. The firm typically booked the present value of speculative or hypothetical future streams as current earnings. Enron had also created thousands of Special Purpose Vehicles (SPVs), which were and remain legal instruments used by many companies ostensibly to hedge risks, lower tax liabilities, and to offload unwanted assets. In contravention of existing laws and accounting standards, senior Enron managers (with the help of in-house legal counsel, external auditors, and investment bankers) used some of these SPVs to aggressively manipulate earnings in order to window dress the balance sheet. What these managers did not wish to be known was that Enron, in many cases, was still legally liable for these debts and that none of the related sales were compliant with existing accounting rules.[23] Where an SPV was set up to provide a hedge for the decrease in the value of certain assets, for example, Enron's management failed to inform markets that Enron was frequently party to both ends of the hedge, which defeated the very purpose of entering such an arrangement.

SPVs are frequently set up by corporations to acquire and finance specific assets. An SPV is typically a subsidiary company with an asset/liability structure and legal status designed to keep its obligations secure and separate from the parent company. Under certain conditions, an SPV's balance sheet does not have to be consolidated into the balance sheet of the parent. Where properly set up, and effectively controlled and financed by outsiders, an SPV can be of economic use to a company. Enron misused some of its SPVs to, among other purposes, hide debts and liabilities, offload unwanted assets (booking their 'sale' as 'earnings', frequently at inflated prices), obtain loans and then declare such loans as assets for the parent company, and book earnings from businesses which had not yet come into being. What made matters worse was the flagrant conflict of interest of Enron's then CFO Andrew Fastow, who set up, owned, and managed several of the more notorious SPVs, personally benefiting from the arrangements. This conflict of interest was conveniently swept aside when Enron's board of directors suspended on several occasions the company's code of conduct to allow Fastow to engage in this business arrangement (Powers *et al.*, 2002). Any hedge function of such deals was illusionary as Enron had typically funded crucial SPVs with its own stock, and ultimately remained responsible for the SPVs liabilities (in contravention of rules regarding the independence of SPVs). Effectively, many such vehicles had been created in order to move assets of poor quality and liabilities off the parent's balance sheet in transactions which technically allowed the booking of paper profits by the parent.

When Enron's stock started to decline, several SPVs became insolvent and liability for the losses reverted to Enron. This subsequently triggered revisions to past earnings reports, a worsening of debt ratings, and rapid declines in the value of Enron stock, resulting in yet more liabilities from other SPVs reverting to the company. Very quickly, Enron suffered a classic bank run, where the loss of credibility rapidly undermined what was left of its financial viability. The discovered manipulations of Enron's financial statements immediately raised concerns regarding the true state of the firm's economic position. A proposed takeover by rival firm Dynergy quickly collapsed after successive revelations of additional liabilities pointed to the possibility of further significant revisions to Enron's true position regarding assets and debts.

Enron's published results for 1998–2000 shed some light on underlying problems and a discerning eye might even then have detected inconsistencies in Enron's financial reporting. According to audited figures, Enron's annual net earnings rose from $125m to $979m between 1985 and 2000.[24] The firm's reported revenues increased to $40bn from 1998 to 1999, and to $100bn the year after. The revenue growth came from Enron's new economy trading business, as revenues from its old economy asset-rich businesses – including pipelines and water companies – stayed flat. Reported earnings, however, increased less steeply in this period than its reported revenues (which were already inflated). Pre-tax profits, for example, increased by $1bn in 1998, and then by only $500m in each of 1999 and 2000.[25] This suggests declining returns in the trading business, reflected in trading margins which collapsed from 5.3 per cent in early 1998 to 1.7 per cent in the third quarter of 2001.[26]

If Enron were simply a story of a business plan gone awry, a derivatives deal gone bad, or an economy which turned against it, the company's demise would remain spectacular, but of relatively little interest to this discussion. Of much greater interest is the story of human fallibility behind Enron's collapse. During much of its existence Enron may have acted within the broad constraints of the law and accounting rules.[27] To the surprise of many observers, the majority of the financial instruments Enron used were perfectly legal (although the way they were used often was not). This includes the SPVs, but not necessarily the way they were set up, operated, and the purpose for which they were created. Certainly, Enron did breach many GAAP and securities rules, but many of the instruments and accounting interpretations used were perfectly legal (at least in part). Arthur Andersen, Enron's auditor, approved the use of many of these instruments, which might have been seen (by Andersen engagement partners) as straining the rules, sometimes to the extreme, but not, necessarily, as breaking them. Ultimately, Andersen came to regret some of these interpretations, and the decisions by its quality control unit at company headquarters to allow them. Shortly before the collapse of Enron, Andersen finally did insist on a number of restatements (which in turn triggered Enron's downward spiral), but this was too late to avert blame from the accounting firm for having agreed to management's interpretations in the first place.

Enron's external auditor was frequently aware of the extremely risky accounting interpretations, but Anderson was not alone in creating or approving the many instruments and financial vehicles which led to Enron's demise. Some of the other big accounting firms were also involved in creating and/or auditing some of these instruments. A number of the more notorious SPVs which brought down the company, including LJM1 and LJM2, had been audited by KPMG (Morrison, 2004). And Anderson was not the lead auditor for some other major SPVs (Raptors I, II, III, IV), or the Braveheart venture (Morrison, 2004). Enron set up several thousand SPVs, partially designed to protect Enron's reported profitability in the two years immediately prior to its collapse. LJM1 ('LJM Cayman LP') and LJM2 ('LJM2 Co-Investment LP') essentially functioned as vehicles to stow and retrieve assets at will, used to move loss-making assets off Enron's balance sheet while allowing the booking of these transactions as 'sales' with related 'earnings'. Since Enron ultimately backed these vehicles financially, none of the sales and earnings were valid. The 'Raptors' were established to shield Enron from mark-to-market losses in various equity investments.[28] Using appreciated Enron stock to ostensibly hedge against volatile assets, this provided a temporary solution at best when Enron's stock started to lose value. Braveheart was devised by Enron in 2000 as a joint venture with Blockbuster (a US video chain) to build a 'video-on-demand' service that would allow customers to download films from the Internet. While the project never got past the test phase, and Blockbuster soon withdrew from the venture, Enron booked hypothetical future revenues through a sale of the involved 'assets' to yet another SPV it had set up specifically for this purpose (violating more GAAP rules on the way). None of these partnerships were legal, as they were never really separate from Enron. Outside investment was in fact guaranteed by Enron. Hence, any sales and profits were imaginary and had to be reversed (i.e. consolidated with Enron's financial books) once the true ownership of the assets and liabilities was revealed.

Compliance of these and many other of Enron's SPVs with US GAAP was largely illusory, and the overall combined effect was a massive distortion of the financial statements. In the opinion of the Enron bankruptcy examiner (Neil Batson), this led to an overstatement of profits by 96 per cent, of operating cash flows by 105 per cent, and an understatement of liabilities by 116 per cent in the final set of fully audited financial statements (Batson, 2003a). The subsequent consolidation with Enron's balance sheet led to massive restatements of its financial figures, and resultant loss of market confidence in the company.[29] Other parties, too, were instrumental in approving these instruments. Koniak (2003a, b), for example, emphasizes the role of lawyers in enabling corporate fraud by providing their seal of approval to corporate contracts and constructs (see also Powers *et al.*, 2002). Sale (2005) notes the key role banks played in the demise of Enron as counterparties to the deals at the centre of the scandal.

The main flaw in Enron's business plan was that, in the later years, much of the company's reported success was based on artificially inflated earnings. Somewhere along the way, Enron executives, bolstered by self-delusions of success and encouraged by a highly competitive winner mentality prevailing within the company, went beyond pushing the boundaries of even the most aggressive interpretations of accounting rules and firmly crossed the line into fraud. There is, however, a fine and ambiguous line between aggressive interpretation and fraudulent misrepresentation. It is often not easy to determine whether a particular financial statement represents accounting fraud until a scandal breaks. The details of Enron's collapse seem to indicate that the principals saw themselves as players in a tournament (Rosen, 1981; Becker and Huselid, 1992). Their job was not just to make money, but to make the most money – to create a firm, where success did not merely mean doing better than anybody else. It meant virtually destroying the next firm (see, for example, McLean and Elkind, 2003). This single-minded pursuit of first place by Enron's managers may have contributed to the firm's destruction. As they did so they firmly shed the behaviour patterns of the rational actor and displayed the behavioural infirmities described in typical cases of corporate fraud (Langevoort, 1996, 1998b; Krawiec, 2000).

The list of parties implicated in the Enron debacle is sobering. Several of the firm's senior managers have since been indicted and/or sentenced for fraud and breaches of financial regulations.[30] Then there are the directors of the company. Well qualified for the job, at least judging by their credentials, they were provided with an enviable governance charter, which, incidentally, would have met most of the stipulations of the US Sarbanes-Oxley Act 2002. Nonetheless, they failed miserably in their task as the ultimate monitors of the firm (Powers *et al.*, 2002). Captured by senior executives, mesmerized by the firm's paper performance and executives, or simply overwhelmed by the complexity of the deals, not a single director voiced any opposition to any of the executive decisions at the centre of the scandal. On several occasions the board waived the firm's code of conduct where this stood in the way of massive conflicts of interest and the self-enrichment of senior executives. Enron directors received above average remuneration for their services, and many had close links to the company or received funds from Enron for work not related to their function as directors. Why they did not raise any objections to questionable deals or to accounting interpretations they did not understand remains an open question. The United States Senate in 2002 commented on the role of the board in Enron's collapse and came to the conclusion that the board of directors was guilty of:

- fiduciary failure
- knowingly allowing Enron to engage in high risk accounting practices
- allowing inappropriate conflicts of interest

- exercising inadequate oversight of transaction and compensation controls and failure to protect Enron shareholders from unfair dealing
- allowing Enron to conduct billions of dollars in off-the-books activity to make its financial condition appear better than it was
- approving excessive compensation for company executives
- being compromised by financial ties between the company and certain Board members, and finally
- failing to ensure the independence of the company's auditor (US Senate 2002b).

The accounting profession's reputation was not enhanced by the Enron debacle. Arthur Andersen had already been disingenuous in its treatment of the many off-balance sheet vehicles set up by Enron. More damaging yet was the decision to shred documents related to its Enron audit after the SEC initiated an investigation of Enron's financial affairs (Cramton, 2002). As the firm's lead auditor, Andersen – once one of the world's five leading accounting firms with 28,000 employees in the United States and 85,000 worldwide – had profited generously from its association with Enron. During the last year of doing business with Enron, Andersen received revenues in excess of $50m, with non-auditing fees forming slightly over half of this figure. While this was less than 1 per cent of total year 2000 revenue for Andersen, Enron was the most substantial client for the firm's Houston office, which, by definition, violated any notion of independence.[31]

Over time, Andersen may have gained a reputation for cutting corners and a tendency to comply with the wishes of clients in its interpretation of auditing rules, as opposed to sticking to the spirit of the law. It was the lead auditor of a string of companies and organizations involved with auditing irregularities and/or spectacular financial collapse across at least three continents, including Boston Chicken, Waste Management, Sunbeam, the Baptist Foundation of Arizona, Global Crossing, WorldCom, as well as Enron (all in the United States), HIH Insurance (Australia), and the Asia Pulp and Paper Company (Asia).[32] A distinctive lack of effective internal controls may long-since have put Anderson on a trajectory with disaster (Turner, 2005).

In June 2002, Andersen's US division was found guilty by federal prosecutors of obstructing the course of justice with regard to the Enron investigation. Pre-empting its official punishment, Andersen had voluntarily agreed to stop auditing public companies in the US. The firm quickly dissolved after the guilty verdict which prevented Andersen from auditing public companies. In an interesting twist, in late May 2005, the Supreme Court overturned the company's 2002 Enron-related conviction by a Houston jury. This, to some degree, vindicated views that the decision by the Houston court to find Andersen guilty of obstruction of justice had less to do with law and more to do with a perceived need to find scapegoats for the demise of Enron (Morrison, 2004). The initial guilty verdict certainly brought down a whole company for the mistakes of a few. The 2005 decision to overturn the verdict, of course, came too late to resurrect the company. Still, as noted, Arthur Andersen had suffered a series of major audit failures, which may indicate some problems with the corporate culture at Andersen, especially with regard to ethics and professionalism (Toffler and Reingold, 2003; Wyatt, 2004; Turner, 2005). Andersen had no exclusive rights to a possible lack of moral or legal fibre within the accounting industry. The accounting industry as a whole, over the last 20-odd years, may have let its quest for consulting fees cloud its judgement on what auditing is about.

Enron's internal and external legal counsel set up and sanctioned the thousands of off-balance sheet vehicles and subsidiaries (at the last count, Enron had created more than 3,000 SPVs) including the infamous Raptors and LJM partnerships. Highly complicated and incredibly numerous, these vehicles had ostensibly been set up to diversify assets Enron no longer perceived as valuable or to offload derivative risk. Effectively, however, many of these vehicles were intentionally created and designed to make Enron's financial situation look better than it was. Many times, Enron was in effect dealing with itself, without divesting risk, and frequently booked paper profits, loans, and imaginary future revenue as real profits.[33] One additional reason for setting up the Byzantine system of subsidiaries and partnerships was outright tax avoidance (US Senate, 2003a, b). It is likely that all of the documents and agreements between the various business parties involved in the setting up and funding of these vehicles had been vetted, and deemed legal, by counsel.

Commercial and investment banks lent Enron much of the money it needed to run its business and issued billions of dollars of the company's bonds. Banks were frequently also counterparties to some of the more questionable deals (Sale, 2005). There is nothing wrong with extending loans to companies, except that some of these banks' officers knew that Enron was using a number of these deals to misrepresent its financial condition (by, for example, disguising loans as income in the years leading to its collapse). The list of banks involved in setting up and investing in the off-balance sheet vehicles represents some of the biggest names in international finance: J.P. Morgan, Morgan Stanley, Merrill Lynch, CE Capital, Canadian Imperial Bank of Commerce, Credit Suisse First Boston, Dresdner, Chase Capital, and Lehman Brothers. Citibank and J.P. Morgan Chase & Co. helped, for example, to devise accounting techniques known as 'prepay transactions', which Enron used to inappropriately count $5bn in loans as income. Both lenders recognized that the prepay transactions were essentially loans (Batson, 2002; Sale, 2005). In a large number of cases, the loans to off-balance sheet entities were guaranteed by Enron. In other cases, investment banks insured the loans with third parties against loss, or insisted that Enron insure these, which in essence made these deals secured loans.[34]

Promises of returns on investment in excess of 60 per cent per annum, and the fact that the CFO of Enron was listed as the manager in control of the LJM vehicles should have sounded alarm bells for most individual investors, bankers, and Enron's directors. Enron's directors waived the firm's ethics code to allow its own CFO to run some of these vehicles. Instead, directors should have asked why Enron should want to enter such an arrangement when the counterpart promised 60 per cent in profits from the deal to prospective investors. Investors and the directors of the board may be able to claim ignorance when it comes to complicated financial transactions. The financial experts and the lawyers of these banks, however, are highly trained and well paid to recognize and avoid what effectively amounted to pyramid schemes, yet not a single one objected to the rosy projections. Nor did these experts object to the fact that the controlling officer of the LJM vehicles was the CFO of Enron, Andrew Fastow (neither did the banks' legal counsels, see Cramton, 2002, and Sale, 2005). There were no objections to the fact that Enron was the sole trading partner of these vehicles, the source of the exorbitant profits, the chief financial supporter, and ultimately responsible for their potential default.

Most financial analysts did not fail to laud Enron up to the day preceding its bankruptcy, first touting the firm as an innovative leader then announcing, in some cases until the day before the public announcement of Enron's bankruptcy, that the firm would rebound. Hardly an analyst downgraded Enron before it entered bankruptcy proceedings. The naïve trust and excessive optimism in all things connected to Enron can be seen in the fact that some of these financial experts invested not only their bank's money in these ventures, but also their own capital.[35] With a few notable exceptions, the financial press followed the lead of these analysts in praising the company nearly to the very end of its existence.[36]

The US Securities and Exchanges Commission (SEC) failed in monitoring the activities of Enron until it was too late. The SEC had also given Enron blanket exemptions from a number of depression era securities laws intended to protect investors. In particular, in 1997, Enron was granted an exemption from key aspects of the Investment Company Act 1940 for present and future projects which allowed the firm to escape accountability and oversight on many of its derivatives deals. This occurred despite the fact that Enron was turning itself into an investment firm, and had received earlier exemptions from oversight with regard to energy derivatives trading.[37]

US politicians and legislators accepted significant contributions to their election funds and projects from Enron, and frequently complied with Enron lobbying efforts. The company was granted exemptions from a number of oversight regulations with regard to reporting on trading in certain derivatives instruments. Of particular note is the role of Wendy L. Gramm and her husband (now former) US Senator Phil Gramm. Wendy Gramm, as chairwoman of the Commodity Futures Trading Commission, pushed through a key regulatory exemption on 14 January 1993, exempting Enron's trading of futures contracts in response to a request for such action by Enron in 1992. Five weeks later, she left her post with the Commission and joined Enron's board of directors, to serve (until 2001) on the audit committee with access to key financial information about the company. Enron was a significant source of campaign financing for (now former) US Senator Phil Gramm. In December 2000, Senator Gramm helped push the Commodity Futures Modernization Act (regulation that deregulated energy commodity trading) through the US Congress. The passage of this Act granted Enron a complete exclusion for energy trading companies from financial or disclosure requirements respecting portfolios of over-the-counter derivative securities. Enron thereby achieved something available to no other leading dealer in derivative contracts, namely, the complete exemption of its activities from federal supervision and oversight, which enabled Enron to operate an unregulated power auction market (Enron Online).

The US Internal Revenue Service (IRS) was and still is lost over the complexity of Enron's tax schemes, and was unable to determine Enron's tax liabilities, or whether the tax schemes were at all legal. According to the US Senate's *Enron: The Joint Committee on Taxation's Investigative Report*, the company, in the four years between 1996 and 1999, told shareholders it had made \$2.3bn in profits, while at the same time reporting \$3bn in losses to the tax authorities (US Senate, 2003b). The report also notes that between 1998 and 2000, total compensation to the top 200 executives at Enron increased from \$193m in 1998 (about \$1m on average each), to \$1.4bn in 2000 (about \$7m each) – which for 2000 represented one and a half times the company's total reported earnings for that year. The Senate report concluded that:

- Eighty per cent of Enron's foreign entities were inactive shells that did not hold, and were not engaged in or associated with, any ongoing business.
- Between 1990 and 1995, Enron paid approximately \$325m in federal income taxes, paid virtually no federal income taxes from 1996–1999 and paid only \$63m in federal income taxes for 2000–2001.
- Ken Lay, Enron's former CEO, was given a \$7.5m revolving line of credit with the company, refreshed immediately upon use. Between 1997 and 2001, Lay withdrew a total of more than \$106m. In 2001 alone he made 25 withdrawals for a total of \$77.5m. While all but \$7.5m was repaid, the loans were usually repaid with Enron stock that had earlier been granted to Lay.
- Just weeks prior to Enron's bankruptcy, a \$105m bonus programme was implemented for 60 key traders and 500 'critical' employees.[38]

Many explanations have been given for the implosion of the company. Bratton (2002) wrote one of the most detailed and thoughtful early pieces on the events surrounding Enron and suggested several possible causes: a company whose business plan simply got into trouble; a derivative play gone bad; the company as a den of thieves and rogues; and finally a story of bad accounting. It is likely that several or all of these factors played a contributing role. Yet, Enron might also be symptomatic of deeper running problems of the system of corporate governance and might have differed from other companies only by degree, rather than in substance (Bratton, 2002). While rogue agents doubtlessly played a role in Enron's demise, this scandal might also reflect an extreme example of more widespread flaws in the corporate governance system. Peasnell (2002) suggests several possible lessons to be learnt from the Enron debacle and interprets their relevance for accounting, governance, organizational design, and ethics:

- The pace of changes in the company may simply have overwhelmed any internal oversight and control mechanisms. The company had set up thousands of off-balance sheet vehicles to offload assets, leading to a situation where nobody within the company really knew the real state of the firm's finances.
- In reference to the board of directors who subsequently used the ignorance defence when questioned on the failure of the company, it is suggested that directors do not sign off on things they do not understand.[39] Hence, directors, as monitors, should not all too easily abrogate their control function.
- Persistent attempts to get around rules ultimately lead to breaking them.
- Without solid ethical foundations, a company cannot persist in the market.
- The auditor must not be caught up in the same mentality as the firm, especially when it comes to interpreting the propriety and legality of accounting decisions.

The preceding chapters have argued that the question of whether or not the top executives at Enron were aware of rules being broken could be of relatively minor importance to the dynamics of the firm's ultimate destruction. Instead it was suggested that behavioural factors common throughout corporate environments can lead to corporate disaster, without agents being criminally inclined or necessarily engaged in fraud (at least initially). This would also make gatekeeper failure less sinister than commonly assumed after scandals break. In essence, the question is whether cases such as Enron, WorldCom, Adelphia, ImClone, Xerox, Sunbeam, and so forth are mere outliers and examples of aberrant behaviour, or display patterns common to corporate environments.[40]

Germany's Neuer Markt

Despite the headlines concerning the Enron cohort of earnings manipulations, the United States has not been alone in suffering recent corporate scandals. An entire market for technology stocks in Germany, the Neuer Markt, modelled on the NASDAQ of the US, was abandoned in late 2002 because of the impact of a string of accounting scandals concerning companies listed on the exchange. When this stock exchange was finally closed down, it had collapsed by more than 95 per cent in market value from its peak. Prior to the early 1990s, shares had played a relatively minor part in the investment decisions of the average German investor. This changed with the initial public offering in 1996 of then state-owned Deutsche Telekom. Equity investment was further encouraged with the internet and telecom boom that took hold of the country in the late 1990s. A contributing development was the broad adoption of the Anglo-Saxon concept of shareholder value as the defining feature of corporate existence. A crucial factor in winning investors over to the merits of share ownership was that most companies' initial public offerings at the time were enthusiastically recommended and marketed by Germany's most respectable banks. Less encouraging for the banks' reputation was the fact that many newly listed companies (in many cases newly created) were soon found to have issued unsustainably optimistic forecasts, manipulated their accounts, and knowingly issued misleading financial statements. The destruction of billions of Euros in shareholder value, while chief executives were busy selling off their own shares not long before the fall from grace of the companies they managed, for a time tarnished the very idea of equity investment in Germany.

The weaknesses of the corporate governance system in Germany were exposed through a large number of corporate frauds which surfaced during the early years of the current decade. These frauds involved firms which had invented nearly all of their revenues (Comroad,[41] Flowtex), overstretched their finances (Kinowelt, Brokat), and made widely inaccurate earnings forecasts while falsifying financial statements (EM.TV). One of the most egregious accounting frauds in Germany concerned Comroad, which made up nearly 100 per cent of its revenues by reporting sales to businesses that did not exist. What really hit investors' confidence in German corporate governance was that officially Comroad's auditor KPMG, supervisory agencies, banks, and analysts were not aware of this until a journalist broke the story after having tried, and failed, to locate the company's major customers in Asia (Daum, 2003).

For the most part, the committed frauds were audacious, but hardly innovative. Flowtex leased out machinery that it did not possess, to customers it did not have, and then leased it out again, resulting in Germany's largest accounting and corruption scandal to date.[42] EM-TV purchased the broadcasting rights to the Formula One car racing franchise and Jim Henson Co. of the United States,[43] and subsequently issued grossly misleading revenue figures. Brokat purchased other companies for close to €1bn with inflated stock, only to sell them off 12 months later for €25m, and finally went into bankruptcy only two years after having been named 'Entrepreneur of the Year' by auditors Ernst & Young. Metabox repeatedly announced the successful sale of hundreds of millions of Euros worth of products without having any actual sales.

Not on this list of firms disgraced by malfeasance and outright theft is Deutsche Telekom, which caused the greatest destruction of share value in German corporate history to date. More an example of hubris and incompetence than outright fraud, the company paid some $50bn for vastly overpriced overseas telecom companies (e.g. Voicestream of the US), and 3G telecom licences auctioned off by the German government.[44] Ron Sommer, the former CEO responsible for these misallocations, did not face substantial negative financial consequences for these mis-steps, other than being asked to retire from the firm in 2002, at the age of 50, with a full multi-million Euro severance and pension package.[45] That the various boards of directors, external auditors, and regulators did not notice a thing amiss (or if they did, kept it to themselves), or investigate until after the frauds were discussed in the popular press, says much about the weak state of corporate governance in Germany. Corporate governance in Germany had led to a perverse incentive system where the rewards for fraud were massive, while potential punishments were negligible. The profession of public auditors, meanwhile, gained a reputation for being too liberal in signing off audits for firms. As noted, Germany's leading banks did not improve their image during that time either.

It was the profession of auditors who received most of the blame, as they did not in a single instance uncover the frauds their clients had committed. This is a sad verdict for a profession. The large number of companies that brought the Neuer Markt into disrepute (to the extent that international fund managers were no longer allowed to invest in that market) gave the entire German stock market a reputation for lawlessness. The collapse of the Neuer Markt wiped out some €250bn in shareholder value in just two years and, for a while, effectively destroyed the German capital market for newly created companies. It ultimately led to the demise of an entire segment of the country's stock markets; even Germany's main stock exchange suffered a 70 per cent decline in market value (at its worst in 2002). Some blue chip companies suffered declines up to 90 per cent in capitalization, in part due to scandals of their own and the general decline in market valuations, but in part also due to a general mistrust of corporate Germany.

The fraudulent activities of company executives and the gross failure of the entire corporate governance system in Germany led to the introduction of the Transparency and Disclosure Law (Germany, 2002), and the German Corporate Governance Code (GCCC) 2007 (Germany, 2007). These sought to address some of the perceived shortcomings of the system of managerial control in Germany. Established to 'promote the trust of international and national investors, customers, employees and the general public in the management and supervision of listed German stock corporations' (Germany, 2007, Foreword), the GCCC combines statutory regulations with recommendations and suggestions to promote 'good' and 'responsible' corporate governance for the management and supervision of listed companies. The code is primarily an example of self-regulation by the corporate sector, and complements the 'comply-or-explain' rule of the Transparency and Disclosure Law 2002. Deviations from the listed recommendations must be disclosed and explained in annual financial statements.

Parmalat

The late 2003 bankruptcy of Italian food giant Parmalat, revealing debts of over €14bn, was the largest corporate failure in European history to date. Until Parmalat collapsed, the 66-year-old founder and lifetime CEO, Calisto Tanzi, was a highly regarded business man in Italy. By early 2003, Parmalat was the largest Italian food company and the fourth largest in Europe, controlling some 50 per cent of the Italian market in milk and milk-derivative products. Behind Parmalat's façade as an international company with some 36,000 employees, however, was a financial scheme to siphon off funds through a network of 260 international offshore entities. Parmalat's finances were in poor shape from the late 1980s, as the result of a number of ill-conceived investments.[46] Parmalat drew on a network of international banks to provide it with funds to run unprofitable ventures and to repay earlier credits. The list of banks includes some of the biggest in the international financial system and includes Bank of America, Citigroup, J.P. Morgan, Morgan Stanley, UBS, Deutsche Bank, Banco Santander, and ABN. Some of Italy's largest banks were also represented: Capitalia (Rome), S. Paolo-IMI (Turin), Intesa-BCI (Milan), Unicredito (Genoa-Milan), Monte dei Paschi (Siena).[47]

While accumulating losses, and with debts to the banks rising, Parmalat relied on a network of offshore companies to conceal losses by reclassifying them as assets. The company continued to issue bonds, the security for which was supposedly being provided by the liquidity represented by the offshore schemes and fictitious assets held in offshore accounts. The largest banks to place bonds included Bank of America, Citigroup, and J.P. Morgan. These banks, like their European and Italian partners, rated Parmalat bonds as sound financial paper, when they should have known that they were of questionable quality (Citigroup, for example, had been instrumental in setting up Parmalat's accounting system). Parmalat used various methods to move debts off the company's consolidated financial statements including fictitious sales of Parmalat products to subsidiaries using falsified invoices and charging costs and fees to make the sales look legitimate; issuing credit notes for the amount the subsidiaries supposedly owed it, and taking these to banks to raise money; and transferring resultant liabilities to off-book subsidiaries, based in offshore tax havens. In entangling itself in costly financial operations in order to hide its state of insolvency, Parmalat followed a tradition well rehearsed at Enron. While this provided a public impression of a successful and growing company, such transactions aggravated an already unsustainable position.

By the late 1990s, the first warning signs were raised by financial observers. In 1999, a partner in the Buenos Aires offices of accountants Deloitte & Touche internally filed concerns about Parmalat's Latin American operations. Parmalat subsequently threatened to terminate Deloitte's Parmalat business in Argentina, and Deloitte – having taken over as Parmalat's worldwide auditor in the previous year – ultimately certified the accounts.[48] Other Deloitte partners also had serious concerns. In March 2003, Deloitte's Maltese partners questioned a $7bn intercompany transfer (subsequently revealed to have been fictitious). Similar concerns were raised to Deloitte's New York Headquarters by Deloitte's engagement partner for Parmalat Brazil. These objections were rejected, and the Brazil engagement partner was eventually taken off the Parmalat account. Deloitte insists that it behaved properly, pointing out that the official investigation of Parmalat began only after Deloitte Italy, in October 2003, drew attention to irregularities in Parmalat's financial dealings.[49] In 1999, Parmalat executives had transferred the activities of three shell companies to Bonlat, the Cayman Islands firm at the centre of a fictitious Cuban milk deal.[50] By 2002, Bonlat's fictitious assets had grown to a point that the company had to set up another Cayman Islands-based investment fund (Epicurum) to take over some of its recorded assets. Epicurum finally attracted the attention of auditors and Italy's stock market regulator in November 2003. On 19 December 2003, suspicions were further raised when Parmalat failed to make a €150m bond payment. This was odd, as Parmalat had claimed to have nearly €4bn in cash in a Bank of America account held by Bonlat. When Bank of America disputed the existence of such an account, Parmalat was forced to admit that the €4bn did not exist. This was the first revelation in the scandal that turned Parmalat into Europe's Enron. Total debts of over €14bn, eight times the amount on the books, were ultimately revealed.

Summary

Investors, whether based in Asia, Europe, or the United States, desperately wanted to believe in the tale of never-ending profit increases that a large number of companies and market players had so successfully spun during the second part of the 1990s. Regardless of any over-optimism that may exist in the market at any one time, investors should be able to have reasonable confidence in published financial accounts, experts' legal opinions, and boards of directors. Hence, investors should be able to trust the verification process which oversees the senior management of listed companies. This is, after all, one of the reasons for the publication of financial statements. The reputational intermediaries who sign off on the legal compliance of specific corporate transactions and their ultimate accounting treatment provide a seal of approval on which the investor must be able to rely.

That the trust of investors and the general public was betrayed in so many instances leaves the monitoring system of corporate governance and the underlying theory open to severe criticism. How good is a corporate system if it allows massive periodic and unexpected failures?[51] Enron in particular will leave an indelible mark in corporate history and in the minds of auditing partners. With the passage of the Sarbanes-Oxley Act 2002, the creative accounting of Enron and WorldCom has already led to the biggest changes to company rules in the United States since the 1930s. It also led to the demise of one of the former Big-5 accounting firms. Whether this Act will prevent future Enrons is another question. The implications of having fewer big accounting firms will also need to be taken into account. Chapter 8 discusses the implications of the analysis of the preceding chapters for corporate governance policy and offers suggestions on how a behavioural approach can add value to the rational actor approach.

8 Implications for governance policy

> Financial statements can conform to every technical rule and be accompanied by clean audit opinions. But if they don't paint a true and understandable picture of the actual financial condition of a company, they can be materially misleading and fraudulent.[1]

The reputational intermediary model of corporate governance is put to question when accountants, lawyers, and board directors engage in reputation-depleting activities to a degree not predicted by the model. Standard economic theory on choice behaviour would especially appear to conflict with observed behaviour where the potential damage to reputation and wealth far exceeds expected rewards. With regard to recent corporate scandals, neither reputational concerns nor potential penalties prevented reputational intermediaries from engaging in activities which caused damage to themselves and investors. A lack of rationality in agent behaviour is not the only reason for this. Rationality may in part prevail, but individuals take into account factors that lead them into not fulfilling their role as gatekeepers. While it might be possible to reconcile some of these factors with a rational decision-making framework by suitably modifying the utility function, it has been stressed in the preceding text that judgement and decision-making may systematically depart from the predicted outcomes of standard economic choice theory because of the subjective nature of perception and updating.

Concerns about gatekeeper independence have a long history in the United States and elsewhere, auditor independence being at the centre of such concerns (Goldman and Barlev, 1974). Implemented after the financial frauds of the 1920s, the US Securities Exchange Acts 1933 and 1934 stressed the need for auditor independence. More recently, auditor independence issues were again raised in the 1970s, with the sudden collapse of a number of major companies whose certified financial reports had provided no indication of financial difficulties.[2] This scrutiny continued into the 1980s with important court cases against auditing firms and a number of US Congressional hearings.[3] The growing importance of non-audit service provision by accounting firms during the 1990s again raised questions with regard to the feasibility of auditor independence.[4] These concerns were re-emphasized at the turn of the new century when the SEC found that more than 85 per cent of the audit partners of PricewaterhouseCoopers LLP had violated SEC independence rules (SEC, 2000a). About the same time, perceived abuses in the field of financial reporting increased worries about the reliability of corporate disclosure (see then SEC Chairman Arthur Levitt, 1998). The Enron cohort of scandals once more brought these concerns to the forefront of the discussion.

From the late 1980s onwards there has developed a paradigmatic approach to 'good' corporate governance for companies in terms of an overall focus on appropriate internal control and risk management procedures within the relevant entity. Responsibilities for such procedures lie with board members (both executive and non-executive) supported by a formal structure of board committees, and also by increased emphasis given to the role of audit, both internal and external, as a mechanism for ensuring appropriate governance procedures. The development of this paradigm was given significant impetus by the influential COSO report (COSO, 1992) in the US, and in the UK the work of the Cadbury Committee (see Collier, 1997), as subsequently revised and taken forward by the Greenbury[5] and Hampel Committees,[6] led to the development of the Combined Code covering various aspects of corporate governance.[7] The Code is not statutory and adherence to the Code is not mandatory – but the Stock Exchange listing rules issued under the aegis of the Financial Services Authority require disclosure of non-adherence.

The Sarbanes-Oxley Act further strengthened the regulatory underpinnings of the governance paradigm outlined above, requiring management to report on the effectiveness of internal controls and the external auditor to give an opinion as to the suitability of that management assertion. The Act also requires the external auditor to report directly to the audit committee with respect to accounting policies which are critical to the overall picture presented by the financial statements, and further strengthens the position of the audit committee in terms of investigatory powers, resourcing, and the appointment and removal of the external auditor.[8]

In the UK, post-Enron, the government together with the Financial Reporting Council set up a number of investigatory committees and commissioned reports *re* the role and duties of non-executive directors (Higgs, 2003)[9] and *re* the role and duties of audit committees (Smith, 2003).[10] In July 2003 a revised version of the Combined Code was published by the Financial Reporting Council. This, although not radically different from the previous version, did *inter alia* require that for larger listed companies non-executive directors should comprise at least half the board. The 2003 revision also provided for 'a strengthened role for the audit committee in monitoring the integrity of the company's financial reporting, reinforcing the independence of the external auditor and reviewing the management of financial and other risks'.[11]

However, although this paradigm commands widespread support from companies, the investing community, regulators, and other stakeholders,[12] it has not gone entirely unchallenged. These challenges have come from those who consider such a framework to be both costly and likely to stifle enterprise and risk-taking, from those who question the ability of non-executive directors to satisfactorily perform the variety of roles expected of them,[13] and from those who argue that the 'approved' governance mechanisms put in place have been demonstrably ineffective in checking corporate irregularity to date and are unlikely to be any more effective in the future (Clarke *et al.*, 2003).

It is also questionable whether general declines in morality can fully explain corporate scandals and the failure of gatekeepers to prevent them. There is no convincing argument to suggest that the Enron cohort of corporate scandals, for example, differs from earlier waves of corporate wrongdoing by more than detail and degree.[14] Instead, the present discussion stresses the failure of rational choice models of judgement and choice-making to fully account for agent behaviour. This is a key factor contributing to gatekeeper failure, which this research considers to be at the heart of corporate governance breakdowns (see Coffee, 2002, for an elaboration of this argument). What has been termed 'infectious greed' may well have contributed to the wave of corporate scandals of the recent past.[15] However, the main contribution of greed to governance failure may be through a distorting effect on rational judgement and decision-making (Cunningham, 2002).

Regulatory regimes play a major part in (minority) shareholder protection (Black, 2001a, b; Masulis, 2006; Mullineux, 2007). The level of protection varies across countries, and for the purpose of a policy review it is useful to note crucial differences between the UK (and other EU) and US regulatory regimes. Creditors are traditionally favoured in the UK, while the US offers relatively strong protection to debtors, including Chapter 11 protection. *Ex post* litigation by shareholders in the US is strongly emphasised over *ex ante* scrutiny in the UK, and disclosure requirements in the US are generally deemed to be lower than in the UK (Mullineux, 2007).

The Sarbanes-Oxley Act 2002 prescribes a large body of rules to which adherence is mandatory (including Section 404 which imposes heavy penalties on CEOs and CFOs if a corporation's internal controls are found to be inadequate). The Combined Code on Corporate Governance of the UK, in contrast, is a set of principles to which major corporations must adhere on a voluntary comply-or-explain basis. This provides considerable flexibility in terms of adoption of the various principles and recommendations. Audit and accountancy standards in the UK, too, are different from those in the US. With regard to boardroom duties the UK approach relies less on detailed rules and regulations, and more on principles-based best practice codes.

The significant differences between the US and the UK systems have given rise to the argument that there may not be an identifiable Anglo-American corporate governance model, especially with regard to the purpose and focus of the financial accounts (Bush, 2005). The focus of financial accounts in the UK may be closer to serving the interests of the shareholders than is the case in the US, which has been interpreted to be focused on assuring accurate market pricing (Bush, 2005; Mullineux, 2007). This difference is significant and would imply a concentration in the US on the accounts being consistent with the value of shares traded, contrasted with the focus of the UK approach on the accounts being an indicator of capital being used efficiently (Bush, 2005).[16] The British reporting model gives the shareholders the right to know anything that is of significance to form an opinion on a firm's stewardship, as distinct from forward valuation.

UK accounting standards and codes apply to all companies, not merely to listed companies only as in the US. Supplementing company law, the UK approach defines key accounting principles with an emphasis on substance rather than form, and its focus on a true and fair view of a company's state of financial affairs goes beyond the relatively simple checks for compliance of the audit regime in the US. Public oversight of auditors has undergone significant changes post-Enron, away from the traditional self-regulatory oversight by professional bodies. This is done by the Public Accounting Oversight Board (PAOB) in the US, and by the Financial Reporting Council (FRC) in the UK.

Post-Enron, the FRC assumed the functions of the Accountancy Foundation for oversight of the accounting profession, replacing traditional self-regulatory oversight by a professional body. This has led to a unified, independent UK regulator with the roles of setting accounting and audit standards and practices, pro-actively enforcing and monitoring these, and overseeing self-regulatory professional bodies. Within the FRC, the Public Oversight Board is the operating body responsible for independent oversight of the regulation of statutory auditors, monitoring the quality of the auditing function, oversight of the regulatory activities of the professional accountancy bodies, and reviews of audits of sample firms. Professional accounting bodies in the UK changed their regulations with the effect that the lead audit partner has to be rotated within five years, and partners and senior employees of audit firms are not allowed to take up employment with a company they audit within two years of leaving their audit firm.[17] Following the recommendations of the Smith Report (Smith, 2003), the key audit relationship has been transferred from executive directors to the independent audit committee, and the independence of the audit committee has been strengthened by the inclusion of at least one independent non-executive director with significant financial experience.

The significant differences in regulatory regime between the UK and the US call in question the existence of an Anglo-Saxon corporate governance model. Nevertheless, while the regulatory regime undoubtedly will have an influence on the level of protection of non-controlling shareholders against self-dealing (as is demonstrated in cases where governance is practically absent – see Black, 2001a, b), this book has stressed that no matter what system is in place and how strongly it is enforced, cognitive and social factors may interfere with the operation of even the best (if one existed) corporate governance system.

It is suggested that the inclusion of behavioural insights can add significantly to the understanding of the causes of governance failures. This book is intended to complement the important discussion of the impact on governance quality of differences between governance systems (La Porta *et al.*, 1998; Bush, 2005; Masulis, 2006; Mullineux, 2007) and as a result of particular accounting issues (Clarke *et al.*, 2003). The nature of human behaviour allows no room for complacency. This is particularly relevant if the confidence in the effectiveness of a particular governance system is based on a significantly simplified, and in many aspects flawed, model of human choice behaviour. As long as policy relies on a model of decision-making which ignores important aspects of agent behaviour, any governance model is likely to be less effective than hoped for.

Before focusing on the implications of behavioural decision theory for governance policy, it is useful to note the importance of two additional gatekeepers in corporate governance. These two agents do not appear to have come under as much scrutiny for their crucial role in the more recent corporate scandals as have accountants and board directors. Apart from an extensive academic discussion (and a number of Enron-related US Senate hearings), investment bankers and securities lawyers have largely escaped public discussion and the blame has been allocated to other gatekeepers, external auditors in particular.[18] This omission is not critical to the conclusions offered by the present research. Very similar cognitive and behavioural aspects of human decision-making can be invoked to help explain monitor failure by these two agents. It is suggested that the relative lack of discussion on the key role of these two intermediaries is detrimental to designing a more effective system of corporate oversight. What follows is a brief investigation of these two agents with a focus on Enron and the US. It is recognized that the legal and regulatory environment of, say, the EU is vastly different from that of the US. Nonetheless, the importance and role of bankers and lawyers in the EU (and elsewhere) as agents of corporate governance would seem to be broadly comparable.[19]

Bankers and lawyers in corporate governance

Accountants and board directors carry important monitoring and gatekeeping roles in corporate governance and bear key responsibility for accurate disclosure, the defining characteristic of US securities regulation (and a central ingredient to that in the United Kingdom, and elsewhere as well). In contrast, the roles and responsibilities of lawyers and bankers with regard to corporate scandals have not been the focus of broader discussion.[20] Lawyers and legal counsel are central players without whom very few of these scandals could have reached their destructive proportions. Legal opinion is sought for every major corporate transaction.[21] Lawyers are party to the drafting of corporate documents and contracts, and hardly a single securities document gets filed without review by legal counsel.[22] Investment banks are frequently counterparty to corporate transactions through which firms may later come to grief. These banks, in turn, rely on legal counsel for advice on the legality of respective corporate transactions.

Lawyers, bankers and Enron

The Texas-based law firm of Vinson & Elkins represented Enron and approved many of the transactions and instruments which, subsequently found illegal and in violation of securities laws, ultimately played a significant role in Enron's demise.[23] Meanwhile, Kirkland & Ellis, a Chicago-based law firm, represented numerous Enron partnerships, including many of the SPVs (including the 'Raptors' and 'Condor') at the heart of the financial frauds committed at Enron.[24] Investment banks Citigroup and J.P. Morgan, involved in numerous transactions, deals, and vehicles used by Enron to manipulate its earnings, testified in hearings before the US Congress that they relied on their own legal counsel for approval of these transactions (US Senate, 2002d).

Confirming this close working relationship and dependence on legal opinion by corporations, the court-appointed examiner for the Enron bankruptcy proceedings, Neil Batson, noted that Enron's external auditors (Arthur Andersen) demanded approving legal opinion by Enron counsel before signing off on specific accounting treatment and transactions (Batson, 2002). Batson (2002, 2003b) also provides evidence that Enron's bankers, led by Citigroup and J.P. Morgan, were not only aware of the company's wrongful conduct in handling certain transactions, but knowingly helped it, at times against internal objections. Many of Enron's transactions (including the infamous SPVs) were in conflict with existing laws and accounting standards. Specifically, some partnerships were buying assets from Enron (in a three-way deal via banks), and making trades with Enron, which Enron itself was financing.[25] Enron frequently booked loans as 'revenues', with the full knowledge of the involved banks, as Enron guaranteed the entire transaction (promising to pay back banks the original 'cost' of the transaction plus a fee – hence, the transaction constituted a loan). By obscuring the true level of debt it was carrying, this allowed Enron to present its finances in a better light to investors and ratings agencies. Investment banks assisted in setting up many of these vehicles (and in some cases owned or controlled them) which allowed the sham transactions to occur.[26]

Testimony (under oath) by banks' representatives (e.g. of Citigroup and Merill Lynch) corroborated the verdict that banks' officers were aware of the fraudulent intent of the transactions. This also confirmed that the banks were in full control of some of the intermediate vehicles set up to conduct some of these transactions, failing the arm's length criteria required for such vehicles (Enron controlled the remaining intermediate vehicles, and in very few instances did these SPVs meet the independence criteria as defined by regulations) (US Senate, 2002d). Enron's counsel, and that of Merill Lynch and Citigroup (and other banks) endorsed these transactions all the way. The legal terminology for this type of conduct is 'aiding and abetting' and 'co-conspiracy'.[27] Loans by these banks, packaged and booked by Enron as 'sales' in order to strengthen Enron's balance sheet, were guaranteed by Enron, and incorporated a guaranteed return (see Batson, 2003b).[28] The banks, in turn, ostensibly relied on legal opinions before signing the deals. However, the involved bankers were frequently aware that these 'sales' were hardly more than disguised loans.[29] This makes these banks, as knowledgeable principals to the specific transactions, accessories to the frauds committed by Enron's management. Legal counsel, advising on all of these transactions, in turn, share the blame for failing fiduciary duties to the firms they represented (i.e. the banks, leaving aside fiduciary duties to investors, and any concerns about legality).

Legal liability of corporate lawyers

The legal environment in which these two additional intermediaries (bankers and lawyers) operate in the United States differs from that faced by accountants and directors of the board. Nonetheless, a number of US laws and legal decisions from the 1990s have a common (negative) effect on deterrence of reputational intermediaries. Corporate lawyers in the US, for example, have for various reasons benefited from virtual immunity when it comes to litigation for their role in corporate collapse (Cramton, 2002; Koniak, 2003a, b). This group of lawyers is sometimes seen to operate in a 'law-free' zone (Koniak, 2003a). This refers to the fact that it is difficult (and rare) to successfully hold lawyers and law firms liable for financial frauds committed by their clients (Gordon, 2002; see also Sargent, 2004; Spiegel and Ohl, 2005). It is of interest to note that European bankers and lawyers (also accountants and members of the board), too, have escaped significant penalties for their involvement in the governance failures that, for example, led to the demise of Germany's Neuer Markt, Parmalat's bankruptcy, and the near collapse of UK insurer Equitable Life.

Corporate lawyers in the United States are largely shielded from litigation in a number of ways. The prospect for criminal prosecution, either by the SEC or the respective State Bar, is minimal (Koniak, 2003a; see also Macey and Sale, 2003). Private litigation against law firms would also appear to be largely ineffective, as private cause of action for liability against lawyers for aiding and abetting in securities fraud have been blocked by the Supreme Court since 1994.[30] The deterrent value of law suits was further undermined by legislation passed in 1995 which eliminated joint and several liability, and established heightened pleading requirements for plaintiffs.[31] Strong application of the *in pari delicto* doctrine effectively shields corporate and security lawyers in the US from malpractice liability by corporate clients, as long as some of the corporate client's employees can be shown to have committed a wrongful act (Spiegel and Ohl, 2005). The application of the *in pari delicto* doctrine applies despite the requirement of the Sarbanes-Oxley Act

2002 for legal counsel to report up-the-ladder where corporate wrongdoing is suspected (SEC, 2003f). In plain English, the *in pari delicto* doctrine provides the lawyer with a strong defence when it can be shown that asserted injuries arose out of illegal conduct on the part of the plaintiff's agents. This is almost always the case, as in securities cases the plaintiff frequently is the corporation which claims to have been harmed by the lawyer's conduct, and it typically was the corporation's own executives which caused the harm.[32]

As a result of these laws and legal decisions, securities lawyers frequently find that their profession provides a significant degree of protection from prosecution. Nancy A. Temple, the author of the (ambiguously phrased) email sent to David Duncan (then Andersen's engagement partner responsible for the Enron audit), urging compliance with the firm's 'documentation and retention policy' (interpreted by Duncan as an instruction to 'shred it all'), was still practising law in Chicago as this book was drafted.[33] Her email was central to Andersen's subsequent obstruction of justice conviction. Temple was the author of another email to Duncan, in which she advised amendments to an earlier draft memo by Duncan (where he indicated doubt about some of Enron's accounting entries). Specifically, she recommended deleting passages that might suggest that Andersen had concluded that Enron's release was misleading. She also asked for any references to herself to be removed from these communications. This may well have been the single most important document considered by the jury in its decision to find Andersen guilty.

It can be argued that lawyers (both in-house counsel and outside attorneys) are frequently at least passively involved in managerial wrongdoing.[34] A confusion of the roles of the corporate lawyer contributes to the ambiguity of position and duties. The securities lawyer may be seen as either totally committed to the client firm's management, or, alternatively, as a gatekeeper with responsibilities to the firm's owners and other stakeholders. Regardless of the controversy surrounding counsel's potential role and duties in client corporate governance, the notion of corporate lawyers as gatekeepers is not new. Prominent securities attorneys and law academics have regularly emphasized the corporate lawyer's duty to the public.[35] The SEC has long held the view that lawyers who know about clients' wrongdoing have a duty to prevent and/or report this.[36] Lawyers can withhold cooperation (including withdrawal) with client's agents (senior management) who are perceived as committing a wrongdoing, report up-the-ladder, and deny the provision of legal opinions.[37] A refusal by this reputational intermediary to vouch for the client sends a signal to third parties about the value of the transaction (Sommer, 1974; Sargent, 2003). Ironically, an ethical aspect of a counsellor's role, which advocates refusal to cooperate with a wrongdoing client, was expressly invoked in the American Bar Association's first Canons of Ethics of 1908,

> Canon §32: No client, corporate or individual, however powerful, nor any cause, civil or political, however important, is entitled to receive,

> nor should any lawyer render, any service or advice involving disloyalty to the law, whose ministers we are . . . or deception or betrayal of the public.
>
> (ABA, 1908)

Refusal by legal counsel to perceive the investors (and other stakeholders, excluding senior management) of client companies as the true client of the law firm, and thus to be shielded from harm, is hardly a tenable position for a profession. There is sufficient support for the view that the duties of the securities lawyer are sufficiently different from those of the criminal defence advocate to allow for gatekeeping roles by corporate lawyers.[38] The use of illicit methods of investigation against members of the board, authorized by Hewlett-Packard's senior management and initially defended by outside counsel Wilson Sonsini Goodrich & Rosati (WSG&R) as within legal limits (which it was not), illustrates the close relationship and resulting potential for conflicts of interest between lawyers and their corporate clients.[39] WSG&R represents about half of Silicon Valley's public companies, counselled many firms now under scrutiny for backdating stock options, and in some cases also served on their boards. The idea that WSG&R faced a conflict of interest by simultaneously acting both on the board and as legal adviser to some firms cannot be dismissed (*The Economist*, 16 September 2006).

Sarbanes-Oxley and lawyers

A number of provisions of the Sarbanes-Oxley Act required the SEC to issue rules governing the conduct of securities lawyers. Of relevance to the present discussion, section 307 of the Act specifies the inclusion of a rule requiring a lawyer to report to the company's chief legal officer or CEO if said lawyer possesses evidence that company agents are violating securities laws or in breach of their fiduciary duties.[40] Further, if the reporting lawyer does not receive an appropriate response after presenting such evidence, the lawyer is required to continue reporting up-the-ladder and notify the company's board of directors or an appropriate committee of that board of the alleged breach. The SEC subsequently drafted the rule in early 2003. A requirement for a lawyer to report to an outside agency if there is no appropriate response from the board was discussed at the time but not implemented by the SEC. The requirement for a 'noisy withdrawal' by counsel following an inappropriate response from senior executives or the board was not strongly implemented. The usefulness of the report-up-the-ladder requirement of the Sarbanes-Oxley Act is the subject of intense discussion, as it may fail to address the incentives that motivate corporate attorneys (Fisch and Rosen, 2003; Koniak, 2003a, b). One concern is centred on the wording of the portion of the adopted rule which deals with the definition of what constitutes a material violation. Specifically, a lawyer must report, first to the CEO or chief legal officer,

> credible evidence, based upon which it would be unreasonable, under the circumstances, for a prudent and competent attorney not to conclude that it is reasonably likely that a material violation has occurred, is ongoing, or is about to occur.[41]

This definition of what should actually trigger a response from a lawyer is not merely subjective but confused by the use of a double-negative in its formulation. A further criticism deals with the events that would require resignation of counsel (i.e. the specific conditions for a 'noisy withdrawal'). Assuming a lawyer came to the conclusion that the conditions of the standard defining a material violation were met, and evidence of fraud was subsequently reported to the CEO, the chief legal officer, or the board of directors, a lawyer still need not resign if he or she is informed that the board or a 'qualified legal compliance committee' (QLCC, set up by client firm) has received a second legal opinion which has concluded that the securities lawyer,

> may, consistent with his or her professional obligations, assert a colorable defense on behalf of the issuer (or the issuer's officer, director, employee, or agent, as the case may be) in any investigation or judicial or administrative proceeding relating to the reported evidence of a material violation.[42]

This means that a client firm can largely avoid its lawyer ever having to noisily withdraw by adopting a 'qualified legal compliance committee' (QLCC), since a lawyer's reporting obligations are, effectively, terminated with a report to that committee. Even if a lawyer were to overcome the convoluted definition of what constitutes a material violation, this part of the adopted rule would appear to largely prevent any signalling by the lawyer to agents outside the firm. Thus, where a board of directors is complacent or complicit, this may void much of the original thrust of section 307. As Koniak suggests,

> The SEC's rule states that the existence of a second lawyer, hired by the board, will relieve the reporting lawyer of the obligation to resign (or to go to the board personally and report the evidence), if the second lawyer either investigates the matter, recommends rectification, and sees that the company substantially implements those recommendations, or can come up with a colorable defense that 'may' be asserted in a subsequent proceeding. These are not alternatives. If rectification is required to stop a fraud, the existence of a colorable defense is simply not a sufficient alternative response.
>
> (Koniak, 2003b: 1277)

Rules and regulations prior to Sarbanes-Oxley would seem to prohibit lawyers from helping a client to commit fraud (Fisch and Rosen, 2003), and existing laws already made lawyers liable to SEC enforcement action (with evidently little effect in the past). It would also appear that section 307 may not have prevented Enron, as the level of complacency and complicity within that company had run all the way to the top and permeated the board. Therefore, criticisms with regard to section 307 of the Sarbanes-Oxley Act focus on the potential for success of the reporting requirement for legal counsel who suspects management fraud. For a number of reasons, there is merit in questioning the requirement of legal counsel to report up-the-ladder where a board of directors is compromised, as was the case at Enron and likely elsewhere.[43] A consciously fraudulent lawyer will hardly be induced to report on own fraudulent conduct, but cognitive biases work against self-indictment even for an honest lawyer.

One could ask what section 307 contributes to existing incentives for lawyers to report on fraud. However, this may not be the reason why this reporting requirement was created. Under earlier Canons of Professional Ethics (ABA, 1968) and the subsequently drafted Model Code of the American Bar Association (ABA, 1969, and revised thereafter), both of which define lawyerly conduct in the United States, a lawyer is encouraged to rectify or report incidences of fraud of deception by a client (thought it is not clear to whom). This would also appear to be the interpretation of most US State laws responsible (prior to section 307) for regulating and supervising lawyerly conduct (Koniak, 2003b). In sharp contrast, the American Bar Association, and many lawyers, have routinely insisted (and in later versions of the Model Code effectively formulated so) that client confidentiality trumps disclosure.[44] The report-up-the-ladder provision of section 307 of the Sarbanes-Oxley Act finally makes an explicit point of the legal requirement to report fraud and puts the force of federal law behind it. Section 307, as operationalized by the SEC, may not go far enough, but it is a step in the right direction for it emphasizes that legal counsel cannot hide behind attorney/client confidentiality concerns to ignore managerial fraud.[45]

Lawyers and cognitive bias

The operational effectiveness of requirements such as those incorporated in section 307 of the Sarbanes-Oxley Act is subject to many of the behavioural biases discussed in this book. This applies both to the interpretation of what triggers the requirement to report, as well as to what constitutes fraud, and how rigorously to respond to it. As always, the existence of a law does not ensure compliance to it. Cognitive biases act against discovery and action against managerial wrongdoing by counsel. Confirmatory bias, for example, may motivate counsel to 'interpret information in ways that serve their interests or preconceived notions' (Korobkin and Ulen, 2000: 1093). This refers the reader back to the two-stage model discussed earlier. Dissonance reduction by a lawyer associating with a client makes it less likely for the lawyer to recognize client misconduct, as this would be inconsistent with both the lawyer's self-interest, and the lawyer's self-image (of, say, being honest and competent). Self-serving biases typically 'arise when there is a reasonably high level of ambiguity surrounding a situation' (Langevoort, 2002b: 574), and there is no reason to assume that this should not also apply to the lawyer–client relationship. Taken together, such systematic biases generate a form of cognitive conservatism that makes a lawyer 'likely to dismiss as unimportant or aberrational the first few negative bits of information that she receives regarding the client or situation' (Langevoort, 1993 100–1). Escalation of commitment can be expected to further strengthen the belief in the accuracy of past decisions and the appropriateness of own conduct. It should be added that if reputational intermediaries (including lawyers) found ways to ignore existing laws and penalties before Sarbanes-Oxley, what is to prevent them from ignoring these now?[46]

Still, the up-the-ladder reporting rule is a step in the right direction (however convoluted a guide this may be, particularly with respect to what constitutes a trigger for such action). Potentially even more important would have been a 'noisy withdrawal' provision discussed in the early drafting of section 307 of the Act (but subsequently deferred by the SEC). This would have required counsel to terminate representation of the client if management persisted in misconduct, although further caveats apply with regard to the interpretation of events that should trigger such a response.[47] Notwithstanding the various concerns as to the role of lawyers in corporate governance, lawyer complacency in face of client misconduct/fraud is a disgrace and directly contributed to the recent corporate scandals: 'people and institutions broke the law: lots of people, lots of institutions, lots of laws . . . and many had lawyers showing them the way' (Koniak, 2003b: 1237).

Causes of gatekeeper failure

With reference to corporate governance in the United States, gatekeeper failure may be grouped into two broad, complementary, classes. The first group is economic in nature and refers to the decline in liability during the 1990s due to changes in the legal environment in which some groups of gatekeepers operate. A second group of reasons for gatekeeper failure has psychological foundations.

'Rational' causes for gatekeeper failure

The decision to commit a crime is a type of decision-making under uncertainty to which deterrence theory can be applied. Individuals will more likely commit crimes if the expected benefits exceed the expected penalties, defined as the product of subjective probability of being caught and the severity of the punishment.[48] Standard economic theory would, thus, predict that if liability risks decline, or when benefits of acquiescence increase, monitors and gatekeepers may be tempted to increasingly turn a blind eye to managerial wrongdoing. The relative low threat of legal liability in the United States from the mid-1990s onwards may have been a contributing factor to the acquiescence to, and direct involvement in, corporate frauds by gatekeepers (Coffee, 2002). Such causes for corporate failures are systemic in nature, referring to the legal framework within which agents move.[49] Sanctions can only do their (limited) job if they exist, are clearly defined, severe enough, and effectively and swiftly imposed (Wells, 2004). If a crime carries no real punishment, or the punishment is not systematically imposed, then agents can be expected to engage in higher levels of objectionable activities. Changes in the legal framework on legal liability which reduced the likelihood of being a defendant in corporate fraud class action suits may well have led to more risky behaviour by particular agents of corporate governance (Coffee, 2002; Koniak, 2000, 2003a, b). By decreasing the prospect of private and public enforcement, such changes in the legal and operating environment significantly reduced the risk of liability to specific gatekeepers in the US during the 1990s (see summary in Box 8.1).[50]

These changes may have altered the rational cost/benefit equation of acquiescence, direct fraud and/or sub-par performance vs. the potential and cost of litigation against gatekeepers. Making acquiescence less costly (while the benefits increased tremendously at the same time) partially explains why reputational intermediaries might be tempted to aggressively liquidate reputational capital (Coffee, 2002). Put simply, it paid them to do so, at least for a while, as potential risks and costs had been reduced.

Auditors and lawyers particularly benefited from these provisions, although, as Arthur Andersen was to find out, this benefit ultimately came at a significant cost. Given that deterrence can be framed in standard economic cost/benefit theory, the conventional remedy for this cause of corporate scandals is relatively straightforward, if not necessarily easy to implement given the considerable opposition from the affected gatekeepers. If agents respond in a rational manner to such incentives, increasing the risk of liability and the penalties for acquiescence to and participation in corporate fraud (and/or lowering the rewards gained from this) may help restore the link between undesirable behaviour and penalties. This link was certainly weakened by the cited laws and legal decisions. With reference to the United States, incentives towards acquiescence should be diminished by reversing or significantly curtailing some of the protection provided by the above listed acts and court decisions. Specifically this refers to the restoration of private litigation actions against reputational intermediaries for aiding and abetting securities fraud, and also a lowering of pleading standards and the re-introducing of a form of joint and several liability. This argues for Congressional overruling of the *Central Bank of Denver*, and the *Lampf, Pleva* decisions, which has not taken place to date. This argument also supports a reformulation of PSLRA and SLUSA to firmly allow private litigation in securities cases. In sum, these reversals or reformulations of existing law would increase the costs of negligence, acquiescence and complicity by accountants,

Box 8.1 Changes in the US legal environment with relevance to gatekeeper liability

1 Shorter statute of limitations applicable to securities fraud (*Lampf, Pleva, Lipkind, Prupis & Pettigrow* v. *Gilbertson* decision of 1991).[i]
2 Elimination of private aiding and abetting liability in securities fraud cases (the *Central Bank of Denver* decision, 1994).
3 The raising of pleading standards for securities class actions, disallowing joint and several liability, restricting the applicability of the RICO statute to securities fraud class actions, and adopting a protective safe harbour for forward-looking information (the Private Securities Litigation Reform Act (PSLRA) 1995).
4 The abolishing of state court class actions alleging securities fraud (the Securities Litigation Uniform Standards Act (SLUSA) 1998).

Factors that play into the effects of these four legal changes include

1 The increase in the provision and importance of profitable services not primarily related to the gatekeeper function (e.g. consulting services of accounting firms). This may yield a certain 'commodification' of auditors and lawyers. This is generally deemed to have had a negative impact on the quality of the provision of verification and certification services to the public by these reputational intermediaries.[ii]
2 The increase in the limited liability partnership (LLP) form of corporation of legal and accounting firms, reducing the incentive to monitor partners who might excessively defer to a client. This has an effect on the principal/agency setting within a gatekeeper firm, and exacerbates the internal monitoring problem. Both accounting firms and law firms in the United States increasingly adopted this corporate form during the 1990s.

Notes

i *Lampf* v. *Gilbertson* (90–333), 501 US 350 (1991).
ii Coffee (2002); Cramton (2002); Macey and Sale (2003); Koniak (2003a, b).

lawyers, and bankers. As a straightforward application of utility maximizing analysis, this would be expected to deter some negligence of duty and law breaking, and may contribute towards righting the cost/benefit scale which seems to have been tipped too far towards the perceived benefits of acquiescence and complicity at the cost of punishment.

Congress (with the passage of the Sarbanes-Oxley Act 2002) and the SEC (by implementing various sections) have partially acted upon some of these points, by increasing penalties for some acts and criminalizing certain other activities. Auditors are now barred from the provision of a comprehensive set of consulting services to their audit clients, and are also subject to regulation and oversight by a new public oversight office, moving auditing away from self-monitoring, which was seen to have failed to adequately monitor professional conduct of the industry.[51] Section 307 of the same Act (and subsequent formalization by the SEC) introduced the report-up-the-ladder requirement for securities lawyers when they suspect corporate fraud in a client firm. Further imposed were standards of internal monitoring and professional conduct on legal firms.[52] Congress also increased allocation of funds to the SEC, which may serve to enhance securities law enforcement. The Act did not, however, redraft the PSLRA, nor SLUSA. Neither was the *Central Bank of Denver* decision reversed. If a general lack of deterrence was the problem, this Congressional response may be deemed to be somewhat insufficient in reach and effect.[53]

'Irrational' causes for gatekeeper failure

Reforms which primarily emphasize enhanced enforcement of securities laws, increasing penalties for their violation, and pleas for more ethical behaviour by corporate players are a response which appeals to the rational side of individuals. As outlined throughout this research, these may fall critically short in preventing future governance failures. It is suggested that many standard prescriptions regarding the agency problem in governance are based on models of human judgement and choice behaviour which seriously underestimate the effect of bias. If gatekeeper problems were solely related to issues of deterrence, and agents largely adhered to the rational actor model, then changes to relevant laws and enforcement (including the changes introduced by Sarbanes-Oxley and suggested reversals of laws and decisions) could provide a significant and sufficient response by effectively raising the cost of acquiescence and fraud. No doubt such changes to the legal and regulatory environment are important, as there indeed would appear to be a need for a significant rebalancing of the acquiescence/compliance cost–benefit equation. This would, at the very least, narrow the degrees of freedom in which gatekeeping agents operate. However, there are many reasons why deterrence and reputational concerns may not have the effect expected by standard choice theory. Hence, it should not be expected that legal changes based primarily on increased penalties and enhanced detection efforts will provide a panacea to corporate governance problems.[54]

Scholars and practitioners increasingly feel the need to take into account how actors may deviate in their decision-making behaviour from the predictions of rational choice theories. The need for a more realistic account of human behaviour does not, however, imply that actors always fail to evaluate information in an unbiased way or make decisions which are always in conflict with axioms of utility maximization.[55] Individuals and groups can, given appropriate conditions and selected decision tasks, form judgements and make decisions in broad agreement with the predictions of rational expectations models. It is, however, important to recognize that deviations from the predicted outcomes of rational choice theories are significant, widespread, persistent, and systematic in everyday decisions.

Rational expectations models allow for a neat parameterization of variables, and formalization into mathematical models, which explains their widespread appeal. Yet, as useful as such models are for an analysis of choice decisions, they would seem to constitute a somewhat impoverished view of the spectrum of human choice behaviour, which may lead to misinterpretations of the causes of governance breakdowns. In particular, the interpretation of the individual as a basically rational actor may support the view that corporate scandals are primarily due to rogue executives, morally challenged gatekeepers, regulatory loopholes, and insufficient penalties. Such an interpretation is misleading, as it tends to overlook other fundamental causes underlying the neglect of laws, regulations, and duties by individuals and groups.

An investigation into the incentive effects of rules and regulations on individuals (and groups) requires an account of how these agents will form judgements and make decisions. A sound understanding of human choice behaviour, in turn, is fundamental to effective law and economic policy making. It was common, until not long ago, for researchers, policy-makers, and legal experts to base their analysis of human behaviour largely on assumptions consistent with standard rational choice theories.[56] The growing dissatisfaction with the empirical weaknesses of rational theories on choice has more recently led to the incorporation of insights from psychology and behavioural decision theory into academic research and policy prescriptions.[57] Such insights question the efficiency and effectiveness of the traditional incentives provided by the legal, regulatory, and financial framework within which agents operate. The brief discussion on lawyers and bankers in corporate governance has demonstrated that there are behavioural causes for the neglect of duties in addition to weak enforcement and ambiguous rules and regulations.

While the traditional economic model of decision-making focuses on choice rather than perception, the two cannot be separated. Any 'objective reality' that exists is perceived only after interpretation, and frequently misinterpretation, by the observer. This indicates that an individual's interpretation of reality can diverge from objectively defined reality. Once an economic agent (auditor or board member) has made a decision or formed an opinion, future information may be used selectively in a manner which tends to support that original decision or confirm the original view.[58] Langevoort's stockbroker (1996), Prentice's accountant (2000), Krawiec's rogue trader (2000), Koniak's lawyer (2003a), and Sale's banker (2005) all represent the traditional rational maximizer who weighs the risk and costs of breaking rules against the potential gains. This applies cost–benefit analysis to an action and is part of the traditional economic approach to the analysis of choice. However, economic agents also make use of mental tools and shortcuts, which affect their perception, judgement, and decision-making. An individual facing a loss (or who perceives falling behind) may well decide that higher levels of risk are necessary to re-coup a loss (or achieve a target). While success can lead to over-optimism and neglect of risk, failure (or the perception of this) may lead to active risk preference. In either case, the individual is prone to failing to perceive and assess risk in the probabilistic way suggested by theories of utility maximization. Other cognitive biases and social pressures may reinforce this. Optimistic, self-serving impressions of competence and expertise can resist downward revision for unusually long periods of time.

Once committed to a course of action (say an auditor who accepted management's views on an accounting interpretation), many subsequent motivations and judgements operate at an unconscious level to reinforce self-respect and future investment (e.g. a repeat audit), and to ignore signals which would suggest termination of the activity. Not only would such a termination question the agent's competence and resolve, but it would also jeopardize the agent's self-respect. Motivated reasoning reinforces self-serving inference and wishful thinking, to affect the decision-making process. An economic agent can be expected to be sensitive to the adverse effects on remuneration and standing from the loss of a major client (or position on a board). These desires are typically masked from consciousness by selective perception and rationalizations, as an individual prefers to interpret own decisions as reasonable and rational.

Cognitive and motivational bias can distort perceived reality to uphold an original decision or an original view. New information may, on the other hand, be overweighed, through the application of the representativeness heuristic. Either phenomenon leads to a bias in the interpretation of new information. As noted, such functional tools serve to preserve self-esteem, motivation, confidence, and, within limits, can be a sign of mental health, but they may also move the agent away from an objective perception of a situation or own action. For an agent in a corporate setting, the path to fraudulent behaviour might be taken in small incremental steps, and be paved with good intentions, fear, and a series of rationalizations. What, in hindsight, might appear as foolish risks may all along have been perceived as only moderately risky, or as a rational reaction to avoid losses (real or imaginary). This can be reinforced by observations of similar actions by, and pressures from, peers.

Specific policy recommendations

Auditors

In the Statement on Auditing Standards No. 99 ('SAS 99', AICPA, 2002b), AICPA recognized bias in accounting to be a persistent problem. SAS 99 reminds auditors that they need to overcome natural tendencies – such as an overconfidence in client statements – and suggests an audit be approached with a sceptical attitude and questioning mind. A 'fraud triangle' explicitly outlines the incentives, opportunities, and rationalizations when a fraud is being committed. A detailed set of procedures is aimed at increasing the auditor's ability to identify and detect fraud. Steps include communication among engagement partners, with management and the audit committee about the risk of material misstatement, with particular reference to fraud. Consideration of fraud risk factors, accounting estimates for biases, and significant unusual transactions are specifically highlighted. This intuitive approach reflects a comprehensive understanding of the potential for bias in the auditor–client relationship. SAS 99 focuses on new responsibilities and new procedures aimed at improving the likelihood that auditors will detect material misstatements. As such, it would appear to be a step in the right direction. How successful SAS 99 will be in practice, in countering the inevitable bias introduced by the close client/auditor working relationship, remains, of course, a matter for future investigation.

The significance of bias has not always been recognized in court decisions on accountants' aiding and abetting charges. In deciding against plaintiffs courts frequently assumed that because by violating the law a defendant would have subjected him or herself to the risk of the expense and notoriety of a jury trial, it was 'unthinkable' that the defendant would have done so.[59] This rationale presumes that people (including auditors and directors) are so rational and law-breaking so irrational that fraud and recklessness cannot occur. In contrast, if fraud and recklessness do occur, then courts and corporate governance policy-makers ought to consider the possibility that (a) people (and firms) are not as rational as the *DiLeo* adherents and a rational choice decision theory would assume, or (b) sometimes it is rational to defraud others, or (c) both (Prentice, 2000).[60] Prentice (2000) argues that the reasoning resulting in *DiLeo* type decisions embodies two significant dangers of theorizing in law and economics. First, law and economics analysis is sometimes predicated on flawed core assumptions. In this case, the core assumptions are that (1) auditors are rational actors, and (2) audit firms are rational actors. The second danger lies in translating these core assumptions into reality, by insisting that (3) it would be irrational for individual auditors to audit fraudulently or recklessly, and that (4) it would in particular be irrational for audit firms to audit fraudulently or recklessly.[61]

Much of conventional law and economics, and its manifestation in *DiLeo*, rests on the critical assumption that people are rational maximizers of self-interest.[62] However, a refusal to pay attention to non-rational elements of human judgement and choice behaviour places economists and those who use economic models in their own profession at risk of ignoring empirical evidence which demonstrates that individuals frequently behave in ways which violate rational choice models. Worse yet, this may lead to policy recommendations which are unrealistic and possibly counter-productive with regard to intended objectives. Closeness to client, limitations on information and processing capacity, and an extremely complex and variable subject make auditors especially prone to bias. Hence, the question is whether auditors can adhere to the ideal of rational choice models of traditional economic thought. Economists (and others, including judges) have frequently modelled them as such (see, for example, Antle, 1982; Baiman *et al.*, 1987). Yet, the evidence is, by now, overwhelming in support of the view that the rationality of the individual economic actor is overstated in the standard economic model. As useful as rational choice models may be for the economic analysis of choice and decision-making, they cannot claim an exclusive right to describing human judgement and choice behaviour, perhaps not even a predominant one, and their dominance in the analysis of choice and decision-making should be questioned (Conlisk, 1996).

Bias frequently comes with the role individuals play. The minimization of conditions that create bias would thus appear to be a crucial element in producing better audits (and better board decisions). One recommendation would hence be that governance policy should seek to reduce an auditor's dependence on a client's opinion of the results of an audit. Full divestiture of consulting and tax services is one step towards establishing functional auditor independence (Bazerman *et al.*, 2002a, b). Even then, the fact that auditors are hired and fired by the companies they audit will make it difficult to escape bias in auditing. To eliminate this source of bias, the threat of being fired for delivering an unfavourable audit might have to be removed. As noted, the Sarbanes-Oxley Act 2002 (and related legislation in the UK and at EU level) mandates auditor rotation only at the partner level. The board of directors, and by extension the firm, remains responsible for selecting and supervising the auditor, who in turn (in the first instance) remains accountable to senior management.

It remains questionable how independent the 'independent audit' is, given the fact that an auditor is likely to regard the company as his client (Caparo, 1990), and mainly acts as an agent of the board (Dallas, 1988; Bazerman, 1997; Bazerman *et al.*, 2002a, b; Turnbull, 2005). This is partially the result of too close an alignment of the auditor with management, and problems arising from the increasingly uncompetitive market, now dominated by just four firms (Hayward, 2003). The presence of an audit committee may not be able to alleviate this conflict of interests because of conceptual and practical reasons (Hatherly, 1995). Auditors would have to be independent of the board (and management) in order to be free of the conflict created by the control of directors over auditors, and this may require auditors to be elected and controlled by shareholders (Hatherly, 1995; Coffee, 2005; Turnbull, 2005). Neither the UK Combined Code, nor Sarbanes-Oxley addresses the potential for conflict of interest between auditors and directors (Turnbull, 2005).

It is suggested that mandatory auditor rotation at firm level after a fixed term might be a necessary first step to further reduce bias in the auditor–client relationship. This presumes that the audit function remains in the private sector. A more radical suggestion would be to nationalize the external audit and make this function part of the remit of a government agency. The implications of an increasing concentration in the audit market may require the break-up of the Big-4. In any case, care should be taken to rotate people (and firms) on a regular basis to minimize the biases that come from a) working closely with the people to be monitored; b) being responsible for the interpretations during an earlier audit; and c) worrying about negative personal repercussions from a qualified audit report. Additional attention will need to be paid to repeat audits and future employment with a client. Both can be expected to influence present judgement.

Directors

Legal practice and scholars place importance and trust in the role of the board of directors as a governance mechanism, despite serious questions about the effectiveness and ability of this institution in fulfilling its gatekeeper functions.[63] Most boards undoubtedly do a reasonably good job of monitoring the performance of senior management. Yet, the massive failures of firms which periodically interrupt the tranquillity of efficient market theories reveal a serious weakness in the board of directors as a governance mechanism (see, for example, Dallas, 2003 and Langevoort, 2002b). This weakness particularly threatens the basis for the role of the independent director in corporate governance (Mace, 1986).

A board of directors, under pressure to concur with proposals put forth by the chief executive, is subject to a dynamic that binds the group together in ways that frequently obscure the shortcomings of the quality of group decision-making (see Forbes and Milliken, 1999 and Bainbridge, 2002). Rather than active or indirect participation in wrongdoings (although there might have been plenty of that), directors may more frequently find themselves blind to questionable managerial actions, or reluctant to oppose them. As a close-knit group, a board of directors may be particularly prone to the problem that, 'Smart people working together collectively can be dumber than the sum of their brains' (Schwartz and Wald, 2003). This refers to the dangers of groupthink, where groups make faulty decisions because group pressures lead to a deterioration of the critical features of decision-making.[64]

A degree of group cohesion would appear to be necessary to enable a board to make decisions. This, however, also exposes the board to the potentially pathological shortcomings of group decision-making. Group cohesion, while necessary for the functioning of the board, may eventually blind the group to faults in group judgement, and to improprieties of the behaviour of senior management. The Enron board is a good example of an overly permissive board. Blatantly conflicted due to numerous financial connections with Enron not related to their duty as directors, the board also seemed to have been excessively close to management:

> The Subcommittee investigation did not substantiate the claims that the Enron Board members challenged management and asked tough questions. Instead, the investigation found a Board that routinely relied on Enron management and Andersen representations with little or no

effort to verify the information provided, that readily approved new business ventures and complex transactions, and that exercised weak oversight of company operations. The investigation also identified a number of financial ties between Board members and Enron which, collectively, raise questions about Board member independence and willingness to challenge management.

(US Senate 2002a: 14)

Heuristics and group social dynamics may thus, to a degree, explain the acquiescence of board members to the accounting manipulations which brought down the firm or their reluctance to intervene when they noticed these. In general, the greater group cohesion, the more prevalent the problems related to group decision-making, and the poorer the quality of decisions. This is reflected in larger pressure towards conformity and majority decision-making, rationalization of decisions taken, deference to the group leader (i.e. the CEO/Chairman), and a general aversion to question decisions made by the CEO.[65] The pressure for consensus can be reflected in negative reactions to critical outside assessments of a group's decisions. In extreme forms, this leads to tendencies for self-perpetuation at the cost of the firm's shareholders and other stakeholders. The pathological elements of group decision-making can be reinforced by cognitive biases of the individual, which can lead to further polarization in judgement.[66] While group decision-making has the potential to surpass the quality of individual decision-making, few groups live up to this potential. Designating a single director as a devil's advocate with the task of consistently probing for weaknesses in the group's decision-making process and questioning existing views may prove difficult. An openly adversarial stance towards the chief executive by a member of the board may not be appreciated, or yield the desired result, as this runs counter to the traditional atmosphere of mutual respect and congeniality which dominates boards.

The potential shortcomings of group decision-making have a particular impact on the rationale underlying the use of independent directors.[67] The ideal of the independent director may fall significantly short where the individual's objectivity is diminished by group psychology. Such pressures act on the individual to quickly adopt the identity of the group, with the independent director becoming part of an in-group which emphasizes consensus and cohesion over critical assessment. There is a clear distinction between true outsiders, chosen, say, from an approved list of professional directors, rotated at regular intervals, and 'independent' directors, as currently defined.[68] Outsiders may be less prone to assuming in-group behaviour, which may enhance their independence and objectivity. This refers back to the distinction between functional and formal independence. The significance of this difference is reflected in reviews of the literature on boards of directors which fail to find conclusive evidence for a correlation of specific board characteristics and various measures of firm performance (Johnson *et al.*, 1996; Larcker *et al.*, 2005).[69]

In order to instil a true sense of independence it may also be necessary to increase the diversity on a board. One way to achieve this might be to widen the pool from which directors are drawn.[70] This follows recommendations of the Higgs Review (Higgs, 2003), which proposed drawing on greater pools of talent, experiences, and perspectives than is traditionally the case. The need for greater diversity in the backgrounds, skills and experiences of non-executive directors was noted in the Tyson Report (Tyson, 2003), which suggests that this would have a positive effect on firm performance, strategy, and risk management. Highlighted in both the Higgs Review and the Tyson Report was the need for non-executive directors to possess a number of personal attributes in order to be effective and to be able to carry out the responsibilities of their role, including integrity and high ethical standards, sound judgement, the ability and willingness to challenge and probe, and strong interpersonal skills.[71] There is no doubt that integrity and high ethical standards are essential qualities for effective board members. Where these characteristics are not present, there is no oversight by the board. Sound judgement, too, would appear to be a necessary ingredient in order to recognize flawed decision-making and risk, and function as a sounding board for executive management. Of crucial importance is the ability and willingness to challenge and probe information presented by executive management and to raise difficult issues. This has not gone unnoticed. Higgs (2003), for example, suggests that non-executive directors should have 'sufficient strength of character to seek and obtain full and satisfactory answers within the collegiate environment of the board' (Higgs, 2003: 6.15). Nonetheless, it would appear that this willingness to challenge and to confront is in short supply in actual boardrooms, and it is suggested that board capture and social bonding are key issues in this lack of critical assessment of executive decisions in the traditional boardroom.

There have been calls for a mandated minimum number of professional directors on boards (and the various committees), drawn from a list approved by a government regulatory body (Fanto, 2004). This is intended to break the tendency for 'inner circles' to form. Inner circles (or in-groups) are particularly subject to potentially disastrous decision-making due to the high degree of cohesion of such groups. By preventing the entrenchment of an insider group, a core of public directors on boards could be a safeguard against directors falling into the groupthink trap. This may be further enhanced by appointing directors from non-traditional backgrounds to the list of public directors.

Essentially, the emphasis on selecting individuals from outside the traditional pool of directors, and mandating the use of public directors, may enhance the monitoring function of boards. This partially reflects the need for a devil's advocate in group decision-making to counter excessive self-interest focus and groupthink tendencies which arise from excessive group cohesion. At the same time, this would prevent feelings of alienation (and potential isolation) of a designated individual taking on such a role. Moderate levels of cognitive conflict (i.e. differences in views and judgement) in a board may serve to counter the negative effects of excessive cohesion (Janis, 1982; Forbes and Milliken, 1999).

The notion of a public director, drawn from an approved list and accountable to a public body, had been suggested after earlier waves of corporate scandals. William O. Douglas, for example, in a response to the financial scandals of the 1920s, proposed the appointment of public directors to boards, to truly monitor management and represent the various stakeholders (Douglas, 1940).[72] Gilson and Kraakman (1991) propose that public companies draw professional directors from a list drawn up by institutional investors. More recently, Stone (2004) has called for general public directors to be nominated by a Federal Commission and then selected by the company's board.

The function of board members in providing business advice, connections, and expertise can still be met by the traditional director candidate. The monitoring of senior executives, however, might be more efficiently done by true outsiders. The key to successful group decision-making on corporate boards may rest in the diversity of the board members, combined with a mandate of the public directors to focus on the interests of those outside the small inner circle of executive management.[73] Insisting on diversity of board members (by, for example, choosing public directors from non-traditional director backgrounds) may help prevent a contagious spread of poor business practices, including complacency, by board members (Darley, 1996; Maccoby, 2000; Demski, 2003).

Greater independence of external directors from the company and its senior management should be encouraged and mandated. Perhaps they could be registered with, and licensed by, government so that in order to keep their position they will need to satisfy government as well as the company. Arguably, with regard to the more recent corporate scandals, it was in the monitoring role that boards of directors failed the most. Board capture will likely continue to be a serious and persistent problem (Bebchuk *et al.*, 2002b). This points to a motivational component in the neglect of duty by directors, which indicates a need to cut the link between the election to, and tenure on, a board from a firm's senior management. Again, this may not necessarily refer to all members of the board, but would have implications for the election of non-executive directors. To counter the formation of an in-group, it might be a good idea to increase the diversity of the pool from which directors are drawn. Diversity in backgrounds, with respect to, say, function, education, social experience, age, and gender, may further contribute to better decision-making and better monitoring of this group (Cohen and Bailey, 1997). A mandated minimum of truly outside directors, drawn from a government approved list, with a single fixed-term tenure, with a clear mandate to monitor senior executives, and regularly vetted for performance, should assist in countering groupthink tendencies.

The selection process of members to a board of directors typically draws from a small corporate elite (Cook, 2003). As highly qualified as these individuals might be with respect to business matters, their ability to monitor the actions and performance of senior management appears to be less well developed. The current wisdom of improving the gatekeeping function of boards rests on conventional suggestions, for example increasing the technical knowledge of individual directors in areas including finance and accounting, and more stringent (but still conventional) independence criteria with regard to directors and board committees. However, highly specialized knowledge will not necessarily yield better monitors. While the view that well-qualified directors might be better at giving business advice and spotting obviously inadvisable transactions is not without merit, a prescription resting on better qualifications alone misses the point that it is difficult for boards to critically judge and challenge the decisions of senior management. This questions the quality of monitoring of existing boards and their ability to effectively supervise the activities of executive management. The lack of experience, and financial and accounting expertise of, say, the Enron board, does not explain the many breaches of fiduciary duty identified by subsequent investigations (see US Senate, 2002a). With hindsight, Enron's directors, who were impressively well qualified in business and finance matters, provided fundamentally unsound business advice. The managerial activities resulting in the more recent corporate scandals did not, for the most part, rest on highly intricate constructs. Instead, boards of directors waived codes of ethical conduct to allow for dubious self-dealings via even more dubious SPVs (Enron), allowed the declaration of current expenses as capital assets (WorldCom), accepted the booking of hypothetical future revenues as current income (Enron, Xerox), and granted executives massive benefits without commensurate performance (Tyco, NYSE, Adelphia).

This takes the discussion back to the monitoring function of this gatekeeper, and how to enhance monitoring without interfering with the other roles of the board. It is suggested that the main problem with the failure of boards of directors in their duty to monitor managerial conduct is in large part the result of potential flaws in individual and group decision-making, which are insufficiently addressed in the standard governance discussion. These are also largely ignored by the economist's standard model of judgement and choice. The passivity and silence of many boards during crucial decisions and presentations of company executives underscores the fundamental difference between traditional metrics of independence and competence, and the ability to critically assess (and oppose where necessary) the activities and judgements of senior management. It is this issue which needs to be resolved in efforts to turn directors into better gatekeepers.

To merely demand better qualified directors, or to call for representatives of other stakeholders (say, employees or institutional investors) on the board, may not go far enough. Such proposals are still largely based on a model of a self-interested rational actor, free from bias and cognitive short-cuts, and immune to social and group pressures. Such a simple manipulation of board composition ratios will bring some benefits, but it is unlikely to go far enough in enhancing the monitoring quality of this gatekeeper. Technically qualified non-executive directors failed their duties as gatekeepers at Enron primarily because they did not ask critical questions.

Concluding thoughts and caveats

This discussion could be seen to regard models of rationality (broadly defined) of being of two types only. The familiar neo-classical maximization model on the one hand, and everything else, including bounded rationality, heuristics and bias, framing error, institutionalism, affect, emotion, and more, on the other. These alternative models have of course very different sets of assumptions. The main purpose of this book is to introduce to the governance discussion recent findings from cognitive and behavioural research which undermine the strict applicability of the assumptions of the utility maximization model. It is recognized that an independent development of, say, bounded rationality could possibly yield conflicting conclusions to a development of models based on, say, cognition or affect biases.

Bounded rationality, for example, highlights human limitations with regard to cognitive ability and time, and emphasizes the dependence of decision-making on situation and environment. According to this interpretation of rational behaviour, models of judgement and decision-making should be based on what the mind is capable of. Of crucial importance is the decision context. Simon's vision of bounded rationality (1956, 1991) is based on two complementary components: the cognitive and processing limitations of the human mind, and the environment in which it operates. For Simon, these cannot be separated, nor can the concept of bounded rationality be reduced to optimization under constraints (Simon, 1991). The first component suggests that the human mind does not have the computational capacities required for selecting what might be an optimal choice. Even when and where an optimal strategy or outcome exists (in well-defined situations), it is frequently not possible to calculate an optimal decision in a reasonable amount of time. Quite often, the search for an optimal choice might ultimately be illusive, which necessitates the use of an 'approximate method to handle most tasks' (Simon, 1990: 6). The nature of the environment is the second component of Simon's view of bounded rationality. The key idea is that the usefulness and efficiency of a choice method or strategy can only be judged against the environment in which it is used.[74] Hence, the usefulness of a particular strategy depends on the specific environment or situation to which it is applied. Central to this concept of bounded rationality is the notion of satisficing (rather than optimizing, which is fundamental to concepts of utility maximization). Satisficing is a rule for ending the search for alternatives or further information. The individual, rather than engaging in near limitless search (and calculations) for what might be an optimal choice, selects an option from a limited set of alternatives encountered sequentially. Satisficing suggests setting an (adjustable) aspiration level and settling for the first alternative which meets or exceeds this level, economizing on computational and time effort (Simon, 1956).

There is also a political aspect to the more recent corporate scandals. Enron, for one, was highly successful in lobbying for a legal and regulatory environment that suited its immediate objectives. Changes to the system of corporate governance, including the legal setting with regard to liability, the oversight of particular activities, and changes in the organizational structure of gatekeepers, were major contributors to the latest wave of corporate misconduct in the United States. Exemptions from oversight in trading certain energy-related derivatives (Enron) and the ease with which SPVs could be set up are potential examples of regulatory failure. The weakening of liability threats to auditors (and lawyers) is likely to have contributed to the increased risk-taking of that profession (Coffee, 2002). The spread of the limited liability partnership (LLP) is thought to have reduced the efficiency of internal monitoring of auditing and law firms (Koniak, 2003b; Macey and Sale, 2003). These developments destabilized the corporate governance system and changed the incentives of senior executives and gatekeepers, in particular the auditing and legal professions. The literature on the changing regulatory environment is an important one, and is a crucial element in our understanding of corporate governance failures.[75] Structural deficiencies of a system of corporate governance and its functioning can play into the hands of heuristics and social psychological pressures.

The importance of heterogeneity among agents, and a need to provide for flexibility in designing incentives should not be underestimated. For example, individuals who have self-control problems in the form of a present bias typically fail to fully incorporate future costs into their decision equation, and, hence, may not always act in their own long-term interest. In addition to differences in intrinsic tastes for different activities, individuals are likely to vary in their susceptibility to bias, and their degree of awareness of potential self-control problems. Some individuals may come close to the economist's ideal of the rational maximizer. Other individuals, in contrast, may be fully unaware of, say, their future self-control problems. The rest may fall somewhere in between, where individuals are somewhat aware of their future control problems, but underestimate their magnitude (O'Donoghue and Rabin, 2001). Moreover, individual agents are typically uncertain about their own future preferences, needs, options, and constraints. Heterogeneity among agents may, thus, require flexibility in optimal incentive design. This highlights the potential importance of the detailed structure of incentives.[76] Incentive design which does not account for agent heterogeneity may generate inefficient, and even perverse, responses.[77]

Measures which can help counter the biases and socio-psychological pressures likely to arise in the work of gatekeepers include the revolving of gatekeepers (auditors, board members) on a regular basis. These measures would also need to include the rotation of firms, for example, the external auditor. It is suggested that regularly changing auditors, directors, and also lawyers and bankers would reduce problems in two ways. First, the new gatekeeper would be less encumbered by the weight of decisions made by the previous gatekeeper. Second, knowing that one will only be in a particular position (or office) for a just few years before someone else comes in to check the books means that any gambles taken must pay of in that short period. A prohibition of (immediate) repeat services with the same client is expected to assist in further reducing the dependence of reputational intermediaries on clients.[78]

Further, there is the need for a regular (say once a decade) high powered review of the state of corporate governance in individual countries. At the moment, such reviews tend to follow on the heels of corporate scandals, that is, they are reactive in nature. An anticipatory rather than an *ex post* review is suggested, to detect and fix weaknesses before they are used for fraudulent purposes. New types of firms pose new regulatory challenges. A new legislation system has an effective shelf life, after which time ways around it will be found. This may require a periodic regulatory overhaul, rather than simply waiting for the next wave of scandals before initiating changes.

Perhaps, too, a change in corporate culture is needed. It may be difficult to engineer this, but a start can be made in business schools with a much higher emphasis on ethical training, with an additional focus on the problems with practices such as tournaments, valuing flexibility of mind as much as steadiness of purpose (i.e. asking: 'What do you do when you find out you are wrong?'), and encouraging criticism within the corporate environment rather than the evolution of a group identity. Such training may provide an anchor for a valuation of the ethics of own decision-making. An additional positive side-effect of more ethical training, especially in combination with an emphasis on diversity in groups and the inclusion of true outsiders, could be the minimization of apathy in the face of actions of others (Moscovici *et al.*, 1969; Latané and Darley, 1969, 1970; Messick and Bazerman, 1996; Luban, 2006).

Finally, the conclusions drawn here may be seen as extremely negative, and might be interpreted to indicate that changes in corporate governance will not work because people will always seek ways around new rules.[79] Certainly, a committed fraudster is likely to eventually find a way around most rules and regulations. This tendency would appear to be part of human nature which we cannot presume to change. While it cannot be hoped that we will reach a situation where such scandals will never happen, there are things that can be done over and above punitive action (which has its place, but a limited one) to reduce the occurrence of such scandals to a minimum. The insights presented here provide a focus on what else can be done to minimize serious breaches of corporate governance, although we will never be able to predict fundamentally irrational behaviour.

9 Conclusions

The human capacity for rationalization of own or observed behaviour can be a formidable barrier to rational judgement and decision-making. Examples of non-rational behaviour include commitment to lost causes, belief perseverance, and the underestimation of risk. Cognitive dissonance (the clash between conduct and principles) frequently leads to beliefs and judgements being adapted to conform with own conduct, which further distorts perception and judgement.[1] Even when individuals realize own bias in a particular judgement (and are explicitly asked to watch out for this), they are frequently unable to sufficiently adjust for it. Compounding such deviations from rational decision-making is the tendency for individuals to readily recognize biases in others that they do not recognize in themselves.

A large body of literature describes the mental rules of thumb used by the human mind to arrive at judgements under uncertainty. In general, heuristics allow for quick and efficient decision-making, but these cognitive mechanisms can also lead to systematically flawed judgements. It would be difficult to understand how individuals were able to learn at all, if biases dominated decision tasks at all times. Obviously, learning can take place. Individuals can learn from past mistakes, and are capable of applying analysis along the lines suggested by rational choice models. Nonetheless, four decades of research into decision-making demonstrate that human inference is subject to a set of cognitive and motivational filters which can interfere with an objective interpretation of information. The biases that do occur are not evenly distributed, but lead to systematic diversions from the outcomes predicted by rational choice models. While there might be some room for discussion of what is meant by 'objective', the results from behavioural research and social psychology warrant the view that the rational model is an inadequate description of the spectrum of human decision-making.[2]

This research develops the argument that an over-reliance on rational choice models of decision-making may prevent a more thorough discussion on unexpected corporate collapse, and corporate governance in general. A related argument is made with respect to the use of conventional numeric variables to measure the quality of corporate governance. Numeric variables and models of rational behaviour have a poor record in the detection, prevention, and forecasting of earnings management and accounting fraud. The need to move beyond strictly numerical benchmarks in gauging the quality of corporate governance is noted in the literature (see, for example, Larcker *et al.*, 2005).

Policies based on the assumptions of rational models of choice-making may underestimate the intrusion of bias in the decision-making of agents in corporate governance. Conventional responses to corporate fraud, such as stronger penalties and additional layers of oversight or regulation, have been tried in the past with little apparent success in terms of preventing future corporate scandals. The discussion on psychological causes for monitor failure provides some reasons for this. To develop the argument, a discussion on the weak empirical foundations of earnings management research was combined with an analysis of behavioural decision-making by gatekeepers in corporate environments. The discussion on gatekeepers primarily focused on the judgement and choice behaviour of the external auditor and the directors of the board, with a particular emphasis on the feasibility of independence and objectivity. The crucial role of lawyers and bankers, as two important gatekeepers in corporate governance, was outlined.

Common underlying causes of corporate disasters are at the focus of the investigation presented here. Specifically, it is asked why the gatekeeping and monitoring function is less reliable than generally assumed and predicted by models of rational choice. The assumptions of rational decision-making models are compared with those of a behavioural approach. The behavioural approach seems to explain some paradoxes on which the rational approach founders, or at best provides arduous explanations. This ability to better explain why actors behave in a particular way may explain the increasing appeal of the behavioural approach to academics, practitioners, and legal experts.

Accurate disclosure is one of the defining characteristics of the corporate governance system in the United States, and a key ingredient elsewhere. It relies on independent certification and verification of financial disclosure by reputational intermediaries. The monitoring model of corporate governance, in turn, depends to a significant degree on the liability and reputational concerns of agents to deter negligence and fraudulent behaviour. Recent corporate scandals, however, highlight the apparent ease with which existing systems of corporate governance can be undermined. Gatekeeper failure is identified as a key factor in this breakdown. One potential cause of this is the inadequacy of the rational model of judgement and decision-making in describing human choice behaviour in a corporate setting. The frequent incidence of governance failures emphasizes the importance of understanding the limits of independence, objectivity, and impartiality of monitors and gatekeepers.

A large body of research comments on ways to minimize conflicts of interest between principal and agent. This has identified many important factors which contribute to an understanding of the issues at hand. Identified are, for example, board characteristics (e.g. the proportion of independent directors and the presence of specialized board committees), stock ownership, influence of debt-holders, composition of executive compensation, anti-takeover defences, and audit client diversification.[3] This book suggests, however, that this important debate on corporate governance is somewhat incomplete. Until fairly recently, the effects of human psychology on judgement and choice behaviour received little attention in the broader discussion. Frequently ignored, or dismissed as irrelevant, were the effects of cognitive limits, heuristics, bias, emotion, and affect on human perception, judgement, and decision-making. This is odd, as the debate on corporate governance mechanisms should be particularly concerned with the response of individuals to measures and incentives aimed at minimizing the agency problem. Agents' perception of governance measures, their judgement and decision-making, and their ultimate response within the given legal and incentive framework is important in order to gauge the efficiency of such tools.

There is a growing awareness by academics as well as practitioners of the importance of a better understanding of human decision-making than is provided by the neo-classical rational choice model alone (Jones and Goldsmith, 2005). An over-reliance of legal and economic theory on the rational model of choice behaviour may yield an overconfidence with regard to the feasibility of independence of gatekeepers. This may also result in overconfidence in the deterrence value of rules and legislation. To the extent that individuals are rational economic actors who weigh cost and benefits before committing legal transgressions, increased expected penalties would add to deterrence. However, the rational model of decision-making may not always (and not even primarily) be a useful description of how individuals perceive their situation, form judgements, and make-decisions in a corporate environment (or elsewhere). Choice behaviour is not solely based on logical reasoning, but is also influenced by biases, schemata, framing, and cognitive and judgmental heuristics (Jolls *et al.*, 1998; Prentice, 2000; Rabin, 2002). If the rational actor model is an inadequate paradigm for describing human judgement and decision-making, reputational concerns and penalties may fail to sufficiently deter legal transgressions.

The insights presented here would seem to be of importance to the formulation of governance legislation and codes of best practice.[4] The assumption of the rationality of actors is fundamental to past and current rules and regulations, underlies legal interpretations of conduct, and is still reflected in more recent legislation and academic research on corporate governance. A time-honoured response to major corporate failures is the establishment of committees of inquiry, the recommendation of new laws and codes of best practice, changes in legislation, and the imposition of additional layers of oversight. These measures typically react post hoc to problems, and new waves of corporate debacles tend to shake public confidence in the existing system of corporate governance just a few years thereafter. It is suggested that the recurrence of waves of fraud, and the predictable pattern of responses, should prompt the question of whether some crucial elements in human nature are being somewhat disregarded in the standard approach to the agency problem.

Traditional regulatory responses with regard to actual or alleged acquiescence (or direct involvement) of monitors and gatekeepers may underestimate the effects of bias on the efficiency of the monitoring model in its current form. This is particularly evident with regard to rules and legislation which merely serve up more of the same, that is, stronger penalties, greater oversight, more rules, and so forth, for behaviour that is to be discouraged. This at best provides temporary relief, and there is no reason to assume that such an approach should work any better with regard to current scandals. In contrast, it can be shown that bias and social pressures in the auditor/client relationship and in the work of a board of directors can severely compromise their respective monitoring/gatekeeping functions (Bazerman *et al.*, 2002a, b; Langevoort, 2001b). This also applies to the functioning of the two other groups of gatekeepers, lawyers and investment bankers, without whom none of the recent scandals could have reached their devastating proportions.

Contemporary economics, to a large degree, is concerned with the mean reaction, that is, the reaction of the representative individual. Deviations from that mean are frequently deemed to be balanced by deviations in the opposite direction.[5] In contrast, the heuristics and biases literature (and also that on affect and emotions) suggests that individuals (and small groups) are subject to forces which can cause systematic deviations from the predictions of the standard economics model of choice. Individual decisions may not automatically or quickly be corrected to meet the predicted outcomes of rational choice models.[6] This is of particular importance for the present discussion, as decisions in corporate governance are often made at the individual level or in small groups. While the legal and regulatory environment sets the framework within which choices are made, important decisions within corporate settings ultimately come down to a few individuals. In addition, these individuals frequently form a closely knit group, which tends to view the world around it in very similar ways.

For the individual, there may frequently be little opportunity to learn from own or others' past mistakes. This would seem to particularly apply to situations where the ultimate success of an action is still potentially possible, or can be imagined to be so.[7] Success, real or apparent, is highly rewarded in corporate settings. Failure to live up to expectations, in contrast, can be devastating to a career. Cognitive and social cues frequently serve to reinforce the apparent validity of own judgement and decisions, regardless of objective validity or potential long-term viability of the decision. When the realization of a bad choice finally occurs to the decision-maker (and others), it is frequently too late to undo the damage. This potential for deviation from the predictions of the standard model of human decision-making should be of interest to academics and policy-makers alike.

Emotions, affect, heuristics, bounded rationality, cognitive dissonance, group pressures, escalation of commitment, and more can lead to systematic bias in perception and judgement. Policy recommendations, laws, and rules might be more effective with a greater appreciation of actual individual reactions to particular risk/reward systems. If the remedy for corporate scandals rested solely on finding an optimal level of penalties and enforcement (as the traditional economic analyses of crime and punishment would suggest), the solution would be relatively straightforward: increase penalties, strengthen enforcement, and lower rewards. This lowers the expected payoff for undesirable behaviour, that is, it increases the cost and lessens the benefit of a legal transgression. By lowering the rewards of a particular activity (say, acquiescence to fraud) and effectively raising its price, such responses would be expected to tip the balance in a rational cost–benefit analysis away from the activity.

However, an individual first has to realize that a particular conduct violates rules, needs to subjectively estimate the probability of getting caught, and finally measure the severity of the expected penalties. People generally tend to be unrealistically optimistic in their predictions and expectations, and typically assign higher probabilities to the attainment of desirable outcomes than warranted by objective analysis. In comparison to others, individuals, on average, view themselves more likely to experience positive outcomes, less likely to experience negative ones, and typically overestimate their control over a situation (Weinstein, 1980).[8] Behavioural research further shows that the future costs of an activity tend to be heavily discounted against the present benefits of this activity. A combination of over-optimism and unwarranted discounting of future costs drastically lowers the expected costs (say, in terms of penalties) of a present activity. An underestimation of risk and the heavy discounting of future costs have implications for the deterrence value of sanctions and reputation.

More vexing yet, the individual first needs to realize that a particular act is in contravention of existing rules and laws. Individuals are frequently unable to perceive an activity as a legal transgression (or properly judge its severity) at the time it takes place, and they frequently do not realize when they cross the line between acceptable and unacceptable behaviour. This is compounded by the fact that the choices which may ultimately lead to fraudulent activities usually do not carry prominent warning signs. At least, any warning signs are frequently not obvious to the individual in question. As bright and obvious as 'red flags' may seem to be with hindsight, especially to the uninvolved observer, they are typically of little use to the individual at the centre of the activities at the time they take place. For the most part, an individual may be aware of a small infringement here, a minor transgression there. This may appear to be nothing more than cutting some corners and part of everyday business life. To the individual's perception, this path might look slippery or perhaps merely cutting edge, but not obviously fraudulent, and absolutely not criminal.

There is no doubt that conscious frauds were committed in the discussed cases, and that particular actors lacked moral aptitude. However, most corporate wrongdoers do not fit the profile of a career criminal, and most people at the centre of corporate scandals are likely to have an ethical make-up not much different from that of anybody else.[9] Most of these individuals would probably react indignantly to the accusation that they must think cheating and lying to be an acceptable business tool. In contrast to a view that corporate scandals are mainly due to fraud, rogue agents, and a lack of ethics, situational, social, psychological, and cognitive effects may intervene in actors' judgement of what is acceptable behaviour, and what is not. There is no reason why these insights cannot be used to find better ways to stop as many corporate scandals as possible.

There is a contextual dimension to corporate fraud and acquiescence. Managers and gatekeepers find themselves in a highly competitive environment which rewards success above all. These actors are typically surrounded by peers who appear to agree with any and all of their decisions, are faced with flexible (i.e. uncertain) accounting rules, and cater to an investing public which, at times, pays scant regard to warning signs.[10] That human judgement (including moral judgement) is heavily influenced by peer pressure and situation was strikingly demonstrated by Milgram's 1963 experiment on obedience to authority, which analysed the effect of peer pressure on behaviour.[11] The Stanford Prison Experiment in 1971 further demonstrated the impact of situation and role play on perception, judgement, moral conscience, and behaviour.[12] This strongly suggests that corporate fraudsters and gatekeepers of poor quality may not all be inherently evil, at least not initially. Instead, agents in corporate governance may frequently fall victim to common social and cognitive judgement traps which diminish their capacity for rational objective analysis.[13]

Ignorance of the law can, of course, be no defence against prosecution. Neither is the existence of heuristics and biases. Other individuals, in similar circumstances and with similar opportunities, did not go down that fraudulent path (whether by luck or by volition is left open). Not all boards of directors fell victim to groupthink, and some auditors voiced their misgivings about a particular accounting treatment. However, heuristics and situational context do help explain how ordinary people, who may never previously have come into conflict with the law, may come to be implicated in massive corporate scandals. Socio-psychological pressures also help explain why firms may do a poor job of minimizing the internal agency problem. If the insights from the behavioural view are useful in describing how executive managers and their monitors behave, then this seriously brings into question the efficacy of existing rules and regulations on corporate governance. At the very least, it suggests the need for significant modifications to the monitoring model of corporate governance. A better understanding of what drives managerial and monitor conduct should allow the design of better systems of corporate governance.

Neither the possible loss of reputation, nor the potential of jail time prevented individuals implicated in corporate scandals from perpetrating what subsequently turned out to be fraudulent acts. Further, in some cases, the potential benefits were in no relation to the subsequent damage to reputation, wealth, and personal freedom. That is, a rational cost–benefit analysis should have prevented an individual from engaging in a particular activity. That this did not happen, or was not applied appropriately, has important repercussions for governance analysis and policy-making. Instead of holding on to an ideal model of decision-making (useful as such a model may be for theoretical reasons), there is a need to investigate how actual decisions are being made.

Deviations from the rational model of decision-making can be significant and persistent. Specifically, the rational model would appear to be flawed for two reasons: (1) while people behave rationally overall, they do so in a more complex manner than captured by simple rational choice models (which indicates the need for an expansion of the model, for example into various interpretations of bounded rationality, heuristics and biases, and affect) and, (2) people simply do not always behave rationally.[14] Reforms based on the standard monitoring model may possibly be little more than cosmetic sticking plaster to give the appearance of having righted the corporate ship while leaving it still fundamentally unsteady.

The Sarbanes-Oxley Act 2002 goes some way towards mitigating bias in auditing by, for example, making engagement partner rotation mandatory, prohibiting the provision of some services by accounting firms to their audit clients, and by strengthening the formal independence of boards.[15] The punitive legislation incorporated in the Sarbanes-Oxley Act is, however, also evidence of a long-established, but relatively ineffective, tradition of raising the cost of crime. No doubt there should be penalties for breaking the rules, but behavioural research and experience shows how easily individuals may inappropriately rationalize personal risks from engaging in an activity to a minimum. This interpretation is supported by the literature on crime and punishment, which suggests that the impact of an increase in the level of penalties for an offence may be limited (see, for example, Polinsky and Shavell, 1999 and Eide, 2000).

Rational choice models of human decision-making and conventional numeric measures can at best partially explain unexpected corporate collapses. A similar argument extends to the measurement, detection, and prediction of earnings management. Traditional structural indicators of corporate governance quality may be very limited guides to managerial behaviour and firm performance (Larcker *et al.*, 2005). The failure of earnings management models to predict future corporate frauds underlines the difficulties of measuring the quality of corporate governance. Enron scored high on typical governance indicators (e.g. the separation of the roles of CEO and chairman, the use of high-profile independent directors, the presence of a competent audit committee), and yet failed miserably in the stewardship of shareholders' funds.

Despite such criticisms, research on abnormal accruals shows that specific numeric metrics can still be useful warning signs of impending financial difficulties (Sloan, 1996; Palepu *et al.*, 2000; Dechow and Dichev, 2002; Richardson *et al.*, 2004a). Assessing attributes in the distribution of earnings in large samples can provide further evidence consistent with earnings management (Degeorge *et al.*, 1999; Dechow and Skinner, 2000; Myers *et al.*, 2006). The earnings benchmarks hierarchy identified by Degeorge *et al.* (1999) may provide an additional guide. The same goes for long periods of smooth earnings growth, which may be an indication of efforts to avoid the severe declines in market valuations when such a string is broken (Myers *et al.*, 2006). Restating firms tend to have deteriorating financial performance in the period around the restatement (Callen *et al.*, 2006). This identifies inferior financial performance as an additional motivator for aggressive reporting practices of management.

Such metrics may not be foolproof, but they can serve as red warning flags of potential trouble. Nevertheless, there would appear to be no alternative to closely examining the financial statements of each individual firm (Larcker *et al.*, 2005). Investors should bear in mind that managers have an incentive to improve the scores of the very benchmarks on which markets focus. Managers are very good at discovering new instruments which void the usefulness of existing benchmarks. This demonstrates the character of corporate governance as a 'regulatory game', with a sequence of events as follows. Scandals occur which, at least in part, can be traced to particular procedural instruments. This results in changes in the law to make such use of procedures and instruments more difficult. As a reaction, corporate agents evolve new instruments, and finally, new scandals result once again in the introduction of new laws or changes to existing laws. This process is also facilitated by technical changes which continually provide new opportunities. A changing environment and the emergence of new types of firms pose new regulatory challenges. As a result, any legislation would appear to have an effective shelf life, after which agents can be expected to find ways around it. One possible conclusion to draw from this is the need for a proactive regulatory overhaul every few years.

One might finally ask whether massive corporate debacles can happen again, and the somewhat pessimistic conclusion reached here is that they can and will. An alternative view would suggest that the system, overall, is working well and requires little more than fine-tuning at the margins. While it is not suggested here that the system is fatally broken or that the confidence placed in it is mistaken, the author does not share the optimistic interpretation that the system works well, and would argue that there are too many such scandals, and that the damage they cause is far too large to allow for complacency. Corporate scandals will occur, but this is inevitable and should not surprise observers. It is unlikely that any system of corporate governance will be able to prevent all instances of fraud. A committed fraudster, with willing accomplices, will always find a way around existing rules.[16] However, future unexpected corporate failures are more likely if the inclusion of crucial features of human nature is being resisted in efforts to maintain cherished models of choice behaviour. Much of the existing confidence in the potential functioning of corporate governance mechanisms may be based on an incomplete view of the social psychological basis of human behaviour.[17]

It is hoped that the analysis presented here adds to the literature by providing fresh insights into the human nature of judgement and decision-making in corporate governance. The inclusion of behavioural insights may assist in minimizing the incidence of catastrophic fraud. In particular, it is hoped that such insights and their incorporation in governance mechanisms will help prevent frauds committed by non-career criminals. Dismissing modifications to models that improve psychological realism is not helpful. As messy as the insights of behavioural analysis may be, practitioners, policy-makers, and scholars will benefit from a better understanding of how individuals behave in the real world. Incorporating such insights in models of corporate governance may, at the very least, assist in the detection of corporate frauds before they become irreversible.[18]

Notes

1 Introduction

1 Coffee (2001) refers to reputational intermediaries in corporate governance as gatekeepers, defined as independent professionals who protect the interests of investors and shareholders against self-dealing behaviour of insiders by providing verification and certification functions. Auditors, corporate lawyers, investment bankers, and directors of the board can be gatekeepers. Earlier important contributions on gatekeepers include Gilson (1984), Kraakman (1986), and Bushman and Smith (2001).

2 For the details on the WorldCom case, see Thornburgh (2002, 2003, 2004).

3 Xerox, for example, overstated profits by $1.4bn and equipment sales by $6.4bn in the period 1997–2001 (BBC News, 28/6/2002). Lucent had earlier admitted to having overstated earnings by $700m in Q4 of 1999 (Fortune, 7/7/2003). Both companies subsequently lost over 90 per cent of their stock valuation. Both firms had been in the 10th (uppermost) decile of firms, which accrue more revenues (and/or less expenses) than firms in lower deciles. This makes accruals a larger component of the earnings of the higher decile firms (Baron and Richardson, 2004, referring to the Criterion Accrual Model, developed by Criterion Research Group in conjunction with accounting professors of the Wharton Business School. The model assigns accruals scores to listed companies). This matches findings that accruals can be a useful leading indicator for measures including the likelihood of SEC enforcement action, poor future earnings, future stock underperformance, and the likelihood of financial restatements (Sloan, 1996; Bradshaw *et al.*, 2001; Richardson *et al.*, 2004b).

4 The 1997/1998 Asian financial crisis, rooted in dismal corporate governance, had preceded this, of course. Entire economies were pushed towards financial meltdown as the result of fraudulent or highly impudent management of firms and a distinctive lack of supervision.

5 Since July 1998, APRA has been the regulator of the Australian financial services industry. It oversees banks, building societies, credit unions, general insurance and reinsurance companies, life insurance, friendly societies, and most members of the superannuation industry. See www.apra.gov.au.

6 A mere six weeks passed from the first publication of accounting irregularities to the demise in late 2001 of what was once one of world's leading electricity, natural gas, pulp and paper, and communications companies with claimed year 2000 revenues in excess of $100bn and a peak market capitalization of close to $70bn.

7 There is also an extensive academic literature reviewing and interpreting aspects of the Enron saga – examples of which include Bratton (2002), Gordon (2002), Benston *et al.* (2003), Benston (2003b, c; 2006), Coffee (2003a, b).

8 The ability to purchase both external and internal audit from the same firm has been a source of controversy for some time and the SEC had brought into force rules (likely unworkable) limiting the extent to which clients could purchase internal audit from their external auditor. Post Sarbanes-Oxley there is now a complete prohibition of joint provision.

9 Wendy Gramm is the wife of a (now former) US Senator and as chair of the Commodities Futures Trading Commission in 1993 she had overseen significant deregulation of Enron's trading in energy futures – just ahead of leaving the Commission and joining Enron as a non-executive director.

10 Now a requirement of the Combined Code in the UK.

11 Batson (2003b: 131–55) provides detail as to Andersen's interaction with the Enron audit committee.

12 It is sometimes assumed by users of financial data that external auditors actually draft the financial reports of a company. This is not so. The senior management of a company produces these reports, to which the external auditor affixes his or her signature. In an ideal case, this signature provides a seal of approval that the figures contained in a financial report represent the true financial state of the company. Corporate scandals remind us that this is an ideal which is not always met.

13 Bratton (2002) refers to a darker side of the shareholder value norm. Instead of maximizing productivity and thus increasing the value of the firm, managers and shareholders may place too great an emphasis on short-term performance numbers and on meeting the requirements of accounting standards rather than providing a reliable overview of the true financial state of the firm. This can lead to the perverse result of concentrating on immediate results at the cost of long-term performance and even survival of the firm. It also increases the pressure to engage in earnings manipulations. Senior executives may frequently view shareholder value as a constraint, rather than an objective.

14 'irrational exuberance' – Annual Dinner and Francis Boyer Lecture of The American Enterprise Institute for Public Policy Research, Washington, DC, 5 December 1996. 'infectious greed' – Congressional Hearing, Washington, DC, 16 July 2002.

15 Banner (1997, 1998) argues that most major legislation regulating securities markets has come about following a sustained financial market crash. See also Clarke *et al.* (2003) who make a similar point with regard to securities regulation in Australia.

16 Where accounting fraud is involved, the various corporate scandals mostly differ by variations of a similar tune, for example, incorrect recognition of earnings, underestimates (i.e. hiding) of liabilities, booking imaginary future earnings, and so forth (for further examples of specific instruments used in manipulating financial figures, see Clarke *et al.*, 2003).

17 'Principal' and 'agent' generally refers to the separation of ownership and control. The principal–agent problem arises whenever a principal hires an agent to perform certain tasks, which highlights the necessity of aligning the interests of these two parties (Smith, 1776). Berle and Means (1932) referred to the alignment of the interests between management and the holders of the firm's capital. More broadly defined, 'principal' need not necessarily be equated with ownership (especially share ownership).

18 Clarke *et al.* (2003) emphasize the role of specific features of the accounting system which in their view are at the centre of many of the frauds under observation.

19 It may well be, however, that the boundaries of what is considered proper behaviour are pushed outward when stock markets are booming. A similar argument can be made with regard to a decrease in due diligence and proper objectiveness. Auditing might, for example, be considered more of a nuisance than a necessity when earnings growth seems limitless.

20 The discussion of 'rules vs. principles', with regard to what may constitute a better system for financial reporting and the external audit is also of relevance (see, for example, ICAS, 2006).

2 Overview of corporate governance

1 Under US federal bankruptcy law, for example, holders of common stock of a company in Chapter 11 are given the lowest priority in bankruptcy and come after secured and general unsecured creditors in terms of their ability to receive a recovery on their claim.

2 Shareholder wealth maximization refers to a view of corporate governance according to which directors have a fiduciary duty to maximize shareholder wealth. Traditionally, this is justified by ownership of the firm by shareholders.

3 Further examples of research on the impact of different corporate governance structures on executive behaviour and/or organizational performance include Core *et al.* (1999), and Gompers *et al.* (2003).

4 Not that the Japanese model, supposedly being more supportive of long-term investment activities of corporations, necessarily provides a better guide to long-term firm performance. This research cannot possibly do justice to the rich field of investigation that discusses the question of whether an emphasis on 'shareholder value' allows for the perpetuation of societal prosperity. Engelen (2002) may serve as an introduction to some of these issues. For an elaboration and critique of shareholder theory and practice, see O'Sullivan (2000).

5 Beginning in mid-2002, the SEC required US listed companies to disclose options grants within two days of their being granted to comply with the Sarbanes-Oxley Act 2002. By the end of October 2006, more than 140 companies had disclosed internal or regulatory probes of their option grants, including investigations by the SEC and/or the US Department of Justice, and some 34 top executives had resigned or been asked to resign over issues of options backdating (Reuters News, 29 October 2006). A small number of former top executives have had charges related to backdating brought against them. The backdating of options describes a range of activities related to the granting of options, and includes the changing of the date used to set options and their exercise price to one where the underlying stock's value is low enough to make the option valuable. Heron and Lie (2006) estimate that nearly 30 per cent of their sample of over 7,700 US listed firms manipulated grants to top executives at some point between 1996 and 2005.

6 Dechow and Skinner (2000) argue that managers successfully affect benchmark levels by influencing the analysts who follow the firm's progress, and in turn have considerable control over meeting those benchmark figures as the latter are accounting figures subject to earnings management.

7 The efficient market hypothesis asserts that financial markets are efficient and that prices of traded assets reflect all known information and are therefore accurate (or best unbiased estimators). EMH is commonly stated in three forms – weak form efficiency, semi-strong form efficiency and strong form efficiency – each with different and increasingly restrictive implications for how markets work.

8 A similar comment would appear valid for executive compensation from 1993–2003. Bebchuk and Grinstein (2005) found that if the relationship of compensation to various corporate performance measures and company profit had remained stable, mean compensation in 2003 would have been about half of actual size. In 2005 executive compensation vastly outstripped growth in earnings in the United States (*Wall Street Journal Europe*, 7 January 2006).

9 Empirical research generally finds that performance benchmarking in top executive compensation is asymmetric. Garvey and Milbourn (2003: 3) found evidence that 'executives are . . . insulated from bad luck, while they are rewarded for good luck'.

10 Examples of guaranteed compensation regardless of performance include rewarding mediocrity and failure, golden goodbyes in excess of contractual obligations, at-the-money options, the resetting and reloading of options, guaranteed bonuses, and gratuitous payments.

11 The reputation of monitors is also subject to asymmetric information and the free rider problem. Any one reputational intermediary cannot capture all of his or her own investment in reputation and some of this investment accrues to the profession. This reduces interest in reputational investment, and also limits the ability of reputational intermediaries to vouch for the quality of financial disclosure (Black, 2001b).

12 This might be a rational argument for self-dealing.

13 It is argued later in this research that the economist's classical assumption of rationality may not necessarily be the best framework in which to assess agents' behaviour. In particular, I will propose that judgement and decisions may not always be based on a trade-off between ethics and profits, as assumed in a rational framework, but may also, and perhaps primarily so, be due to poor decision-making as the result of psychological, social, and cognitive factors.

14 Of the three most senior executives at Enron, former long-time CEO Ken Lay passed away before sentencing, former CEO Jeff Skilling has been sentenced (in appeal), and former CFO Andrew Fastow was incarcerated, as of October 2006, to serve a six-year sentence. Fastow had to surrender a large part of the gains he made through illegal Enron ventures. Skilling, sentenced to 24 years, was also ordered to surrender some $60m in personal wealth. Both orders were in appeal at the time this book went to press.

15 For a summary of Enron insider trading, see the website of law firm Lerach, Coughlin, Stoia, Geller, Rudman & Robbins, at <www.enronfraud.com/insider.html> (accessed 16 August 2007).

16 See, for example, Gottfredson and Hirschi (1990); Pfohl (1994); Polinsky and Shavell (1999); Goode (2005). The value of deterrence in corporate governance will be further discussed in subsequent chapters.

17 See, for example, Cornish and Clarke (1986) and Posner (2003). For the classic text on crime as an economic activity, and the traditional behavioural assumptions behind the costs and benefits of crime, see Becker (1968). For an overview of research on social deviance, see Pontell (2005).

18 Some results of research on tax evasion, for example, suggest that both penalties and audit probabilities may have significant impacts on evasion (Klepper and Nagin, 1989), although the probability of detection may be more important as a deterrent than the level of sanctions (Kinsey, 1992). Hessing *et al.* (1992), in contrast, find no evidence of a deterrent effect with respect to tax evasion. I would also like to refer to issues relating to morals and civic duty, which have been shown to affect law abidance (see Orviska and Hudson, 2003). One must ask, however, why agents should suddenly have become less moral or lost some of their civic duty, compared to former times. There is no strong reason to assume that there has been a general decline in business morals among senior executives. Corporate scandals are as old as corporations, and the relative size of scandals also shows no clear trend in terms of magnitude (Clarke *et al.*, 2003).

19 US data suggests that over 70 per cent of inmates are rearrested within three years of being released (US Department of Justice, 2004). I earlier referred to the diminished value of deterrence in white collar crime. Punishment for securities fraud, for example, frequently bears no relation to the magnitude of the damage caused. Michael Milken, of 1980s junk-bond market fame, may have paid a $600m fine and served 20 months in a federal prison, but this still left him with an estimated $600m from ill-gotten gains. This is not a bad return, and positively favours white-collar crime over, say, holding up a bank, not that either activity is to be encouraged.

20 Institutional investors are entities which invest own or clients' funds in public companies and include private and public pension funds, mutual funds, insurance companies, banks, and private equity firms. Main factors which affect the level of engagement of the various types of institutional investors are fund size, investment time horizon, performance expectations, proportion invested in equity, legal restraints, active/passive investing, internal/external management, defined-benefit/defined-contribution (*re* pensions). Hartzell and Stark (2003), for example, found that institutional ownership is positively related to the pay-for-performance sensitivity of executive compensation and negatively related to the level of compensation, and suggest that these institutions serve a monitoring role, and mitigate agency problems. See DTI (2005b) for a recent overview of the literature on institutional investors.

21 This abstracts from considerations of heterogeneity of this investor class, which has implications on the likely level and direction of engagement. A complex set of characteristics, including fund size, investment time horizon, performance expectations, and the proportion of funds invested in equity, influences institutional investors' propensity for, and level and type of, engagement. See DTI (2005b) for a more detailed discussion.

22 See speech by Ethiopis Tafara, Director, Office of International Affairs, SEC, *Remarks on UK and US approaches to Corporate Governance and on the Market for Corporate Control*, delivered at the Institute of Chartered Accountants in England and Wales, London, United Kingdom, 9 January 2007. Available HTTP: <http://www.sec.gov/news/speech/2007/spch020807et.htm> (accessed 15 August 2007).

23 Hermes, a London-based fund, is especially active in this respect.

24 Theoretically, 'a board of directors is the equilibrium solution (albeit possibly second best) to some agency problems confronting the firm' (Hermalin and Weisbach, 2003: 9–10).

25 Earnings management is not restricted to income-increasing behaviour. Managers may prefer to engage in income-decreasing earnings management. Managers may systematically manipulate reported earnings downwards when pre-managed earnings exceed threshold earnings by a substantial amount (Degeorge *et al.*, 1999), or when managers' accounting-based bonuses are at their maximum (Healy, 1985; Gaver *et al.*, 1995; Holthausen *et al.*, 1995). For example, Freddie Mac, the US mortgage finance firm, was fined $125m in 2003 for understating its profits by some $5bn over several years. See OFHEO (2003).

26 Specifically, these authors found that accrual quality is negatively related to the absolute magnitude of accruals, the length of the operating cycle, loss incidence, and the standard deviation of sales, cash flows, accruals, and earnings, and positively related to firm size.

27 Borokhovich, *et al.* (1996) analysed stock returns around succession announcements and found that shareholders tend to benefit from outsider appointments.

28 The Committee on the Financial Aspects of Corporate Governance, chaired by Sir Adrian Cadbury, made recommendations on the role of directors and auditors in response to financial scandals in the 1980s. The Committee also produced a Code of Best Practice, which primarily related to the composition of the board, composition of board committees, establishment of an audit committee, the role of independent directors, and related company financial reporting and controls. The London Stock Exchange subsequently introduced the requirement for UK listed companies to issue a statement of compliance with the provisions of the Code, or explain their non-compliance.

29 AICPA was, until 1973, in one form or another, solely responsible for the pronouncement of US accounting principles (GAAP). From 1973 onward, the non-government Financial Accounting Standards Board (FASB) became the SEC designated organization responsible for setting accounting standards. AICPA

retained some standard-setting functions in a number of areas, including financial statement auditing, professional ethics, attest services, CPA firm quality control, CPA tax practice, and financial planning practice. Following the Sarbanes-Oxley Act 2002, passed in response to massive perceived failures of the auditing process, the newly created Public Company Accounting Oversight Board and the SEC were given some of the powers and duties previously residing with AICPA (particularly with regard to quality assurance of public audits).

30 Independence, in part, depends on the diversification of the client base. Arthur Andersen, for example, had many other clients apart from Enron and income from this particular client constituted only about 1 per cent of total revenue for this accounting firm. For the engagement partner however, Enron was the major (and only significant) client and thus the individual auditor was hardly independent on the basis of this definition. It is now apparent that Andersen's independence was compromised in additional ways. This problem was and is not specific to Andersen but is an industry-wide issue.

31 *In re Enron Corp. Sec., Derivative & ERISA Litigation*, 235 F. Supp., 2d, 549, 675 (S.D. Tex. 2002).

32 Ibid., at 675–6.

33 See testimony of David Duncan, Andersen's Enron engagement partner (*United States* v. *Duncan*, CRH-02-209 (S.D. Tex. Apr. 9, 2002) (charging Andersen's lead partner on the Enron engagement team with one count of obstruction of justice); *United States* v. *Andersen*, CRH 02-121 (S.D. Tex. Mar. 7, 2002) (charging Arthur Andersen with one count of obstruction of justice). Mr Duncan pled guilty, and Andersen was convicted after a six-week jury trial (conviction overturned by the Supreme Court in 2005, *Arthur Andersen LLP* v. *United States* 544 US 696). 'A number of surviving Arthur Andersen documents reveal that Arthur Andersen knew, was concerned about, yet covered up or ignored fraudulent accounting practices by Enron' (*In re Enron Corp. Sec., Derivative & ERISA Litigation*, 235 F. Supp., 2d, 549, 675 (S.D. Tex. 2002)).

34 Macey and Sale's argument (2003) is based on work by Eisenberg and Macey (2003), who investigated the distribution of restatements across major accounting firms.

3 Earnings management

1 See Denis (2001) for an insight into the breadth of the literature.

2 This argument is sometimes formulated in terms of visibility of earnings management: as long as earnings management is visible and transparent, rational investors will take this into consideration and adjust their judgements and decisions accordingly. This yields the argument that earnings management is not important as long as it is clearly visible. Alternatively, earnings management might be a positive activity if it conveys privileged information to market participants.

3 Jiambalvo (1996) discusses a range of forms of earnings management. See also, National Association of Certified Fraud Examiners (1993). Holthausen *et al.* (1995) discuss actions including changes in expenditures on research and development, and capital expenditures, as means of earnings manipulations.

4 Conservative accounting can be defined as the differential verifiability required for recognition of profits versus losses, that is, a higher degree of verification is required for gains than for losses. Effectively, costs and losses are booked immediately, while income and earnings enhancing items are booked only when their receipt can unequivocally be confirmed. This typically leads to a systematic understatement of net assets and typically yields positive earnings surprises rather than negative ones. As an example, Freddy Mac, the US mortgage finance firm, was found to have understated its profits by some $5bn over several years (OFHEO, 2003).

5 See Clarke *et al.* (2003) for a review of such cases in Australia.

6 Several studies found that earnings reported by firms making stock offers tend to contain abnormally high levels of positive accruals around offer dates (DuCharme, 1994; Friedlan, 1994; Shivakumar, 2000), and that these accruals tend to reverse in later reporting periods and are significantly negatively related to post-offer stock returns (Rangan, 1998; Teoh *et al.*, 1998a, b).

7 See Kahneman and Tversky (1992) for a detailed discussion of the status-quo bias and prospect theory, and Kahneman and Tversky (1986) for loss framing.

8 For a detailed exploration of the effects of this bias on the accounting area, see Bazerman *et al.* (2002a, b).

9 Ideally, contracts for senior managers are designed to align their interests with the long-term success of the firm (Langevoort, 1998b). How this can, if at all, be achieved, is quite a different matter.

10 The human preference for immediate gratification over future rewards is well documented. See Loewenstein (1996); Rabin (1998, 2002); Thaler (2000); O'Donoghue and Rabin (2001, 2003, 2005).

11 In a different context, but eminently relevant to our discussion, this was put as follows: 'Men endowed with the properties of angels do not have to anticipate disappointing outcomes; nor do they have to enter disappointment into calculations, but mortals must' (Landau and Chisholm, 1995: 69).

12 Defined as the variability in flows due to timing effects.

13 Earnings were deemed in Dechow's study (1994) to have a lower first order annual autocorrelation than either cash from operations or net cash flows; noise decreases as the reporting period increases.

14 It should be noted that cash flows and aggregate earnings can both be biased predictors for future cash flows. Cash flow measures tend to suffer less than accruals-based earnings measures from the potential for earnings manipulation, but introduce typical distortions in the financial flow patterns over time. This suggests that the mixed results of prior research may, in part, be due to sample composition which may influence the magnitude of the respective biases (Barth *et al.*, 2001).

15 This refers to accruals which tend to reverse over time periods. Some accruals tend to reverse much slower, or not at all. This research will address the implication of non-reversal slightly further on in the discussion.

16 Understanding what causes the market to fail to fully incorporate the future earnings implications of current accruals and cash flow signals is a perplexing issue that deserves further investigation. It has implications for the efficient market hypothesis and the rationality assumptions of market participants. While related to the present investigation, it is not possible to pursue this matter in detail at this point.

17 One obvious problem, of course, is that perpetrators of earnings management with intent to mislead the users of financial information hardly wish to advertise the fact. Managerial intent itself is largely unobservable. Yet, as will be shown, the intention to mislead is a central component of this manipulation of financial information.

18 The reader will recall the distinction between outright fraud and earnings management. Clearly, corporate fraud is typically based on earnings management. However, not all incidences of earnings management constitute fraud. Where managerial discretion ends and fraud begins remains debatable.

19 Abnormal accruals are frequently also referred to as unexpected or discretionary, although conceptually there are slight differences between these terms.

20 See Thomas and Zhang (2000) for a comparison of accruals prediction models. A somewhat simpler approach looks at changes in total accruals as a proxy for unexpected accruals.

21 It should be noted that not all abnormal accruals should be identified as discretionary accruals.

22 For examples of this approach, see Healy (1985); Jones (1991); Dechow (1994); Peasnell *et al.* (2000a, b, 2001, 2002); Klein (2002), DaDalt *et al.* (2003). A somewhat simpler approach looks at changes in total accruals as a proxy for unexpected accruals. See Thomas and Zhang (2000) for a comparison of accruals prediction models.

23 Dechow and Skinner (2000) point to the trade-off this approach makes vis-à-vis research using discretionary accruals methods. While discretionary accruals models tend to lack power and tend to use small sample sizes, studies on the attributes of earnings distributions (e.g. Burgstahler and Dichev, 1997) crucially depend on the assumption that the detected empirical irregularities are evidence of earnings management.

24 Myers *et al.* (2006) interpret the existence of a long string of consecutive quarters of growth in earnings-per-share resulting from accruals (rather than from cash flows) as prima facie evidence of earnings management.

25 See Dechow *et al.* (1995) for a detailed discussion of strengths and weaknesses of several competing models; also Kang and Shivdasani (1995) and more recently, Moreira and Pope (2006).

26 Dechow *et al.* (1995) found that all the models under investigation produced reasonably well-specified tests, but that the power of these tests was low for fairly high levels of earnings management (5 per cent of assets). Application to firms that experienced extreme financial performance led to mis-specified tests for all models. Instead of focusing on managerial use of discretional accruals, Dechow and Skinner (2000) suggest that the identification of firms engaging in earnings management may benefit from concentrating on managerial incentives.

27 Hribar and Collins (2002) suggest that the most important and pervasive factors for this error in the balance sheet approach to accruals measurement are due to mergers and acquisitions, divestitures, and foreign currency translation of foreign subsidiary account balances. The authors recommend using accruals measures taken directly from the cash flow statement instead.

28 An additional finding in this study was that investors do not seem to fully anticipate the lower earnings persistence of the various types of accruals.

29 Richardson *et al.* (2004a) contend that Healy's definition of accruals (1985) excludes several important categories of accruals with low reliability (hence low persistence), which, if ignored by the market, can lead to significant mispricing. An example of the type of accruals frequently omitted in the accruals literature is the capitalization of operating costs, at the heart of the accounting scandal at WorldCom.

30 Dharan (2003) suggests focusing on accruals which reverse more slowly as an alternative to working capital accruals (traditionally investigated in the literature).

31 The reader is reminded of Enron's use of thousands of Special Purpose Vehicles to shift liabilities and low quality assets off its books, and to record largely fictitious revenues.

32 For a discussion of the differences in views on this topic, see Dechow and Skinner (2000).

33 This is in addition to the question of whether earnings management is a problem of sufficient severity to justify such a wide discussion. See Denis (2001) for an introduction to the breadth of this literature.

34 This would appear to closely relate to the phenomenon of escalation of commitment. This refers to an over-commitment to a failing cause, where a prior approving decision increases the psychological pressure for continued support of this decision, regardless of evidence that would support view reversal and termination of support (see Staw, 1976; Garland, 1990; Brockner, 1992; Bromiley *et al.*, 2002).

35 Participants of the survey included a quarter of FTSE 100 listed companies and larger private companies in the UK, with a combined revenue of over £500bn (RSM Robson Rhodes Press release, 18 October 2004. Available HTTP: <http://www.rsmi.co.uk/> (accessed 15 March 2007)).

36 The surveys do not include reference to the large corporate scandals which emerged during 2001/2002. The Enron fraud alone led to losses in the region of \$60–70bn. Losses associated with the WorldCom fraud were approaching the \$100bn mark.

37 It should be noted that sensitivities towards earnings manipulations, particularly overstatements, might have increased due to the financial scandals of the recent past and it is possible that any increase in sensitivity might just be a temporary phenomenon.

38 Partially as a result of accruals reversing in subsequent periods.

39 Former White House chief economic advisor Larry Lindsay was recorded as calling the Enron debacle a 'tribute to American capitalism', while former US Treasury Secretary Paul O'Neill made the point that 'Companies come and go' and 'Part of the genius of capitalism is people get to make good decisions or bad decisions, and they get to pay the consequence or to enjoy the fruits of their decisions. That's the way the system works.'

40 This interpretation goes further than that usually assumed in econometric models which investigate an association between accounting discretion and poor corporate governance. Later models assume that a correlation between these two (broad) variables cannot automatically lead to an interpretation of opportunism as this should lead to an observation of subsequent loss of shareholder wealth.

41 Clarke *et al.* (2003), in part, make a related argument with regard to accounting principles in Australia.

42 See also Wells' argument (2004) for auditors to use a much more critical approach to the detection of corporate fraud. With particular reference to the use of models for fraud detection, Wells suggests that auditors should address how clients fare in areas including internal controls, financial condition, corporate structure, cultural and ethical reward systems, and executive integrity. Wells continues to argue the case for an analysis of fraud with the objective of preventing it, instead of reacting to fraud which has already occurred. He suggests that antifraud investigators, in coordination with the auditors, should try to identify key risk areas during an audit. In an earlier paper, Professor Benston had proposed that a large auditing firm would be strongly averse to conducting a misleading audit, dismissing the possibility of acquiescence (Benston, 1985). In fact, Benston had deemed it inconceivable that an auditor would be tempted to participate in a client's fraud on account of the reputational damage that this would incur on exposure. Benston and Hartgraves provide some recognition of a lack of insufficient exercise in 'the requisite scepticism that auditors should adopt' (2002: 126). After the Enron/Andersen debacle, Professor Benston would appear to allow for the possibility that auditing partners may sometimes conduct audits of poor quality and produce misstatements for personal gain, even where the potential costs of such actions vastly outweigh any possible gains (Benston, 2003a).

43 Andersen partner testimony. United States Senate (2002b: 19).

44 That supposedly non-recurring events often re-appeared in subsequent years' reports apparently did not deter investors.

45 Enron frequently placed crucial information in the footnotes of its financial reports. Admittedly, the wording used in those footnotes may not always have been the most comprehensible, and at times might have been downright obscure, but determined observers could nonetheless have extracted valuable information from them. Still, apparently much more important in the average investor's mind (and that of analysts and other experts) than these informational gems hidden

in footnotes were the headline figures provided by the firm, irrespective of their validity. Thus, highly visible figures, even where considered to be a poor estimator of true underlying realities may act as an anchor from which investors and other observers insufficiently adjust.

46 'It is the peculiar and perpetual error of the human understanding to be more moved and excited by affirmatives than by negatives' (Francis Bacon).

47 Section 404 of the Act requires the annual report of the issuer to contain a management assessment with regard to adequate internal control structure and procedures for financial reporting. This has to be attested and reported on by the issuer's auditor.

48 In January 2004, US regulators voted to propose new rules requiring mutual fund advisers to adopt and enforce codes of ethics and requiring new disclosures by fund employees (Reuters, 14 January 2004). This followed an investigation by Eliot Spitzer, the Attorney General for New York, into illegal or unethical trading schemes within the mutual fund industry, which holds $7 trillion in investors' assets.

49 *Herald Tribune*; Reuters; Bloomberg News, 24 May 2006.

4 Rationality or rational behaviour?

1 See, for example, Daws and Hastie (2001) who trace the maximization of expected utilities concept to the classic piece by von Neuman and Morgenstern (1944).

2 See Ellickson (1998) for the impact of social norms on law and economics.

3 Bayes' theorem describes the relationships that exist within an array of conditional probabilities. Bayesian updating is based on joint probability – the probability of two events occurring together – and is applied to a prior probability estimate to obtain an improved posterior probability estimate. One application is to situations where probability is defined according to strict relative-frequencies. It is also applied to situations where probability is constructed in terms of subjective confidence. In this latter form, the subjective confidence in the truth of a particular hypothesis is adjusted upward or downward in accordance with confirmatory or disconfirmatory observations with regard to a prior. Bayesian probabilities can be interpreted as a measure of the degree of belief a rational person has in the proposition or belief in question. Bayesian inference uses Bayes' theorem to update the probability of an original set of beliefs in light of new information.

4 A subjective interpretation of probability theory based on Bayesian updating was earlier described by Ramsey and Braithwaite (1931) who began to axiomatize choice under uncertainty. This task was subsequently developed into a theory of subjective and personal probability by Savage (1954).

5 Waller provides a simplified summary of the rational actor model of individual choice making:

> Individuals are assumed to act as if they maximize expected utility. That is, an individual's preferences are taken as given, consistent, and representable in the form of a utility function. An individual knows a priori the set of alternative actions and chooses the action with the highest utility or expectation thereof. When uncertainty exists as to the actions' consequences, an individual can assess the probability distribution corresponding to his or her knowledge. When new information may be collected from the environment, an individual knows the information's possible content and can assess, in accord with Bayes' theorem, the probability distribution conditioned on the conjunction of such content and his or her prior knowledge.
>
> (Waller, 1995: 32)

6 Formalism, according to Blaug, 'gives priority to the form of expression of theories at the expense of content' (1998: 30).

7 See also Simon (1983: 13): 'Conceptually, the SEU [Subjective Expected Utility] Model is a beautiful object deserving a prominent place in Plato's heaven of ideas. But vast difficulties make it impossible to employ it in any literal way in making actual human decisions.'

8 Most economists seem to take for granted that rationality in its most fundamental and robust form is a valid description of human choice-making. As an abstraction, this model is, of course, not expected to work perfectly under all circumstances, which may partially explain the reluctance to accept the challenges from cognitive psychology and behavioural economics which investigate deviations from its predictions. This may leave many economists agnostic to behavioural evidence which challenges this construct on a fundamental level. The view that preference maximization is synonymous with choice also tends to ignore the potential importance of heterogeneity among agents for the design of incentives (O'Donoghue and Rabin, 2005).

9 This assumption is part of Prospect Theory (Kahneman and Tversky, 1979).

10 See O'Donoghue and Rabin (2005), who conclude that optimal incentive design should pay attention to details that the standard model would assume to be irrelevant.

11 For example, see Strotz (1955); Slovic and Lichtenstein (1971); Tversky and Kahneman (1974); Kahneman and Tversky (1979, 1984, 1986); Nisbett and Ross (1980); Staw (1981); Thaler (1981); Slovic *et al.* (1982, 2004); Taylor and Brown (1988); Rabin (2002); Westen *et al.* (2006).

12 Important texts include *Judgement Under Uncertainty: Heuristics and Biases* (Kahneman *et al.*, 1982); *The Psychology of Judgement and Decision Making* (Plous, 1993); *Research on Judgment and Decision Making* (Goldstein and Hogarth, 1997); *A Behavioural Approach to Law and Economics* (Jolls *et al.*, 1998); *Judgment in Managerial Decision Making* (Bazerman, 2005); *Heuristics and Biases* (Gilovich *et al.*, 2002a); *A Perspective on Psychology and Economics* (Rabin, 2002).

13 Rabin (2002) provides a detailed overview of the integration of psychology and economics in order to achieve a greater degree of realism in the economic analysis of human decision-making and behaviour.

14 Base rates refer to the relative frequency of an event within a population, and have to be taken into account to correctly update a prior with new information (as when applying Bayes' rule).

15 This demonstration of base rates is an adaptation of work done by David Lane who produced the example for The Connexions Project. Licensed for use under the Creative Commons Attribution License. See <http://cnx.org> and <http://creativecommons.org/licenses/by/1.0/> (accessed 15 August 2007).

16 Base rates frequently do influence probability judgements of course, but the literature on base rate neglect demonstrates that individuals may often place relatively less weight on base rate information than on descriptive, individual information, and on mental shortcuts (heuristics) in updating. New information may either be overweighed or underweighted, relative to the prior. The discussion will return to this important point.

17 While people would typically be considered to be risk averse over gains, they frequently appear to be risk-loving over losses. Kahneman and Tversky (1979) found that 70 per cent of subjects would prefer a 3/4 probability of losing nothing and 1/4 probability of losing \$6,000 to a 2/4 probability of losing nothing and 1/4 probability of losing \$4,000 or \$2,000. As a mean-preserving spread of the less preferred lottery, the responses of 70 per cent of the subjects in the preferred lottery question are inconsistent with the standard concavity assumption. Tversky and Kahneman (1991) suggest that individuals value moderate losses approximately

twice as much as same-sized gains. The standard concave utility function in contrast implies risk-neutrality for small stakes.

18 In a paper published in 1960 (cited in his 1991 Nobel Price speech), which more explicitly dealt with the question of asset allocation, Coase emphasizes that transactions costs could not be neglected and that the initial allocation of property rights very well mattered in the presence of such costs. The endowment effect impacts on the valuation of assets, and thus may affect allocation efficiency, just as transactions costs do.

19 Tversky and Kahneman (1992: 297) found evidence for 'a distinctive fourfold pattern of risk attitudes: risk aversion for gains and risk seeking for losses of high probability; risk seeking for gains and risk aversion for losses of low probability'.

20 Alternatively, p(A | new info) = (p(new info | A)/p(new info)) * p(A). Where, a prior is the initial estimate of probability of hypothesis, and the posterior is the estimate of probability after incorporating new evidence.

21 A simple application of Bayes' rule was provided earlier when the calculation of the likelihood of 'Disease X' was used to demonstrate the use of base rates.

22 See also Tversky and Kahneman (1983), who find that representations in terms of frequencies can eliminate conjunction errors.

23 If memory were unbiased, and had all relevant information available, then this heuristic would not lead to such errors. However, memory retrieval is never unbiased, as it is based on retrieval cues, and likely also to be subject to further influences. One such influence can be seen in the confirmation bias, the tendency to seek out and overweigh information which supports a prior view, while disregarding contradictory data (Wason, 1960, 1966). Westen *et al.* (2006) present results of a study showing the brain activity for confirmation bias. Their results suggest the unconscious and emotion driven nature of this form of bias. Specifically, emotion-biased motivated reasoning would appear to be qualitatively distinct from reasoning where no emotional stake is present.

24 [With reference to psychological theories of the choice process:] 'In these theories, the economists' calculus of utility assessment and maximization is reduced to one of many factors in the decision making environment, with an influence that may be overridden by context effects, emotion, and errors in perception and judgment' (McFadden, 2000: 345).

25 'People may be rationalizing rather than rational' (anonymous referee). In an early paper on the impact of affect (also put in terms of 'experiental thinking') Cajon (1980: 155) noted that '*We sometimes delude ourselves that we proceed in a rational manner and weigh all the pros and cons of the various alternatives. But this is probably seldom the case. Quite often, "I decided in favor of X" is no more than "I liked X." . . . We buy the cars we "like," choose the jobs and houses we find "attractive," and then justify these choices by various reasons.*' Also, '*Decisions . . . are often reached by focusing on reasons that justify the selection of one option over another*' (Shafir *et al.*, 1993: 34).

26 This is referred to as the 'fundamental attribution error', coined by Ross (1977). See the classic experiments by Jones and Harris (1967). See also Kelley (1967, 1973). On the use of accountability to reduce attribution error, see Tetlock (1985).

27 The reader is referred to Rabin (2002), who provides a detailed overview of the integration of psychology and economics to achieve a greater degree of realism in economic analysis.

28 '[T]here is considerable evidence that people tend to interpret subsequent evidence so as to maintain their initial beliefs' (Lord *et al.*, 1979: 2099).

29 In an investigation of self-serving bias in auditing, King (2002) shows that social pressure to conform to group norms can counterbalance self-serving bias. King criticizes Bazerman *et al.* (2002a) who conclude that auditors find it difficult to

be independent due to unconscious bias. However, pressure to conform to norms may also induce or reinforce individual bias. Whether group pressure works to lessen or to enhance bias would appear to depend on what norms the group emphasizes. In general, see Stoner (1961) on risky shift; Moscovici and Zavalloni (1969) on group polarization; Staw (1976) on flaws of group decision-making; Myers (1978, 1982) on polarization in social environments; and Sullivan and Kida (1995) on the effect of prior gains and losses on risky decision-making.

30 Hyperbolic discounting refers to the empirically observed phenomenon that discount rates are often not constant over time, but appear to decline. That is, individuals appear to have a declining rate of time preference. This is in contrast to exponential discounting typically used in discounted utility models, which assume a constant discounting rate over time. For a critical review of discounting and inter-temporal consistency, see Frederick *et al.* (2002). Consistent with the predictions of hyperbolic discounting, visceral influences on behaviour can also explain time inconsistencies. Visceral factors may better explain impulsivity in some forms of consumption and the importance of sensory contact (i.e. physical proximity to the object) as cues. See Zajonc (1980); Loewenstein (1996).

31 Mitchell's views are contrasted by Prentice (2004). Mitchell is of course correct when he stresses the need for empirically verifiable claims. There is no argument on this point.

32 What Mitchell (2002: ii) calls the 'equality of incompetence', refers to the relatively recent movement in legal scholarship known as behavioural law and economics.

33 De-biasing efforts can, under some circumstances exacerbate biases. Seidenfeld (2001) investigated possible accountability effects of political review in administrative agency settings. Camerer and Hogarth (1999) reviewed experiments involving financial incentives to investigate the impact of material consequences on behaviour. These studies confirm that incentives (aimed at de-biasing) sometimes improved performance, but may sometimes exacerbate existing bias.

34 Possible explanations cited by Heifetz and Spiegel (2001) refer to the perceived benefits of overconfidence with regard to, among others, motivation and self-esteem (Taylor and Brown, 1988; Camerer and Lovallo, 1999). Another benefit might be related to the lower time cost of decision-making based on heuristics as opposed to using Bayesian updating. Samuelson and Zhang (1992) earlier found that a regular payoff-monotonic dynamics wipes out serially dominated strategies for the case of finite numbers of strategies. The potential of strategic advantage from a biased objective function was investigated in early work by Schelling (1960), and has also been applied to economics, see, for example, Akerlof and Dickens (1982); Rogoff (1985). For applications to macroeconomics, see Akerlof (2002).

35 An early suggestion of intrinsic optimism as an explanation for investment decisions was suggested by Keynes ([1936] 1967). One explanation for the emergence of a biased perception depends on interaction between agents and externalities imposed by an action in a strategic (say, competitive) setting. Actions by 'optimists' can induce others to change their behaviour with a positive impact on the optimists. Individuals who hold (moderately) optimistic beliefs about their prospects and fail to update them in a Bayesian fashion can gain a strategic advantage over other individuals. This, incidentally, provides an explanation as to why individuals may not learn over time to update their beliefs in a Bayesian fashion. A similar logic may be applied to a pessimistic stance. Another explanation may rest on the time costs of Bayesian updating. An alternative explanation of optimism and self-confidence is based on dynamic inconsistency. Brocas and Carrillo (1999) explain overinvestment (resulting in excessive business failure rates) without recourse to boundedly rational or over-optimistic agents, and make use of

the concept of dynamically inconsistent preferences (see Strotz, 1955) to explain their findings.

36 Jolls *et al.* (1998) note that nearly 200 studies support this descriptive claim; see also Weinstein (1980).

37 Hubris might be an extreme form of this reinforcement process.

38 'The mentally healthy person appears to have the enviable capacity to distort reality in a direction that enhances self-esteem, maintains beliefs in personal efficacy, and promotes an optimistic view of the future' (Taylor and Brown, 1988: 203).

39 This would appear to make the realist a sorry specimen of humanity.

40 Landau and Chisholm (1995) cite the 1986 loss of the US Challenger space shuttle as an example of over-optimism in management leading to flawed decision-making.

41 The specific attributes Williamson (1999) refers to are bounded rationality and opportunism, which he sees distributed across the human population in variable degree.

5 Introducing behaviour to corporate governance

1 'The trouble with Homo Economicus is that he has really very little to do with his emotional, dim-witted half brother Homo sapiens, who bought Petsmart.com on a hunch' ('The Why of Buy', *TIME* magazine, 8 March 2004).

2 See also SEC (2003e) on global settlement related to analyst conflict of interest.

3 See Koniak (2002, 2003a, b) and Cramton (2002) for a discussion of legal and ethical aspects of lawyers in corporate governance.

4 In an additional twist to loss aversion behaviour, Douma *et al.* (2004) found that goal-setting can motivate unethical behaviour and motivated communication, especially when individuals are just short of reaching specific goals. Explained in terms of reference point adoption and loss aversion (Kahneman and Tversky, 1979; Heath *et al.*, 1999), Douma *et al.* posit that the closer to the goal individuals are, the higher may be the potential and incidence of unethical behaviour.

5 The perverse effects of Enron's incentive system on ethical behaviour and compliance with rules within Enron Corp. have been described, for example, by Bratton (2002), and harshly condemned by Spector (2003). Enron practised an extreme form of tournament, the 'rank-and-yank' system, under which units were each year required to identify (and fire) those at the bottom 15 per cent of performance. Those who came out in the top 15 per cent range were highly rewarded and promoted.

6 Motivated reasoning refers to the tendency for individuals to draw a particular conclusion through a process of biased reasoning. Utilizing a biased subset of the relevant beliefs, rules, and cognitive mechanisms, the individual interprets evidence in a manner designed to confirm an initial view. An initial hypothesis may itself be constructed through biased cognitive processes designed to 'reason' towards a desired conclusion: 'Motivation may affect reasoning through reliance on a biased set of cognitive processes: strategies for accessing, construing, and evaluating beliefs . . . Motivation can be construed as affecting the process of reasoning: forming impression, determining one's beliefs and attitudes, evaluating evidence, and making decisions' (Kunda, 1990: 481). And elsewhere, 'Strong evidence suggests that individuals generate, revise, and sustain personal hypotheses in ways designed to provide "support" for desired conclusions. The cart, essentially, is before the horse' (Hanson and Kysar, 1999: 727).

7 If the situation, despite the odds, ultimately turns out positively, it is not obvious that the principle of sunk costs was ignored, as the outcome would then likely be interpreted a success. Indeed, a positive outcome may then be seen as evidence of consistency in decision making, which is often rewarded (Staw, 1981).

8 A time budget refers to the time constraints imposed by audit firm management in which audit tasks should be completed. This may reflect a balancing of 'costs vs. quality' due to professional and competitive constraints faced by auditing firms.
9 See Bernardi and Arnold (1997), who find that the average moral development scores for male managers of the five largest accounting firms fell between those expected for senior high school and college students. Female accountants scored somewhat higher.
10 See Dunegan *et al.* (1992) for an application in business settings.
11 This may partially explain the underestimation of the difficulties of quitting an addiction (Loewenstein, 1999).
12 This sheds light, for example, on why some conflicts break down and the parties fail to identify a resolution, relevant to board decisions as well as to decisions on internal monitoring.
13 Recall the discussion in the previous chapter on over-optimism as an indicator of mental health, and as a potential motivator for creative thinking and effort.
14 Individuals often prefer the larger and later of two prizes when both are distant in time, but prefer the smaller, earlier one when both are near (Slovic *et al.*, 2002).
15 For a review of emotion and its interplay with cognition and social behaviour, see Zajonc (1998). For a review of the role of emotion in decision-making, see Loewenstein and Lerner (2003).
16 Such as, for example, evaluating ambiguous information more negatively in a negative mood and more positively in a positive mood. Affect intensity has been found to enhance the influence of emotion in the decision-making process (Loewenstein and Lerner, 2003).
17 Slovic *et al.* provide a good summary of Damasio's work:

> One of the most comprehensive and dramatic theoretical accounts of the role of affect in decision making is presented by the neurologist, Antonio Damasio (1994), in his book *Descartes' Error: Emotion, Reason, and the Human Brain*. Damasio's theory is derived from observations of patients with damage to the ventromedial frontal cortices of the brain that has left their basic intelligence, memory, and capacity for logical thought intact but has impaired their ability to 'feel' – that is, to associate affective feelings and emotions with the anticipated consequences of their actions. Close observation of these patients combined with a number of experimental studies led Damasio to argue that this type of brain damage induces a form of sociopathy (Damasio *et al.*, 1990) that destroys the individual's ability to make rational decisions; that is, decisions that are in his or her best interests. Persons suffering this damage became socially dysfunctional even though they remain intellectually capable of analytical reasoning.
>
> (2002: 399)

18 Fungibility refers to the ease by which one good can be interchanged with another identical good. With regard to consumption behaviour, this is interpreted to imply the interchangeability of assets, income streams, and other sources of wealth, hence these are assumed to be perfect substitutes. The mental accounts model argues that accounting decisions such as to which category to assign a particular income or purchase, the possible combination of outcomes, and the frequency of updating mental accounts can affect the perceived attractiveness of choices. Hence, money in one mental account is not a perfect substitute in another account, which violates fungibility. The mental accounts model shares several features with Kahneman and Tversky's Prospect Theory (1979), including the definition of the value function over gains and losses relative to a reference point, diminishing sensitivity of the loss and gain functions, and loss aversion (Thaler, 1980, 1985).

19 The mental accounts model has been used to explain, for example, differing time horizons, issues of self-control, budgeting decisions, individual consumption choice decisions, savings, the appeal of savings plans and flat-rate plans, the equity premium puzzle, attention to sunk costs, risk aversion, decisions to quit early once a certain amount of income has been earned, and more. For an overview of the mental accounts model, see Thaler (1999).

20 For classic accounts of life-cycle theory, see Modigliani and Brumberg (1954). Friedman (1957) proposed a permanent-income hypothesis, which leaves out assets but introduces lags into the consumption function. While both theories have greatly enhanced our understanding of consumption behaviour, empirical analyses suggest that neither theory is a complete explanation.

21 Kahneman and Tversky (1984: 347) proposed three alternatives in which outcomes might be framed: in terms of a minimal account, a topical account, or a comprehensive account. The comprehensive account incorporates all elements of wealth: current income and assets, future earnings, probabilities of such future earnings and other future assets, etc. Conventional economic theory typically assumes that decisions are based on such a comprehensive account. A minimal account concentrates on differences between options, while a topical account relates consequences of possible choices in relation to a reference point.

22 Financial analysts, for example, may base their judgements of risk and return for unfamiliar stocks upon a global attitude (Ganzach, 2000). Ganzach (2000) suggests that in situations where stocks were perceived as 'good', they were judged to have high return and low risk, whereas if they were perceived as bad, they were judged to be low in return and high in risk. However, for familiar stocks, perceived risk and return were positively correlated, rather than being driven by a global attitude.

23 Even the Big-4 accounting firms suggest that the existing audit system is 'broken'. While their motivation for this suggestion is likely different from that of this research, it does highlight persistent questions regarding the relevance of published financial data ('Big Four in call for real-time accounts', *Financial Times*, 8 November 2006).

24 External audits were also not good at predicting or preventing earlier cases of corporate fraud or mismanagement. Clarke *et al.* (2003) chronicled and analysed four decades of unexpected corporate collapse in Australia (and elsewhere) for commonalities. These authors maintain that the auditing profession has a long history of failure with regard to its monitoring role.

25 Lynn Turner was the chief accountant for the Securities and Exchange Commission from 1998 to 2001, and is a director of the Center for Corporate Financial Reporting at Colorado State University.

26 Selected settlement deals and years include Colonial Realty (1999: $90m); Waste Management (2000/01: part of $229m, plus $20m to Waste Management, plus $7m to the SEC); Sunbeam (2001: $110m); Baptist Foundation of Arizona (2002: $217m); Boston Chicken (2002: $19.4m); Bond Corp. (2002: est. Aus$100m); Qwest (2004: $250m); Global Crossing (2005: $25m); WorldCom (2005: $65m) (various press and online sources).

27 *Arthur Andersen LLP* v. *United States*, 125 S. Ct. 2129, 2005.

28 The relatively low impact of litigation on the then Big-5 auditing firms (with Arthur Andersen being an exception) has also been shown to hold for law firms. Langevoort (1993) proposes that law firms suffer relatively minor reputational damage from being caught assisting fraudulent clients. This may be indicative of a kind of reputation which is normally ignored, namely that some clients may be drawn to attorneys and auditors apparently willing to go along with clients' fraudulent intentions.

29 While this does not absolve an individual from blame, it does suggest that measures aimed at deterrence may not always be as powerful as generally assumed.

Where an individual is not aware of a transgression, or vigorously rationalizes own actions, deterrence effects would appear to be limited.

30 Some selectivity may also apply to the strength of the norm against self-dealing brought to bear in the financial community. The public's objections to self-dealing appear to be negatively related to corporate results. Put bluntly, in an up-market, not much attention may be given to evidence of gross self-dealing, perhaps taking this type of behaviour as 'the price of success'. The operative norm appears to be that self-dealing transactions in such a market are acceptable so long as these stay in the same range as that of comparable transactions. Since everyone is making money, magnanimity is shown to what may be perceived as minor breaches in conduct rules. On the downside, everything is different. The same officer hailed as an entrepreneurial genius on the upside starts to look like a villain and his or her self-dealing transactions cause a scandal even though these might already have been disclosed in published financial reports.

31 Although individuals tend to frequently assume bias in other people's judgement and behaviour, own perception and processing of information is typically deemed to be free of bias.

32 One such cognitive aid to rationalizing risk to a minimum is the overconfidence bias. Where a gatekeeper (whether this be an auditor, director, legal counsel, or banker) is subject to this bias, their judgement will be skewed against believing that respective clients are committing a fraud. A closely related bias is the confirmatory bias, the tendency for actors to 'interpret information in ways that serve their interests or preconceived notions' (Korobkin and Ulen, 2000: 1093).

33 Some of these recommendations (see, for example, Treadway, 1987; Cadbury, 1992) have been taken up in legislative and regulatory efforts in response to the Enron cohort of corporate scandals (as, for example, in the US Sarbanes-Oxley Act 2002 and the UK Combined Code, FRC, 2006). See also Cadbury Compliance Report (1995).

34 This new auditing standard will be further discussed.

35 See Gulati *et al.* (2003) for a discussion of the hindsight bias, the tendency to judge events predictable after they have unfolded. See also Bukszar and Connolly (1988) on the potential pitfalls of learning from experience.

36 Hanson and Kysar (1999) pay particular attention to affect and other judgement heuristics with regard to the manipulation of consumers by the packaging, marketing, and public relations practices of manufacturers. They call into question the consumer's ability to comprehend risk given an inability of individuals to consistently follow axioms of rationality under certain conditions. These findings can readily be applied to studying the effectiveness of product warnings, and general risk assessments.

37 Andersen would not survive the investigation, trial, and verdict. See Morrison's spirited defence of Arthur Andersen's involvement with Enron (2004) and an account of the alleged politics behind the case against Andersen. The belated reversal in May 2005 by the US Supreme Court of the obstruction of justice verdict adds some credence to Morrison's point that Andersen was made a scapegoat. Of course, this reversal came too late to revive Andersen as a firm.

38 Naïve optimism can arise from a confluence of factors including positive past experiences, a perception that risks are of low frequency and that the potential harm is preventable by human intervention.

6 Independence of auditors and directors

1 The board of directors and outside auditors are complemented in their task by supervision of areas of corporate activity by government and non-government agencies and other private sector agents (for example institutional investors, analysts,

public supervisory bodies, lawyers, and bankers). Legal counsel, too, has a central role, which has been somewhat neglected in the governance debate. Investment banks frequently facilitated corporate wrongdoing. The role of lawyers and legal counsel, as well as that of bankers in corporate governance will be discussed in Chapter 8.

2 Using a sample of UK firms, Peasnell *et al.* (2001) found that the demand for outside directors is a decreasing non-linear function of managerial ownership.

3 These papers report an insignificant relationship between various accounting measures of firm performance and the proportion of formally independent directors on the board. The use of Tobin's Q as the performance measure also does not appear to yield a significant correlation in this respect (Bhagat and Black, 2000).

4 What Krugman (2002b) calls the 'invisible handshake' in the boardroom.

5 The contract of Robert Annunziata of Global Crossing is one example of a weak pay/performance link and poor board oversight. Annunziata's tenure as CEO ended on 3 March 2000, after just one year on the job. As the company's performance levelled off, Mr Annunziata's compensation did not diminish commensurately (the company ultimately filed for Chapter 11 bankruptcy protection in January 2002). Annunziata's options for that period amounted to \$170m. A post-Enron example of the continued hold of the CEO on the board of directors resulting in a weak link between pay and performance was the nearly \$190m compensation package of former New York Stock Exchange Chairman and CEO Richard Grasso. Grasso's compensation had grown even as the exchange's income dwindled.

6 The Board on at least two occasions waved the Enron conflict-of-interest code to allow Enron's Chief Financial Officer to be in charge of some the special purpose vehicles used to obscure Enron's debt position (see Powers *et al.*, 2002).

7 'The Crisis in Corporate Governance', *Business Week*, 6 May 2002, pp. 71–2.

8 According to Senator Joseph Lieberman, member of the Senate Permanent Investigations Committee on Enron, 10 out of 15 of the most recent outside directors had conflicts of interest, including contracts with Enron, shared links with charities, and memberships of the boards of companies doing business with Enron (see United States Senate, 2002b).

9 Robert K. Jaedicke had also been the dean of the Graduate School of Business at Stanford University from 1983–1990, acting dean in 1979–1980, and associate dean for academic affairs from 1969 to 1981. Jaedicke joined the accounting faculty at the School in 1961 (Source: Stanford Graduate School of Business).

10 The discussion will return to this two-stage model.

11 This makes the simplifying assumption that reputation is not of value in itself, which of course it might be. In addition, potential reputational damage has no deterrence value in cases where the reputation is already lost.

12 Directorship reports on a survey of 17,000 listed companies. Other results include an average tenure of 5.4 years, with an average of 6 to 12 members per board, 91.2 per cent of which are male.

13 'The audit process and its environment are complex and variable. An audit takes several months to complete and is itself part of an ongoing process incorporating past audits, intervening events and expectations about events that may occur subsequent to the audit' (Gibbins and Wolf, 1982: 107).

14 See also, 'Auditors express opinions based on investigations that, no matter how thorough, inevitably involve subjective judgments' (Hogarth, 1991: 277). Jiambalvo and Wilner (1985) find that there is often substantial disagreement among trained auditors regarding the proper outcome for a particular problem.

15 Bazerman *et al.* (2002a, b) argue that very little association with a client is required to produce biased judgements.

16 Moreno *et al.* (2002) find that subjects reject decision alternatives which elicit negative affect in favour of alternatives which elicit positive affect. Subjects appear

to consider both financial data and affective value when considering alternatives, even if this is at the cost of economic value. This indicates that decision behaviour may be the result of a complex interaction between default strategies (such as prospect theory), the decision context, and affective reaction.

17 I am grateful to Professor John Hudson for suggesting this framework.

18 However, salient or representative new information may be overweighed with respect to its validity.

19 This, in part, refers the reader to an auditor's utility function outlining the costs and benefits of engaging in fraudulent practice presented earlier in the text, where it was suggested that the utility gained from an adverse report is path dependent. If the individual has previously given the firm a clean bill of health, then suddenly failing to do so may raise questions about previous decisions.

20 With regard to auditor independence, see SEC (2001), *Final Rule: Revision of the Commission's Auditor Independence Requirements*; and SEC (2003a), *Strengthening the Commission's Requirements Regarding Auditor Independence.* These, inter alia, define and detail cooling off periods of one year before a member of an audit team can join a client firm in certain key positions, list categories of prohibited non-audit services, mandate partner rotation, and enhance various disclosure and certification requirements.

21 By implication, this would also seem to apply to any other gatekeeper, especially, given their proximity to management, the members of a board.

22 The Sarbanes-Oxley Act 2002 legislates rotation (after five years) of the lead auditing partner only. Rotation of the auditing firm is not required. The lead partner may also not join the audit client in a 'financial reporting oversight' position for at least one year after leaving the audit engagement team.

23 CPAs working for audit firms frequently join the firms they have previously audited. The reader may recall that even the whistleblower in the Enron case was a former Andersen employee, as were many of her colleagues in internal auditing at Enron. This is not an isolated case:

> Until 1997, for example, every CFO and chief accounting officer hired by Waste Management worked previously at Arthur Andersen – Waste Management's independent auditor. All told, 14 former Andersen employees went to work for the Houston-based waste treatment and disposal company during the '90s. According to the SEC, most of the former Andersen auditors took jobs in key financial and accounting positions at the waste treatment and disposal company.
>
> (Craig Schneider, CFO.com (3 April 2002) *When Accountants Switch Sides*. Available HTTP: <http://www.cfo.com/printable/article.cfm/3004152> (accessed August 15 2007))

24 Feroz *et al.* (1991) found that 10 of the 25 large accounting firms censured by the SEC suffered no penalty to the firm or its personnel.

25 This study concentrated on second-tier firms, not what then were the Big-8.

26 The US Racketeer Influenced and Corrupt Organizations Act (RICO) provides for penalties for organized crime acts. Enacted by section 901(a) of the Organized Crime Control Act of 1970, Pub. L. No. 91–452, 84 Stat. 922.

27 *Lampf, Pleva, Lipkind & Petigrow* v. *Gilbertston*, 501 US 350, 359–61 (1991).

28 *Central Bank of Denver*, N.A. v. *First Interstate of Denver*, N.A., 511 US 164 (1994).

29 Pub. L. No. 105–353, 112 Stat. 3227.

30 See Coffee (2001) for a detailed discussion of the impact of these acts and other legislation passed in the mid to late 1990s with regard to the threat of litigation for accountants. Suggesting that the threat of litigation diminished during that time, Coffee cites several factors which might explain why the expected costs of

capture, or acquiescence, declined in the US prior to Enron. First, the apparent risk of litigation had fallen with the passage of certain laws and court decisions. Second, auditing had become a less significant source of income for the big accounting firms. Third, the compensation structure of partners had taken on a commission feature.

31 As has been pointed out earlier, liability for the firm is not the same as liability for the partner. There may be relatively little deterrence to the individual partner from the threat of fines against, or even closure of, the firm.

32 The term 'audit failure' is related to audit quality, which is unobservablc. Audit failure usually becomes known in the context of business failure, or substantial restatements.

33 Berardino did take the personal consequences by resigning on 26 March 2002, shortly after the unprecedented criminal indictment of the firm for obstruction of justice on 14 March 2002 which led to the demise of Andersen. Of course, he would have lost his job in any case after the firm was dissolved.

34 Gordon (2002) in particular points to the bundling of auditing plus tax planning, due to what he perceives as the carryover mindset from tax planning into accounting planning. It is quite revealing that Enron paid virtually no corporate taxes in the five years prior to its demise, despite reporting nearly $2bn in earnings from 1996 through 2000.

35 An evolution from a partnership of accounting professionals, constrained by a strong sense of professional ethics, to a profit-maximizing limited partnership organization using high-powered incentive compensation schemes is seen as one of the factors in the profession's morphing from 'watchdogs to lapdogs' (quote from US Congressional hearings on the role of Arthur Andersen in the failure of Enron Corp). For a discussion of the effect of changes to the legal and organizational setup of accounting firms, see Macey and Sale (2003). For a shorter account of the cultural change in the accounting profession, see Jeanne Dugan 'Did You Hear the One About the Accountant? It's Not Very Funny', *Wall Street Journal*, 14 March 2002, p. A1.

36 An accounting firm may lose a significant part of income from objecting to an accounting treatment, if the accounting firm loses a major consultancy contract as a result of the perceived obstruction.

37 Not surprisingly, the auditing profession in the US was for a long time vehemently opposed to a) the separation of audit and non-audit services, and b) anything other than self-regulation and self-monitoring.

38 See, for example, Frankel *et al.* (2002), who detect evidence for a loss of independence, contrasted by the response by Ashbaugh-Skaife *et al.* (2003), who strongly dispute these results. In general, see Larcker *et al.* (2005) who suggest that the typical structural indicators of corporate governance used in academic research have very limited ability in explaining managerial behaviour and organizational performance. This was noted in the discussion on the difficulty of detecting and measuring earnings management. This caveat would appear to be of equal importance in measuring the effects of auditor independence, which are frequently based on similar structural indicators.

39 Going concern opinions are issued by an auditor if there are questions regarding the financial viability of a firm. As these send a negative signal to markets and indicate financial distress, firms are expected to resist the issuance of such an opinion. Studies have also looked into the relationship between non-audit services and abnormal accruals (Chung and Kallapur, 2003) and between non-audit services and earnings management (Frankel *et al.*, 2002).

40 A situation where either outcome is less than desirable has been characterized by Kahneman and Lovallo (1997) as one likely to lead to excessive risk-taking and escalation of commitment.

41 *The Times* (London) reported David Duncan, Andersen's Houston partner in charge of the Enron account, as having had an estimated $1m per year salary (*The Times*, 19 January 2002).

42 With the major exception of Arthur Andersen, accounting firms may not have suffered heavy penalties from poor audits (see Wilson and Grimlund, 1990; Feroz *et al.*, 1991; Painter and Duggan, 1996). Fines imposed by oversight bodies such as the SEC can be substantial, but on the whole do little harm to the balance sheet. Individual partners may suffer even less. Even where the firm is destroyed due to its poor accounting practices, these individuals' careers are likely to suffer very little. They have a good chance of joining one of the remaining firms, who will need to hire more accountants as they pick up the business of the closed accounting firm.

43 Sarbanes-Oxley Act 2002 §201(a) (providing unlawful non-auditing services).

7 Recent corporate governance failures

1 ChuoAoyama, once Japan's third-largest audit firm, which used to count Sony, Toyota and Softbank among its clients, was in September 2006 renamed Misuzu after PricewaterhouseCoopers had separated from its Japanese affiliate. The fact that two more of the firm's former clients have admitted accounting irregularities since July 2006 (Nikko Cordial, Japan's third-largest broker, and Sony) has accelerated this accounting firm's demise. In February 2007 Misuzu asked other leading auditing firms to take on its remaining clients, as it prepared to close down permanently (*Washington Post*, 7 December 2006; *The Asahi Shimbun*, 21 February 2007; *The Economist*, 24 March 2007).

2 Fannie Mae (the 'Federal National Mortgage Association'), a federally chartered corporation owned by shareholders but run as a quasi-governmental agency, is mandated to provide liquidity in the secondary mortgage market.

3 As suggested in the preceding chapters, this recurrence of scandals and the apparent surprise of market participants and researchers is more of a problem for a rational view of agent behaviour than for an interpretation which allows the intrusion of behavioural effects in choice making.

4 In accruals accounting, incorrect estimates in one year typically lead to accrual reversions in following periods. Where management gets into the habit of issuing unsustainably positive financial figures, this sets up a process where the next periods' figures have to be managed even higher to postpone the need to restate earnings. While this may go on for surprisingly long periods, decades even, ultimately it is hardly sustainable (Clarke *et al.*, 2003).

5 For a detailed review of the LTCM case and implications for assessments of systemic risk, see GAO (1999).

6 Earnings management is central to most large cases of corporate fraud.

7 The various reports of the Enron bankruptcy examination run to more than two thousand pages, and the cost of the Enron bankruptcy examination enquiry approached $100m.

8 This term derives from the insurance literature and involves the increased probability of negligent behaviour once insured. Moral hazard is frequently fundamental to corporate financial disasters.

9 The $200(+)bn US Savings and Loan disaster of the 1980s provides an illustrative blue print of the moral hazard problems created by the confluence of a conducive legal framework, government guarantees, careless deregulation, and easily available money, where the owners of financial institutions had nothing to lose from making risky loans, but could gain handsomely if the loans were (however unlikely) successful (for a detailed discussion, see Milgrom and Roberts, 1992).

10 See Milgrom and Roberts (1992) for a discussion of financial decision making under moral hazard. International financial institutions may have performed a similar mental arithmetic, hoping for an international bailout by the IMF if a borrower country were to become insolvent. As things turned out, this reasoning worked out quite nicely for international lenders who suffered only minimal losses as the IMF bailed out one country after another with unprecedented emergency loans, and national authorities saddled the broad public with the debts that private operators had raised. The privatization of gains was thus balanced with a socialization of the losses, in a classic demonstration of the successful application (by the private financial actors) of moral hazard.

11 The Bank of Thailand had sold its dollar reserves in the forward market in efforts to prop up the baht. To Thailand's credit, the IMF loan was not taken up in full, and was repaid ahead of schedule.

12 It was the result of this effort by factory workers, labouring 12 hours a day, 6 days a week, in 40 degrees heat, for a wage of less than $200 a month, which created this economic miracle. Sheer sweat turned the country from an agricultural economy into one of the success stories of the 1980s/1990s. The effort of these workers, primarily young females from the countryside, had created the $32bn in reserves, which the Bank of Thailand in less than six months spent most of on the ill-fated defence of the Thai currency.

13 During 1996, my colleague Peter Gastreich, now with UBS, and I published a series of articles on the sustainability of the boom in the Bangkok-based *Asia Times*. By late 1996, we predicted (somewhat bravely) that the baht would likely be set loose from its peg against the US dollar within some six months. We were not very popular at the Bank of Thailand after that. The peg was finally abandoned on 2 July 1997 and quickly led to a 50 per cent devaluation of the currency.

14 As a result, not a single financial actor who had contributed to the financial collapse of the country was ultimately taken to court, penalized, or had his/her assets confiscated. The message this sends out to the next generation of financial fraudsters is obvious.

15 The final cost of the crisis to Thailand is still debated. Official estimates of non-performing loans on the books of the financial sector ranged about 50 per cent by mid-1999 (Sussangkarn, 2000). The cost of resolving the banking crisis alone has been estimated to be in the region of 40–50 per cent of 1997 GDP, a greater proportion than the Mexican financial crisis of 1994 (DFAT, 1999). Griffith-Jones and Gottschalk (2004) estimate the cumulative output loss for Thailand between 1997 and 2002 at over $305bn (in 2002 dollars). At twice the country's 1997 GDP, this was nearly three times the similarly estimated absolute loss for Mexico, and the highest loss for any country affected by a financial crisis in the 1990s, bar Indonesia (at $345bn).

16 Admittedly, the siphoning off part is somewhat based on conjecture as no official data exists to back this assertion. The fact remains that most of these loans were never paid back to the government, nor were these funds ever traced. It can be assumed that much of these funds did not stay in Thailand. Most of the recipient finance companies were subsequently nationalized or closed down, with the public sector taking on their debt.

17 I interviewed several of the key private sector players at the time. Many finance institutions and corporations had long given up even the pretence of intending to repay their outstanding loans.

18 By mid-1997, the country's foreign debt rapidly approached more than 200 per cent of GDP. Non-performing loans held by private commercial banks exceeded 40 per cent of their loan portfolio, a figure which went up to 70 per cent in the case of state-owned banks (Siamwalla, 2000).

19 Enron was, for example, named 'America's Most Innovative Company' by *Fortune* magazine for six consecutive years, from 1996 to 2001. In February 2001,

Fortune magazine's ranking of America's most admired companies listed Enron as No. 1 for 'innovativeness' and No. 2 for 'quality of management'.

20 However, it was never perfect. The company had come under scrutiny for irregularities long before 2001. In 1987, for instance, Enron was at the centre of a trading scandal that nearly consumed the company. The 1985 merger that Kenneth Lay engineered with InterNorth, a much larger rival, to form the new Enron saddled the firm with massive debts. Through the rest of the 1980s, Enron tried to sell some holdings, citing the need to reduce its debt. The debt problem was obscured during the 1990s, but never went away and ultimately contributed to its bankruptcy.

21 The site is said to have handled 550,000 transactions with a notional value of $345bn in its first year (*The Economist*, Energy Survey, 10 February 2001).

22 In essence, the firm attempted to do this through a combination of moving non-performing assets off the books while registering these as 'sales', and by booking hypothetical future earnings in present periods. Unfortunately, most of these 'sales' and 'earnings' were illusionary and did not involve any real or viable transactions. When these transactions were reversed, actual profits had to be restated downwards for a number of periods to a magnitude which destroyed confidence in the company.

23 That some of these executives controlled these SPVs, and benefited from their transactions with Enron was also not exactly emphasized in communications with the public. The obvious conflicts of interests this represented, and the substantial profits these executives derived from these deals, added to the subsequent outrage.

24 Eventually it was discovered that some $630m of the 2000 figure came from improper accounting involving LJM and other partnerships. Another $296m in 'profit' came from hidden tax-cutting transactions, hardly normal business operations (Powers *et al.*, 2002).

25 'Special Report, Enron, The Amazing Disintegrating firm', *The Economist*, 8 December 2001, at pp. 61, 62.

26 Ibid.

27 In contrast to the general view that fraud is the main culprit in corporate scandal, Clarke *et al.* (2003) make a strong case that the very adherence to existing accounting rules may be one of the major contributors to the waves of corporate scandals witnessed in the recent past, in the US, Australia, and elsewhere.

28 Mark-to-market refers to the recording of the price or value of a security, portfolio, or an asset to reflect its current market value rather than its book value. A hypothetical sale of such assets at an inflated price to another party allows for the booking of this higher value. In Enron's case, assets and liability were effectively just shifted from one Enron entity to another, providing an illusion of value.

29 See Powers *et al.* (2002) and Batson (2002, 2003a, b) for detailed analyses of these vehicles and their impact on Enron's balance sheet.

30 Enron founder, and long-time CEO and Chairman, Kenneth Lay was found guilty on charges of fraud and conspiracy in May 2006, but passed away in July of that year, before he could be sentenced. Andrew Fastow, former CFO, received a six-year prison sentence in September 2006. Jeffrey Skilling, senior executive and briefly CEO, was sentenced to 24 years in prison in October 2006. Richard Causey, the firm's former chief accounting officer, was sentenced to five-and-a-half years in November 2006 for his role in covering up fraudulent accounting practices at Enron (source: various news reports).

31 Source of revenue figures: *Time* Magazine, 13 January 2002.

32 Drexel Burnham Lambert (DBL) had been another earlier Andersen client. DBL collapsed under the weight of its own creation – the 1980s junk bond market in the US. Another infamous Andersen client was Lincoln Savings and Loan, a symbol of the US Savings & Loan debacle, which failed due to fraud in 1989 at an eventual cost to the taxpayer of $2.9bn.

33 Booking of future profits for current period earnings is a common practice and legitimate under current accounting rules. In fact, this is one feature of accruals accounting. The use of special purpose vehicles (SPVs) is also widespread. However, Enron's financial officers turned this into an art form and, for example, booked highly improbable future revenues (in some cases 20 years into the future) as current earnings, classified loans it took out as sales (and hence revenues), and classified assets that were merely shunted from one subsidiary to another (via SPVs) as sales (again booking them as revenues for Enron).

34 Investment bank J.P. Morgan Chase in late 2002 sought $1.1bn from insurers after Enron declared bankruptcy. Through joint ventures, pre-paid trades through Mahonia Ltd (a Channel Island registered energy trading business created and controlled by J.P. Morgan Chase and used by Enron as a tax shelter and a vehicle to hide loans disguised as trades), and other securities, J.P. Morgan Chase had a financial exposure to Enron in excess of $2.1bn. About half of this exposure had been insured by 11 insurance companies which had underwritten some $1bn worth of transactions between Enron and Mahonia Ltd. The insurance companies refused to pay off the insurance, arguing that the bank had deceived them into believing that the transactions between J.P. Morgan and Enron were trades, while effectively these constituted loans. In early 2003, the insurers agreed to pay $654m (some 60 per cent of the amount underwritten) to settle the lawsuit. (*Houston Chronicle*, 3 January 2003; see www.chron.com/disp/story.mpl/special/enron/1722999.html).

35 Some 100 Merrill Lynch executives, for example, invested more than $16m of their personal funds in one of the controversial SPVs (CNN, 30 January 2002). Executives at Germany's Dresdner Bank were known to have invested $1m of their own money in such partnerships (TheStreet.com, 12/27/2002). In 2002, the US Justice Department charged three former British (NatWest) bankers with wire fraud for investing in Enron SPVs (*The Washington Times*, 28 June 2002).

36 Bethany McLean, co-author of *The Smartest Guys in the Room: The Amazing Rise and Scandalous Fall of Enron* (McLean and Elkind, 2003), is credited as being one of the first to question Enron's stock value. Richard Grubman, founding analyst with Highfields Capital, had questioned Enron's balance sheet earlier in 2001. John Olson, senior vice president and director of energy research at the Houston-based investment firm of Sanders Morris Harris, had been critical of Enron's accounting for a decade before the company's fall. In recognition that some auditors at Andersen did a good job, Carl Bass, an auditor at Andersen involved in internal quality control, had raised serious questions about Enron's accounting practices as early as 1999, and was subsequently taken off the Enron case by senior Andersen management.

37 Commodity Futures Trading Commission, regulatory exception granted on 14 January 1993.

38 It should also be noted that rank and file employees were barred by management from selling their 401(k)s, frequently invested in Enron stock, around the time Enron revealed a third quarter loss of $638m. A 401(k) is a type of retirement plan used in the United States that allows employees to save and invest for their own retirement. As an employer established plan, a 401(k) is generally funded with before-tax salary contributions, and frequently supplemented by employer contributions. Investment options include employers' stock, mutual funds, money market funds, and bonds.

39 This implies a scathing indictment of the analyst community who agreed upon and widely discussed the fact that Enron's financial structure was highly complex and that many of the financial details were buried in off-balance sheet entities that were cryptically described in Enron's disclosure documents. As one analyst reportedly put it, Enron was a 'faith' stock (Gordon, 2002).

40 Langevoort (2003: 1140) asks: 'were Enron and the others just exceptions that prove the rule, the unavoidable handful of bad apples in a barrel of otherwise sweet corporate fruit?'

41 Comroad is a particularly gross case of fraud. Less than 2 per cent of its revenues actually existed. The firm's main business partner and even its main supplier were invented. Comroad's long time external auditor, KPMG, terminated its audit relationship only after press reports questioned the existence of Comroad's main (and only) customer in Hong Kong, and, as is customary, denied any fault or blame in the fraud.

42 For nearly a decade, Flowtex leased largely non-existing machines to leasing companies, falsifying invoices, defrauded some 120 banks and leasing companies in the process, and allegedly bribed local officials and politicians, without raising the suspicion of the banks, the auditors, or the authorities. The firm's lead auditor, KPMG, ultimately paid some €50m compensation (a mere 5 per cent of damages sought) to banks and leasing companies, without admitting guilt or blame for the fraud it did not detect. The State of Baden-Württemberg, where the company was located, is currently being sued for over €1.1bn for its involvement in covering up the fraud. Flowtex CEO Manfred Schmider, the main culprit in the fraud, was sentenced to 12 years in jail. He has since July 2006 been allowed to leave jail on day-release, and could be a free man as early as October 2007. Some €100m of the fraudulently obtained funds could not be traced.

43 Jim Henson Co. is the production unit famous for the Muppet Show – bought by EM-TV for close to $700m and sold back to the Henson family in 2003 for one tenth of that sum.

44 The auction in 2000 raised some €50bn with each firm paying around €8.5bn for its slice of the German 3G market. Alongside T-Mobil (the subsidiary of Deutsche Telekom), the winners included E-Plus Hutchison (a consortium made up of KPN, NTT, and Hutchison), Group 3G (Sonera and Telefonica), Mannesman Multimedia, MobilCom Multimedia (then partially owned by France Telecom) and the 90 per cent BT-owned Viag. MobilCom and Group 3G pulled out of the German 3G market in 2002 (source: various news reports).

45 Mr Sommer is currently a member of the Board of Directors of Motorola, a member of the Supervisory Board at Munich Re and of Celanese AG, and a member of the International Advisory Board of The Blackstone Group. He has been serving as Chairman of the International Advisory Council of Sistema since May 2003, and was elected to the Board of Directors of Sistema in June 2005 (source: company websites).

46 In 1987, for example, the firm had spent €130m on a TV station (Odeon TV) that its senior management hoped to build into Italy's third major network but which collapsed just three years later. From the early 1990s, Parmalat began to engage in earnings management to mask its problems with a mixture of fictitious transactions and aggressive acquisitions in Italy, Brazil, Argentina, Hungary, Canada, and the United States.

47 In 1999, for example, Citigroup set up a Delaware company by the name of Buco Nero, the Italian for 'black hole', through which Parmalat was able to funnel a set of complex and misleading financing schemes. Buco Nero typically loaned money to subsidiaries of Parmalat which then redistributed the money to other Parmalat companies. In an ongoing lawsuit against Citigroup, which seeks $10bn in damages, Parmalat administrator Enrico Bondi alleges that Buco Nero was used to disguise loans as equity, in order to hide Parmalat's true financial situation.

48 *Time* Magazine, December 2004. *Time* Bonus Section December 2004: Global Business.

49 In March 2003, some nine months before the company collapsed, Joanna Speed, Merrill Lynch's food industry analyst in London, became the first big bank

analyst to issue a 'sell' recommendation on Parmalat stock, as she found the accounts impossible to understand (newratings.com, New York, 31 March 2003).

50 The general scheme of the Cuban milk transactions appears to have worked like this: Parmalat obtained loans on the basis of fictitious or double invoices to retailers, subsequently hiding the debt through transfers to shell companies based in offshore tax havens. This seems to have gone on for over a decade. The Cuban deal involved a fictitious supply of 300,000 tons of milk powder to a Cuban importer (via a Cayman Islands subsidiary) by a non-existent milk producer in Singapore. Worth $1.3bn, this, apparently, would have been enough to supply each Cuban citizen with over 200 litres a year. Neither this magnitude, nor the fact that Singapore is hardly known for its milk expertise, raised any concerns.

51 One of the latest financial scandals in Germany would appear to support this concern. Phoenix Kapitaldienst GmbH, a firm promising high returns from investments in options and other derivatives, was closed down by Germany's financial supervisory authority (BaFin) in 2005, after the firm had misappropriated some €600–700m of some 30,000 investors' capital. Accounting firm Ernst & Young had in 2002 been tasked with a special audit of the firm by BaFin, and criticized organizational weaknesses in the firm, but failed to notice the key fraud. Phoenix's long-time auditor, Godehard Puckler, refuses to accept any responsibility for the failure to detect anything amiss.

8 Implications for governance policy

1 Mary Jo White, partner in the law firm of Debevoise & Plimpton in New York City, and former US attorney for the Southern District of New York. Speech given at the 13th Annual Fraud Conference & Trade Show Aug. 4–9, 2002. Available HTTP: <http://www.acfe.com/fraud/view.asp?ArticleID=201> (accessed 15 August 2007).

2 Including the demise of National Student Marketing, audited by Peat Marwick which later became part of KPMG. The US Senate, in 1977, raised serious concerns over the lack of independence of accountants who performed public audits, and noted that 'The accounting profession must improve its procedures for assuring independence in view of the public's needs and expectations . . . The best policy . . . is to require that independent auditors of publicly owned corporations perform only services directly related to accounting' (United States Senate, 1977).

3 For example, Congressional hearings chaired by Representative John Dingell questioning the accounting profession's ability to self-regulate itself; of importance also is the accounting profession's efforts at the end of the decade to persuade the SEC to modify independence rules to allow expanded business relationships with audit clients, including the provision of non-audit services (*United States* v. *Arthur Young & Co.* 465 US 805, 1984). Although it initially rejected these, the SEC relented in 1990 by allowing Arthur Andersen to perform non-audit services (via its Andersen Consulting branch) (see SEC, 2000b; and also SEC 1990).

4 Provision of non-audit services by auditors was deemed even by an AICPA committee report to 'erode auditor independence', and that financial statement users 'are concerned that auditors may accept audit engagements at marginal profits to obtain more profitable consulting engagements. Those arrangements could motivate auditors to reduce the amount of audit work and to be reluctant to irritate management to protect the consulting relationship' SEC (2000b). A 1999 report commissioned by the Independent Standards Board found that 'Most [interviewees] felt that the evolution of accounting firms into multi-disciplinary business service consultancies represents a challenge to the ability of auditors to maintain the reality and the perception of independence' (Earnscliffe Research and Communications, 1999).

5 1995. Available HTTP: <http://www.ecgi.org/codes/code.php?code_id=131> (accessed 15 August 2007).

6 1998. Available HTTP: <http://www.ecgi.org/codes/documents/hampel_index.htm> (accessed 15 August 2007).

7 The most recent version of the Combined Code, issued by the Financial Reporting Council in June 2006. Available HTTP: <http://www.frc.org.uk/corporate/combinedcode.cfm> (accessed 15 August 2007).

8 For a summary of the Act prepared by the AICPA, see HTTP: <http://thecaq.aicpa.org/Resources/Sarbanes+Oxley/> (accessed 15 August 2007).

9 Available HTTP: <http://www.dti.gov.uk/bbf/corp-governance/higgs-tyson/page23342.html> (accessed 15 August 2007).

10 Available HTTP: <http://www.football-research.org/docs/smithreport-30-01-03.pdf> (accessed 15 August 2007).

11 FRC press notice, 23 July 2003. Available HTTP: <http://www.frc.org.uk/press/pub0311.html> (accessed 15 August 2007).

12 A number of empirical studies have provided evidence supportive of the benefits of separate aspects of the corporate governance 'package'. For example, Becker *et al.* (1996) report higher audit quality to be associated with less earnings management activity. Beasley (1996) presents evidence that the presence of an audit committee is associated with a reduction in the probability of fraudulent financial reporting. Peasnell *et al.* (2001) found that in the UK more outside directors on the board are associated with reduced levels of earnings management (but found no such association with the presence or otherwise of an audit committee). Carcello and Neal (2003a) report that in the US the presence of executive directors on audit committees is associated with optimistic disclosures for companies experiencing financial distress, Carcello and Neal (2003b) report that more independent audit committees are better able to protect external auditors from dismissal. Beekes *et al.* (2004) found that firms with a higher proportion of outside directors are more likely to recognize bad news in earnings on a timely basis (but are not more conservative in respect to recognizing good news). Gramling *et al.* (2005) suggest that internal audit has 'a positive influence on the corporate governance, including reporting quality and firm performance'. Although this stream of research may link 'better' corporate governance with certain features of 'better' financial reporting and disclosure, it does not directly address policy-related issues as to whether the benefits from the imposition of corporate governance structures are likely to exceed the costs.

13 See, for example, Ezzamel and Watson (1997), see also Spira (2003) and Spira and Bender (2004) for further discussion of this issue.

14 Clarke *et al.* (2003) make a similar point with respect to corporate scandals in Australia.

15 'An infectious greed seemed to grip much of our business community' (Former Federal Reserve Chairman Alan Greenspan, quoted by Floyd Norris, 'The Markets: Market Place; Yes, He Can Top That', *New York Times*, 17 July 2002 at A-1).

16 'Because of a constitutional quirk, the US federal reporting model does not address in enforceable law the fundamental capitalist proposition "do the accounts show how efficiently a company is run on its capital resources?" This proposition requires that internal accounting and external reporting address the intra vires objectives of a company (acting within the powers of the company). Instead the federal model poses a legally very different, and actually far more ambiguous question, "are the accounts consistent in showing what a company might be worth when a share is exchanged?" ' (Bush, 2005: 6).

17 The requirement for auditor rotation is also part of EU Directive 2006/43/EC, on statutory audit. This directive is partly a response to the recent accounting

scandals, but originated in a 1996 Green paper on the role and responsibility of the statutory auditor in the EU. Broadly designed to reinforce the statutory audit function and provide for some harmonization within the EU, the directive sets out to enhance the audit quality, clarifies the duties of statutory auditors, their independence and ethics, introduces a requirement for external quality assurance, and suggests public oversight of the audit profession. This broadened the scope of the Eighth Council Directive on Company Law, which primarily dealt with the approval of statutory auditors. The directive also provides a basis for international cooperation between regulators in the EU and with regulators in third countries, such as the US Public Company Accounting Oversight Board (PCAOB). The 2006 Directive applies not only to EU auditors and audit firms but also to audit firms from third countries, with implementation primarily being a matter for EU Member States. See EU Directive 2006/43/EC. Available HTTP: <http://europa.eu.int/eur-lex/lex/JOHtml.do?uri=OJ:L:2006:157:SOM:EN:HTML> (accessed 15 August 2007).

18 While investment banks were fined for their involvement in the Enron scandal, the accounting profession bore the brunt of criminal prosecution and public and regulatory criticism, as well as new regulation. For insights on the contribution of investment bankers and securities lawyers to corporate governance failures, see, for example, Painter (1994); Powers *et al.* (2002); Batson (2002, 2003a, b, c); Cramton (2002); Coffee (2003a); Fisch and Rosen (2003); Koniak (2003a, b); Macey and Sale (2003); Song (2003); Sargent (2004); Sale (2005); Spiegel and Ohl (2005).

19 This would also seem to apply to concerns about legal liability.

20 The settlements agreed by some investment banks regarding their involvement with Enron notwithstanding. See Koniak (2003a, b) for a discussion of the role of lawyers in corporate governance. Also, see Cramton (2002) for a detailed exposé of the conduct of legal counsel with respect to the Enron/Andersen case. See Sale (2005) on the role of investment banks in corporate fraud, and on the appropriateness of the various settlements.

21 During statements by the two US Senators sponsoring section 307 ('Rules of Professional Responsibility for Attorneys') of the Sarbanes-Oxley Act 2002, Senator Enzi commented, 'One of the thoughts that occurred to me was that probably in almost every transaction there was a lawyer who drew up the documents involved in that procedure' (148 Cong. Rec. S6554). Senator Corzine, former chief executive of Goldman Sachs, added, 'In fact, in our corporate world today – and I can verify this by my own experiences – executives and accountants work day to day with lawyers. They give them advice on almost each and every transaction. That means when executives and accountants have been engaged in wrongdoing, there have been some other folks at the scene of the crime – and generally they are lawyers' (148 Congressional Record S6556).

22 'No major corporate transaction goes forward without a lawyer's okay; no securities documents get filed without a lawyer's review; and no private placement memoranda are issued without a lawyer's input, if not a lawyer's drafting them herself. We had laws on the books that prohibited most and maybe all of the damaging conduct engaged in by companies like Enron. But it takes lawyers to bring that law to bear on transactions and corporate activities, as they are being planned and implemented. When lawyers use their skills instead to circumvent those laws, we end up here. Unless we rein in the lawyers, what use is it to write new laws or to enact reforms? As long as lawyers stand ready to interpret our laws out of existence to serve management's goals, our new laws will be as ineffective as our old ones. Take away the lawyer's law-free zone and the law-free zones lawyers build for others will shrink too' (Koniak, 2003a: 227).

23 See Ellen Joan Pollock, 'Lawyers for Enron Faulted Its Deals, Didn't Force Issue', *Wall Street Journal*, 22 May 2002, at A1. See also Powers *et al.* (2002).

24 See pp. 656–74, 704–6, *in re. Enron Corp. Securities, Derivative & ERISA Litigation*, 235 F. Supp. 2d 549 (S.D. Tex. 549 2002), also regarding the involvement of Vinson & Elkins.

25 For further examples of 'structured financing', such as loans disguised as asset sales (Enron's prepay scheme), see US Senate (2002d), in particular the testimony of Robert Roach, Chief Investigator, Permanent Subcommittee. Available HTTP: <http://www.senate.gov/~gov_affairs/072302roach.pdf> (accessed 15 August 2007). The reader may also wish to consult: HTTP: <http://www.senate.gov/~gov_affairs/072302roach_a.pdf> (Accounting Treatment of Prepays – accessed 15 August 2007); and, HTTP: <http://www.senate.gov/~gov_affairs/072302roach_b.pdf> (Knowledge and Participation of Financial Institutions in Enron Prepays) (accessed 15 August 2007).

26 'There is evidence that some of the banks "knowingly allowed investors" to rely on Enron financial statements they knew were misleading' (see Testimony of Robert Roach, Chief Investigator Permanent Subcommittee on Investigations, the US Senate, 2002d). Available HTTP: <http://www.senate.gov/~gov_affairs/072302roach.pdf> (accessed 15 August 2007).

27 See, for example, the SEC charges against Merrill Lynch executives regarding aiding and abetting the Enron accounting fraud (SEC, 2003b). See also SEC (2003c).

28 The ordinary investor may be forgiven for mistaking such transactions for 'sales'. Investment bankers, in contrast, are highly skilled financial experts who are far less likely to be misled by obfuscation. In the particular case of these Enron transactions, banks insisted on guarantees by Enron that the funds lent to Enron SPVs would be paid pack. This hardly qualifies as a sale, and is, in fact, a loan. When Enron booked such transactions as 'sales' during financial disclosure, the banks knowingly aided in misinforming investors.

29 Investment bank Merill Lynch, for example, emphasized to would-be investors that some of the SPV partnerships it tried to market were controlled by Enron's CFO Andrew Fastow. Trading on inside information is a civil and criminal offence of course (see US Senate, 2002d). That it never occurred to Merill Lynch or its legal counsel that this might implicate the bank is astonishing. For detailed case studies on the involvement of lawyers in corporate scandals of recent and earlier vintage, see Hazard *et al.* (2004). Also, for a discussion of lawyer involvement in Lincoln Savings & Loan, one of the major thrift failures of the $200bn Savings and Loan (S&L) debacle in the United States, see Simon (1998).

30 *Central Bank of Denver* v. *First Interstate Bank of Denver*, 511 US 164, 177–78 (1994). For an elaboration, see Coffee (2002).

31 Private Securities Litigation Reform Act (PSLRA) 1995, Pub. L. No. 104–67, 109 Stat. 737 (1995). This Act, as well as the *Central Bank of Denver* decision, also applies to other agents including bankers and accountants. 'Joint and several liability' refers to recovery of all damages from any of the negligent defendants regardless of their individual share of the liability. The reader will recall the discussion on *Central Bank of Denver* and the PSLRA with regard to liability deterrence on accounting firms. For a general discussion of the impact of these and other changes in the legal environment in the US, see Coffee (2002).

32 For a critical discussion on the likely impact of the Sarbanes-Oxley Act on attorney responsibility, see, for example, Cramton (2003); Fisch and Rosen (2003); Koniak (2003a, b).

33 See <http://www.martindale.com/xp/Martindale/home.xml> (accessed 1 March 2007).

34 For a summary of basic types of lawyers' involvement in managerial wrongdoing, see Sargent (2004).

35 Prominent amongst these are A.A. Sommer, Jr., a former SEC Commissioner and leader of the securities bar (US), who summarized the duties of the corporate lawyer in a 1974 speech:

> I would suggest that in securities matters (other than those where advocacy is clearly proper) the attorney will have to function in a manner more akin to that of auditor than to that of the attorney. This means several things. It means that he will have to exercise a measure of independence that is perhaps uncomfortable if he is also the close counsellor of management in other matters, often including business decisions. It means he will have to be acutely cognizant of his responsibility to the public who engage in securities transactions that would never have come about were it not for his professional presence. It means that he will have to adopt the healthy scepticism toward the representation of management which a good auditor must adopt. It means that he will have to do the same thing the auditor does when confronted with an intransigent client – resign.
>
> (Sommer, 1974)

Former Harvard Law School Professor Louis Loss suggested that the job of the securities lawyer involves asking 'searching questions' about client's proposed disclosures (quoted in Loss and Seligman, 2003).

36 See *SEC* v. *National Student Marketing*, 457 F. Supp. 682 (D.D.C. 1978). Also, *in re. William R. Carter & Charles J. Johnson, Jr.* [1981 Transfer Binder] Fed. Sec. L. Rep. (CCH), 82,847, 1981 SEC LEXIS 1940 (1981). The SEC's position was strongly opposed by the American Bar Association, and the SEC subsequently desisted from enforcing its view. Enron changed this, and the Sarbanes-Oxley Act 2002 (via section 307) provided the SEC with a strong mandate to force lawyers to see what they would prefer not to see. The imposition of an affirmative whistleblowing obligation (the report-up-the-ladder requirement), and associated sanctions for failure to do so, intends to make more difficult the wilful ignorance, negligence, and deliberate insensitivity to conflicts of interest which frequently characterize lawyers' involvement in clients' corporate fraud. See Sargent (2003) and Koniak (2003a, b) for elaboration.

37 For a wider gatekeeper definition which would seem to apply to lawyers, see Kraakman (1986), where gatekeepers are defined as private parties able to prevent misconduct by withholding their cooperation from wrongdoers.

38 For an introduction to this discussion, see Campbell and Gaetke (2003); Coffee (2003); Fisch and Rosen (2003); Koniak (2003a, b); Loss and Seligman (2003); Song (2003); Spiegel and Ohl (2005); and earlier contributions by Sommer (1974).

39 Former Hewlett-Packard chairwoman Patricia C. Dunn authorized an investigation into board-level leaks in 2005/2006. During this investigation some of the hired investigators obtained the personal telephone records of HP board members through illegal means. The charges against Dunn, dismissed in March 2007, centred on her knowledge and authorization of the illegal means used to obtain the telephone records. The scandal lead to the resignations of a number of senior HP managers, including Chairwoman Dunn, Ann Baskins (HP general counsel), and Kevin T. Hunsaker (HP senior counsel and director of ethics). HP's Board of Directors also dropped law firm Wilson, Sonsini, Goodrich & Rosati as outside counsel to the board (*Washington Post*, 29 September 2006; *International Herald Tribune*, 14 December 2006; *New York Times*, 22 September 2006; 15 March 2007).

40 Sarbanes-Oxley Act 2002, Pub. L. No. 107–204, 116 Stat. 745 § 307, 15 USC.A. § 7245.

41 Implementation of Standards of Professional Conduct for Attorneys, Securities Act Release No. 33–8185, 68 Fed. Reg. 6296, 6321 (Feb. 6, 2003) (codified at 17 C.F.R. pt. 205.2(e)).

42 Implementation of Standards of Professional Conduct for Attorneys, 68 Fed. Reg. at 6320 (codified at 17 C.F.R. pt. 05.2(b)(3)(ii)).

43 This is made evident by the fact that Enron's board repeatedly waived the firm's own code of conduct to allow transactions by senior management that were laden with conflicts of interest. The investigation chaired by Senator Lieberman determined that 10 of the 15 most recent Enron 'independent' directors were suffering from conflicts of interest (see US Senate, 2002a). The 'noisy withdrawal' requirement, discussed at the time of the SEC's implementation of section 307, might have added to the arsenal of legal counsel against clients suspected of wrongdoing. This requirement would have required counsel to terminate representation of the client if management persisted in misconduct. Unfortunately, the bar successfully lobbied against the inclusion of this requirement.

44 See Koniak (2003a, b) and Cramton (2003) for a detailed discussion of this argument.

45 See Koniak (2003a, b) for a detailed discussion of section 307.

46 Increasing penalties may do little to deter crime. White-collar crimes are likely to have a low probability of detection and the expected sentence of a complex fraud is not dramatically increased by raising maximum sentences. Further diminishing the potential deterrence value of penalties is the notion that individuals may discount the disutility of future imprisonment and the risk of being caught. See, for example, Polinsky and Shavell (1999) and also Eide (2000), noting studies which found no statistical effect from an increase in the severity of punishment.

47 Under the final rule (Rule 307), attorneys who appear or practise before the Commission in the representation of an issuer are required to report evidence of material violations of the US securities laws or a breach of fiduciary duty by an issuer or its agent to the chief legal officer (or chief legal officer and chief executive officer) of the issuer, or alternatively to report such evidence to a qualified legal compliance committee of the issuer. Attorneys (other than those who report directly to a qualified legal compliance committee) must then report up-the-ladder to the audit committee, another committee of directors not employed by the issuer, or directly to the board of directors in the event that the chief legal officer or chief executive officer fails to respond appropriately. An attorney *may* still report failure to respond appropriately to the Commission, but is now not required to do so. Under the earlier noisy withdrawal proposal, an attorney would have been required to withdraw from representing the company if, after reporting evidence of a material violation, and this did not receive an appropriate response, the attorney reasonably believed that a material violation was ongoing or about to occur and was likely to result in substantial injury to the financial interest or property of the company or investors. Originally proposed was notification of the SEC within one day of withdrawal, and disaffirmation of any opinion, document, representation, affirmation, or characterization in any document submitted to or filed with the SEC that the attorney had prepared and now reasonably believed to be false or misleading. In addition, the up-the-ladder reporting requirement is significantly weakened by the final rule which provides that an attorney who reports evidence of a material violation to a QLCC will fully satisfy his or her reporting obligations and will have no additional obligation to further report a suspected violation.

48 See Becker (1968) for the seminal application of economic principles to crime and optimal punishment.

49 Reduced liability and a probably reduced likelihood of prosecution resulting from changes to the legislative framework apply to several gatekeepers, and are frequently invoked in analyses of behaviour of accounting and law firms. See Coffee (2002) for a discussion on the impact on gatekeeper liability of a raft of legislative changes in the US, arguing that gatekeeper verification and certification functions lost operational value due to declining liability risk during the 1990s. See Cramton (2002) and Koniak (2002, 2003a, b) with reference to reduced liability of lawyers. Macey and Sale (2003) discuss the effects of the spread of the LLP

corporate form on the independence and governance of accounting firms. The move to the limited liability partnership of these two agents may have contributed to the weakening of their effectiveness as gatekeepers. Bromberg and Ribstein (2005) provide a general analysis of the LLP on limiting partner liability.

50 '[T]he Supreme Court and Congress have eviscerated private actions against lawyers for aiding and abetting under the securities laws' (Gordon, 2003: 1188), referring to the PSLRA and the *Central Bank of Denver* decision.

51 See Sarbanes-Oxley Act, sections 101–105, establishing of the Public Company Accounting Oversight Board; sections 201–204, with regard to non-audit services, audit partner rotation, reports to audit committees. All accounting firms who perform audits of listed companies must belong and report to the Public Company Accounting Oversight Board (PCAOB) (see Title I of Sarbanes-Oxley (Public Company Accounting Oversight Board)). The PCAOB is an independent non-profit organization under the jurisdiction and oversight of the SEC (and funded by mandatory fees from accountants and issuers) (see Sections 101, 107, 109 of Sarbanes-Oxley). The board sets accounting guidelines, reviews and inspects accounting firms' auditing performance, and disciplines public accountants (see Sections 103–105 of Sarbanes-Oxley). This board is thus intended to provide external oversight of the public accounting industry to foster independence from management. See www.pcaobus.org for further information on rules, proceedings, and organization of the oversight board.

52 See Sarbanes-Oxley, section 307, directing the SEC to establish minimum rules of professional responsibility for securities lawyers.

53 Coffee (2003) notes, however, that the judicial response since Enron may partially make up for this perceived shortfall of Sarbanes-Oxley. By restoring 'aiding and abetting' liability of gatekeepers (see *in re. Enron Corp. Secs., Derivative & ERISA Litig.*, 235 F. Supp. 2d 549 (S.D. Tex. 2002)) the judiciary may have bypassed the Supreme Court's *Central Bank of Denver* decision. Private class action may also be more feasible following federal court decisions involving Lernout & Hauspie (e.g. *in re. Lernout & Hauspie Sec. Litig.*, 236 F. Supp. 2d 161 (D. Mass. 2003)). Cunningham (2004) makes the point that the new disclosure requirements for auditors concerning the effectiveness of internal control over financial reporting of clients (Sarbanes-Oxley Act 2002, §404(a) and §404(b)) may counter the Supreme Court's 1994 *Central Bank* decision, which largely insulated auditors from liability.

54 Of course, efforts to minimize divergences in interests of agents from those of principals form the basis of traditional financial and legal scholarship based on agency theory. The goal to prevent self-dealing by corporate agents is uncontroversial. One can certainly also argue that particular reforms to address specific wrongdoings may be appropriate. These would include regulations aimed at reducing obvious conflicts of interests. However, many such rules were already in place prior to the Enron cohort of scandals, and did not sufficiently deter gatekeepers.

55 See, for example, Mitchell (2002) who claims that behavioural decision theory asserts that individuals always act inconsistently with rational choice theories; and Prentice's (2004) reply. There is indeed no call anywhere in the behavioural literature to replace rational choice theory with something one might call irrational choice theory.

56 Well-known concerns with regard to the general applicability of the utility optimization paradigm have been raised over the years. See, for example, Simon (1955, 1956) and Williamson (1973).

57 For a recent application, see Langevoort (2006).

58 The conservation bias inclines the individual to overlook or dismiss information that conflicts with a prior. This also typically leads to overconfidence (Rabin and Schrag, 1999). In contrast, the use of the representative heuristic would tend to

overemphasize new information at the cost of earlier information. Overweighting (due to representativeness) or underweighting (due to conservatism) the relevance of new information leads to upward-biased and downward-biased posteriors respectively (Bartoli, 2005). The prior itself, may of course have been formed under the influence of bias.

59 For example, *in re. Banca Cremi, S.A.* v. *Alex Brown & Sons, Inc* 132 F.3d 1017 (4th Cir. 1997), it was held, in a case involving the plaintiffs' claim that the law required the defendant broker-dealer to disclose its mark-ups, that the plaintiffs' interpretation of the law must be incorrect or the defendant would already be doing it (132 F.3d 1017 (4th Cir. 1997), at 1035). This reasoning is comparable to Judge Easterbrook's decision in *DiLeo* v. *Ernst & Young* (901 F.2d 624, 7th Cir. 1990), see Chapter 6.

60 *DiLeo* v. *Ernst & Young* (901 F.2d 624, 7th Cir. 1990).

61 'Conventional law and economics and its manifestation in *DiLeo* rest wholly on the critical assumption that people are rational maximizers of their self-interest' (Prentice, 2000: 139).

62 See, for example, Posner (2003). See also Noll and Krier (1990), who summarize core assumptions of the standard model, and Viscusi (1996: 636), who notes that the 'foundation of economic analysis of choice is based on the rationality of individual decision-making'.

63 For an overview of such arguments see Lin (1996).

64 The deterioration of 'mental efficiency, reality testing, and moral judgement' Janis (1972: 9). The following symptoms of groupthink, identified by Janis (1972), would appear to be of particular importance with regard to the quality of decision-making of boards:

- collective rationalization (the discounting of warnings and refusal to reconsider assumptions or review options)
- direct pressures on dissenters (pressures not to express arguments which are seen to go against the group's views)
- illusions of unanimity (expressed views are assumed to be unanimous, silence is interpreted as consent)
- self-censorship (doubts and deviations from the perceived group consensus are not raised by the individual, or deemed to be irrelevant)
- self-appointed mindguards (group members who protect the group and the leader from information which threatens group cohesion).

65 In a 2002 letter to Berkshire Hathaway's stockholders, Warren Buffett summed this up as follows:

> Why have intelligent and decent directors failed so miserably? The answer lies not in inadequate laws – it's always been clear that directors are obligated to represent the interests of shareholders – but rather in what I'd call 'boardroom atmosphere.' It's almost impossible, for example, in a boardroom populated by well-mannered people, to raise the question of whether the CEO should be replaced. It's equally awkward to question a proposed acquisition that has been endorsed by the CEO, particularly when his inside staff and outside advisors are present and unanimously support his decision. (They wouldn't be in the room if they didn't.) Finally, when the compensation committee – armed, as always, with support from a high-paid consultant – reports on a megagrant of options to the CEO, it would be like belching at the dinner table for a director to suggest that the committee reconsider.
>
> (available HTTP: <http://www.berkshirehathaway.com/letters/2002pdf.pdf> (accessed 15 August 2007))

66 See, for example, Bazerman *et al.* (2000), arguing that individual biases or cognitive limitations can magnify the shortcomings of group decision-making; Lev (2003) linking earnings manipulation to managers' optimism; Kahneman and Lovallo (2003) demonstrating the potentially devastating effect of over-optimism on executive decisions; Myers (1982) on polarization of group judgement.

67 Empirical research on the effect of independent board directors on firm performance has generally been inconclusive. See Hermalin and Weisbach (2003) for a survey of empirical results. See also Bhagat and Black (1999). By extension, these concerns also affect the various board committees, ostensibly created as a counterweight to the CEO's influence. As committee members are selected from the board, one must question the oppositional power of these sub-groups.

68 Fanto (2004), for example, proposes that public companies be mandated to take on a significant minority of public directors. The author suggests that these be chosen from a list of individuals identified by a government oversight board. The main aim of these outsiders would be to enhance the board's monitoring function by forming a counterweight to the firm's inner circle.

69 Johnson *et al.* (1996) conclude that there is no clear consensus on the relationship between demographic board characteristics and particular performance measures. This would suggest that the influence of boards on firm performance is more complex and indirect than might often be presumed. The reliability of many of the assumptions underlying direct composition–performance links has repeatedly been questioned (see, for example, Lawrence, 1997).

70 At the end of 2002, less than 13,000 individuals held the directorships of the 1,700 largest corporations in the US, with a significant number of interlocks, where an individual sits on more than one board (Cook, 2003).

71 These characteristics have been succinctly summarized by Aviva Chairman Pehr Gyllenhammar in guidelines for the selection of non-executive directors with the phrase 'no crooks, no cronies, no cowards' (quoted in Tyson, 2003).

72 Douglas was a professor of law, Chairman of the SEC in 1939, and was from 1940 elected to the US Supreme Court.

73 Forms of diversity include differences in industry background, educational background, social background, and functional background. See Forbes and Milliken (1999) for a discussion on the complex interaction of board demography, board performance, and firm performance. See also Cohen and Bailey (1997) and Dallas (2002).

74 Any good statistician will adapt a model to a particular problem, rather than try to force one model onto all problems. Why should one decision-making strategy be applicable to any and all problems of choice under uncertainty?

75 See Coffee (2003a) for a detailed analysis of the impact of these changes in the regulatory environment.

76 See O'Donoghue and Rabin (2005) for a detailed discussion on self-control problems, present bias, agent heterogeneity, and incentive design. This discussion in particular investigates differences in incentive design for exponential discounters in contrast to individuals who display present bias. Their work picks up on, and extends, the discussion on time-inconsistent preferences. See Strotz (1955); Phelps and Pollak (1968); Thaler (1981); and especially Laibson (1997). For a recent overview, see Frederick *et al.* (2002).

77 Heterogeneity may exist between agents and within a single agent over time or with respect to situational context, that is, a person may have different preferences at different points in time, and unstable preferences as a result of different solicitation processes.

78 Where, due to consolidation, only a small number of firms remain in an industry to conduct a particular service, as may be the case in the auditing industry where the Big-4 dominate audits of listed companies, this may indicate a need to break up large firms in order to enhance competition.

79 This is reminiscent of one critique of the heuristics and biases approach which alleges that this portrays the human mind in an overly negative, and hopelessly incompetent, light. See Cohen (1981); Gigerenzer (1994); the reply to Gigerenzer by Kahneman and Tversky (1996); and the return reply by Gigerenzer (1996).

9 Conclusions

1 One implication is that preferences and beliefs may frequently not be formed prior to observations of own behaviour. Hence the causation may, at times, run from behaviour to beliefs.
2 Camerer *et al.* (2004a) suggest that agents differ in their degree of rationality and that economic models should take this into consideration.
3 For extensive reviews of the corporate governance literature see, for example, Shleifer and Vishny (1997a) and Bhagat and Black (2002).
4 They would also appear to be of relevance to the way accounting and auditing is being taught and conducted.
5 More formally, interactions in markets are thought to correct or offset abnormal individual behaviour. This is based on a number of underlying assumptions, which include the following: deviations from rationality are random, individuals will learn from mistakes, arbitrage will take care of anomalies, and rational agents will drive irrational agents from the market. For a recent discussion of the validity of these assumptions and the interplay between individual irrationality and aggregate outcomes, see Fehr and Tyran (2005).
6 Bias may persist even in competitive markets (see Hirschey *et al.*, 2005, who suggest that investors typically react insufficiently to negative restatements). See also Shleifer and Vishny (1997b); Langevoort (1998a, b); Rabin (1998); Shleifer (2000); and Porter and Smith (2003).
7 This is apart from the realization that more information may not always lead to better decision-making. Given various cognitive filters and interpretation mechanisms aimed at preserving prior beliefs, additional information may be interpreted to support a prior view, regardless of the value of this new data in supporting the prior.
8 Perceived susceptibility describes one's belief about the likelihood of risk (say to personal harm, the risk of being caught, etc.). Personal risk perceptions seem to be quite immune to debiasing efforts, see Weinstein and Klein (1995); also Armor and Taylor (2002).
9 This matches the findings of the Report to the Nation on Occupational Fraud and Abuse by the Association of Certified Fraud Examiners (ACFE, 1996, 2002, 2004, 2006), which suggests that the vast majority of individuals accused of occupational fraud are first-time offenders.
10 See Luban (2006) for a discussion of ethical, cultural, economic, and psychological explanations for the moral breakdowns in corporate settings.
11 Milgram's 1963 study evaluated how social pressure affects conscience. Specifically the study induced behaviour which the test persons would not normally have condoned or engaged in (Milgram, 1963).
12 Zimbardo *et al.*'s 1971 Stanford Prison Experiment investigated the effects of role play and situation on individuals' behaviour. The experiment demonstrated that environment and situation, rather than individual disposition, can be responsible for pathological behaviour (Zimbardo *et al.*, 1973a, b).
13 Testimony during various Enron hearings amusingly highlights the disparity between interpretation and fact. For example, see Statement of David Bushnell, Citigroup Managing Director (US Senate, 2002d):

> But let me be clear. While we regret our relationship with Enron, we acted in good faith at all times. Our employees, including the bankers who are here

> today, are honest people doing honest business. They did transactions that were common throughout Wall Street, and they believed those transactions were entirely appropriate.

Further, see Statement of J.P. Morgan Chase (US Senate, 2002d):

> It is our understanding that Enron recorded these transactions on its balance sheet; in other words, they were not off balance sheet transactions. As stated earlier, however, the manner in which Enron accounted for these transactions on *its* books of account and in *its* financial statements was a matter for Enron and *its* management and auditors [original emphasis].

To put these denials of responsibility and guilt into some perspective, see Sale (2005) for a detailed discussion on banks' knowledge of and involvement in Enron's frauds. The Enron Examiner's final report also makes it clear that banks frequently knew that their dealings with Enron were not above board (Batson, 2003c). See also US Senate (2003c) for a detailed discussion of direct and knowing involvement of banks in fraudulent transactions by Enron. Any doubts about culpability and credibility of the testimony of the representatives of two banks in particular were quickly dispersed by documents produced by the Senate's Governmental Affairs Committee's Subcommittee on Investigation, showing the total control of Citibank and J.P. Morgan Chase over the respective vehicles used to facilitate specific Enron deals (see US Senate, 2002d).

14 While this research illustrated causes for the divergence between behaviour predicted by rational models and actual choice behaviour, people sometimes do not even appear to be rational in the dictionary sense. Obviously self-destructive behaviour exists, as do insane acts. However, it is expected that these are in the minority.

15 The UK auditing regime post-Enron has also responded to concerns about auditor independence by requiring rotation of lead auditor and by imposing some restrictions on lead auditor employment in the audited firm (FRC, 2003, 2006). This mirrors similar responses in EU legislation (see EU Directive 2006/43/EC, on statutory audit).

16 This would suggest the need for a periodic overhaul of the regulatory system. Further, as Alan Greenspan has noted, market participants seem to be prone to periodic irrational exuberance which may trump corporate safeguards. For a reflection on the likely effectiveness of the Sarbanes-Oxley Act, see Cunningham (2003).

17 The impoverished basis of corporate law jurisprudence with respect to behavioural insights is reflected in a recent decision by the Delaware Chancery Court:

> Delaware law should not be based on a reductionist view of human nature that simplifies human motivations on the lines of the least sophisticated notions of the law and economics movement. *Homo sapiens* is not merely homo economicus . . . Nor should our law ignore the social nature of humans. To be direct, corporate directors are generally the sort of people deeply enmeshed in social institutions. Such institutions have norms, expectations that, explicitly and impli-citly, influence and channel the behaviour of those who participate in their operation. Some things are 'just not done,' or only at a cost, which might not be so severe as a loss of position, but may involve a loss of standing in the institution. In being appropriately sensitive to this factor, our law also cannot assume – absent some proof of the point – that corporate

> directors are, as a general matter, persons of unusual social bravery, who operate heedless to the inhibitions that social norms generate for ordinary folk.
> (Delaware Chancery Court Vice Chancellor Leo Strine, *In re Oracle Corp. Derivative Litigation*, 824 A.2d 917; 2003 Del. Ch. LEXIS 55 at 938. Decision to deny motion to terminate)

Judge Strine questioned the impartiality of two directors on the special litigation committee (SLC) formed by Oracle's board of directors in response to a stockholder derivative suit on improper insider trading by Oracle management. Judge Strine argued that the two directors (both Stanford professors) had significant ties to the defendants whom they were investigating (all with ties to Stanford University).

18 For an introduction to the dynamics of disasters, see Rudolph and Repenning (2002).

Bibliography

ABA (American Bar Association) (1908). *1908 Code of Professional Ethics, Canon 32.*

ABA (American Bar Association) (1968). *1968 Canons of Professional Ethics.*

ABA (American Bar Association) (1969). *1969 Model Code of the American Bar Association.*

Abramson, L.Y. and Alloy, L.B. (1981). Depression, Non-Depression and Cognitive Illusions: A Reply to Schwartz. *Journal of Experimental Psychology*, 110(3), 436–47.

ACFE (Association of Certified Fraud Examiners) (1996). *1996 Report to the Nation on Occupational Fraud and Abuse.* Austin, Texas: ACFE.

ACFE (Association of Certified Fraud Examiners) (2002). *2002 Report to the Nation on Occupational Fraud and Abuse.* Austin, Texas: ACFE.

ACFE (Association of Certified Fraud Examiners) (2004). *2004 Report to the Nation on Occupational Fraud and Abuse.* Austin, Texas: ACFE.

ACFE (Association of Certified Fraud Examiners) (2006). *2006 Report to the Nation on Occupational Fraud and Abuse.* Austin, Texas: ACFE.

AICPA (American Institute of Certified Public Accountants) (2002a). *Code of Professional Conduct. Rule 102 – Integrity and Objectivity*, as adopted January 12, 1988. New York: AICPA.

AICPA (American Institute of Certified Public Accountants) (2002b). *Statement on Auditing Standards No. 99 (SAS 99): Consideration of Fraud in a Financial Statement Audit.* New York: AICPA.

Ainslie, G.W. (1975). Specious Reward: A Behavioural Theory of Impulsiveness and Impulsive Control. *Psychological Bulletin*, 82(4), 463–96.

Ainslie, G.W. (2001). *Breakdown of Will.* Cambridge: Cambridge University Press.

Ainslie, G.W. and Haslam, N. (1992). Self-control, in *Choice Over Time*, ed. Loewenstein, G. and Elster, J. New York: Russell Sage Foundation Press.

Akerlof, G.A. (1991). Procrastination and Obedience. Richard T. Ely lecture. *American Economic Association Papers and Proceedings*, 81(2), 1–19.

Akerlof, G.A. (2002). Behavioural Macroeconomics and Macroeconomic Behaviour. *American Economic Review*, 92(3), 411–34.

Akerlof, G.A. and Dickens, W.T. (1982). The Economic Consequences of Cognitive Dissonance. *American Economic Review*, 72(3), 307–19.

Alhakami, A. and Slovic, P. (1994). A Psychological Study of the Inverse Relationship between Perceived Risk and Perceived Benefit. *Risk Analysis*, 14(6), 1085–96.

Antle, R. (1982). The Auditor as an Economic Agent. *Journal of Accounting Research*, 20(2), 503–27.

Archer, M. and Tritter, J. (eds) (2000). *Rational Choice Theory*. London: Routledge.

Archer, M. and Tritter, J. (eds) (2001). *Rational Choice Theory Resisting Colonization*. London: Routledge.

Argenti, J. (1976). *Corporate Collapse*. Maidenhead: McGraw-Hill.

Argenti, J. (1985). Predicting Company Failure. *Accountants' Digest*, 93.

Arlen, J.H. (1998). Comment: The Future of Behavioural Economic Analysis of Law. *Vanderbilt Law Review*, 51, 1765–88.

Arlen, J.H. and Carney, W.J. (1992). Vicarious Liability for Fraud on Securities Markets: Theory and Evidence. *University of Illinois Law Review*, 691, 724–7.

Arlen, J.H., Spitzer, M., and Talley, E. (2001). *Endowment Effects within Corporate Agency Relationships*. Yale Law School. Program for Studies in Law, Economics, and Public Policy. Working Paper No. 261.

Armor, D.A. and Taylor, S.E. (2002). When Predictions Fail: The Dilemma of Unrealistic Optimism, in *Heuristics and Biases*, ed. Gilovich, T., Griffin, D., and Kahneman, D. Cambridge: Cambridge University Press.

Aronson, E. (1968a). Dissonance Theory: Progress and Problems, in *Theories of Cognitive Consistency*, ed. Abelson, R., Aronson, E., McGuire, W., Newcomb, T., Rosenberg, M., and Tannenbaum, T. Chicago: Rand McNally.

Aronson, E. (1968b). *The Social Animal*. San Francisco: Freeman.

Asare, S.K. and Wright, A.M. (1997). Evaluation of Competing Hypotheses in Auditing. *Auditing: A Journal of Practice and Theory*, 16(1), 1–12.

Asch, S.E. (1951). Effects of Group Pressure upon the Modification and Distortion of Judgement, in *Groups, Leadership and Men*, ed. H. Guetzkow. Pittsburgh: Carnegy Press.

Asch, S.E. (1955). Opinions and Social Pressure. *Scientific American*, 193(5), 31–5.

Ashbaugh-Skaife, H., LaFond, R., and Mayhew, B.W. (2003). Do Non-Audit Services Compromise Auditor Independence? Further Evidence. *The Accounting Review*, 78(3), 611–39.

Ashby, F.G., Isen, A.M., and Turken, U. (1999). A Neuropsychological Theory of Positive Affect and its Influence on Cognition. *Psychological Review*, 106(3), 529–50.

ASIC (Australian Securities and Investments Commission) (2004). *Corporate Law Economic Reform Program (Audit Reform and Corporate Disclosure) Act 2004* (also known as CLERP 9). Available HTTP: <http://www.asic.gov.au/asic/asic_polprac.nsf/byheadline/CLERP+9?openDocument> (accessed 12 August 2007).

ASX (Australian Stock Exchange) (2003). Principles of Good Corporate Governance and Best Practice Recommendations. Available HTTP: <http://www.asx.com.au/supervision/governance/index.htm> (accessed 13 October 2007).

ASX (Australian Stock Exchange) (2007). Corporate Governance Principles and Recommendations. Available HTTP: <http://www.asx.com.au/supervision/governance/Revised_Corporate_Governance_Principles_and_Recommendations.htm> (accessed 13 October 2007).

Atkinson, J.W. (1964). *An Introduction to Motivation*. Princeton: Van Nostrand.

Babcock, L. and Loewenstein, G. (1997). Explaining Bargaining: The Role of Self-serving Biases. *Journal of Economic Perspectives*, 11(1), 109–26.

Babcock, L., Wang, X., and Loewenstein, G. (1996). Choosing the Wrong Pond: Social Comparisons that Reflect a Self-Serving Bias. *Quarterly Journal of Economics*, 111(1), 1–19.

Babcock, L., Camerer, C., Issacharoff, S.C., and Loewenstein, G. (1993). Self-serving Assessments of Fairness and Pretrial Bargaining. *Journal of Legal Studies*, 22(1), 135–59.

Babcock, L., Camerer, C., Issacharoff, S.C., and Loewenstein, G. (1995). Biased Judgments of Fairness in Bargaining. *American Economic Review*, 85(5), 1337–43.

Bacon, F. (1960). *The New Organon and Related Writings*. New York: Liberal Arts Press. (Originally published in 1620.)

Baiman, S., Evans, J.H., and Noel, J. (1987). Optimal Contracts with a Utility-maximizing Auditor. *Journal of Accounting Research*, 25(3), 217–44.

Bainbridge, S.M. (2002). Why a Board? Group Decision Making in Corporate Governance. *Vanderbilt Law Review*, 55, 1–55. Available HTTP: <http://ssrn.com/abstract=266683> (accessed 1 August 2007).

Ball, R. and Shivakumar, L. (2006). Earnings Quality at Initial Public Offerings. Working paper. Available HTTP: <http://ssrn.com/abstract=918421> (accessed 1 August 2007).

Banner, S. (1997). What Causes New Securities Regulation? 300 Years of Evidence. *Washington University Law Quarterly*, 75(2), 849–55.

Banner, S. (1998). *Anglo-American Securities Regulation: Cultural and Political Roots, 1690–1860*. New York: Cambridge University Press.

Bar-Gill, O. and Bebchuk, L.A. (2003). *Misreporting Corporate Performance*. Discussion Paper, John M. Olin Center for Law, Economics, and Business, Harvard University. Available HTTP: <http://papers.ssrn.com/abstract_id=354141> (accessed 1 August 2007).

Baron, J., Bazerman, M.H., and Shonk, K. (2006). Enlarging the Societal Pie through Wise Legislation: A Cognitive Perspective. *Perspectives on Psychological Science*, 1(2), 123–32.

Baron, N. and Richardson, S. (2004). Danger Lurks in Accruals. *Directorship* (June).

Baron, R.S. (2005). So Right It's Wrong: Groupthink and the Ubiquitous Nature of Polarized Group Decision Making, in *Advances in Experimental Social Psychology*, 37, ed. Zanna, M.P. San Diego, Calif.: Elsevier Academic Press.

Barth, M.E., Cram, D.P., and Nelson, K.K. (2001). Accruals and the Prediction of Future Cash Flows. *Accounting Review*, 76(1), 27–58.

Bartoli, F. (2005). Attitudes Towards Information and Beliefs: How Do Biased Perceptions Influence Individuals' Behaviour? Università di Siena working paper.

Bartov, E., Givoly, D., and Hayn, C. (2002). The Rewards to Meeting or Beating Earnings Expectations. *Journal of Accounting and Economics*, 33, 173–204.

Basioudis, I.G., Geiger, M.A., and Papanastasiou, V. (2006). *Audit Fees, Non-audit Fees and Auditor Reporting on UK Stressed Companies*. Paper Presented at the National Auditing Conference, University of Manchester, March 2006. Copy with author.

Batson, N. (2002). *First Interim Report of Neal Batson Court Appointed Examiner*. Available HTTP: <http://www.enron.com/corp/por/pdfs/InterimReport1ofExaminer.pdf> (accessed 14 August 2007).

Batson, N. (2003a). *Second Interim Report of Neal Batson Court Appointed Examiner*. Available HTTP: <http://www.enron.com/corp/por/pdfs/examiner2/InterimReport2ofExaminer.pdf> (accessed 14 August 2007).

Batson, N. (2003b). *Third Interim Report of Neal Batson Court Appointed Examiner*. Available HTTP: <http://www.enron.com/corp/por/pdfs/examiner3/ExaminersReport3.pdf> (accessed 14 August 2007).

Batson, N. (2003c). *Final Report of The Court Appointed Bankruptcy Examiner.* Available HTTP: <http://www.enron.com/corp/por/examinerfinal.html> (accessed 14 August 2007).

Bazerman, M.H. (1986). *Managerial Decision Making*. New York: John Wiley & Sons.

Bazerman, M.H. (2005). *Judgment in Managerial Decision Making* (6th edition). Hoboken, NJ: John Wiley & Sons.

Bazerman, M.H., Curhan, J.R., and Moore, D.A. (2000). The Death and Rebirth of the Social Psychology of Negotiation. In *Blackwell Handbook of Social Psychology: Interpersonal Processes*, ed. Fletcher, G.J.O. and Clark, M.S. Oxford: Blackwell.

Bazerman, M.H., Loewenstein, G., and Moore, D.A. (2002a). *Auditor Independence, Conflict of Interest and the Unconscious Intrusion of Bias.* Harvard NOM Research Paper No. 02-40. Available HTTP: <http://ssrn.com/abstract_id=324261> (accessed 1 August 2007).

Bazerman, M.H., Loewenstein, G., and Moore, D.A. (2002b). Why Good Accountants Do Bad Audits. *Harvard Business Review*, 80(11), 97–102.

Bazerman, M.H., Loewenstein, G., and Morgan, K. (1997). The Impossibility of Auditor Independence. *Sloan Management Review*, 38(4).

Bazerman, M.H., Tenbrunsel, A.E., and Wade-Benzoni, K.A. (1998). Negotiating with Yourself and Losing: Making Decisions with Competing Internal Preferences. *Academy of Management Review*, 23(2), 225–41.

Bazerman, M.H., Barry, B., O'Connor, K.M., De Dreu, C.K.W., Lituchy, T.R., and Schroth, H.A. (2002c). *What We Want to Do Versus What We Think We Should Do: An Empirical Investigation of Intrapersonal Conflict.* Harvard NOM Research Paper No. 02-18. Available HTTP: <http://ssrn.com/abstract_id=310199> (accessed 1 August 2007).

Beasley, M. (1996). An Empirical Analysis of the Relation between the Board of Director Composition and Financial Statement Fraud. *Accounting Review*, 71(4), 443–65.

Bebchuk, L.A. (1999). *A Rent-Protection Theory of Corporate Ownership and Control.* Harvard Law and Economics Discussion Paper, No. 260, EFA 0285. Available HTTP: <http://ssrn.com/abstract=168990> (accessed 1 August 2007).

Bebchuk, L.A. and Fried, J.M. (2003). Executive Compensation as an Agency Problem. *Journal of Economic Perspectives*, 17(3), 71–92.

Bebchuk, L.A. and Grinstein, Y. (2005). The Growth of Executive Pay. *Oxford Review of Economic Policy*, 21(2), 283–303.

Bebchuk, L.A., Fried, J.M., and Walker, D.I. (2002a). Executive Compensation in America: Optimal Contracting or Extraction of Rents? *The University of Chicago Law Review*, 69, 751–846.

Bebchuk, L.A., Fried, J.M., and Walker, D.I. (2002b). Managerial Power and Rent Extraction in the Design of Executive Compensation. *University of Chicago Law Review*, 69, 751–846.

Becker, B.E. and Huselid, M.A. (1992). The Incentive Effects of Tournament Compensation Systems. *Administrative Science Quarterly*, 37 (June), 336–50.

Becker, C., Defond, M., Jiambalvo, J., and Subramanyam, K. (1996). The Effect of Audit Quality on Earnings Management. *Contemporary Accounting Research*, 15, 1–24.

Becker, G.S. (1968). Crime and Punishment: An Economic Approach. *Journal of Political Economy*, 76, 169–217.

Bedard, J. and Wright, A. (1994). The Functionality of Decision Heuristics: Reliance on Prior Audit Adjustments in Evidential Planning. *Behavioural Research in Accounting*, 6 (Supplement), 62–89.

Beekes, W., Pope, P., and Young, S. (2004). The Link between Earnings Timeliness, Earnings Conservatism and Board Composition: Evidence from the UK. *Corporate Governance*, 12(1), 47–59.

Benston, G.J. (1985). The Market for Public Accounting Services: Demand, Supply and Regulation. *Journal of Accounting and Public Policy*, 4(1), 33–79.

Benston, G.J. (2003a). *The Role and Limitations of Financial Accounting and Auditing for Financial Market Discipline*. Presented at the Conference on Market Discipline, Federal Reserve Bank of Chicago, 31 October 2003.

Benston, G.J. (2003b). The Quality of Corporate Financial Statements and their Auditors Before and After Enron. *Policy Analysis*, 497, 1–29. Washington, DC: Cato Institute for Policy Analysis.

Benston, G.J. (2003c). The Regulation of Accountants and Public Accounting Before and After Enron. *Emory Law Journal*, 52(3), 1325–51.

Benston, G.J. (2006). Fair-value Accounting: A Cautionary Tale from Enron. *Journal of Accounting and Public Policy*, 25, 465–84.

Benston, G.J. and Hartgraves, A.L. (2002). Enron: What Happened and What We Can Learn from it. *Journal of Accounting and Public Policy*, 21(2), 105–28.

Benston, G., Bromwich, M., Litan, R., and Wagenhofer, A. (2003). *Following the Money: The Enron Failure and the State of Corporate Disclosure*. AIE Brookings Joint Center for Regulatory Studies.

Berle, A.A. and Means, G.C. (1932). *The Modern Corporation and Private Property*. New York: Macmillan.

Bernard, V.L. and Skinner, D.J. (1996). What Motivates Managers' Discretionary Accruals? *Journal of Accounting and Economics*, 22(1–3), 313–25.

Bernardi, R. and Arnold, D.F. (1997). An Examination of Moral Development within Public Accounting by Gender, Staff Level and Firm. *Contemporary Accounting Research*, 14(4), 653–68.

Bhagat, S. and Black, B.S. (1999). The Uncertain Relationship between Board Composition and Firm Performance. *Business Lawyer*, 54, 921–63.

Bhagat, S. and Black, B.S. (2000). *Board Independence and Long-term Firm Performance*. Stanford Law School John M. Olin Program in Law and Economics Working Paper no. 188. Available HTTP: <http://papers.ssrn.com/paper.taf?abstract_id=133808> (accessed 1 August 2007).

Bhagat, S. and Black, B.S. (2002). The Non-correlation between Board Independence and Long-term Firm Performance. *Journal of Corporation Law*, 27(2), 231–73.

Bickel, W.K. and Johnson, M.W. (2003). Delay Discounting: A Fundamental Behavioural Process of Drug Dependence, in *Time and Decision*, ed. Loewenstein, G., Read, D., and Baumeister, R.F. New York: Russell Sage Foundation.

Birnbaum, M.H. (2001). *Introduction to Behavioural Research on the Internet*. New York: Prentice-Hall.

Black, B.S. (1998). Shareholder Activism and Corporate Governance in the United States, in *The New Palgrave Dictionary of Economics and the Law*, ed. Newman, P. London: Macmillan.

Black, B.S. (2001a). Does Corporate Governance Matter? A Crude Test Using Russian Data. *University of Pennsylvania Law Review*, 149, 2131–50.

Black, B.S. (2001b). The Legal and Institutional Preconditions for Strong Securities Markets. *University of California Los Angeles Law Review*, 48, 781–855.

Black, B.S., Hasung, J., and Woochan, K. (2003). *Does Corporate Governance Affect Firms' Market Values? Evidence from Korea*. Stanford Law and Economics Olin Working Paper, 237. Available HTTP: <http://ssrn.com/abstract=311275> (accessed 1 August 2007).

Blaug, M. (1998). Disturbing Currents in Modern Economics. *Challenge*, 41(3), 11–34.

Blue Ribbon Committee (1999). *Report and Recommendations of the Blue Ribbon Committee on Improving the Effectiveness of Corporate Audit Committees*. New York: The New York Stock Exchange and the National Association of Securities Dealers.

Bonner, S.E. and Pennington, N. (1991). Cognitive Processes and Knowledge as Determinants of Auditor Expertise. *Journal of Accounting Literature*, 10, 1–50.

Borokhovich, K., Parrino, R., and Trapani, T. (1996). Outside Directors and CEO Selection. *Journal of Financial and Quantitative Analysis*, 31(3), 337–55.

Bowen, R.M., Rajgopal, S., and Venkatachalam, M. (2006). *Accounting Discretion, Corporate Governance and Firm Performance*. Duke Fuqua School of Business Working Paper. Available HTTP: <http://catalyst.merage.uci.edu/tools/dl_public.cat?year=2006&file_id=295&type=cal&name=brv_CAR_Jan06.pdf> (accessed 14 August 2007).

Boycko, M., Shleifer, A., and Vishny, R.W. (1995). *Privatising Russia*. Boston: The MIT Press.

Bradshaw, M.T., Richardson, S.A., and Sloan, R.G. (2001). Do Analysts and Auditors use Information in Accruals? *Journal of Accounting Research*, 39(1), 45–74.

Bratton, W.W. (2002). *Enron and the Dark Side of Shareholder Value*. Public Law and Legal Theory Working Paper No. 035, The George Washington University Law School. Available HTTP: <http://ssrn.com/abstract=301475> (accessed 1 August 2007).

Braun, P.A. and Yaniv, I. (1992). A Case Study of Expert Judgment: Economists' Probabilities vs. Base-Rate Forecasts. *Journal of Behavioural Decision Making*, 5(3), 217–31.

Brenner, M., Sundaram, R.K., and Yermack, D. (1998). *Altering the Terms of Executive Stock Options*. New York University, Center for Law and Business Working Paper No. CLB-98-001. Available HTTP: <http://papers.ssrn.com/paper.taf?abstract_id=114288> (accessed 1 August 2007).

Briloff, A.J. (1972). *Unaccountable Accounting*. New York: Harper & Row.

Briloff, A.J. (1976). *More Debits than Credits: The Burnt Investors' Guide to Financial Statements*. New York: Harper & Row.

Briloff, A.J. (1982). *Truth About Accounting*. New York: Harper & Row.

Briloff, A.J. (2004). Accounting Scholars in the Groves of Academe In Pari Delicto. *Critical Perspectives on Accounting*, 15(6–7), 787–96.

Brocas, I. and Carrillo, J.D. (1999). Entry Mistakes, Entrepreneurial Boldness and Optimism. ECARE and CEPR. Discussion Paper No. 2213. Centre for Economic Policy Research.

Brockner, J. (1992). The Escalation of Commitment to a Failing Course of Action: Toward Theoretical Progress. *Academy of Management Review*, 17(1), 39–61.

Brockner, J. and Rubin, J.Z. (1985). *Entrapment in Escalating Conflicts: A Social Psychological Analysis*. New York: Springer.

Bromberg, A. and Ribstein, L. (2005). *Limited Liability Partnerships, the Revised Uniform Partnership Act and the Uniform Limited Partnership Act (2001)*. Boston: Little, Brown and Co.

Bromiley, P., McNamara, G., and Moon, H. (2002). Banking on Commitment: Intended and Unintended Consequences of an Organization's Attempt to Attenuate Escalation of Commitment. *Academy of Management Journal*, 45(2), 443–53.

Brown, C.L. and Carpenter, G.S. (2000). Why is the Trivial Important? A Reasons-based Account for the Effects of Trivial Attributes on Choice. *Journal of Consumer Research*, 26(4), 373–86.

Brown, L.D. (1998). *Managerial Behaviour and the Bias in Analysts' Earnings Forecasts*. Working paper, Georgia State University. Available HTTP: <http://ssrn.com/abstract=113508> (accessed 1 August 2007).

Brudney, V. (1982). The Independent Director-Heavenly City or Potemkin Village? *Harvard Law Review*, 95(3), 597–660.

Bruner, J.S. (1957). Going Beyond the Information Given, in *Contemporary Approaches to Cognition*, ed. Bruner, J.S., Brunswik, E., Festinger, L., Heider, F., Muenzinger, K.F., Osgood, C.E., and Rapaport, D. Cambridge, Mass.: Harvard University Press.

Bruner, J.S. and Potter, M.C. (1964). Inference in Visual Recognition. *Science*, 144, 424–5.

Bukszar, E. and Connolly, T. (1988). Hindsight Bias and Strategic Choice: Some Problems in Learning from Experience. *Academy of Management Journal*, 31, 628–41.

Bulow, J. and Rogoff, K. (1989). Sovereign Debt: Is to Forgive to Forget? *American Economic Review*, 79(1), 43–51.

Burgstahler, D.C. and Dichev, I.D. (1997). Earnings, Adaptation and Equity Value. *Accounting Review*, 72(2), 187–216.

Burgstahler, D.C. and Eames, M. (2006). Management of Earnings and Analysts' Forecasts to Achieve Zero and Small Positive Earnings Surprises. *Journal of Business Finance & Accounting*, 33(5–6), 633–52.

Burrows, P. and Veljanovski, C.G. (eds) (1981). *The Economic Approach to Law*. London and Boston: Butterworths.

Bush, T. (2005). *Divided by a Common Language. Where Economics Meets Law: US Vs Non-US Financial Reporting Models*. Dialogue in Corporate Governance: Beyond the Myth of Anglo-American Corporate Governance. Institute of Chartered Accountants in England and Wales (ICAEW).

Bushman, R. and Smith, A. (2001). Financial Accounting Information and Corporate Governance. *Journal of Accounting and Economics*, 32(1–3), 237–333.

Byrne, J.A. (1999). The Teddy Roosevelts of Corporate Governance. *Business Week*, 31 May, 75–9.

Cadbury, A. (1992). *Report of the Committee on the Financial Aspects of Corporate Governance*. London: Gee.

Calabresi, G. and Melamed, A.D. (1972). Property Rules, Liability Rules and Inalienability: One View of the Cathedral. *Harvard Law Review*, 85(6), 1089–128.

Callen, J.L., Livnat, J., and Segal, D. (2006). Accounting Restatements: Are They Always Bad News? *The Journal of Investing* (Fall).

Camerer, C.F. and Hogarth, R.M. (1999). The Effects of Financial Incentives in Experiments: A Review and Capital-Labor-Production Framework. *Journal of Risk and Uncertainty*, 19(1–3), 7–42.

Camerer, C. and Lovallo, D. (1999). Overconfidence and Excess Entry: An Experimental Approach. *American Economic Review*, 89(1), 306–18.

Camerer, C.F., Ho, T.-H., and Chong, J.-K. (2004a). A Cognitive Hierarchy Model of Games. *Quarterly Journal of Economics*, 119(3), 861–98.

Camerer, C., Loewenstein, G., and Prelec, D. (2004b). Neuroeconomics: Why Economics Needs Brains. *Scandinavian Journal of Economics*, 106(3), 555–80.

Camerer, C., Loewenstein, G., and Prelec, D. (2005). Neuroeconomics: How Neuroscience Can Inform Economics. *Journal of Economic Literature*, 43(1), 9–64.

Cameron, L. (1995). *Raising the Stakes in the Ultimatum Game: Experimental Evidence from Indonesia*. Industrial Relations Section, Princeton University Working Paper No. 345.

Campbell, R.B. and Gaetke, E.R. (2003). The Ethical Obligation of Transactional Lawyers to Act as Gatekeepers. *Rutgers Law Review*, 56(9).

Caparo (1990). House of Lords Judgment of *Caparo vs. Dickman*, London. Available HTTP: <http://oxcheps.new.ox.ac.uk/casebook/Resources/CAPARO_1.pdf> (accessed 14 August 2007).

Carcello, J. and Neal, T. (2003a). Audit Committee Independence and Disclosure: Choice for Financially Distressed Firms. *Corporate Governance*, 11(4), 289–99.

Carcello, J. and Neal, T. (2003b). Audit Committee Characteristics and Auditor Dismissals Following 'New' Going-concern Audit Reports. *The Accounting Review*, 78, 95–117.

Chapman, L.J. and Chapman, J.P. (1967). Genesis of Popular but Erroneous Psychodiagnostic Observations. *Journal of Abnormal Psychology*, 72(3), 193–204.

Chapman, L.J. and Chapman, J.P. (1969). Illusory Correlation as an Obstacle to the Use of Valid Psychodiagnostic Signs. *Journal of Abnormal Psychology*, 74(3), 271–80.

Chapman, L.J. and Chapman, J.P. (1971). Test Results Are What You Think They Are. *Psychology Today*, 5(6), 18–22. Reprinted in Kahneman, D., Slovic, P., and Tversky, A. (eds), *Judgment under Uncertainty* (1982). New York: Cambridge University Press.

Chase, V.M., Hertwig, R., and Gigerenzer, G. (1998). Visions of Rationality. *Trends in Cognitive Sciences*, 2(6), 206–14.

Chung, H. and Kallapur, S. (2003). Client Importance, Non-audit Services and Abnormal Accruals. *The Accounting Review*, 78(4), 931–55.

Chung, S.H. and Herrnstein, R.J. (1967). Choice and Delay of Reinforcement. *Journal of the Experimental Analysis of Behaviour*, 10(1), 67–74.

Clarke, F.L., Dean, G.W., and Oliver, K.G. (2003). *Corporate Collapse: Regulatory, Accounting and Ethical Failure* (2nd edition). Cambridge: Cambridge University Press.

CNMV (Comisión Nacional del Mercado de Valores) (2003a). *Report by the Special Commission chaired by Enrique de Aldama y Miñón to Foster Transparency and Security in the Markets and in Listed Companies (Aldama Report)*. Available HTTP: <http://www.ecgi.org/codes/code.php?code_id=109> (accessed 14 August 2007).

CNMV (Comisión Nacional del Mercado de Valores) (2003b). *Law 26/2003 – LEY 26/2003, de 17 de julio, por la que se modifican la Ley 24/1988, de 28 de julio, del Mercado de Valores, y el texto refundido de la Ley de Sociedades Anónimas, aprobado por el Real Decreto Legislativo 1564/1989, de 22 de diciembre, con el fin de reforzar la transparencia de las sociedades anónimas cotizadas*. Available HTTP: <http://www.cnmv.es/index.htm> (accessed 2 March 2007).

Coase, R.H. (1937). The Nature of the Firm. *Economica*, 4, 386–405.

Coase, R.H. (1959). The Federal Communications Commission. *Journal of Law and Economics*, 2, 1–40.

Coase, R.H. (1960). The Problem of Social Cost. *Journal of Law and Economics*, 3, 1–44.

Coffee, J.C. (2001). *The Acquiescent Gatekeeper: Reputational Intermediaries, Auditor Independence and the Governance of Accounting*. Columbia Law School Center for Law and Economics Studies Working Paper No. 191. Available HTTP: <http://ssrn.com/abstract=270944> (accessed 1 August 2007).

Coffee, J.C. (2002). *Understanding Enron: It's About the Gatekeepers, Stupid*. Columbia Law School Center for Law and Economic Studies Working Paper No. 207. Available HTTP: <http://ssrn.com/abstract=325240> (accessed 1 August 2007).

Coffee, J.C. (2003a). *What Caused Enron? A Capsule Social and Economic History of the 1990's*. Columbia Law School Center for Law and Economic Studies Working Paper No. 214. Available HTTP: <http://ssrn.com/abstract=373581> (accessed 1 August 2007).

Coffee, J.C. (2003b). *Gatekeeper Failure and Reform: The Challenge of Fashioning Relevant Reforms*. Columbia Law School Center for Law and Economic Studies Working Paper No. 237. Available HTTP: <http://ssrn.com/abstract=447940> (accessed 1 August 2007).

Coffee, J.C. (2005). *A Theory of Corporate Scandals: Why the US and Europe Differ*. The Center for Law and Economic Studies, Columbia University Law School, Working Paper No. 274. Available HTTP: <http://papers.ssrn.com/sol3/Papers.cfm?abstract_id=694581> (accessed 1 August 2007).

Cohen, J.R. and Trompeter, G.M. (1998). An Examination of Factors Affecting Audit Practice Development. *Contemporary Accounting Research*, 15(4), 481–504.

Cohen, J.R., Pant, L.W., and Sharp, D.J. (1995). An Exploratory Examination of International Differences in Auditors' Ethical Perceptions. *Behavioural Research in Accounting*, 7, 37–64.

Cohen, L.J. (1981). Can Human Irrationality be Experimentally Demonstrated? *Behaviour and Brain Sciences*, 4, 317–31.

Cohen, S.G. and Bailey, D.E. (1997). What Makes Teams Work: Group Effectiveness Research from the Shop Floor to the Executive Suite. *Journal of Management*, 23(3), 239–90.

Cohen, S.G. and Edwards, J.R. (1989). Personality Characteristics as Moderators of the Relationship between Stress and Disorder, in *Advances in the Investigation of Psychological Stress*, ed. Neufield, R.W.J. New York: Wiley.

Collier, P. (1997). Corporate Governance and Audit Committees, in *Current Issues in Auditing* (3rd edition), ed. Sherer, M. and Turley, S. London: Sage.

Collins, D.W. and Hribar, P. (2000). Earnings-based and Accrual-based Market Anomalies: One Effect or Two? *Journal of Accounting and Economics*, 29(1), 101–23.

Collins, D.W., Gong, G., and Hribar, P. (2003). Investor Sophistication and the Mispricing of Accruals. *Review of Accounting Studies*, 8(2/3), 251–76.

Conference Board (2007). The 2007 Institutional Investment Report. See: http://www.conference-board.org/publications/describe.cfm?id=1270

Conlisk, J. (1996). Why Bounded Rationality? *Journal of Economic Literature*, 34(2), 669–700.

CONSOB (Commissione Nazionale per le Società e la Borsa) (2005). Legislative Decree no. 58, of 24 February 1998 – Consolidated Law on Financial Intermediation, pursuant to Articles 8 and 21 of Law 52 of 6 February 1996 (as amended by Law 262/2005 'Provisions for the Protection of Savings and the Regulation of Financial Markets').

Cook, J.R. (2003). Corporate and Director Interlocks in the USA: 2003. Staff Report of The Corporate Library. Available HTTP: <http://www.thecorporatelibrary.com/index.php?F=Shop&p=shop&s=srr&sn=ar> (accessed 14 August 2007).

Core, J.R., Holthausen, R.W., and Larcker, D. (1999). Corporate Governance, Chief Executive Officer Compensation and Firm Performance. *Journal of Financial Economics*, 51, 371–406.

Cornish, D.B. and Clarke, R.V. (eds) (1986). *The Reasoning Criminal*. New York: Springer-Verlag.

COSO (Committee of Sponsoring Organizations of the Treadway Commission) (1992). *Internal Control-Integrated Framework*, AICPA.

Cousins, J., Mitchell, A., and Sikka, P. (2004). *Race to the Bottom: The Case of the Accountancy Firms*. Basildon: Association for Accountancy & Business Affairs.

Cox, J.D. and Munsinger, H.L. (1985). Bias in the Boardroom: Psychological Foundations and Legal Implications of Corporate Cohesion. *Law & Contemporary Problems*, 48 (Summer), 83–135.

Cramton, R.C. (2002). Enron and the Corporate Lawyer: A Primer on the Legal and Ethical Issues. *The Business Lawyer*, 58(1), 143–87.

Cunningham, L.A. (2002). Sharing Accounting's Burden: Business Lawyers in Enron's Dark Shadows. *The Business Lawyer*, 57(4), 1421–662.

Cunningham, L.A. (2003). The Sarbanes-Oxley Yawn: Heavy Rhetoric, Light Reform (and It Just Might Work). *Connecticut Law Review*, 35(3), 915–89.

Cunningham, L.A. (2004). Facilitating Auditing's New Early Warning System: Control Disclosure, Auditor Liability and Safe Harbors. Boston College Law School, Public Law and Legal Theory Research Paper Series, no. 35.

DaDalt, P.J., Davidson III, W.N., and Xie, B. (2003). Earnings Management and Corporate Governance: The Roles of the Board and the Audit Committee. *Journal of Corporate Finance*, 9(3), 295–316.

Daily, C.M., Ellstrand, A.E., and Johnson, J. (1996). Boards of Directors: A Review and Research Agenda. *Journal of Management*, 22(3), 409–38.

Dallas, L.L. (1988). Two Models of Corporate Governance: Beyond Berle & Means. *Journal of Law Reform*, 22(1), 19–116.

Dallas, L.L. (2002). The New Managerialism and Diversity on Corporate Boards of Director. *Tulane Law Review*, 76(5/6), 1363–405.

Dallas, L.L. (2003). A Preliminary Inquiry into the Responsibility of Corporations and their Directors and Officers for Corporate Climate: The Psychology of Enron's Demise. *Rutgers Law Journal*, 35(1), 1–68.

Damasio, A.R. (1994). *Descartes' Error: Emotion, Reason and the Human Brain*. New York: Avon.

Damasio, A.R., Tranel, D., and Damasio, H.C. (1990). Individuals with Sociopathic Behaviour Caused by Frontal Damage Fail to Respond Autonomically to Social Stimuli. *Behavioural Brain Research*, 41, 81–94.

Dann, L.Y. and DeAngelo, H. (1988). Corporate Financial Policy and Corporate Control: A Study of Defensive Adjustments in Asset and Ownership Structure. *Journal of Financial Economics*, 20(1/2), 87–128.

Darley, J.M. (1996). How Organizations Socialize Individuals into Evildoing, in *Codes of Conduct*, ed. Messick, D.M. and Tenbrunsel, A.E. New York: Russell Sage.

Daum, R. (2003). *Außer Kontrolle*. Munich: FinanzBuch Verlag.

Davey, P.J. (1991). *Voting Corporate Pension Fund Proxies*. New York: The Conference Board.

Davis, J.H., Kameda, T., Parks, C., Stasson, M., and Zimmerman, S. (1989). Some Social Mechanics of Group Decision Making: The Distribution of Opinion, Polling Sequence and Implications for Consensus. *Journal of Personality and Social Psychology*, 57(6), 1000–12.

Davis, L.R. and Simon, D.T. (1992). The Impact of SEC Disciplinary Actions on Audit Fees. *Auditing: A Journal of Practice and Theory*, 11(1), 58–68.

Daws, R.M. and Hastie, R. (2001). *Rational Choice in an Uncertain World – An Introduction to Judgement and Decision Making*. London: Sage.

Deakin, S. and Konzelmann, S. (2003). *Learning From Enron*. ESRC Centre for Business Research, University of Cambridge Working Paper no. 274.

DeAngelo, L. (1986). Accounting Numbers as Market Valuation Substitutes: A Study of Management Buyouts of Public Stockholders. *The Accounting Review*, 61, 400–20.

DeAngelo, H. and DeAngelo, L. (1985). Management Buyouts of Publicly Traded Corporations. *Financial Analysts Journal*, 43(3), 38–50.

DeAngelo, H., DeAngelo, L., and Skinner, D.J. (1994). Accounting Choice in Troubled Companies. *Journal of Accounting and Economics*, 17(1/2), 113–44.

De Bondt, W.F.M. and Thaler, R.H. (2002). Do Analysts Overreact?, in *Heuristics and Biases*, ed. Gilovich, T., Griffin, D., and Kahneman, D. Cambridge: Cambridge University Press.

Dechow, P.M. (1994). Accounting Earnings and Cash Flows as Measures of Firm Performance: The Role of Accounting Accruals. *Journal of Accounting and Economics*, 18(1), 3–43.

Dechow, P.M. and Dichev, I.D. (2002). The Quality of Accruals and Earnings: The Role of Accrual Estimation Errors. *The Accounting Review*, 77(s-1), 35–59.

Dechow, P.M. and Skinner, D.J. (2000). Earnings Management: Reconciling the Views of Accounting Academics, Practitioners and Regulators. *Accounting Horizons*, 14(2), 235–50.

Dechow, P.M., Hutton, A., and Sloan, R. (1999). An Empirical Assessment of the Residual Income Valuation Model. *Journal of Accounting and Economics*, 26, 1–34.

Dechow, P.M., Kothari, S.P., and Watts, R.L. (1998a). The Relation between Earnings and Cash Flows. *Journal of Accounting and Economics*, 25(2), 133–69.

Dechow, P.M., Richardson, S.A., and Tuna, A.I. (2003). Why Are Earnings Kinky? An Examination of the Earnings Management Explanation. *Review of Accounting Studies*, 8, 355–84.

Dechow, P.M., Sabino, J., and Sloan, R.G. (1998b). *Implications of Nondiscretionary Accruals for Earnings Management and Market-Based Research*. Working paper. Draft, September 1998. Presented at the American Accounting Association 1998 Annual Meeting.

Dechow, P.M., Sloan, R.G., and Sweeney, A.P. (1995). Detecting Earnings Management. *The Accounting Review*, 70(2), 193–225.

Dechow, P.M., Sloan, R.G., and Sweeney, A.P. (1996). Causes and Consequences of Earnings Management: An Analysis of Firms Subject to Enforcement Actions by the SEC. *Contemporary Accounting Research*, 13(1), 1–36.

DeFond, M.L. and Francis, J.R. (2005). Audit Research after Sarbanes-Oxley. *Auditing: A Journal of Practice & Theory*, 24(Supplement), 5–30.

DeFond, M.L. and Jiambalvo, J. (1994). Debt Covenant Violation and Manipulation of Accruals: Accounting Choice in Troubled Companies. *Journal of Accounting and Economics*, 17, 145–76.

DeFond, M.L. and Park, C.W. (1997). Smoothing Income in Anticipation of Future Earnings. *Journal of Accounting and Economics*, 23(2), 115–40.

DeFond, M.L. and Subramanyam, K.R. (1998). Auditor Changes and Discretionary Accruals. *Journal of Accounting and Economics*, 25(1), 35–68.

DeFond, M.L., Raghunandan, K., and Subramanyam, K.R. (2002). *Do Non-audit Service Fees Impair Auditor Independence? Evidence from Going Concern Audit Opinions*. Working paper, USC and Texas A&M.

Degeorge, F., Patel, J., and Zeckhauser, R. (1999). Earnings Management to Exceed Thresholds. *Journal of Business*, 72(1), 1–33.

Del Guercio, D.G. and Hawkins, J. (1999). The Motivation and Impact of Pension Fund Activism, *Journal of Financial Economics*, 52(3), 293–340.

Demski, J.S. (2003). Corporate Conflicts of Interest. *Journal of Economic Perspectives*, 17(2), 51–72.

Denis, D.K. (2001). Twenty-five Years of Corporate Governance Research . . . and Counting. *Review of Financial Economics*, 10(3), 191–213.

Denis, D.K. and Sarin, A. (1999). Ownership and Board Structures in Publicly Traded Firms. *Journal of Financial Economics*, 52, 187–223.

DFAT (Department of Foreign Affairs and Trade, Australia) (1999). *Asia's Financial Markets: Capitalising on Reform*. Available HTTP: <https://www.dfat.gov.au/publications/fin_markets/> (accessed 1 August 2007).

Dharan, B.G. (2003). *Accruals Management with Financing and Investing Transactions*. Work in progress, copy with author.

Dichev, I. and Skinner, D. (2002). Large Sample Evidence on the Debt Covenant Hypothesis. *Journal of Accounting Research*, 40(4), 1091–124.

Diekmann, K.A. (1997). Implicit Justifications' and Self-serving Group Allocations. *Journal of Organizational Behaviour*, 18(1), 3–16.

Diekmann, K.A., Samuels, S.M., Ross, L., and Bazerman, M.H. (1997). Self-interest and Fairness in Problems of Resource Allocation: Allocators Versus Recipients. *Journal of Personality and Social Psychology*, 72(5), 1061–74.

Directorship (2006). Reaching the 'New Era' Director. Available HTTP: <http://www.directorship.com/pdf/DirectorshipMediaKit.pdf> (accessed 1 August 2007).

Doidge, C., Karolyi, G.A., and Stulz, R. (2005). Why Do Countries Matter so Much for Corporate Governance? Working paper, Ohio State University.

Douglas, W.O. (1940). *Democracy and Finance*. New Haven: Yale University Press.

Douma, B., Ordóñez, L., and Schweitzer, M.E. (2004). The Dark Side of Goal Setting: The Role of Goals in Motivating Unethical Decision Making. *The Academy of Management Journal*, 47, 422–32.

Drobetz, W., Schillhofer, A., and Zimmermann, H. (2004). Corporate Governance and Expected Stock Returns: Evidence from Germany. *European Financial Management*, 10(2), 267–93.

DTI (Department of Trade and Industry, United Kingdom) (2005a). *Company Law Reform Bill White Paper*. Available HTTP: <http://www.dti.gov.uk/bbf/co-act-2006/white-paper/page22800.html> (accessed 14 August 2007).

DTI (Department of Trade and Industry, United Kingdom) (2005b). *Investors and Management Practice: A Literature Review*. Available HTTP: <http://www.berr.gov.uk/files/file11032.pdf> (accessed 14 August 2007).

DTI (Department of Trade and Industry, United Kingdom) (2007). *Companies Act 2006, Regulatory Impact Assessment*. Available HTTP: <http://www.dti.gov.uk/files/file29937.pdf> (accessed 14 August 2007).

DuCharme, L.L. (1994). *IPOs: Private Information and Earnings Management*. Dissertation, The University of Washington.

DuCharme, L.L., Malatesta, P.H., and Sefcik, S.E. (2004). Earnings Management, Stock Issues and Shareholder Lawsuits. *Journal of Financial Economics*, 71(1), 27–49.

Dunegan, K.J., Duchon, D., and Barton, S.L. (1992). Affect, Risk and Decision Criticality: Replication and Extension in a Business Setting. *Organizational Behaviour and Human Decision Processes*, 53(3), 335–51.

Durtschi, C. and Easton, P.D. (2005). Earnings Management? The Shapes of the Frequency Distributions of Earnings Metrics are not Evidence Ipso Facto. *Journal of Accounting Research*, 43, 557–92.

Earnscliffe Research and Communications (1999). *Report to the United States Independence Standards Board: Research into Perceptions of Auditor Independence and Objectivity*. Ottawa: Earnscliffe Research and Communications.

Easterbrook, F. and Fischel, D. (1991). *The Economic Structure of Economic Law*. Cambridge, Mass.: Harvard University Press.

Eddy, D.M. (1982). Probabilistic Reasoning in Clinical Medicine: Problems and Opportunities, in *Judgements under Uncertainty: Heuristics and Biases*, ed. Kahneman, D., Slovic, P., and Tversky, A. Cambridge: Cambridge University Press.

Eide, E. (2000). Economics of Criminal Behaviour, in *Encyclopaedia of Law and Economics*, vol. V, ed. Oudewijn, B. and De Geest, G. Cheltenham, UK: Edward Elgar.

Eisenberg, T. and Macey, J.R. (2003). *Was Arthur Andersen Different? An Empirical Examination of Major Accounting Firms' Audits of Large Clients*. Cornell Legal Studies Research Paper No. 04-03 Available HTTP: <http://ssrn.com/abstract=468761> (accessed 1 August 2007).

Eisenberg, T., Sundgren, S., and Wells, M. (1998). Larger Board Size and Decreasing Firm Value in Small Firms. *Journal of Financial Economics*, 48(1), 35–54.

Ellickson, R.C. (1989). Bringing Culture and Human Frailty to Rational Actors: A Critique of Classical Law and Economics. *Chicago-Kent Law Review*, 65, 23–55.

Ellickson, R.C. (1998). Law and Economics Discovers Social Norms. *The Journal of Legal Studies*, 27(2), 537–52.

Engelen, E. (2002). Corporate Governance, Property and Democracy: A Conceptual Critique of Shareholder Ideology. *Economy and Society*, 31(3), 391–413.

Epstein, L.G. and Zin, S.E. (1990). First-order Risk Aversion and the Equity Premium Puzzle. *Journal of Monetary Economics*, 26(3), 387–407.

Epstein, S. (1994). Integration of the Cognitive and Psychodynamic Unconscious. *American Psychologist*, 49(8), 709–24.

Erickson, M. and Wang, S. (1999). Earnings Management by Acquiring Firms in Stock for Stock Mergers. *Journal of Accounting and Economics*, 27(2), 149–76.

Ezzamel, M. and Watson, R. (1997). Wearing Two Hats: The Conflicting Control and Management Roles of Non-executive Directors, in *Corporate Governance: Economic, Management and Financial Issues*, ed. Keasey, K., Thompson, S., and Wright, M. Oxford: Oxford University Press.

Fama, E.F. (1980). Agency Problems and the Theory of the Firm. *Journal of Political Economy*, 88(2), 288–307.

Fama, E.F. and Jensen, M.C. (1983a). Separation of Ownership and Control. *Journal of Law and Economics*, 26, 301–25.

Fama, E.F. and Jensen, M.C. (1983b). Agency Problems and Residual Claims. *Journal of Law and Economics*, 26, 327–49.

Fanto, J. (2004). Whistleblowing and the Public Director: Countering Corporate Inner Circles. *Oregon Law Review*, 83(2), 435–540.

FASB (Financial Accounting Standards Board, United States) (1978). *Statement of Financial Accounting Concepts No. 1.* Norwalk, Conn.: FASB.

FASB (Financial Accounting Standards Board, United States) (2002). *Statement of Financial Accounting Concepts 2, Qualitative Characteristics of Accounting Information.* Norwalk, Conn.: FASB.

Fehr, E. and Tougareva, E. (1996). *Do High Monetary Stakes Remove Reciprocal Fairness? Experimental Evidence from Russia.* Discussion Paper. University of Zurich.

Fehr, E. and Tyran, J. (2005). Individual Irrationality and Aggregate Outcomes. *Journal of Economic Perspectives*, 19(4), 43–66.

FEI (Financial Executives International) (2005). *Committee on Corporate Reporting. Feedback Regarding the Implementation of Section 404 of the Sarbanes-Oxley Act.* File Number 4-497. Morristown, NJ: FEI Research Foundation. Copy with author.

FEI (Financial Executives International) and Wu, M. (2002). *Quantitative Measures of the Quality of Financial Reporting.* Morristown, NJ: Financial Executives International Research Foundation.

Feroz, E.H., Park, K., and Pastena, V.S. (1991). The Financial and Market Effects of the SEC's Accounting and Auditing Enforcement Releases. *Journal of Accounting Research*, 29(Supplement), 107–48.

Ferrarini, G.A. and Giudici, P. (2005). *Financial Scandals and the Role of Private Enforcement: The Parmalat Case.* ECGI – Law Working Paper No. 40/2005 Available HTTP: <http://ssrn.com/abstract=730403> (accessed 1 August 2007).

Ferreira, M.A. and Matos, P.P. (2006). The Colors of Investors' Money: The Role of Institutional Investors Around the World. Working paper. Available HTTP: <http://ssrn.com/abstract=885777> (accessed 1 August 2007).

Festinger, L. (1957). *A Theory of Cognitive Dissonance.* Stanford, Calif.: Stanford University Press.

Finucane, M.L., Alhakami, A., Slovic, P., and Johnson, S.M. (2000). The Affect Heuristic in Judgements of Risks and Benefits. *Journal of Behavioural Decision Making*, 13(1), 1–17.

Firth, M. (1990). Auditor Reputation: The Impact of Critical Reports Issued by UK Government Inspectors. *Rand Journal of Economics*, 21(3), 374–87.

Fisch, J.E. and Rosen, K.M. (2003). Is There a Role for Lawyers in Preventing Future Enrons? *Villanova Law Review*, 48(4), 1097–138.

Fischhoff, B. (2002). Heuristics and Biases in Application, in *Heuristics and Biases*, ed. Gilovich, T., Griffin, D., and Kahneman, D. Cambridge: Cambridge University Press.

Forbes, D.P. and Milliken, F.J. (1999). Cognition and Corporate Governance: Understanding Boards of Directors as Strategic Decision-making Groups. *Academy of Management Journal*, 24(3), 489–505.

Fox, F.V. and Staw, B.M. (1979). The Trapped Administrator: Effects of Job Insecurity and Policy Resistance upon Commitment to a Course of Action. *Administrative Science Quarterly*, 24(3), 449–71.

France (2003). LOI No. 2003-706 du 1er Août 2003 de Sécurité Financière, http://www.legifrance.gouv.fr/WAspad/UnTexteDeJorf?numjo=ECOX0200186L

Francis, J.R. (2004). What Do We Know about Audit Quality? *The British Accounting Review*, 34(4), 345–68.

Francis, J.R. and Krishnan, J. (1999). Accounting Accruals and Auditors Reporting Conservatism. *Contemporary Accounting Research*, 16(1), 135–65.

Francis, J.R. and Schipper, K. (1999). Have Financial Statements Lost their Relevance? *Journal of Accounting Research*, 37(2), 319–52.

Frankel, R., Johnson, M., and Nelson, K. (2002). *The Relation between Auditors Fees for Non-audit Services and Earnings Quality*. MIT Sloan Working Paper No. 4330-02. Available HTTP: <http://papers.ssrn.com/sol3/papers.cfm?abstract_id=296557> (accessed 1 August 2007).

FRC (Financial Reporting Council, United Kingdom) (2003). *Combined Code on Corporate Governance July 2003*. Available HTTP: <http://www.frc.org.uk/corporate/combinedcode.cfm> (accessed 14 August 2007).

FRC (Financial Reporting Council, United Kingdom) (2006). *Combined Code on Corporate Governance June 2006*. Available HTTP: <http://www.frc.org.uk/corporate/combinedcode.cfm> (accessed 14 August 2007).

Frederick, S., Loewenstein, G., and O'Donoghue, T. (2002). Time Discounting and Time Preference: A Critical Review. *Journal of Economic Literature*, 40(2), 351–401.

Friedlan, J.M. (1994). Accounting Choices of Issues of Initial Public Offerings. *Contemporary Accounting Research*, 11(1), 1–32.

Friedman, M. (1953). *Essays in Positive Economics*. Chicago: University of Chicago Press.

Friedman, M. (1957). *A Theory of Consumption Function*. Princeton, NJ: Princeton University Press.

Galbraith, J.K. (1967). *The New Industrial State*. London: Hamish Hamilton.

Ganzach, Y. (2000). Judging Risk and Return of Financial Assets. *Organizational Behaviour and Human Decision Processes*, 83(2), 353–70.

GAO (Government Accounting Office) (1999). *Long-Term Capital Management. Report to Congressional Requesters*. GAO/GDD-00-03. Washington, DC, Government Accounting Office.

GAO (Government Accounting Office) (2002). *Financial Statement Restatements: Trends, Market Impacts, Regulatory Responses and Remaining Challenges*. GAO-02-302. Washington, DC, Government Accounting Office.

GAO (Government Accounting Office) (2006). *Financial Restatements: Update of Public Company Trends, Market Impacts, and Regulatory Enforcement Activities*. GAO-06-678. Washington, DC, Government Accounting Office.

Garland, H. (1990). Throwing Good Money after Bad: The Effect of Sunk Cost on the Decision to Escalate Commitment to an Ongoing Project. *Journal of Applied Psychology*, 75(6), 728–31.

Garrido, M.D.A. (2005). *Government and External Risk Mitigation: Why Was Singapore Less Affected by the Asian Financial Crisis than its Southeast Asian Neighbours?* LSE Working Paper Series. No. 05-54. Available HTTP: <http://www.lse.ac.uk/collections/DESTIN/pdf/WP54.pdf> (accessed 14 August 2007).

Garvey, G.T. and Milbourn, T.T. (2003). *Asymmetric Benchmarking in Compensation: Executives are Paid for (Good) Luck but not Punished for Bad.* AFA 2004 San Diego Meetings. Available HTTP: <http://ssrn.com/abstract=392701> (accessed 1 August 2007).

Gaver, J.J., Gaver, K.M., and Austin, J.R. (1995). Additional Evidence on Bonus Plans and Income Management. *Journal of Accounting and Economics*, 19(1), 3–28.

Germany (2002). *Transparency and Disclosure Law.* Available HTTP: <http://217.160.60.235/BGBL/bgbl1f/bgbl102s-2681.pdf> (accessed 14 August 2007).

Germany (2007). *German Corporate Governance Code* (as amended on 14 June 2007). Available HTTP: <http://www.corporate-governance-code.de/eng/kodex/index.html> (accessed 14 August 2007).

Gibbins, M. and Wolf, F.M. (1982). Auditors' Subjective Decision Environment – the Case of a Normal External Audit. *Accounting Review*, 57(1), 105–24.

Gibbons, R. and Murphy, K. (1990). Relative Performance Evaluation for Chief Executive Officers. *Industrial and Labor Relations Review*, 43(3), 30–51.

Gigerenzer, G. (1994). Why the Distinction between Single-event Probabilities and Frequencies is Relevant for Psychology (and Vice Versa), in *Subjective Probability*, ed. Wright, G. and Ayton, P. New York: Wiley.

Gigerenzer, G. (1996). On Narrow Norms and Vague Heuristics: A Reply to Kahneman and Tversky. *Psychological Review*, 103, 592–6.

Gigerenzer, G. and Goldstein, D.G. (1996). Reasoning the Fast and Frugal Way: Models of Bounded Rationality. *Psychological Review*, 103(4), 650–69.

Gigerenzer, G. and Hoffrage, U. (1995). How to Improve Bayesian Reasoning Without Instruction: Frequency Formats. *Psychological Review*, 102(4), 684–704.

Gigerenzer, G. and Todd, P.M. (and the ABC Research Group) (1999). *Simple Heuristics that Make Us Smart*. New York: Oxford University Press.

Gillan, S.L. and Starks, L.T. (2000). Corporate Governance Proposals and Shareholder Activism: The Role of Institutional Investors. *Journal of Financial Economics*, 57(2), 275–305.

Gillan, S.L. and Starks, L.T. (2002). Institutional Investors, Corporate Ownership and Corporate Governance. Discussion Paper No. 2002/9, United Nations University.

Gilovich, T., Griffin, D., and Kahneman, D. (eds) (2002a). *Heuristics and Biases*. Cambridge: Cambridge University Press.

Gilovich, T., Madey, S.F., and Medvec, V.H. (2002b). When Less is More: Counterfactual Thinking and Satisfaction among Olympic Medalists, in *Heuristics and Biases*, ed. Gilovich, T., Griffin, D., and Kahneman, D. Cambridge: Cambridge University Press.

Gilson, R.J. (1984). Value Creation by Business Lawyers: Legal Skills and Asset Pricing. *The Yale Law Journal*, 94(2), 239–313.

Gilson, R.J. and Kraakman, R. (1991). Reinventing the Outside Director: An Agenda for Institutional Investors. *Stanford Law Review*, 43(4), 863–906.

Givoly, D. and Hayn, C. (2003). Measuring Reporting Conservatism. Working Paper, Pennsylvania State University.

Glimcher, P.W., Dorris, M.C., and Bayer, H.M. (2005). Physiological Utility Theory and the Neuroeconomics of Choice. *Games and Economic Behaviour*, 52, 213–56.

Goldin, H. (2003). Report of Harrison J. Goldin, The Court-Appointed Examiner in the Enron North America Corp. Bankruptcy Proceeding, Respecting His Investigations of the Role of Certain Entities in Transactions Pertaining to Special Purpose Entities, Available HTTP: <http://www.enron.com/corp/por/pdfs/SPEReport11142003.pdf> (accessed 14 August 2007).

Goldman, A. and Barlev, B. (1974). The Auditor–Firm Conflict of Interest: Its Implications for Independence. *The Accounting Review*, 49(4), 707–18.

Goldstein, W.M. and Hogarth, R.M. (eds) (1997). *Research on Judgment and Decision Making*. Cambridge: Cambridge University Press.

Gompers, P., Ishii, J., and Metrick, A. (2003). Corporate Governance and Equity Prices. *Quarterly Journal of Economics*, 118(1), 107–55.

Goode, E. (2005). *Deviant Behaviour* (7th edition). New York: Prentice-Hall.

Gordon, J.N. (2002). What Enron Means for the Management and Control of the Modern Business Corporation: Some Initial Reflections. *University of Chicago Law Review*, 69(3), 1233–51.

Gordon, J.N. (2003). A New Role for Lawyers? The Corporate Counsellor After Enron. *Connecticut Law Review*, 35(3), 1185–216.

Gottfredson, M.R. and Hirschi, T. (1990). *A General Theory of Crime*. Stanford, Calif.: Stanford University Press.

Gramling, A., Maletta, M., Schneider, A., and Church, B. (2004). The Role of the Internal Audit Function in Corporate Governance: A Synthesis of the Extant Internal Auditing Literature and Directions for Future Research. *Journal of Accounting Literature*, 23, 94–223.

Green, D. and Shapiro, I. (1994). *Pathologies of Rational Choice Theory: A Critique of Applications in Political Science*. New Haven: Yale University Press.

Green, L., Fry, A.F., and Myerson, J. (1994). Discounting of Delayed Rewards: A Life Span Comparison. *Psychological Science*, 5, 33–6.

Greenberg, J.S. and Alloy, L.B. (1989). Depression Versus Anxiety: Differences in Self and Other Schemata, in *Cognitive Processes in Depression*, ed. L.B. Alloy. New York: Guilford Press.

Greenspan, A. (1996). *The Challenge of Central Banking in a Democratic Society*. Speech given at the American Enterprise Institute for Public Policy Research in Washington, DC, 5 December 1996.

Griffin, D. and Tversky, A. (1992). The Weighing of Evidence and the Determinants of Confidence. *Cognitive Psychology*, 24(3), 411–35.

Griffin, P. (2003). A League of Their Own? Financial Analysts' Responses to Restatements and Corrective Disclosures. *Journal of Accounting, Auditing and Finance*, 18(4), 519–28.

Griffith-Jones, S. and Gottschalk, R. (2004). *Costs of Currency Crises and Benefits of International Financial Reform Institute of Development Studies*. University of Sussex Research Paper. Available HTTP: <http://www.ids.ac.uk/ids/global/Finance/pdfs/SGJCostofcrises2.pdf> (accessed 14 August 2007).

Griffiths, I. (1986). *Creative Accounting: How to Make Your Profits What You Want Them to Be*. London: Allen & Unwin.

Grossman, S. and Hart, O. (1986). The Costs and Benefits of Ownership: A Theory of Vertical and Lateral Integration. *Journal of Political Economy*, 94(4), 691–719.

Guay, W.P., Kothari, S.P., and Watts, R.L. (1996). A Market-based Evaluation of Discretionary Accrual Models. *Journal of Accounting Research*, 34 (Supplement), 83–105.

Gulati, M., Rachlinski, J.J., and Langevoort, D.C. (2003). *Fraud by Hindsight*. Georgetown University Law Center, Public Law and Legal Theory Working Paper No. 442820. Available HTTP: <http://papers.ssrn.com/abstract=442820> (accessed 1 August 2007).

Guthrie, J. (1992). Critical Issues in Public Sector Auditing. *Managerial Auditing Journal*, 7(4), 28–34.

Guthrie, J. and Turnbull, S. (1995). Audit Committees: Is there a Role for Corporate Senates and/or Stakeholders Councils? *Corporate Governance: An International Review*, 3(2), 78–89.

Hackenbrack, K. and Nelson, M.W. (1996). Auditors' Incentives and their Application of Financial Accounting Standards. *The Accounting Review*, 71(1), 43–59.

Hall, B. and Liebman, J. (1998). Are CEO's Really Paid Like Bureaucrats? *Quarterly Journal of Economics*, 113(3), 653–92.

Hanson, J.D. and Kysar, D.A. (1999). Taking Behaviouralism Seriously: The Problem of Market Manipulation. *New York University Law Review*, 74, 630–749.

Hartzell, J.C. and Starks, L.T. (2003). Institutional Investors and Executive Compensation. *The Journal of Finance*, 58(6), 2351–74.

Hastorf, A.H. and Cantril, H. (1954). They Saw a Game: A Case Study. *Journal of Abnormal and Social Psychology*, 49, 129–34.

Hatherly, D.J. (1995). The Case for the Shareholder Panel in the UK. *The European Accounting Review*, 4(3), 535–53.

Hayn, C. (1995). The Information Content of Losses. *Journal of Accounting & Economics*, 20(2), 125–54.

Haynes, C. and Kachelmeier, S. (1998). The Effects of Accounting Contexts on Accounting Decisions: A Synthesis of Cognitive and Economic Perspectives in Accounting Experimentation. *Journal of Accounting Literature*, 17, 97–136.

Hayward, J. (2003). *Thinking not Ticking: Bringing Competition to the Public Interest Audit*. Centre for the Study of Financial Innovation (CSFI), London.

Hazard, G.C., Koniak, S.P., Cramton, R.C., and Cohen, G.M. (2004). *The Law and Ethics of Lawyering*. University Casebook Series (4th edition). Westbury: Foundation Press.

Healy, P.M. (1985). The Effects of Bonus Schemes on Accounting Decisions. *Journal of Accounting and Economics*, 7, 85–107.

Healy, P.M. and Palepu, K.G. (1993). The Effect of Firm's Financial Disclosure Strategies on Stock Prices. *Accounting Horizons*, 7(1), 1–12.

Healy, P.M. and Palepu, K.G. (1995). The Challenges of Investor Communication. *Journal of Financial Economics*, 38(2), 111–40.

Healy, P.M. and Wahlen, J.M. (1999). A Review of the Earnings Management Literature and its Implications for Standard Setting. *Accounting Horizons*, 13(4), 365–89.

Heath, C., Larrick, R.P., and Wu, G. (1999). Goals as Reference Points. *Cognitive Psychology*, 38, 79–109.

Heifetz, A. and Spiegel, Y. (2000). *On the Evolutionary Emergence of Optimism*. Working Paper. Available HTTP: <http://www.kellogg.northwestern.edu/research/math/papers/1304.pdf> (accessed 14 August 2007).

Heifetz, A. and Spiegel, Y. (2001). *The Evolution Of Biased Perceptions*. Working Paper. Available HTTP: <http://www.tau.ac.il/~spiegel/papers/optimism9.pdf> (accessed 14 August 2007).

Hendrickson, H. and Espahbodi, R. (1991). Second Opinion, Opinion Shopping and Independence. *Managerial Auditing Journal*, 11(9), 4–48.

Hermalin, B.E. and Weisbach, M.S. (1998). Endogenously Chosen Boards of Directors and their Monitoring of the CEO. *American Economic Review*, 88, 96–118.

Hermalin, B.E. and Weisbach, M.S. (2003). Boards of Directors as an Endogenously Determined Institution: A Survey of the Economic Literature. *Economic Policy Review* (Federal Reserve Bank of New York), April, pp. 7–26.

Hermes (2004). Corporate Governance and Performance. Available HTTP: <http://www.hermes.co.uk/pdf/corporate_governance/corporate_governance_and_performance_060105.pdf> (accessed 14 August 2007).

Heron, R.A. and Lie, E. (2006). What Fraction of Stock Option Grants to Top Executives have been Backdated or Manipulated? Working Paper. Available HTTP: <http://www.biz.uiowa.edu/faculty/elie/Grants-11-01-2006.pdf> (accessed 14 August 2007).

Hessing, D.J., Elfers, H., Robben, H., and Webley, P. (1992). Does Deterrence Deter? Measuring the Effect of Deterrence on Tax Compliance in Field Studies and Experimental Studies, in *Why People Pay Taxes: Tax Compliance and Tax Enforcement*, ed. Slemrod, J. Ann Arbor: University of Michigan Press.

Hey, J. (1997). The Economic Journal: Report to the Managing Editor. *Royal Economic Society Newsletter*, January, 3–5.

Higgs, D. (2003). *Review of the Role and Effectiveness of Non-executive Directors.* The Department of Trade and Industry. Available HTTP: <http://www.berr.gov.uk/files/file23012.pdf> (accessed 14 August 2007).

Hirsch, P., Michaels, S., and Friedman, R. (1987). 'Dirty Hands' Versus 'Clean Models'. Is Sociology in Danger of Being Seduced by Economics? *Theory and Society*, 16(3), 317–36.

Hirschey, M., Palmrose, Z.-V., and Scholz, S. (2005). Long-term Market Underreaction to Accounting Restatements. Paper Presented at the 2005 Financial Management Association Annual Meeting, Chicago. With author.

Hirst, D.E. and Koonce, L. (1996). Audit Analytical Procedures: A Field Investigation. *Contemporary Accounting Research*, 13(2), 457–86.

Hochberg, Y.V., Newman, Y.S., and Rierson, M.A. (2003). *Information in the Time-Series Dynamics of Earnings Management: Evidence from Insider Trading and Firm Return.* Working Paper. Available HTTP: <http://www.kellogg.northwestern.edu/faculty/hochberg/htm/EMIT.pdf> (accessed 14 August 2007).

Hoffrage, U. and Gigerenzer, G. (1998). Using Natural Frequencies to Improve Diagnostic Inferences. *Academic Medicine*, 73(5), 538–40.

Hogarth, R.M. (1991). A Perspective on Cognitive Research in Accounting. *The Accounting Review*, 66(2), 277–90.

Holland, J.B. (1997). *Corporate Communications with Institutional Shareholders.* Edinburgh: Institute of Chartered Accountants of Scotland.

Holland, J.B. (1998a). Influence and Intervention by Financial Institutions in their Investee Companies. *Corporate Governance: An International Review*, 6(4), 249–64.

Holland, J.B. (1998b). Private Voluntary Disclosure, Financial Intermediation and Market Efficiency. *Journal of Business Finance and Accounting*, 25(1), 29–68.

Holthausen, R.W. and Watts, R.L. (2001). The Relevance of the Value Relevance Literature for Financial Accounting Standard Setting. *Journal of Accounting and Economics*, 31(1–3), 3–75.

Holthausen, R.W., Larcker, D.F., and Sloan, R.G. (1995). Annual Bonus Schemes and the Manipulation of Earnings. *The Journal of Accounting and Economics*, 19(1), 29–75.

Hribar, P. and Collins, D.W. (2002). Errors in Estimating Accruals: Implications for Empirical Research. *Journal of Accounting Research*, 40(1), 105–35.

Hribar, P. and Nichols, D.C. (2006). The Use of Unsigned Earnings Quality Measures in Tests of Earnings Management. Working paper, University of Iowa and Cornell University.

Hribar, P., Johnson, B., and Jenkins, N. (2006). Stock Repurchases as an Earnings Management Device. *Journal of Accounting and Economics*, 41(1–2), 3–27.

Huron Consulting Group (2003). *An Analysis of Restatement Matters: Rules, Errors, Ethics, for the Five Years Ended December 31, 2002*. Report. Available HTTP: <http://www.huronconsultinggroup.com> (accessed 14 August 2007).

ICAS (The Institute of Chartered Accountants of Scotland) (2006). *Principles not Rules: A Question of Judgement*. Available HTTP: <http://www.icas.org.uk/site/cms/download/rs_Principles_v_Rules.pdf> (accessed 14 August 2007).

Ichheiser, G. (1949). Misunderstandings in Human Relations: A Study in False Social Perception. *American Journal of Sociology*, 55(Part 2), 1–70.

Isenberg, D.J. (1986). Group Polarization: A Critical Review and Meta-Analysis. *Journal of Personality and Social Psychology*, 50(6), 1141–51.

Jameson, M. (1988). *The Practical Art of Creative Accounting*. London: Kogan Page.

Janis, L.I. (1972). *Victims of Groupthink: A Psychological Study of Foreign-policy Decisions and Fiascos*. Boston: Houghton Mifflin.

Janis, L.I. (1982). *Groupthink* (2nd edition). Boston: Houghton Mifflin.

Janis, L.I. (1989). Groupthink: The Desperate Drive for Consensus at Any Cost, in *Classic Readings in Organizational Behaviour*, ed. Ott, J.S. Belmont, Calif.: Wadsworth.

Jegers, M. (1991). Prospect Theory and Risk-return Relation: Some Belgian Evidence. *Academy of Management Journal*, 34(1), 215–25.

Jensen, M.C. (1993). The Modern Industrial Revolution, Exit and the Failure of Internal Control Systems. *Journal of Finance*, 48(3), 831–80.

Jensen, M.C. and Meckling, W.H. (1976). The Theory of the Firm: Managerial Behaviour, Agency Costs and Ownership Structure. *Journal of Financial Economics*, 3(4), 305–60.

Jensen, M.C. and Murphy, K.J. (1990a). Performance Pay and Top Management Incentives. *Journal of Political Economy*, 98(April), 225–64.

Jensen, M.C. and Murphy, K.J. (1990b). CEO Incentives: It's Not How Much You Pay, But How. *Harvard Business Review*, 3(May/June), 138–53.

Jeter, D.C. and Shivakumar, J. (1999). Cross-Sectional Estimation of Abnormal Accruals Using Quarterly and Annual Data: Effectiveness in Detecting Event-specific Earnings Management. *Accounting and Business Research*, 29(4), 299–319.

Jiambalvo, J. (1996). Discussion of Causes and Consequences of Earnings Manipulation: An Analysis of Firms Subject to Enforcement Actions by the SEC. *Contemporary Accounting Research*, 13(1), 37–48.

Jiambalvo, J. and Wilner, N. (1985). Auditor Evaluation of Contingent Claims. *Auditing: A Journal of Practice & Theory*, 5(1), 10–11.

Johnson, E.N. (1994). Auditor Memory for Audit Evidence: Effects of Group Assistance, Time Delay and Memory Task. *Auditing: A Journal of Practice & Theory*, 13(1), 36–56.

Johnson, J.L., Daily, C.M., and Ellstrand, A.E. (1996). Boards of Directors: A Review and Research Agenda. *Journal of Management*, 22(3), 409–39.

Johnson, S.A., Ryan, H.E., and Tian, Y.S. (2006). Managerial Incentives and Corporate Fraud: The Sources of Incentives Matter. EFA 2006 Zurich Meetings (2 November 2006). Available HTTP: <http://ssrn.com/abstract=395960> (accessed 1 August 2007).

Jolls, C., Sunstein, C.R., and Thaler, R.H. (1998). A Behavioural Approach to Law and Economics. *Stanford Law Review*, 50(5), 1471–550.

Jones, C.L. and Weingram, S.E. (1997). *The Effects of Insider Trading, Seasoned Equity Offerings, Corporate Announcements, Accounting Restatements and SEC Enforcement Actions on 10b-5 Litigation Risk*. Working Paper, Stanford University.

Jones, E.E. and Harris, V.A. (1967). The Attribution of Attitudes. *Journal of Experimental Social Psychology*, 3, 1–24.

Jones, E.E. and Nisbett, R.E. (1971). The Actor and the Observer: Divergent Perceptions and the Causes of Behaviour, in *Attribution: Perceiving the Causes of Behaviour*, ed. Jones, E.E., Kanouse, D.E., Kelley, H.H., Nisbett, R.E., Valins, S., and Weiner, B. Morristown, NJ: General Learning Press.

Jones, J. (1991). Earnings Management during Import Relief Investigations. *Journal of Accounting Research*, 29(2), 193–229.

Jones, O.D. and Goldsmith, T.H. (2005). Law and Behavioural Biology. *Columbia Law Review*, 105(2), 405–502.

Joyce, E. and Biddle, G. (1981a). Anchoring and Adjustment in Probabilistic Inference in Auditing. *Journal of Accounting Research*, 19(1), 120–45.

Joyce, E. and Biddle, G. (1981b). Are Auditors' Judgments Sufficiently Regressive? *Journal of Accounting Research*, 19(2), 323–49.

Kahle, J.B. and White, R.A. (2004). Tax Professional Decision Biases: The Effects of Initial Beliefs and Client Preference. *Journal of the American Taxation Association*, 26(s-1), 1–30.

Kahneman, D. (1994). New Challenges to the Rationality Assumption. *Journal of Institutional and Theoretical Economics*, 150, 18–36.

Kahneman, D. and Lovallo, D. (1997). Timid Choices and Bold Forecasts: A Cognitive Perspective on Risk Taking. *Management Science*, 39(1), 17–32.

Kahneman, D. and Lovallo, D. (2003). Delusions of Success. *Harvard Business Review*, 81(7), 56–64.

Kahneman, D. and Snell, J. (1992). Predicting a Changing Taste: Do People Know What They Will Like? *Journal of Behavioural Decision-Making*, 5, 187–200.

Kahneman, D. and Tversky, A. (1979). Prospect Theory: An Analysis of Decision under Risk. *Econometrica*, 47(2), 263–91.

Kahneman, D. and Tversky, A. (1982). The Psychology of Preferences. *Scientific American*, 246(1), 160–73.

Kahneman, D. and Tversky, A. (1984). Choices, Values and Frames. *American Psychologist*, 39, 341–50.

Kahneman, D. and Tversky, A. (1986). Rational Choice and the Framing of Decisions. *59 Journal of Business*, S251.

Kahneman, D. and Tversky, A. (1992). Advances in Prospect Theory: Cumulative Representation of Uncertainty. *Journal of Risk and Uncertainty*, 5(4), 297–323.

Kahneman, D. and Tversky, A. (1996). On the Reality of Cognitive Illusions. A Reply to Gigerenzer's Critique. *Psychological Review*, 103, 582–91.

Kahneman, D., Knetsch, J.L., and Thaler, R.H. (1991). Anomalies: The Endowment Effect, Loss Aversion and Status Quo Bias. *Journal of Economic Perspectives*, 5(1), 197–206.

Kahneman, D., Slovic, P., and Tversky, A. (eds) (1982). *Judgment under Uncertainty: Heuristics and Biases.* New York: Cambridge University Press.

Kang, J. and Shivdasani, A. (1995). Firm Performance, Corporate Governance and Top Executive Turnover in Japan. *Journal of Financial Economics*, 38(1), 29–59.

Katz, D. (1960). The Functional Approach to the Study of Attitudes. *Public Opinion Quarterly*, 24(2), 163–204.

Kelley, H.H. (1967). Attribution Theory in Social Psychology, in *Nebraska Symposium on Motivation*, ed. D. Levine. Lincoln: University of Nebraska Press.

Kelley, H.H. (1973). The Process of Causal Attribution. *American Psychologist*, 28, 107–28.

Kellogg, I. and Kellogg, L.B. (1991). *Fraud, Window Dressing and Negligence in Financial Statements*. Commercial Law Series. New York: McGraw-Hill.

Kent, P. and Weber, R. (1998). Auditor Expertise and the Estimation of Dollar Error in Accounts. *Abacus*, 34(1), 120–39.

Keynes, J.M. (1967). *The General Theory of Employment, Interest and Money*. London: Macmillan. (First published 1936.)

Kida, T. (1984). The Effect of Causality and Specificity on Data Use. *Journal of Accounting Research*, 22(1), 145–52.

Kidd-Steward, J. and Countryman, A. (2002). Local Audit Conflicts Add Up: Consulting Deals, Hiring Practices in Question. *Chicago Tribune*, 24 February 2002, at p. C-1.

King, R.R. (2002). An Experimental Investigation of Self-Serving Biases in an Auditing Trust Game: The Effect of Group Affiliation. *The Accounting Review*, 77(2), 265–84.

Kinsey, K.A. (1992). Deterrence and Alienation Effects of IRS Enforcement: An Analysis of Survey Data, in *Why People Pay Taxes: Tax Compliance and Enforcement*, ed. Slemrod, J. Ann Arbor: University of Michigan Press.

Klapper, L.F. and Love, I. (2003). Corporate Governance, Investor Protection and Performance in Emerging Markets. World Bank. Policy Research Working Paper; No. WPS 2818.

Klein, A. (1998). Firm Performance and Board Committee Structure. *Journal of Law and Economics*, 41(1), 275–303.

Klein, A. (2002). Audit Committee, Board of Director Characteristics and Earnings Management, *Journal of Accounting and Economics*, 33(3), 375–400.

Klein, W.M. and Kunda, Z. (1993). Maintaining Self-serving Social Comparisons: Biased Reconstruction of One's Past Behaviours. *Personality & Social Psychology Bulletin*, 19(6), 732–9.

Klein, W.M. and Kunda, Z. (1994). Exaggerated Self-Assessments and the Preference for Controllable Risks. *Organizational Behaviour & Human Decision Processes*, 59(3), 410–27.

Klepper, S. and Nagin, D. (1989). The Anatomy of Tax Evasion. *Journal of Law, Economics and Organization*, 5(1), 1–24.

Knetsch, J.L. and Sinden, J.A. (1984). Willingness to Pay and Compensation Demanded: Experimental Evidence of an Unexpected Disparity in Measures of Value. *Quarterly Journal of Economics*, 99(3), 507–21.

Knight, J. (2000). Suboptimality and Social Institutions: The Relationship Between Cognition and Context, in *Cognition, Rationality and Institutions*, ed. Steit, M., Mummert, U., and Kiwit, D. Berlin: Springer.

Koniak, S.P. (2002). *Accountability Issues: Lessons Learned From Enron's Fall.* Testimony to the United States Senate Committee on the Judiciary, 6 February 2002.

Koniak, S.P. (2003a). Corporate Fraud: See Lawyers. *Harvard Journal of Law and Public Policy*, 26(1), 195–230.

Koniak, S.P. (2003b). When the Hurlyburly's Done: The Bar's Struggle with the SEC. Symposium – Regulating the Lawyer: Past Efforts and Future Possibilities. *Columbia Law Review*, 103(5), 1236–80.

Korn/Ferry International (2004). 31st Annual Board of Directors Study. Available HTTP: <http://www.kornferry.com/> (accessed 14 August 2007).

Korn/Ferry International (2005). 32nd Annual Board of Directors Study. Available HTTP: <http://www.kornferry.com/> (accessed 14 August 2007).

Korobkin, R.B. (2003). The Endowment Effect and Legal Analysis. *North Western University Law Review*, 97(3), 1227–93.

Korobkin, R.B. and Guthrie, C.P. (2004). *Heuristics and Biases at the Bargaining Table.* Vanderbilt Law and Economics Research Paper No. 04-11; UCLA School of Law, Law & Economics Research Paper No. 04-5.

Korobkin, R.B. and Ulen, T. (2000). Law and Behavioural Science: Removing the Rationality Assumption from Law and Economics. *California Law Review*, 88(4), 1051–144.

Kotchetova, N.V. and Messier, W.F. (2001). *Do Auditors Think as Frequentists?* Preliminary Draft. School of Accountancy, Robinson College of Business Georgia State University, Atlanta, Ga. With author.

Kothari, S.P., Leone, A.J., and Wasley, C.E. (2005). Performance Matched Discretionary Accrual Measures. *Journal of Accounting & Economics*, 39, 163–97.

Kraakman, R.H. (1986). Gatekeepers: The Anatomy of a Third Party Enforcement Strategy. *Journal of Law, Economics and Organization*, 2(1), 53–104.

Krause, L. (1998). *The Economics and Politics of the Asian Financial Crisis of 1997–98.* New York: The Council on Foreign Relations.

Krawiec, K.D. (2000). Accounting for Greed: Unraveling the Rogue Trader Mystery. *Oregon Law Review*, 79(2), 101–52.

Krecké, E. (2003). Economic Analysis and Legal Pragmatism. *International Review of Law and Economics*, 23(4), 421–37.

Kruger, J. and Dunning, D. (1999). Unskilled and Unaware of it: How Difficulties in Recognizing One's Own Incompetence Lead to Inflated Self-assessments. *Journal of Personality and Social Psychology*, 77(6), 1121–34.

Krugman, P. (1994). The Myth of Asia's Miracle. *Foreign Affairs*, November/ December.

Krugman, P. (1998). *What Happened to Asia?* Paul Krugman Web Page: http://www.wws.princeton.edu/pkrugman/

Krugman, P. (2002a). The Outrage Constraint. *New York Times*, 23 August 2002.

Krugman, P. (2002b). For Richer. *New York Times Magazine*, 20 October 2002.

Kuhn, T.S. (1970). *The Structure of Scientific Revolutions*, 2nd edition. Chicago: University of Chicago Press.

Kunda, Z. (1987). Motivated Inference: Self-serving Generation and Evaluation of Causal Theories. *Journal of Personality and Social Psychology*, 53(4), 636–47.

Kunda, Z. (1990). The Case for Motivated Reasoning. *Psychological Bulletin*, 108(3), 480–98.

Kunda, Z. (1999). *Social Cognition: Making Sense of People*. Cambridge, Mass.: A Bradford Book/The MIT Press.

Laibson, D. (1997). Golden Eggs and Hyperbolic Discounting. *Quarterly Journal of Economics*, 112(2), 443–77.

Landau, M. and Chisholm, D. (1995). The Arrogance of Optimism: Notes on Failure Avoidance Management. *Journal of Contingencies and Crisis Management*, 3(2), 67–80.

Langer, E.J. and Roth, J. (1975). Heads I Win, Tails it's Chance: The Illusion of Control as a Function of the Sequence of Outcomes in a Purely Chance Task. *Journal of Personality and Social Psychology*, 32, 951–5.

Langer, E.J., Welch IV, J.C., White, J.B., and Yariv, L. (2006). Frequent Social Comparisons and Destructive Emotions and Behaviours: The Dark Side of Social Comparisons. *Journal of Adult Development*, 13(1), 36–44.

Langevoort, D.C. (1993). Where Were the Lawyers? A Behavioural Inquiry into Lawyers' Responsibility for Clients' Fraud. *Vanderbilt Law Review*, 46, 75–119.

Langevoort, D.C. (1996). Selling Hope, Selling Risk: Some Lessons for Law from Behavioural Economics about Stockbrokers and Sophisticated Customers, *California Law Review*, 84(3), 627–701.

Langevoort, D.C. (1998a). Behavioural Theories of Judgment and Decision Making in Legal Scholarship: A Literature Review. *Vanderbilt Law Review*, 51, 1499–540.

Langevoort, D.C. (1998b). Organized Illusions: A Behavioural Theory of Why Corporations Mislead Stock Market Investors (and Cause Other Social Harms). *University of Pennsylvania Law Review*, 146(2), 101–72.

Langevoort, D.C. (2001a). *Monitoring: The Behaviour Economics of Inducing Agents' Compliance with Legal Rules*. University of Southern California Law School, Center for Law, Economics & Organization. Research Paper No. C01-7. Available HTTP: <http://papers.ssrn.com/abstract_id=276121> (accessed 1 August 2007).

Langevoort, D.C. (2001b). The Human Nature of Boards: Law, Norms and the Unintended Consequences of Independence and Accountability. *The Georgetown Law Journal*, 89, 797–832.

Langevoort, D.C. (2002a). The Organizational Psychology of Hyper-Competition: Corporate Irresponsibility and the Lessons of Enron. *George Washington Law Review*, 70(5/6), 968–75.

Langevoort, D.C. (2002b). When Lawyers and Law Firms Invest in their Corporate Clients' Stock. *Washington University Law Quarterly*, 80(2), 569–88.

Langevoort, D.C. (2003). Managing the 'Expectations Gap' in Investor Protection: The SEC and the Post-Enron Reform Agenda. *Villanova Law Review*, 48(4), 1139–65.

Langevoort, D.C. (2006). *Reflections on Scienter (and the Securities Fraud Case Against Martha Stewart that Never Happened)*. Preliminary draft, with author.

La Porta, R., Lopez-de-Silanes, F., Shleifer, A., and Vishny, R.W. (1998). Law and Finance. *The Journal of Political Economy*, 106(6), 1113–55.

La Porta, R., Lopez-de-Silanes, F., Shleifer, A., and Vishny, R.W. (2002). Investor Protection and Corporate Valuation. *The Journal of Finance*, 57(3), 1147–70.

Larcker, D.F., Richardson, S.A., and Tuna, A.I. (2005). How Important is Corporate Governance? Working Paper. Available HTTP: <http://ssrn.com/abstract=595821> (accessed 1 August 2007).

Latané, B. and Darley, J.M. (1969). Bystander 'Apathy'. *American Scientist*, 57, 244–68.

Latané, B. and Darley, J.M. (1970). *The Unresponsive Bystander: Why Doesn't He Help?* Englewood Cliffs, NJ: Prentice-Hall.

Lawrence, B. (1997). The Black Box of Organizational Demography. *Organization Science*, 8(1), 1–22.

Lazonick, W. and O'Sullivan, M. (2000). Maximizing Shareholder Value: A New Ideology for Corporate Governance. *Economy and Society*, 29(1), 13–36.

Lev, B. (2003). Corporate Earnings: Facts and Fiction. *Journal of Economic Perspectives*, 17(2), 27–50.

Levitt, A. (1998). *The Numbers Game.* Speech Delivered at the New York University Centre for Law and Business, New York (28 September). Available HTTP: <http://www.sec.gov/news/speech/speecharchive/1998/spch220.txt> (accessed 14 August 2007).

Levitt, A. (2000). *Testimony Concerning Commission's Auditor Independence Proposal before the Senate Subcommittee on Securities Committee on Banking, Housing and Urban Affairs.* Available HTTP: <http://www.sec.gov/rules/extra/audmin2.htm> (accessed 14 August 2007).

Lichtenstein, S. and Slovic, P. (1971). Reversals of Preference between Bids and Choices in Gambling Decisions. *Journal of Experimental Psychology*, 89, 46–55.

Lichtenstein, S. and Slovic, P. (1973). Response-induced Reversals of Preference in Gambling Decisions: An Extended Replication in Las Vegas. *Journal of Experimental Psychology*, 101, 16–20.

Lichtenstein, S., Slovic, P., Fischhoff, B., Layman, M., and Combs, B. (1978). Judged Frequency of Lethal Events. *Journal of Experimental Psychology: Human Learning and Memory*, 4(6), 551–78.

Liebrand, W.B.G., Messick, D.M., and Wolters, F.J.M. (1986). Why We are Fairer than Others: A Cross-cultural Replication and Extension. *Journal of Experimental Social Psychology*, 22(6), 590–604.

Lin, L. (1996). The Effectiveness of Outside Directors as a Corporate Governance Mechanism: Theories and Evidence. *Northwestern University Law Review*, 90(3), 898–966.

Lipton, M. and Lorsch, J. (1992). A Modest Proposal for Improved Corporate Governance. *Business Lawyer*, 48(1), 59–77.

Lockhart, J.B. (2006). *Statement of James B. Lockhart III, Acting Director Office of Federal Housing Enterprise Oversight on 'Ofheo's Report of the Special Examination of Fannie Mae' before the Subcommittee on Capital Markets, Insurance and Government Sponsored Enterprises, US House of Representatives*. 6 June 2006. Available HTTP: <http://www.ofheo.gov/News.asp?FormMode=Testimonies&ID=288> (accessed 14 August 2007).

Loewenstein, G.F. (1996). Out of Control: Visceral Influences on Behaviour. *Organizational Behaviour and Human Decision Processes*, 65(3), March, 272–92.

Loewenstein, G.F. (1999). A Visceral Account of Addiction, in *Getting Hooked: Rationality and Addiction*, ed. Elster, J. and Skog, O.J. Cambridge: Cambridge University Press.

Loewenstein, G.F. and Lerner, J.S. (2003). The Role of Affect in Decision Making, in *Handbook of Affective Science*, ed. Davidson, R.J., Goldsmith, H.H., and Scherer, K.R. New York: Oxford University Press.

Loewenstein, G.F. and Prelac, D. (1992). *Choices Over Time*. New York, Russell Sage Foundation.

Loewenstein, G.F. and Schkade, D. (1999). Wouldn't it Be Nice? Predicting Future Feelings, in *Well-Being: The Foundations of Hedonic Psychology*, ed. Diener, E., Schwartz, N., and Kahneman, D. New York: Russell Sage Foundation.

Loss, L. and Seligman, J. (2003). *Fundamentals of Securities Regulation* (5th edition). New York: Aspen.

Lord, C.G., Ross, L., and Lepper, M.R. (1979). Biased Assimilation and Attitude Polarization: The Effects of Prior Theories on Subsequently Considered Evidence. *Journal of Personality and Social Psychology*, 37(11), 2098–109.

Luban, D. (2006). Making Sense of Moral Breakdowns, in *Moral Leadership: The Theory and Practice of Power, Judgement and Policy*, ed. Rhode, D.L. Hoboken, NJ: Wiley.

Maccoby, M. (2000). Narcissistic Leaders. *Harvard Business Review*, 78(1), 69–77.

McDaniel, L.S. and Kinney, W.R. (1995). Expectation-formation Guidance in the Auditors' Review of Interim Financial Statements. *Journal of Accounting Research*, 33(1), 59–67.

Mace, M. (1986). *Directors: Myth and Reality*. Boston: Harvard Business School Press.

Macey, J.R. and Sale, H.A. (2003). Observations on the Role of Commodification, Independence and Governance in the Accounting Industry. *Villanova Law Review*, 48(4), 1167–88.

McFadden, D. (1999). Rationality for Economists? *Journal of Risk and Uncertainty*, 19(1–3), 73–105.

McFadden, D. (2000). *Economic Choices*. Nobel Prize Lecture. Available HTTP: <http://nobelprize.org/nobel_prizes/economics/laureates/2000/mcfadden-lecture.pdf> (accessed 14 August 2007).

McHoskey, J.W. (1995). Case Closed? On the John F. Kennedy Assassination: Biased Assimilation of Evidence and Attitude Polarization. *Basic and Applied Social Psychology*, 17(3), 395–409.

McKenzie, C.R.M. (1994). Base Rates Versus Prior Beliefs in Bayesian Inference. *Psycoloquy*, 5(1). http://www.cogsci.ecs.soton.ac.uk/psycoloquy/

McLean, B. and Elkind, P. (2003). *The Smartest Guys in the Room: The Amazing Rise and Scandalous Fall of Enron*. New York: Portfolio.

McNair, C.J. (1991). Proper Compromises: The Management Control Dilemma in Public Accounting and its Impact on Auditor Behaviour. *Accounting, Organizations and Society*, 16(7), 635–53.

Makar, S.D., Alam, P., and Pearson, M.A. (2000). Earnings Management: When Does Juggling the Numbers Become Fraud? *Fraud Magazine*, 14(1), 60–77.

Mankiw, G.N. (1981). The Permanent Income Hypothesis and the Real Interest Rate. *Economic Letters*, 7, 307–11.

March, J.G. (1978). Bounded Rationality, Ambiguity, and the Engineering of Choice. *Bell Journal of Economics*, 9(1), 587–608.

Masulis, R.W. (2006). *The Law and Economics of Self-Dealing*. Keynote Speech. The 19th Australian Finance and Banking Conference. The University of New South Wales, Sydney, December 2006.

Mayers, D., Shivdasani, A., and Smith, C. (1997). Board Composition and Corporate Control: Evidence from the Insurance Industry. *Journal of Business*, 70(1), 33–62.

Mayhew, A. (1987). Culture: Core Concept under Attack. *Journal of Economic Issues*, 21(2), 587–603.

Mayhew, B.W., Schatzberg, J.W.W., and Sevcik, G.R. (2001). The Effect of Accounting Uncertainty and Auditor Reputation on Auditor Independence. *Auditing: A Journal of Practice and Theory*, 20(2), 49–70.

Mazur, J.E. (1987). An Adjustment Procedure for Studying Delayed Reinforcement, in *Quantitative Analysis of Behaviour: The Effect of Delay and of Intervening Events on Reinforcement Value*, ed. Commons, M.L., Mazur, J.E., Nevins, J.A., and Rachlin, H. Hillsdale, NJ: Erlbaum.

Mehra, R. and Prescott, E. (1985). The Equity Premium Puzzle. *Journal of Monetary Economics*, 15, 145–61.

Mehran, H. (1995). Executive Compensation Structure, Ownership and Firm Performance. *Journal of Financial Economics*, 38(2), 163–84.

Messick, D.M. and Bazerman, M.H. (1996). Ethical Leadership and the Psychology of Decision Making. *Sloan Management Review*, 9–22.

Messick, D.M., Bloom, S., Boldizar, J.P., and Samuelson, C.D. (1985). Why We are Fairer than Others. *Journal of Experimental Social Psychology*, 21, 480–500.

Milgram, S. (1963). Behavioural Study of Obedience. *Journal of Abnormal and Social Psychology*, 67, 371–8.

Milgram, S. (1983). *Obedience to Authority: An Experimental View*. New York: Harper/Collins.

Milgrom, P. and Roberts, J. (1992). *Economics, Organization and Management*. New York: Prentice-Hall.

Miller, D.T. (1976). Ego Involvement and Attribution for Success and Failure. *Journal of Personality and Social Psychology*, 34, 901–6.

Miller, D.T. and Ross, M. (1975). Self-serving Biases in the Attribution of Causality: Fact or Fiction? *Psychological Bulletin*, 82, 213–25.

Miller, G.A., Galanter, E., and Pribam, K.H. (1960). Plans and the Structure of Behaviour. New York: Holt, Rinehart & Winston.

Millstein, I.M. (1999). Introduction to the Report and Recommendations of the Blue Ribbon Committee on Improving the Effectiveness of Corporate Audit Committees. Available HTTP: <http://www.nasdaq.com/about/Blue_Ribbon_Panel.pdf> (accessed 14 August 2007).

Mitchell, G. (2002). Why Law and Economics' Perfect Rationality should not be traded for Behavioural Law and Economics' Equal Incompetence. *Georgetown Law Journal*, 91, 67–167.

Modigliani, F. and Brumberg, R.H. (1954). Utility Analysis and the Consumption Function: An Interpretation of Cross-section Data, in *Post-Keynesian Economics*, ed. Kurihara, K.K. New Brunswick, NJ: Rutgers University Press, 388–436.

Moreira, J.A.C. and Pope, P.F. (2006). *Unequal Impact of Conservatism on Accrual Measures and Drivers: Implications for the Specification of Accrual Models*. Work in progress. Available HTTP: <www.fep.up.pt/investigacao/cete/papers/dp0604.pdf> (accessed 14 August 2007).

Moreno, K., Kida, T., and Smith, J.F. (2002). The Impact of Affective Reactions on Risky Decision Making in Accounting Contexts. *Journal of Accounting Research*, 40(5), 1331–49.

Morgan, R.B. (1993). Self- and Co-worker Perceptions of Ethics and their Relationships to Leadership and Salary. *Academy of Management Journal*, 36(1), 200–14.

Morrison, M.A. (2004). Rush to Judgment: The Lynching of Arthur Andersen & Co. *Critical Perspectives on Accounting*, 15(3), 335–75.

Morrison, M.A. (2005). Reply to Lynn E. Turner. *Critical Perspectives on Accounting*, 16, 65–9.

Moscovici, S. and Zavalloni, M. (1969). The Group as a Polarizer of Attitudes. *Journal of Personality and Social Psychology*, 12(2), 125–35.

Moscovici, S., Lage, E., and Naffrechoux, M. (1969). Influence of a Consistent Minority on the Responses of a Majority in a Color Perception Task. *Sociometry*, 32, 365–80.

Mulford, C.W. and Comiskey, E.E. (2002). *Financial Numbers Game: Detecting Creative Accounting Practices*. New York: Wiley.

Mullineux, A. (2007). Is there an Anglo-Saxon Corporate Governance Model? Working paper (with author). The Business School, University of Birmingham.

Muren, A. (2006). *Unrealistic Optimism about Exogenous Events: An Experimental Test*. Research Papers in Economics, Stockholm University, Department of Economics. Available HTTP: <http://people.su.se/~amure/Murenoptdec06.pdf> (accessed 14 August 2007).

Myers, D.G. (1978). Polarizing Effects of Social Comparison. *Journal of Experimental Social Psychology*, 14(6), 554–63.

Myers, D.G. (1982). *Polarizing Effects of Social Interaction*, in *Group Decision Making*, ed. Brandstatter, H., Davis, J. H., and Stocker-Kreichgauer, G. New York: Academic Press.

Myers, D.G. and Bishop, G.D. (1970). Discussion Effects on Racial Attitudes. *Science*, 169(3947), 778–9.

Myers, L.A., Myers, J.N., and Skinner, D. (2006). *Earnings Momentum and Earnings Management*. University of Michigan Working Paper. Copy with author.

Myners, P. (2001). Institutional Investment in the United Kingdom: A Review ('Myners Report'). Available HTTP: <http://www.hm-treasury.gov.uk./media/1/6/31.pdf> (accessed 14 August 2007).

National Association of Certified Fraud Examiners (1993). *Cooking the Books: What Every Accountant Should Know about Fraud*. New York: NASBA.

Nau, R. (2007). Extensions of the Subjective Expected Utility Model, in *Advances in Decision Analysis*, ed. Edwards, W., Miles, R., and von Winterfeldt, D. New York: Cambridge University Press.

Neisser, U. (1967). *Cognitive Psychology*. New York: Appleton, Century, Crofts.

Neisser, U. (1976). *Cognition and Reality*. San Francisco: W.H. Freeman.

NESDB (National Economic and Social Development Board, Thailand) (1999). *Gross Domestic Product: Third Quarter 1999* (December 1999). Bangkok: NESDB.

Nisbett, R. and Ross, L. (1980). *Human Inference: Strategies and Shortcomings of Social Judgment*. Englewood Cliffs, NJ: Prentice-Hall.

Nisbett, R. and Ross, L. (1991). *The Person and the Situation: Perspectives on Social Psychology*. Philadelphia: Temple University Press.

Nissani, M. (1990). A Cognitive Reinterpretation of Stanley Milgram's Observations on Obedience to Authority. *American Psychologist*, 45, 1384–5.

Noll, R.G. and Krier, J.E. (1990). Some Implications of Cognitive Psychology for Risk Regulation. *Journal of Legal Studies*, 19(2), 747–79.

O'Connor, S.M. (2002). *The Inevitability of Enron and the Impossibility of 'Auditor Independence' Under the Current Audit System*. Berkeley Center for Law, Business and the Economy Working Paper. Available HTTP: <http://www.law.berkeley.edu/centers/bclbe/symposia/postenron/SSRN-id303181.pdf> (accessed 14 August 2007).

O'Connor, S.M. (2004). Be Careful What You wish For: How Accountants and Congress Created the Problem of Auditor Independence. *Boston College Law Review*, 45.

O'Donoghue, T. and Rabin, M. (2001). Choice and Procrastination. *Quarterly Journal of Economics*, 116(1), 121–60.

O'Donoghue, T. and Rabin, M. (2003). Self Awareness and Self Control, in *Time and Decision: Economic and Psychological Perspectives on Intertemporal Choice*, ed. Baumeister, R., Loewenstein, G., and Read, D. New York: Russell Sage Foundation.

O'Donoghue, T. and Rabin, M. (2005). *Incentives and Self Control.* Working Paper. Available HTTP: <http://people.cornell.edu/pages/edo1/incent.pdf> (accessed 14 August 2007).

Oesch, J.M. and Galinsky, A.D. (2003). *First Offers in Negotiations: Determinants and Effects.* 16th Annual IACM Conference Melbourne, Australia. 15–18 June 2003. Available HTTP: <http://ssrn.com/abstract=399722> (accessed 1 August 2007).

OFHEO (Office of Federal Housing Enterprise Oversight) (2003). *Report of the Special Examination of Freddie Mac.* Available HTTP: <http://www.ofheo.gov/media/pdf/specialreport122003.pdf> (accessed 14 August 2007).

OFHEO (Office of Federal Housing Enterprise Oversight) (2006). *Report of the Special Examination of Fannie Mae.* Available HTTP: <http://www.ofheo.gov/media/pdf/FNMSPECIALEXAM.PDF> (accessed 14 August 2007).

Orviska, M. and Hudson, J. (2003). Tax Evasion, Civic Duty and the Law Abiding Citizen. *European Journal of Political Economy*, 19(1), 83–102.

O'Sullivan, M. (2000). *Contests for Corporate Control.* Oxford: Oxford University Press.

Painter, R.W. (1994). The Moral Interdependence of Corporate Lawyers and their Clients. *Southern California Law Review*, 67, 507–84.

Painter, R.W. and Duggan, J.E. (1996). Lawyer Disclosure of Corporate Fraud: Establishing a Firm Foundation. *SMU Law Review*, 50, 225–76.

Palepu, K., Healy, P., and Bernard, V. (2000). *Business Analysis and Valuation.* Cincinnati: South-Western College Publishing.

Palmrose, Z-V., Richardson, V.J., and Scholz, S. (2001). *Determinants of Market Reactions to Restatement Announcements.* University of Kansas Working Paper. Available HTTP: <http://ssrn.com/abstract=265009> (accessed 1 August 2007).

Parisi, F. and Smith, V. (2005). *The Law and Economics of Irrational Behaviour*. Palo Alto, Calif.: Stanford University Press.

Parkinson, J.E. (1995). The Role of Exit and Voice in Corporate Governance, in *Corporate Governance and Corporate Control*, ed. Scheikh, S. and Rees, W. London: Cavendish.

Peasnell, K.V. (2002). What Can We Learn from the Enron Affair? Case study presented at Lancaster University (Fall).

Peasnell, K.V., Pope, P.F., and Young, S. (2000a). Detecting Earnings Management Using Cross-sectional Abnormal Accrual Models. *Accounting and Business Research*, 30, 303–26.

Peasnell, K.V., Pope P.F., and Young, S. (2000b). Accrual Management to Meet Earnings Targets: UK Evidence Pre-and-Post-Cadbury. *British Accounting Review*, 32(4), 415–45.

Peasnell, K.V., Pope, P.F., and Young, S. (2001). *Board Monitoring and Earnings Management: Do Outside Directors Influence Abnormal Accruals?* Lancaster University Working Paper. Available HTTP: <http://ssrn.com/abstract=249557> (accessed 1 August 2007).

Peasnell, K.V., Pope, P.F., and Young, S. (2002). *Managerial Equity Ownership and the Demand for Outside Directors*. Lancaster University Working Paper. Available HTTP: <http://ssrn.com/abstract=314829> (accessed 1 August 2007).

Peecher, M.E. (1996). The Influence of Auditors' Justification Processes on their Decisions: A Cognitive Model and Experimental Evidence. *Journal of Accounting Research*, 34(1), 125–40.

Pellet, J. (1998). Teachers Expands its Curriculum. *The Chief Executive*, 139, 44–9. Available HTTP: <http://findarticles.com/p/articles/mi_m4070/is_139_0/ai_53336308/pg_1> (accessed 14 August 2007).

Perloff, L.S. and Fetzer, B.K. (1986). Self–Other Judgments and Perceived Vulnerability to Victimization. *Journal of Personality and Social Psychology*, 50(3), 502–10.

Pfohl, S. (1994). *Images of Deviance and Social Control: A Sociological History* (2nd edition). New York: McGraw-Hill.

Phelps, E.S. and Pollak, R.A. (1968). On Second-best National Saving and Game-equilibrium Growth. *The Review of Economic Studies*, 35(2), 185–99.

Plous, S. (1993). *The Psychology of Judgement and Decision Making*. New York: McGraw-Hill.

POB (Public Oversight Board) (2000). *The Panel on Audit Effectiveness Report and Recommendations.* Stamford: POB.

Polinsky, A.M. and Shavell, S. (1999). On the Disutility and Discounting of Imprisonment and the Theory of Deterrence. *Journal of Legal Studies*, 28(1), 1–16.

Ponemon, L.A. (1990). Ethical Judgments in Accounting: A Cognitive Development Perspective. *Critical Perspectives on Accounting*, 1(2), 191–215.

Pontell, H. (ed.) (2005). *Social Deviance: Readings in Theory and Research* (5th edition). New York: Prentice-Hall.

Porter, D.P. and Smith, V.L. (2003). Stock Market Bubbles in the Laboratory. *Journal of Behavioural Finance*, 4(1), 7–20.

Posner, R.A. (2003). *Economic Analysis of Law* (6th edition). Boston and Toronto: Little, Brown and Co.

Powers, W., Troubh, R., and Winokur, H. (2002). *Report of Investigation by the Special Investigative Committee of the Board of Directors of Enron Corp.* Available HTTP: <http://news.findlaw.com/wp/docs/enron/specinv020102rpt1.pdf> (accessed 14 August 2007).

Prentice, R.A. (2000). The Case of the Irrational Auditor's Securities Fraud: A Behavioural Insight into Securities Regulation. *Northwestern University Law Journal*, 95, 133–220.

Prentice, R.A. (2003). Enron: A Brief Behavioural Autopsy. *American Business Law Review*, 40, 417–44.

Prentice, R.A. (2004). Chicago Man, K-T Man and the Future of Behavioural Law and Economics. *Vanderbilt Law Review*, 56 (November), 1663–777.

Prevost, A.K. and Rao, R.P. (2000). Of What Value are Shareholder Proposals Sponsored by Public Pension Funds? *The Journal of Business*, 73(2), 177–204.

Professional Bank Services, Inc. (2001). *2001 Corporate Governance Survey*.

Pruitt, D.G. (1971a). Choice Shifts in Group Discussion: An Introductory Review. *Journal of Personality and Social Psychology*, 20(3), 339–60.

Pruitt, D.G. (1971b). Conclusions: Towards an Understanding of Choice Shifts in Group Discussion. *Journal of Personality and Social Psychology*, 20(3), 495–510.

Rabin, M. (1998). Psychology and Economics. *Journal of Economic Literature*, 36(1), 11–46.

Rabin, M. (2000a). *Diminishing Marginal Utility of Wealth Cannot Explain Risk Aversion.* Working Paper E00-287. Economics Department, University of California, Berkeley. Available HTTP: <http://repositories.cdlib.org/iber/econ/E00-287> (accessed 14 August 2007).

Rabin, M. (2000b). Risk Aversion and Expected-utility Theory: A Calibration Theorem. *Econometrica*, 68(5), 1281–92.

Rabin, M. (2002). *A Perspective on Psychology and Economics.* Economics Department, University of California (Berkeley) Working Paper E02-313. Available HTTP: <http://repositories.cdlib.org/iber/econ/E02-313> (accessed 14 August 2007).

Rabin, M. and Schrag, J.L. (1999). First Impressions Matter: A Model of Confirmatory Bias. *The Quarterly Journal of Economics*, 114(1), 37–82.

Rachlin, H. (2000). *The Science of Self-Control.* Cambridge, Mass. and London: Harvard University Press.

Ramsey, F.P. and Braithwaite, R.B. (1931). *The Foundations of Mathematics and Other Logical Essays.* New York: Harcourt, Brace.

Ramsay, R.J. (1994). Senior/Manager Differences in Audit Workpaper Review Performance. *Journal of Accounting Research*, 32(1), 127–35.

Rangan, S. (1998). Earnings Management and the Performance of Seasoned Equity Offerings. *Journal of Financial Economics*, 50(1), 101–22.

Rayburn, J. (1986). The Association of Operating Cash Flow and Accruals with Security Returns. *Journal of Accounting Research*, 24, 112–33.

Rees, L., Gill, S., and Gore, R. (1996). An Investigation of Asset Write-downs and Concurrent Abnormal Accruals. *Journal of Accounting Research*, 34 (Supplement), 157–69.

Rehfeld, B. (1998). A Suite Victory for Shareholders. *Institutional Investor*, 32(7), 37–44.

Reynolds, K. and Francis, J. (2001). Does Size Matter? The Influence of Large Clients on Office-level Auditor Reporting Decisions. *Journal of Accounting and Economics*, 30(3), 375–400.

Richardson, S.A., Teoh, S.H., and Wysocki, P. (1999). Tracking Analysts' Forecasts Over the Annual Earnings Horizon: Are Analysts' Forecasts Optimistic or Pessimistic? Working paper, University of Michigan.

Richardson, S.A., Teoh, S.H., and Wysocki, P. (2004a). The Walk-down to Beatable Analyst Forecasts: The Role of Equity Issuance and Insider Trading Incentives. *Contemporary Accounting Research*, 21(4), 885–924.

Richardson, S.A., Tuna, A.I., and Wu, M. (2003). *Capital Market Pressures and Earnings Management: The Case of Earnings Restatements.* The Wharton School Working Paper. Available HTTP: <http://accounting.wharton.upenn.edu/faculty/richardson/RTW3.pdf> (accessed 14 August 2007).

Richardson, S.A., Tuna, A.I., and Wu, M. (2004b). *Does Corporate Governance Really Matter?* The Wharton School Working Paper. Available HTTP: <http://knowledge.wharton.upenn.edu/papers/1281.pdf> (accessed 14 August 2007).

Rogoff, K. (1985). The Optimal Degree of Commitment to an Intermediate Monetary Target. *Quarterly Journal of Economics*, 100(4), 1169–89.

Romano, R. (2004). *The Sarbanes-Oxley Act and the Making of Quack Corporate Governance.* Yale ICF Working Paper No. 04-37; ECGI – Finance. Available HTTP: <http://papers.ssrn.com/paper.taf?abstract_id=596101> (accessed 1 August 2007).

Rosen, S. (1981). The Economics of Superstars. *The American Economic Review*, 71(5), 845–58.

Rosenstein, S. and Wyatt, J.G. (1990). Outside Directors, Board Independence, and Shareholder Wealth. *Journal of Financial Economics*, 26(2), 175–91.

Rosenthal, R. and Jacobson, L. (1968). *Pygmalion in the Classroom: Teacher Expectation and Pupils' Intellectual Development.* New York: Holt, Rinehart & Winston.

Ross, L. (1977). The Intuitive Psychologist and His Shortcomings: Distortions in the Attribution Process, in *Advances in Experimental Social Psychology*, ed. Berkowitz, L. New York: Academic Press.

Rudolph, J.W. and Repenning, N.P. (2002). Disaster Dynamics: Understanding the Role of Quantity in Organizational Collapse. *Administrative Science Quarterly*, 47(1), 1–30.

Ruehlman, L.S., West, S.G., and Pasahow, R.J. (1985). Depression and Evaluative Schemata. *Journal of Personality*, 53(1), 46–92.

Sale, H.A. (2005). *Banks, the Forgotten (?) Partners in Fraud.* University of Iowa Legal Studies Research Paper No. 05-09. Available HTTP: <http://ssrn.com/abstract=673509> (accessed 1 August 2007).

Salterio, S. and Koonce, L. (1997). The Persuasiveness of Audit Evidence: The Case of Accounting Policy Decisions. *Accounting, Organizations and Society*, 22(6), 573–87.

Samuelson, L. and Zhang, J. (1992). Evolutionary Stability in Asymmetric Games. *Journal of Economic Theory*, 57, 363–91.

Samuelson, W. and Zeckhauser, R. (1988). Status Quo Bias in Decision Making. *Journal of Risk and Uncertainty*, 1(1), 7–59.

Sandroni, A. (2000). Do Markets Favor Agents able to Make Accurate Predictions? *Econometrica*, 68(6), 1303–41.

Sarbanes-Oxley Act 2002. Available HTTP: <http://frwebgate.access.gpo.gov/cgi-bin/getdoc.cgi?dbname=107_cong_bills&docid=f:h3763enr.txt.pdf> (accessed 14 August 2007).

Sargent, M.A. (2003). Lawyers in the Perfect Storm. *Washburn Law Journal*, 43(1), 1–43.

Sargent, M.A. (2004). Lawyers in the Moral Maze. *Villanova Law Review*, 49(4), 475–95.

Savage, L.J. (1954). *Foundations of Statistics.* New York: John Wiley & Sons.

Schelling, T.C. (1960). *The Strategy of Conflict.* Cambridge, Mass.: Harvard University Press.

Schelling, T.C. (1978). Egonomics, or the Art of Self-management. *American Economic Review*, 68(2), 290–4.

Schelling, T.C. (1984). *Choice and Consequence: Perspectives of an Errant Economist.* Cambridge, Mass.: Harvard University Press.

Schilit, H. (2002). *Financial Shenanigans: How to Detect Accounting Gimmicks and Fraud in Financial Reports* (2nd edition). New York: McGraw-Hill.

Schipper, K. (1989). Commentary on Earnings Management. *Accounting Horizons*, 3(4), 91–102.

Schisler, D.L. (1994). An Experimental Examination of Factors Affecting Tax Professionals' Aggressiveness – A Prospect Theory Approach. *The Journal of the American Taxation Association*, 16(2), 124–42.

Schkade, D.A. and Kahneman, D. (1998). Does Living in California Make People Happy? A Focusing Illusion in Judgments of Life Satisfaction. *Psychological Science*, 9(5), 340–6.

Schlesinger, L. (2003). *Coopers Paid £65m in Barings Case. Accountancy Age* (18 June). Available HTTP: <http://www.accountancyage.com/accountancyage/news/2033104/coopers-paid-65m-barings-case> (accessed 14 August 2007).

Schoemaker, P.J.H. (1982). The Expected Utility Model: Its Variants, Purposes, Evidence and Limitations. *Journal of Economic Literature*, 20(2), 529–63.

Schumpeter, J.A. (1934). *The Theory of Economic Development: An Inquiry into Profits, Capital, Credit, Interest and the Business Cycle*. Cambridge, Mass.: Harvard University Press. (Originally written 1911.)

Schwartz, J. and Wald, M.L. (2003). Smart People Working Collectively can be Dumber than the Sum of Their Brains: 'Groupthink' is 30 Years Old, and Still Going Strong. *New York Times* (9 March). Available HTTP: <http://www.mindfully.org/Reform/2003/Smart-People-Dumber9mar03.htm> (accessed 14 August 2007).

Schwarz, N. (2000). Emotion, Cognition and Decision Making, *Cognition & Emotion*, 14(4), 433–40.

Schweitzer, M., Ordóñez, L.D., and Douma, B. (2002). *The Dark Side of Goal Setting: The Role of Goals in Motivating Unethical Behaviour*. Academy of Management Meeting. Denver, Colorado. Copy with author.

SEC (Securities and Exchange Commission) (1990). *Office of the Chief Accountant, Arthur Andersen & Co.* Federal Securities Law Reports. Para. 79,484 (20 June).

SEC (Securities and Exchange Commission) (2000a). *Report of the Internal Investigation of Independence Issues at PricewaterhouseCoopers LLP.* (2000, AP File No. 3-9809) Report prepared by independent consultants Jess Fardella *et al.* of New York law firm Lankler, Siffert & Wohl LLP.

SEC (Securities and Exchange Commission) (2000b). *Background Information: Auditor Independence*. 27 June. Available HTTP: <http://www.sec.gov/news/extra/audback.htm> (accessed 14 August 2007).

SEC (Securities and Exchange Commission) (2001). *Final Rule: Revision of the Commission's Auditor Independence Requirements*. Available HTTP: <http://www.sec.gov/rules/final/33-7919.htm> (accessed 14 August 2007).

SEC (Securities and Exchange Commission) (2003a). *Strengthening the Commission's Requirements Regarding Auditor Independence*. Available HTTP: <http://www.sec.gov/rules/final/33-8183.htm> (accessed 14 August 2007).

SEC (Securities and Exchange Commission) (2003b). Litigation Release No. 18038 (March 17), also Accounting and Auditing Enforcement Release No. 1742 (March 17). Available HTTP: <http://www.sec.gov/litigation/litreleases/lr18038.htm> (accessed 14 August 2007).

SEC (Securities and Exchange Commission) (2003c). *SEC Settles Enforcement Proceedings against J.P. Morgan Chase and Citigroup*. Enforcement Release 2003-87. Available HTTP: <http://www.sec.gov/news/press/2003-87.htm> (accessed 14 August 2007).

SEC (Securities and Exchange Commission) (2003d). Joint Press Release of the SEC, the State of New York Attorney General, NASAA, the NASD and the NYSE: *Ten of Nation's Top Investment Firms Settle Enforcement Actions Involving Conflicts of Interest between Research and Investment Banking* (April 28). Available HTTP: <http://www.sec.gov/news/press/2003-54.htm> (accessed 14 August 2007).

SEC (Securities and Exchange Commission) (2003e). *Statement Regarding Global Settlement Related to Analyst Conflict of Interest* (April 28). Available HTTP: <http://sec.gov/news/speech/spch042803com.htm> (accessed 14 August 2007).

SEC (Securities and Exchange Commission) (2003f). SEC Adopts Attorney Conduct Rule Under Sarbanes-Oxley Act. Available HTTP: <http://www.sec.gov/news/press/2003-13.htm> (accessed 14 August 2007).

Seidenfeld, M. (2001). The Psychology of Accountability and Political Review of Agency Rules. *Duke Law Journal*, 51, 1059–95.

Seligman, M.E.P. (1991). *Learned Optimism*. New York: Alfred A. Knopf.

Shafir, E., Simonson, I., and Tversky, A. (1993). Reason-Based Choice. *Cognition*, 49, 11–36.

Shefrin, H.M. and Thaler, R.H. (1988). The Behavioural Life-Cycle Hypothesis. *Economic Inquiry*, 26(4), 609–43.

Sherman, D.A., Kim, H., and Zajonc, R.B. (1998). *Affective Perseverance: Cognitions Change but Preferences Stay the Same*. Paper Presented at the Annual Meeting of the American Psychological Society, 1998.

Sherman, S.J. and Gorkin, R.B. (1980). Attitude Bolstering When Behaviour is Inconsistent with Central Attitudes. *Journal of Experimental Social Psychology*, 16(4), 388–403.

Shivakumar, L. (2000). Do Firms Mislead Investors by Overstating Earnings before Seasoned Equity Offerings? *Journal of Accounting and Economics*, 29(3), 339–72.

Shivdasani, A. and Yermack, D. (1999). CEO Involvement in the Selection of New Board Members: An Empirical Analysis. *Journal of Finance*, 54(5), 1829–53.

Shleifer, A. (2000). *Inefficient Markets: An Introduction to Behavioural Finance*. Oxford: New York.

Shleifer, A. and Vishny, R.W. (1997a). A Survey of Corporate Governance. *The Journal of Finance*, 52(2), 737–83.

Shleifer, A. and Vishny, R.W. (1997b). The Limits of Arbitrage. *Journal of Finance*, 52(1), 35–55.

Siamwalla, A. (2000). *Anatomy of the Thai Economic Crisis*. TDRI Report. Available HTTP: <http://www.info.tdri.or.th/reports/unpublished/anatomy.pdf> (accessed 14 August 2007).

Simon, H.A. (1955). A Behavioural Model of Rational Choice. *Quarterly Journal of Economics*, 69(1), 99–118.

Simon, H.A. (1956). Rational Choice and the Structure of the Environment. *Psychological Review*, 63(2), 129–38.

Simon, H.A. (1957). *Models of Man*. New York: Wiley.

Simon, H.A. (1959). Theories of Decision-making in Economics and Behavioural Science. *The American Economic Review*, 49(3), 253–83.

Simon, H.A. (1961). *Administrative Behaviour* (2nd edition). New York: The Macmillan Company.

Simon, H.A. (1978). Rationality and Process and Product of Thought. *American Economic Review*, 68(2), 1–16.

Simon, H.A. (1983). *Reason in Human Affairs*. Oxford: Basil Blackwell.

Simon, H.A. (1990). Invariants of Human Behaviour. *Annual Review of Psychology*, 41, 1–19.

Simon, H.A. (1991). Cognitive Architectures in a Rational Analysis: Comment, in *Architectures for Intelligence*, ed. VanLehn, K. Hillsdale, NJ: Lawrence Erlbaum Associates.

Simon, W.H. (1998). The Kaye Scholer Affair: The Lawyer's Duty of Candor and the Bar's Temptations of Evasion and Apology. *Law & Social Inquiry*, 23(2), 243–90.

Simonson, I. and Tversky, A. (1992). Choice in Context: Tradeoff Contrast and Extremeness Aversion. *Journal of Marketing Research*, 29(3), 281–95.

Skinner, D. and Sloan, R. (2002). Earnings Surprises, Growth Expectations and Stock Returns. *Review of Accounting Studies*, 7(2–3), 289–312.

Sloan, R.G. (1996). Do Stock Prices Fully Reflect Information in Accruals and Cash Flows about Future Earnings? *The Accounting Review*, 71(3), 289–315.

Slovic, P. and Lichtenstein, S. (1971). Comparison of Bayesian and Regression Approaches to the Study of Information Processing in Judgment. *Organizational Behaviour and Human Performance*, 6(6), 649–744.

Slovic, P., Fischhoff, B., and Lichtenstein, S. (1982). Facts versus Fears: Understanding Perceived Risk, in *Judgement under Uncertainty: Heuristics and Biases*, ed. Kahnemann, D., Slovic, P., and Tversky, A. Cambridge: Cambridge University Press.

Slovic, P., Finucane, M.L., Peters, E., and MacGregor, D.G. (2002). The Affect Heuristic, in *Heuristics and Biases*, ed. Gilovich, T., Griffin, D., and Kahneman, D. Cambridge: Cambridge University Press.

Slovic, P., Finucane, M.L., Peters, E., and MacGregor, D.G. (2004). Risk as Analysis and Risk as Feelings: Some Thoughts about Affect, Reason, Risk, and Rationality. *Risk Analysis*, 24(2), 311–22.

Slovic, P., MacGregor, D.G., Malmfors, T., and Purchase, I.F.H. (1999). *Influence of Affective Processes on Toxicologists' Judgements of Risk*. Unpublished study. Eugene, Oreg.: Decision Research.

Smedslund, J. (1963). The Concept of Correlation in Adults. *Scandinavian Journal of Psychology*, 4, 165–73.

Smith, A. (1776). *The Wealth of Nations*, ed. Edwin Cannan, 1904. Reprint edition 1937. New York: Modern Library.

Smith, J.F. and Kida, T. (1991). Heuristics and Biases: Expertise and Task Realism in Auditing. *Psychological Bulletin*, 109(3), 472–89.

Smith, Sir Robert (2003). Audit Committees – Combined Code Guidance. Available HTTP: <http://www.football-research.org/docs/smithreport-30-01-03.pdf> (accessed 15 August 2007).

Smith, V.L. (1991). Rational Choice: The Contrast between Economics and Psychology. *Journal of Political Economy*, 99(4), 877–97.

Snyder, M. (1984). When Beliefs Create Reality, in *Advances in Experimental Social Psychology*, ed. Berkowitz, L. New York: Academic.

Snyder, M., Tanke, E.D., and Berscheid, E. (1977). Social Perception and Interpersonal Behaviour: On the Self-fulfilling Nature of Social Stereotypes. *Journal of Personality and Social Psychology*, 35(9), 656–66.

Solomon, I. and Shields, M.D. (1995). Judgment and Decision-Making Research in Auditing, in *Judgement and Decision-making in Accounting and Auditing*, ed. Ashton, R.H. and Ashton, A.H. Cambridge: Cambridge University Press.

Sommer, A.A., Jr. (1974). The Emerging Responsibilities of the Securities Lawyer. Address to the Banking, Corporation & Business Law Section, N.Y. State Bar Association (24 January), reprinted in Soderquist, L.D. and Gabaldon, T.A. (2006). *Securities Regulation* (6th edition). Van Nuys, Calif.: Foundation Press.

Song, D. (2003). The Laws of Securities Lawyering after Sarbanes-Oxley. *Duke Law Journal*, 53, 257–89.

Spector, B. (2003). HRM at Enron: The Unindicted Co-conspirator. *Organizational Dynamics*, 32(2), 207–20.

Spiegel, J.H. and Ohl, A.H.G. (2005). The In Pari Delicto Defense and Attorney Misconduct, or It Is Time to Get Rid of the 'Law-Free Zone'. *Journal of Business and Securities Law*, 1(1), 65–80.

Spira, L. (2003). Audit Committees: Begging the Question, *Corporate Governance*, 12(4), 489–99.

Spira, L. and Bender, R. (2004). Compare and Contrast: Perspectives on Board Committees, *Corporate Governance*, 11(3), 180–8.

Stasser, G., Kerr, N.L., and Davis, J.H. (1989). Influence Processes and Consensus Models in Decision-Making Groups, in *Psychology of Group Influence*, ed. Paulus, P.B. Hillsdale, NJ: Lawrence Erlbaum.

Stasson, M.F., Ono, K., Zimmerman, S.K., and Davis, J.H. (1988). Group Consensus Processes on Cognitive Bias Tasks: A Social Decision Scheme Approach. *Japanese Psychological Research*, 30(2), 68–77.

Staw, B.M. (1976). Knee Deep in the Big Muddy: A Study of Escalating Commitment to a Chosen Course of Action. *Organizational Behaviour & Human Performance*, 16(1), 27–44.

Staw, B.M. (1981). The Escalation of Commitment to a Course of Action. *Academy of Management Review*, 6(4), 577–87.

Staw, B.M. and Ross, J. (1987). Knowing When to Pull the Plug. *Harvard Business Review*, 65(2), 68–74.

Stone, C.D. (2004). *Corporate Responsibility: Law and Ethics.* Washington: Beard Books.

Stoner, J.A.F. (1961). *A Comparison of Individual and Group Decisions Involving Risk.* Unpublished Master's Thesis, Massachusetts Institute of Technology.

Strotz, R.H. (1955). Myopia and Inconsistency in Dynamic Utility Maximization. *Review of Economic Studies*, 23(3), 165–80.

Stulz, R. (2005). The Limits of Financial Globalization. *Journal of Finance*, 60(4), 1595–1638.

Subramanyam, K.R. (1996). The Pricing of Discretionary Accruals. *Journal of Accounting and Economics*, 22(1–3), 249–81.

Sullivan, K. and Kida, T. (1995). The Effect of Multiple Reference Points and Prior Gains and Losses on Managers' Risky Decision Making. *Organizational Behaviour and Human Decision Processes*, 64(1), 76–83.

Sussangkarn, C. (2000). *Thailand: Toward a Sustainable Recovery.* Paper Presented at the Regional Outlook Forum 2000, Singapore, 6 January 2000. Available HTTP: <http://www.info.tdri.or.th/reports/unpublished/sing00.htm> (accessed 14 August 2007).

Svenson, O. (1981). Are We Less Skillful Than Our Fellow Drivers Are? *Acta Psychologica*, 47, 143–8.

Taylor, S.E. and Brown, J.D. (1988). Illusion and Well-being: A Social Psychological Perspective on Mental Health. *Psychological Bulletin*, 103(2), 193–210.

Taylor, S.E., Kemeny, M.E., Reed, G., Bower, J.E., and Gruenewald, T.L. (2000). Psychological Resources, Positive Illusions, and Health. *American Psychologist*, 55(1), 99–109.

Teger, A.I. (1980). *Too Much Invested to Quit.* New York: Pergamon Press.

Teoh, S.H., Welch, I., and Wong, T.J. (1998a). Earnings Management and the Underperformance of Seasoned Equity Offerings. *Journal of Financial Economics*, 50(1), 63–99.

Teoh, S.H., Welch, I., and Wong, T.J. (1998b). Earnings Management and the Long-run Market Performance of Initial Public Offerings. *Journal of Finance*, 53(6), 1935–74.

Tetlock, P.E. (1985). Accountability: A Social Check on the Fundamental Attribution Error. *Social Psychology Quarterly*, 48(3), 227–36.

Thaler, R.H. (1980). Toward a Positive Theory of Consumer Choice. *Journal of Economic Behaviour and Organization*, 1, 39–60.

Thaler, R.H. (1981). Some Empirical Evidence on Dynamic Inconsistency. *Economics Letters*, 8(3), 201–7.

Thaler, R.H. (1985). Mental Accounting and Consumer Choice. *Marketing Science*, 4, 199–214.

Thaler, R.H. (1990). Anomalies: Saving, Fungibility and Mental Accounts. *Journal of Economic Perspectives*, 4(1), 193–205.

Thaler, R.H. (1999). Mental Accounting Matters. *Journal of Behavioural Decision Making*, 12(3), 183–206.

Thaler, R.H. (2000). From Homo Economicus to Homo Sapiens. *The Journal of Economic Perspectives*, 14(1), 133–41.

Thaler, R.H. and Benartzi, S. (1995). Myopic Loss Aversion and the Equity Premium Puzzle, *Quarterly Journal of Economics*, 110(1), 73–92.

Thaler, R.H. and Benartzi, S. (2004). Save More Tomorrow: Using Behavioral Economics to Increase Employee Saving. *Journal of Political Economy*, 112(1), Part 2, 164–87.

Thaler, R.H. and Loewenstein, G. (1989). Anomalies: Intertemporal Choice. *Journal of Economic Perspectives*, 3(4), 181–93.

Thomas, J. and Zhang, X. (2000). Identifying Unexpected Accruals: A Comparison of Current Approaches. *Journal Accounting and Public Policy*, 19(4–5), 347–76.

Thompson, L. (1995). They Saw a Negotiation: Partisanship and Involvement. *Journal of Personality and Social Psychology*, 68(5), 839–53.

Thornburgh, D. (2002). *First Interim Report of Dick Thornburgh, Bankruptcy Court Examiner.* Available HTTP: <http://news.findlaw.com/hdocs/docs/worldcom/thornburgh1strpt.pdf> (accessed 14 August 2007).

Thornburgh, D. (2003). *Second Interim Report of the Court Appointed Bankruptcy Examiner.* Available HTTP: <http://www.klng.com/files/tbl_s48News/PDFUpload307/8838/Worldcom_Report2.pdf> (accessed 14 August 2007).

Thornburgh, D. (2004). *Third and Final Report of Dick Thornburgh, Bankruptcy Court Examiner.* Available HTTP: <http://www.klng.com/files/tbl_s48News/PDFUpload307/10129/WorldCom_Report_final.pdf> (accessed 14 August 2007).

Toffler, B.L. and Reingold, J. (2003). *Final Accounting*, New York: Broadway Books.

Treadway, J.C. (1987). *The Report of the National Commission on Fraudulent Financial Reporting.* Commonly referred to as 'The Treadway Commission's Report', or 'The Treadway Report'. Available HTTP: <http://www.coso.org/Publications/NCFFR.pdf> (accessed 14 August 2007).

Turnbull, S. (2000). Corporate Governance: Theories, Challenges and Paradigms. *Gouvernance: Revue Internationale*, 1(1), 11–43.

Turnbull, S. (2005). How US and UK Auditing Practices Became Muddled to Muddle Corporate Governance Principles. ICFAI *Journal of Audit Practice*, 2(3).

Turner, L.E. (2005). Reply to Mary Morrison. *Critical Perspectives on Accounting*, 16(1), 63–4.

Turner, L.E., Dietrich, R., Anderson, K., and Bailey, A. (2002). *Accounting Restatements.* Working paper, SEC, University of Illinois, and Ohio State University.

Tversky, A. and Kahneman, D. (1973). Availability: A Heuristic for Judging Frequency and Probability. *Cognitive Psychology*, 5(September), 207–32.

Tversky, A. and Kahneman, D. (1974). Judgment under Uncertainty: Heuristics and Biases. *Science*, 185(4157), 1124–30.

Tversky, A. and Kahneman, D. (1981). The Framing of Decisions and the Psychology of Choice. *Science*, 211(4481), 453–8.

Tversky, A. and Kahneman, D. (1982). Evidential Impact of Base Rates, in *Judgment under Uncertainty: Heuristics and Biases*, ed. Kahneman, D., Slovic, P., and Tversky, A. Cambridge: Cambridge University Press.

Tversky, A. and Kahneman, D. (1983). Extension versus Intuitive Reasoning: The Conjunction Fallacy in Probability Judgment. *Psychological Review*, 90(4), 293–315.

Tversky, A. and Kahneman, D. (1991). Loss Aversion in Riskless Choice: A Reference Dependent Model. *Quarterly Journal of Economics*, 106(4), 1039–61.

Tversky, A. and Kahneman, D. (1992). Advances in Prospect Theory: Cumulative Representation of Uncertainty. *Journal of Risk and Uncertainty*, 5(4), 297–323.

Tversky, A. and Thaler, R.H. (1990). Anomalies: Preference Reversals. *Journal of Economic Perspectives*, 4(2), 201–11.

Tversky, A., Slovic, P., and Kahneman, D. (1990). The Causes of Preference Reversal. *American Economic Review*, 80(1), 204–17.

Tyson, L. (2003). *The Tyson Report on the Recruitment and Development of Non-Executive Directors.* The Department of Trade and Industry. Available HTTP: <http://facultyresearch.london.edu/docs/TysonReport.pdf> (accessed 14 August 2007).

Tyson, T. (1990). Believing that Everyone Else is Less Ethical: Implications for Work Behaviour and Ethics Instruction. *Journal of Business Ethics*, 9(9), 715–21.

Uecker, W.C. and Kinney, W.R. (1977). Judgmental Evaluation of Sample Results: A Study of the Type and Severity of Errors Made by Practicing CPAs. *Accounting, Organizations and Society*, 2(3), 269–75.

United Kingdom (2006). Companies Act 2006. Available HTTP: <http://www.opsi.gov.uk/acts/acts2006/ukpga_20060046_en.pdf> (accessed 14 August 2007).

United States Congress (2000). *Commodity Futures Modernization Act 2000.* Pub. L. No. 106-554, 114 Stat. 2763. Available HTTP: <http://www.cftc.gov/files/ogc/ogchr5660.pdf> (accessed 14 August 2007).

United States Department of Justice (2004). *Office of Justice Programs Bureau of Justice Statistics.* Re-entry Trends in the United States. Available HTTP: <http://www.ojp.usdoj.gov/bjs/reentry/reentry.htm> (accessed 14 August 2007).

United States House of Representatives (2001). *Joint Hearing: The Enron Collapse: Impact on Investors and Financial Markets.* Available HTTP: <http://commdocs.house.gov/committees/bank/hba76958.000/hba76958_0.HTM> (accessed 16 October 2007).

United States Senate (1977). *Improving The Accountability of Publicly Owned Corporations and Their Auditors.* Subcommittee on Reports, Accounting and Management, Committee on Government Affairs (Metcalf Subcommittee Report).

United States Senate (2002a). *The Role of the Enron Board in the Collapse of Enron Corporation: Hearing of the Permanent Investigations Subcommittee of the Senate Governmental Affairs Committee*, 108th Congress.

United States Senate (2002b). *Report of the Senate Permanent Subcommittee on Investigations on the Role of the Board of Directors in Enron's Collapse.* Report No. 107-70.

United States Senate (2002c). *Sarbanes Releases Result of Probe into Proliferation of 'Restatements of Earnings' and Faulty Accounting Practices.* Committee on Banking, Housing and Urban Affairs. Press Release 23 October 2002. Available HTTP: <http://banking.senate.gov/prel02/1023rest.htm> (accessed 14 August 2007).

United States Senate (2002d). *The Role of the Financial Institutions in Enron's Collapse before the Permanent Subcommittee on Investigations of the Senate Committee on Government Affairs*, 107th Congress, 2nd Session (July 23). Available HTTP: <http://www.gpo.gov/congress/senate/senate12sh107.html> (accessed 14 August 2007).

United States Senate (2003a). *Report of Investigation of Enron Corporation and Related Entities regarding Federal Tax and Compensation Issues and Policy Recommendations.* Committee on Finance. Available HTTP: <http://www.house.gov/jct/s-3-03-vol1.pdf> (accessed 14 August 2007).

United States Senate (2003b). *Enron: The Joint Committee on Taxation's Investigative Report.* Hearing 108–117, 2003. Available HTTP: <http://finance.senate.gov/hearings/89349.pdf> (accessed 14 August 2007).

United States Senate (2003c). *Fishtail, Bacchus, Sundance and Slapshot: Four Enron Transactions Funded and Facilitated by US Financial Institutions.* S. Prt. 107–82. Available HTTP: <http://hsgac.senate.gov/_files/121102report.pdf> (accessed 14 August 2007).

Useem, M. (1996). *Investor Capitalism: How Money Managers are Changing the Face of Corporate America.* New York: HarperCollins.

Viscusi, W.K. (1992). *Smoking: Making the Risky Decision.* New York: Oxford University Press.

Viscusi, W.K. (1996). Individual Rationality, Hazard Warnings and the Foundations of Tort Law. *Rutgers Law Review*, 48(3), 625–71.

Von Neumann, J. and Morgenstern, O. (1944). *Theory of Games and Economic Behaviour*. Princeton: Princeton University Press.

Walker, R.G. (1989). Ten (Legal) Ways to Cook Your Books. *Business Review Weekly*, 2 June, 50–3.

Walker, R.G. (1991a). Audit Excuses Rest on the Expectation Gap. *Business Review Weekly*, 11 January, 59–61.

Walker, R.G. (1991b). Why So Many Audits Have Been Failing. *Business Review Weekly*, 18 January, 82–4.

Waller, W.S. (1995). Decision-Making Research in Managerial Accounting: Return to Behavioural-Economics Foundations, in *Judgment and Decision-Making Research In Accounting and Auditing*, ed. Ashton, R.H. and Ashton, A.H. New York: Cambridge University Press.

Waller, W. and Felix, W.L. (1984). The Auditor and Learning from Experience: Some Conjectures. *Accounting, Organization and Society*, 9(3/4), 383–406.

Wan, K.M. (2003). Independent Directors, Executive Pay and Firm Performance. *Employee Benefits, Compensation & Pension Law*, 4(12), E-journal issue 19 June.

Wason, P.C. (1960). On the Failure to Eliminate Hypotheses in a Conceptual Task. *Quarterly Journal of Experimental Psychology*, 12(3), 129–40.

Wason, P.C. (1966). Reasoning, in *New Horizons in Psychology*, ed. Foss, B.M. Harmondsworth: Penguin.

Wason, P.C. (1968). Reasoning about a Rule. *Quarterly Journal of Experimental Psychology*, 20(3), 273–81.

Watson, D. (1982). The Actor and the Observer: How are their Perceptions of Causality Divergent? *Psychological Bulletin*, 92(6), 682–700.

Watson, D. and Clark, L.A. (1984). Negative Affectivity: The Disposition to Experience Aversive Emotional States. *Psychological Bulletin*, 96(3), 465–90.

Watts, R.L. (2003a). Conservatism in Accounting Part I: Explanations and Implications. *Accounting Horizons*, 17(3), 207–21.

Watts, R.L. (2003b). Conservatism in Accounting – Part II: Evidence and Research Opportunities. *Accounting Horizons*, 17(4), 287–302.

Watts, R.L. and Zimmerman, J.L. (1986). *Positive Accounting Theory*. Edgewood Cliffs, NJ: Prentice-Hall.

Watts, R.L. and Zimmerman, J.L. (1990). Positive Accounting Theory: A Ten Year Perspective. *Accounting Review*, 65(1), 131–58.

Weick, K.E. (1964). Reduction of Cognitive Dissonance through Task Enhancement and Effort Expenditure. *Journal of Abnormal & Social Psychology*, 68(5), 533–9.

Weick, K.E. (1983). Stress in Accounting Systems. *The Accounting Review*, 58(2), 350–69.

Weick, K.E. (1995). *Sensemaking in Organizations*. Thousand Oaks, Calif.: Sage.

Weinstein, N.D. (1980). Unrealistic Optimism about Future Life Events. *Journal of Personality and Social Psychology*, 39(5), 806–20.

Weinstein, N.D. (1984). Why it Won't Happen to Me: Perceptions of Risk Factors and Susceptibility. *Health Psychology*, 3(5), 431–57.

Weinstein, N.D. and Klein, W.M. (1995). Resistance of Personal Risk Perceptions to Debiasing Interventions. *Health Psychology*, 14(2), 132–40.

Weisbach, M. (1988). Outside Directors and CEO Turnover. *Journal of Financial Economics*, 20(1/2), 413–60.

Wells, J. (2004). New Approaches to Fraud Deterrence. *Journal of Accountancy*, 197(2), 72–6.

Westen, D., Kilts, C., Blagov, P., Harenski, K., and Hamann, S. (2006). The Neural Basis of Motivated Reasoning: An FMRI Study of Emotional Constraints on Political Judgment during the US Presidential Election of 2004. *Journal of Cognitive Neuroscience*, 18(11), 1947–58.

Williams, P.F. (2004). You Reap What You Sow: The Ethical Discourse of Professional Accounting. *Critical Perspectives on Accounting*, 15(6–7), 995–1001.

Williamson, O.E. (1973). Markets and Hierarchies: Some Elementary Considerations. *American Economic Review*, 63(2), 316–25.

Williamson, O.E. (1988). Corporate Finance and Corporate Governance. *Journal of Finance*, 43(3), 567–91.

Williamson, O.E. (1991). Economic Institutions: Spontaneous and Intentional Governance. *Journal of Law, Economics and Organization*, 7(Special issue), 159–87.

Williamson, O.E. (1996). *The Mechanisms of Governance*. New York: Oxford University Press.

Williamson, O.E. (1999). *Human Actors and Economic Organization*. Business and Public Policy Working Paper, BPP-72, Institute of Management, Innovation & Organization, University of California, Berkeley.

Wilson, P. (1987). The Incremental Information Content of the Accrual and Funds Components of Earnings after Controlling for Earnings. *The Accounting Review*, 62(2), 293–322.

Wilson, T.E. and Grimlund, R.A. (1990). An Examination of the Importance of an Auditor's Reputation. *Auditing: Journal of Practice and Theory*, 9(2), 43–59.

Wilson, T.D. and Schooler, J.W. (1991). Thinking Too Much: Introspection can reduce the Quality of Preferences and Decisions. *Journal of Personality & Social Psychology*, 60(2), 181–92.

Winkielman, P., Zajonc, R.B., and Schwarz, N. (1997). Subliminal Affective Priming Resists Attributional Interventions. *Cognition and Emotion*, 11(4), 433–65.

Wu, M. (2002). *Earnings Restatements: A Capital Markets Perspective.* New York University Working paper.

Wyatt, A.R. (2004). Accounting Professionalism – They Just Don't Get It! *Accounting Horizons*, 18(1), 45–53.

Xie, H. (2001). The Mispricing of Abnormal Accruals. *Accounting Review*, 76(3), 357–74.

Yariv, L. (2002). *I'll See It When I Believe It – A Simple Model of Cognitive Consistency*. California Institute of Technology Working Paper. Available HTTP: <http://www.hss.caltech.edu/~lyariv/Papers/Believe.pdf> (accessed 14 August 2007).

Yermack, D. (1996). Higher Market Valuation of Companies with a Small Board of Directors. *Journal of Financial Economics*, 40(2), 185–212.

Yermack, D. (1997). Good Timing: CEO Stock Option Awards and Company News Announcements. *Journal of Finance*, 50(2), 449–76.

Young, M.R. (2001). *Accounting Irregularities and Financial Fraud: A Corporate Governance Guide.* San Diego: Harcourt Brace Professional Publishing.

Zafirovski, M. (2001). From Market Catallactics to Universal Social Theory: Another Look at the Paradigm of Rational Choice. *Theory & Science*, 2(1), electronic journal.

Zafirovski, M. (2003). Human Rational Behaviour and Economic Rationality. *Electronic Journal of Sociology*, 7(2), electronic journal.

Zajonc, R.B. (1968). Attitudinal Effects of Mere Exposure. *Journal of Personality and Social Psychology Monograph*, 9(2), 1–27.

Zajonc, R.B. (1980). Feeling and Thinking: Preferences Need No Inferences. *American Psychologist*, 35(2), 151–75.

Zajonc, R.B. (1998). Emotions, in *The Handbook of Social Psychology* (4th edition), ed. Gilbert, D.T., Fiske, S.T., and Gardner, L. Boston: McGraw-Hill.

Zarowin, S. (2005). Golden Business Ideas. *Journal of Accountancy*, 200(1), 109.

Zeff, S.A. (1978). The Rise of Economic Consequences. *Journal of Accountancy*, 146(6), 56–63.

Zimbardo, P.G., Haney, C., Banks, W.C., and Jaffe, D.A. (1973a). The Mind is a Formidable Jailer: A Pirandellian Prison. *New York Times Magazine*, 8 April, Section 6, 36.

Zimbardo, P.G., Haney, C., Banks, W.C., and Jaffe, D.A. (1973b). The Psychology of Imprisonment: Privation, Power and Pathology. Unpublished manuscript, Stanford University.

Author index

Subject index